Optimiz
Criminal Law

OPTIMIZE LAW REVISION

Titles in the series:
Contract Law
Criminal Law
English Legal System
Equity and Trusts
EU Law
Land Law
Public Law

Forthcoming:
Tort Law

The Optimize series' academic advisors are:

– Michael Bromby, Higher Education Academy Discipline Lead for Law 2011–2013, Reader in Law, GCU.

'The use of visualisation in Optimize will help students to focus on the key issues when revising.'

– Emily Allbon, Law Librarian and creator of Lawbore, City University.

'Partnering well-explained, comprehensive content with visual tools like maps and flowcharts is what makes the Optimize series so unique. These books help students take their learning up a notch; offering support in grappling with the subject, as well as insight into what will help make their work stand out.'

– Sanmeet Kaur Dua, Lecturer in Law, co-creator of Lawbore, City University.

'This series sets out the essential concepts and principles that students need to grasp in a logical way by combining memorable visual diagrams and text. Students will find that they will not easily forget what they read in this series as the unique aim higher and interaction points will leave a blueprint in their minds.'

– Zoe Swan, Senior Lecturer in Law, University of Brighton.

'The wide range of visual material includes diagrams, charts, tables and maps, enabling students to check their knowledge and understanding on each topic area, every step of the way ... When combined with carefully explained legal principles and solid, understandable examples, students will find this series provides them with a win–win solution to the study of law and developing revision techniques.'

Optimize
Criminal Law

John Hendy and Odette Hutchinson

Routledge
Taylor & Francis Group

LONDON AND NEW YORK

First published 2015
by Routledge
2 Park Square, Milton Park, Abingdon, Oxon OX14 4RN

and by Routledge
711 Third Avenue, New York, NY 10017

Routledge is an imprint of the Taylor & Francis Group, an informa business
© 2015 John Hendy and Odette Hutchinson

The right of John Hendy and Odette Hutchinson to be identified as authors of this work has been asserted by them in accordance with sections 77 and 78 of the Copyright, Designs and Patents Act 1988.

Trademark notice: Product or corporate names may be trademarks or registered trademarks, and are used only for identification and explanation without intent to infringe.

British Library Cataloguing in Publication Data
A catalogue record for this book is available from the British Library

Library of Congress Cataloging in Publication Data
Hendy, John, 1980– author.
Optimize criminal law / John Hendy, Odette Hutchinson.
pages cm. — (Optimize series)
Summary: "Criminal Law volume of the new Optimize revision series"— Provided by publisher.
ISBN 978-0-415-85712-3 (paperback) — ISBN 978-1-315-84898-3 (ebk)   1. Criminal law—Great Britain.
I. Hutchinson, Odette.   II. Title.   III. Title: Criminal law.
KD7869.H46 2015
345.41—dc23
2014030106

ISBN: 978-0-415-85712-3 (pbk)
ISBN: 978-1-315-84898-3 (ebk)

Typeset in TheSans
by RefineCatch Limited, Bungay, Suffolk

Contents

Optimize – Your Blueprint for Exam Success

Why Optimize?

In developing the *Optimize* format, Routledge have spent a lot of time talking to law students like you, and to your lecturers and examiners about assessment, about teaching and learning, and about exam preparation. The aim of our series is to help you make the most of your knowledge to gain good marks – to optimise your revision.

Students

Students told us that there was a huge amount to learn, and that visual features such as diagrams, tables and flowcharts made the law easier to follow. Learning and remembering cases was an area of difficulty, as was applying these in problem questions. Revision guides could make this easier by presenting the law succinctly, showing concepts in a visual format and highlighting how important cases can be applied in assessment.

Lecturers

Lecturers agreed that visual features were effective to aid learning, but were concerned that students learned by rote when using revision guides. To succeed in assessment, they wanted to encourage them to get their teeth into arguments, to support their answers with authority, and show they had truly understood the principles underlying their questions. In short, they wanted them to show they understood how they were assessed on the law, rather than repeating the basic principles.

Assessment criteria

If you want to do well in exams, it's important to understand how you will be assessed. In order to get the best out of your exam or essay question, your first port of call should be to make yourself familiar with the marking criteria available from your law school; this will help you to identify and recognise the skills and knowledge you will need to succeed. Like course outlines, assessment criteria can differ from school to school and so if you can get hold of a copy of your own criteria, this will be invaluable. To give you a clear idea of what these criteria look like, we've collated the most common terms from 64 marking schemes for core curriculum courses in the UK.

research
reading
Evidence
Understanding
Structure Critical Argument
Application Use sources
Analysis
Originality
Knowledge
Presentation

Common Assessment Criteria, Routledge Subject Assessment Survey 2012

Optimizing the law

The format of this *Optimize Law* volume has been developed with these assessment criteria and the learning needs of students firmly in mind.

- ❖ **Visual format:** Our expert series advisors have brought a wealth of knowledge about visual learning to help us to develop the book's visual format.
- ❖ **Tailored coverage:** Each book is tailored to the needs of your core curriculum course and presents all commonly taught topics.
- ❖ **Assessment-led revision:** Our authors are experienced teachers with an interest in how students learn, and they have structured each chapter around revision objectives that relate to the criteria you will be assessed on.
- ❖ **Assessment-led pedagogy:** The Aim Higher, Common Pitfalls, Up for Debate and Case precedent features used in these books are closely linked to common assessment criteria – showing you how to gain the best marks, avoid the worst, apply the law and think critically about it.
- ❖ **Putting it into practice:** Each chapter presents example essay or problem questions and template answers to show you how to apply what you have learned.

Routledge and the *Optimize* team wish you the very best of luck in your exams and essays!

Guide to Using the Book and the Companion Website

The Routledge *Optimize* revision series is designed to provide students with a clear overview of the core topics in their course, and to contextualise this overview within a narrative that offers straightforward, practical advice relating to assessment.

Revision objectives

These overviews are a brief introduction of the core themes and issues you will encounter in each chapter.

Chapter topic maps

Visually link together all of the key topics in each chapter to tie together understanding of key issues.

Illustrative diagrams

A series of diagrams and tables are used to help facilitate the understanding of concepts and interrelationships within key topics.

Up for Debate

Up for Debate features help you to critique current law and reflect on how and in which direction it may develop in the future.

Case precedent boxes

A variety of landmark cases are highlighted in text boxes for ease of reference. The facts, principle and application for the case are presented to help understand how these courses are used in legal problems.

Aim Higher and Common Pitfalls

These assessment-focused sections show students how to get the best marks, and avoid the most common mistakes.

Case grid

This draws together all of the key cases from each chapter.

Companion website

www.routledge.com/cw/optimizelawrevision

Visit the Optimize Law Revision website to discover a comprehensive range of resources designed to enhance your learning experience.

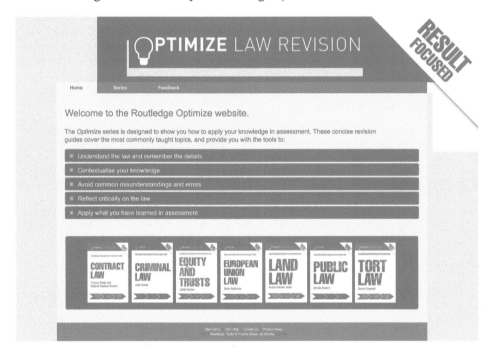

Resources for Optimize Law Revision

❖ Up for Debate podcasts
❖ Aim Higher and Common Pitfalls podcasts
❖ Subject maps for each topic
❖ Downloadable versions of chapter maps and other diagrams

Resources for Routledge Q&As

❖ MCQ questions
❖ Flashcard glossary
❖ The good, the fair and the ugly podcasts

Table of Cases and Statutes

■ Cases

■ Statutes

1

Introduction – What is Criminal Law and What is a Crime?

Understand the law

- Do you understand the nature and purpose of the criminal law?
- Do you understand the general building blocks of criminal liability?

Remember the details

- Can you remember the meaning of the terms *actus reus* and *mens rea*?
- Can you remember the burden and standard of proof in criminal proceedings?

Reflect critically on areas of debate

- Do you understand the significance of the **Human Rights Act 1998** in relation to criminal proceedings?

Contextualise

- Are you able to contextualise your knowledge and identify overlap and distinctions in relation to civil law?

Apply your skills and knowledge

- Can you apply this knowledge to the rest of this text?

Introduction to Criminal Law

Welcome to *Optimize Criminal Law*! Criminal law is a dynamic and fascinating area of law, and it is a subject that the majority of students enjoy studying. It is not however, a subject without challenges. The criminal law consists of a vast range of complex, sometimes conflicting and contradictory rules. The good news is that this textbook has been designed to support you in navigating this challenging but exciting area of law. *Optimize Criminal Law* is result-focused; we have one primary objective and that is to use our experience and knowledge to help you achieve an outstanding result in criminal law.

In the forthcoming chapters we will help you understand the substantive criminal law and how it is applied in real and hypothetical situations. We will show you how to break down individual offences into the core elements of criminal liability. You will learn how to construct criminal liability and how to identify relevant defences. We will illustrate how to maximise your marks by adopting a strategic and structured approach to answering problem questions. We will also support you in articulating and demonstrating a critical understanding of the criminal law in essay-style questions.

Throughout this book you will find a number of features, which will assist you in developing your knowledge and understanding of the criminal law. Some of these result-orientated features include:

* Aim Higher points;
* Tips and suggestions on how to answer problem questions;
* Suggested solutions to essay and problem questions;
* Examiner insight boxes, with contributions from experienced criminal law examiners;
* Read for success suggestions to enhance your critical understanding of the criminal law.

Defining criminal law

Criminal law is a branch of public law. A straightforward way of understanding criminal conduct is by viewing it as conduct which gives rise to legal proceedings through the prospect of state punishment. In short:

1. The criminal law is enforced by the state;
2. Infringements of the criminal law are punishable by the state.

Professor Andrew Ashworth defines criminal conduct in the following terms:

> There are certain wrongs which are criminal in most jurisdictions, but in general there is no straightforward moral or social test of whether conduct is criminal. The most reliable test is the formal one: is the conduct prohibited, on pain of conviction and sentence?
>
> *Andrew Ashworth, Principles of Criminal Law*

What functions does the criminal law perform?

The criminal law performs a number of different functions. Knowing and under-standing the functions that the criminal law performs is important, in so far as it provides students with a tool by which to critically evaluate cases, legislation and policy decisions.

Functions of the criminal law:

1. A mechanism of social control
2. Protects individual and public interests
3. Protects individuals and property from harm
4. Punishes people convicted of criminal wrongdoing
5. Educates individuals as to acceptable conduct and behaviour
6. Enforces morals

It is worth noting that functions 5 and 6 are particularly controversial. There is disagreement as to whether the criminal law is really an effective tool by which to educate members of society (point 5). There is also disagreement as to whether the criminal law should seek to enforce the morals and values of society (point 6). More detailed consideration of point 6 can be found in Martin and Storey, *Unlocking the Criminal Law*, 4th Edition, 2013, Routledge.

Aim Higher

Every criminal law course is different. It is not unusual for there to be significant vari-ation between courses in terms of content and focus. One of the first things you should do is look at the syllabus for YOUR criminal law course! Do not assume that certain topics are included in your course, just because your course textbook contains material on these subjects! If you incorrectly make this assumption you may spend valuable time revising material that is not covered by your course and therefore material that is not examinable!

Where does the criminal law come from?

There are a number of different sources of criminal law as illustrated in the following diagram.

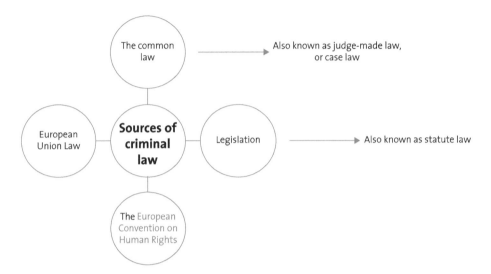

The most important sources of law, or at least the ones that you will be using most frequently throughout your criminal law studies, are:

Criminal liability versus civil liability

Criminal liability and civil liability can, and frequently do, cross over. An act or an omission (which simply means a failure to act) may give rise to civil and/or criminal liability. For example, if Odette hits Matt this could constitute the criminal offence of assault. It could also give rise to a civil action for trespass to the person (tort – civil law). Therefore, if Odette hits Matt and is convicted of a criminal offence Odette may have to pay a fine. She might be sentenced to a term in prison or receive some other form of punishment for the offence. Odette may also have to pay damages under civil law.

The important thing for you to remember, is that a criminal prosecution does not preclude a victim from pursuing a civil action against the wrongdoer and vice versa; that is, a civil action against a wrongdoer does not preclude the state from taking action against a defendant or defendants.

Criminal liability

In simplistic terms, criminal liability exists where a defendant is responsible for conduct (this could take the form of an act, an omission or a state of affairs) that breaches the criminal law, and at the time the conduct was committed, or occurred, the defendant had a particular state of mind (there are some offences for which the defendant's state of mind is irrelevant; we refer to these as strict or absolute liability offences which we will discuss later); and, finally, the defendant has no valid defence.

Let's break this down in order to understand the building blocks of criminal liability more clearly. The building blocks of criminal liability consist of:

In criminal law some of the building blocks have special terms. For example, the conduct element of an offence is referred to as the *actus reus*; this Latin term means 'guilty act'. The state of mind element of criminal liability is referred to as the *mens rea*, this Latin term means 'guilty mind'. It is important that you use these Latin terms in your assessments. So let's re-draft the above diagram accordingly.

We will consider *actus reus* and *mens rea* in more detail in Chapter 1 and Chapter 2, but at the moment we simply want you to understand that these terms are the building blocks of criminal liability.

Key points of criminal liability

Before you embark on your journey through the criminal law there are a number of key points that you need to be aware of at this juncture. When constructing criminal liability you must bear the following critical points in mind:

❖ The defendant's motive is irrelevant to the question of constructing criminal liability. Do not get caught up with or preoccupied with WHY the defendant committed the offence.

❖ The substantive criminal law is not concerned with HOW the prosecution will PROVE the defendant's guilt. Again if you spend time considering this you will be wasting valuable time!

❖ You are not the judge, or the jury. Your job is to construct criminal liability, not to determine whether the defendant will be convicted. That is for the jury, or magistrates to determine. In an assessment you must put forward arguments for both sides **unless** specifically asked to do otherwise.

Common Pitfalls

❖ Your role is to demonstrate to the examiner a detailed knowledge of the substantive criminal law. Many students spend valuable time focusing on the motive(s) of the defendant, or agonising over how the prosecution in practical terms will be able to prove the defendant's state of mind.

❖ These are both 'red herrings'. When answering a problem question your job is to identify potential offences and to construct liability for those offences, before considering likely available defences.

❖ If you decide to complete the professional stage of training through the Bar Professional Training Course (BPTC) or the Legal Practice Course (LPC) you will study criminal litigation and procedure. You will also study the complex rules of evidence. For now, at least, focus only on the substantive criminal law!

Fundamental principles of criminal law

1. A key principle running throughout the criminal law is that the defendant is **innocent until proven guilty**.
2. Another key principle in English criminal law is that the **prosecution** (in most cases the Crown Prosecution Service) **bears the burden of proof**.
3. The standard of proof in criminal prosecutions is 'beyond a reasonable doubt'.

The presumption of innocence
This means that the defendant is innocent until proven guilty. This fundamental principle is protected by the common law *R v Woolmington* [1935] AC 462 and by Art 6 of The European Convention on Human Rights

The prosecution bears the burden of proof
This means that the prosecution must prove the defendant committed the alleged offence. The defendant does not have to prove he, or she is innocent.

The burden of proof is 'beyond a reasonable doubt'
This is a very high standard of proof, much higher than the civil standard of proof.

The burden and standard of proof

In practice the burden and standard of proof operates in the following way. If Amy kills Bob, the prosecution must prove beyond a reasonable doubt that Amy killed

Bob. If the prosecution succeeds in doing this, then the jury should convict Amy. If the jury are sure that Amy did not kill Bob, they must acquit Amy. If the jury are not sure either way, then the jury must acquit the defendant.

The prosecution bears the burden, then, of proving the defendant's guilt. It also bears the burden of disproving any defence that the accused may raise.

Case precedent – *Woolmington* [1935] AC 462

Facts: In this case the defendant claimed that he had accidently shot his wife. The prosecution argued that the defendant must prove that the shooting was an accident. The defendant was convicted of murdering his wife.

Principle: On appeal the House of Lords held that a defendant is innocent until proven guilty. It is for the prosecution to prove beyond a reasonable doubt that the shooting was not an accident. It was not for the defendant to prove he was not guilty.

Application: Use this case to illustrate the principle that a defendant is innocent until proven guilty. You can also use this case to illustrate that the prosecution bears the burden of proof.

Reverse burden of proof

In certain situations the burden of proof will shift from the prosecution to the defence. This can happen where the defence has raised a certain defence such as insanity or diminished responsibility. In the event that the accused raises one of these defences the standard of proof changes from 'beyond a reasonable doubt' to on the 'balance of probabilities'. The table below will help you break down these important points.

	The burden of proof	The standard of proof	Rule	Authority
The prosecution	The prosecution bears the burden of proof in most criminal prosecutions. A defendant is innocent until proven guilty. This means they must prove that the defendant is guilty. It also means that the prosecution must disprove the existence of any defence that the accused raises.	Beyond a reasonable doubt	This is the general rule. It is often referred to as 'the golden thread running through the criminal law'.	*Woolmington* [1935] AC462 **Article 6 ECHR**

	The burden of proof	The standard of proof	Rule	Authority
The defence	In the event that the defence raises the defence of insanity or diminished responsibility, the burden of proof shifts from the prosecution to the defence. The defence must prove the existence of the defence. The prosecution must then attempt to disprove it!	Where the burden of proof shifts, the standard of proof changes to the lower standard of proof, the civil standard – on the balance of probabilities.	This is an exception to the general rule that the prosecution bears the burden of proof.	**Diminished responsibility** – **s 2** Homicide Act 1957 as amended by **s 52** of the Coroners and Justices Act 2009 **Insanity** – Reverse burden of proof established by the common law rather than statute In *Sheldrake v DPP* [2005] 1 AC 264 it was held that a reverse burden of proof does not automatically violate **Art 6** of the **ECHR**

Human rights and the criminal law

It is important to understand that the rules and processes of the criminal law do not exist in isolation and as such English criminal law is affected by the Legislation, which was incorporated into domestic law in the form of the Human Rights Act 1998.

The following provisions are particularly important in the context of the criminal law:

> Article 2: The right to life

> Article 6: The right to a fair trial

> Article 7: No punishment without law

Key Points Checklist

Criminal law is a branch of public law. The preoccupation of the criminal law is conduct which gives rise to legal proceedings through the prospect of state punishment. The criminal law is enforced by the state and punishable by the state.	✔
The criminal law performs a number of different functions including: the protection of individuals and property; the maintenance of social and public order; the enforcement of morals; the punishment of individuals who have committed criminal offences; education.	✔
The criminal law is derived from a number of different sources including: the common law; statute law; EU law.	✔
Criminal law differs from civil law. The terminology can be different. The standard and burden of proof are also different in criminal and civil proceedings.	✔
The building blocks of criminal liability are **actus reus** (guilty act), **mens rea** (guilty mind) and the absence of a valid defence.	✔

@ **Visit the book's companion website to test your knowledge**

❖ Resources include a subject map, revision tip podcasts, downloadable diagrams, MCQ quizzes for each chapter, and a flashcard glossary

❖ www.routledge.com/cw/optimizelawrevision

Understand the law
- Can you define the terms *actus reus* and *mens rea*, and how they interact?
- Can you identify the *actus reus* and *mens rea* in different offences?

Remember the details
- Can you remember the different types of *actus reus* and *mens rea* and their meaning?
- Can you identify case law examples for each type of *actus reus* and *mens rea*?

Reflect critically on areas of debate
- Can you demonstrate that you understand the term strict liability and that you are able to offer examples of offences that are strict liability offences?
- Can you reflect on the meaning of intention and recklessness and the distinctions between recklessness and intention using case law to illustrate the differences?

Contextualise
- Do you understand the context in which *actus reus* and *mens rea* operate?
- Do you understand the significance of a break in the chain of causation?

Apply your skills and knowledge
- Can you complete the problem questions for *actus reus* and *mens rea* providing case law and statutory illustrations to support your answer?

Chapter Map

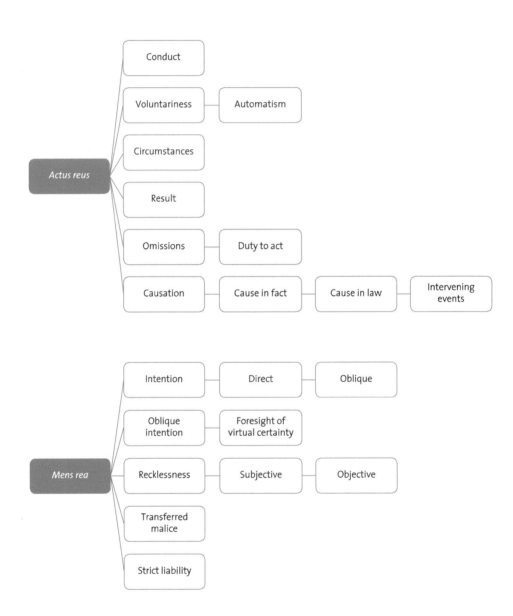

Introduction

In the last chapter we considered two key terms: *actus reus* and *mens rea*. In this chapter we are going to consider these terms in more detail. In particular we are going to consider how these crucial elements come together to construct criminal liability.

The physical element of criminal liability is referred to as *actus reus*, a Latin term which translates as 'guilty act'. The term *mens rea* refers to the mental element of criminal liability. A literal translation of this Latin term is 'guilty mind'.

Therefore there are three ingredients to criminal liability.

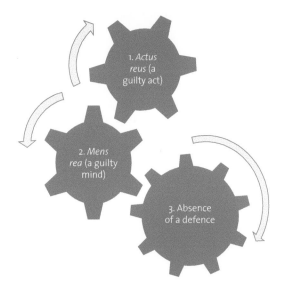

These first two elements will be considered in detail in this chapter. We will consider defences in relation to specific offences throughout the book. We will also consider general defences in the two chapters on general defences,

We will start our consideration of the substantive content in this chapter by considering *actus reus* as a concept.

Actus reus

We are going to start this section of the chapter by considering the importance of voluntariness to the *actus reus* as a concept. Then we will move on to consider the different types of *actus reus* before considering failures to act, also known as omissions. The final *actus reus* topic we will consider together is key concept in criminal liability known as causation.

Voluntariness

In order to construct liability for a criminal offence you will need to be satisfied that the defendant's conduct or omission was voluntary. As a general rule there can be no liability for serious criminal offences unless D's conduct was *voluntary*.

Aim Higher

You should bear in mind that this is not applicable to state of affairs crimes, which are crimes committed when the defendant (D) finds themselves in a particular prohibited situation, such as in possession of a controlled substance (drugs). The nature of a state of affairs case is that it doesn't matter how D came to find himself in that situation. A good illustration can be found in the case of *Winzar v Chief Constable of Kent* The Times 28 March (1983).

Involuntary movements or conduct cannot form the basis of criminal liability. For example, let's imagine that Kaya has very severe hay fever, and as a result of the very high pollen count he begins to sneeze uncontrollably. Whilst sneezing he head-butts his friend Jack. Jack sustains a large bruise to his head. In this scenario Kaya could be argued to have committed the *actus reus* of the offence of battery or actual bodily harm. However, his sneezing is an involuntary action and as such, despite the fact that Jack has suffered physical harm, Kaya would not be liable for either battery or actual bodily harm.

The defendant's inability to control their movements may be the result of a number of different factors including:

❖ illness – physical or mental;
❖ reflex body actions;
❖ the result of injury – having been rendered in an unconscious state.

For example, in *Hill v Baxter* (1958), D lost control of the car that he was driving because he was attacked by a swarm of bees. Another case that you can use to illustrate this principle of law is *Burns v Bidder* (1967).

Case precedent – *R v Quick & Paddison* [1973] 3 AER 397

Facts: D was affected by hypoglycaemia, and had a fit where he was not in control of his arms or legs. During this fit, D assaulted V.

Principle: Voluntariness and automatism

Application: D was found guilty, but on appeal the judge ruled that automatism was a possible defence open to D and that the critical part should have been considered in the original trial. As a result, D's conviction was quashed.

Now we are going to consider the different types of *actus reus* that exist in English criminal law.

Types of *actus reus*

The *actus reus* of a criminal offence consists of all the external elements of that offence. The *actus reus* of a crime can be defined in a number of different ways, for example a conduct crime or a result crime. This has given rise to a typology of criminal offences, the most common of which are conduct crimes and result crimes.

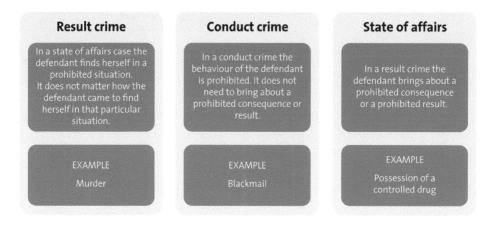

Result crime	Conduct crime	State of affairs
In a state of affairs case the defendant finds herself in a prohibited situation. It does not matter how the defendant came to find herself in that particular situation.	In a conduct crime the behaviour of the defendant is prohibited. It does not need to bring about a prohibited consequence or result.	In a result crime the defendant brings about a prohibited consequence or a prohibited result.
EXAMPLE	EXAMPLE	EXAMPLE
Murder	Blackmail	Possession of a controlled drug

It is worth noting that some offences, such as arson under the **Criminal Damage Act 1971**, are both result and conduct offences.

In the case of a conduct crime it is the defendant's behaviour that is prohibited irrespective of the result or consequences.

For example:

> Cameron discovers some information about Ben and then demands money with menaces. This is blackmail – it is the **conduct which is prohibited**. As such it does not matter whether Ben goes to the police or pays the money.

> Ben is angry with Cameron for having blackmailed him. Intending to cause Cameron serious harm Ben hits Cameron on the head with a spade. The result is the unlawful death of Cameron – **the result is prohibited**. B caused C's death.

The term *actus reus* as we have seen, translates literally to mean 'guilty act'. The term is potentially misleading because it can give rise to an assumption that the *actus reus* of an offence must always be the result of a positive act. You need to be careful because this literal translation of the Latin term is potentially misleading because it suggests that the *actus reus* of an offence is always the result of a positive action. For example, Ben hitting Cameron on the head with a spade. In reality liability for a criminal offence can arise where the defendant fails to act. The term we use in criminal law to describe a failure to act is *omission*. We will now consider the circumstances in which a failure to act can give rise to criminal liability in English criminal law.

Topic Map: Omissions

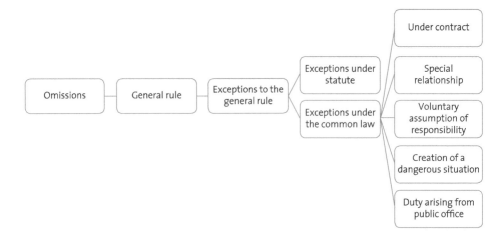

Omission

The general rule in English criminal law is that failing to act cannot give rise to criminal liability. Whilst this is the general rule there are exceptions to this rule there are a number of situations in which a failure to act can give rise to criminal liability. Many of the textbooks give the following illustration of an omission.

A sees B drowning. In these circumstances A is under no legal obligation to assist B. It doesn't even matter if it would be perfectly safe for A to assist B. So where A is a strong swimmer or where B is a small child drowning in very shallow water. A is under no legal obligation to assist B.

Aim Higher

It is important here to note that there is a difference between a legal and a moral obligation to assist a person in need. Most people would recoil at the concept of an adult standing by and watching a child – or indeed anyone – drown when they could have offered assistance without putting their own life in danger.

Having considered the general rule we are now going to consider the exceptions to the general rule.

Exceptions

An exception to the general rule that there is no liability for a failure to act can arise under one of two headings:

1. An exception under statute
2. An exception under common law

We will consider each of these in turn.

Exception under statute
A statute can impose liability for omissions to act. There are lots of examples of statutes imposing criminal liability for an omission to act. You can use the following to support this point in an essay or problem question.

❖ Section 170 of the **Road Traffic Act** – failure to report an accident;
❖ Section 7 of the **Road Traffic Act** – failure to provide a specimen of breath.

Exceptions under the common law
There are a number of points that you need to be aware of in relation to exceptions created by the common law.

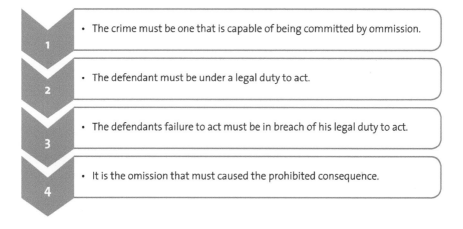

1. The crime must be one that is capable of being committed by ommission.

2. The defendant must be under a legal duty to act.

3. The defendants failure to act must be in breach of his legal duty to act.

4. It is the omission that must caused the prohibited consequence.

1. Not all crimes are capable of being committed by omission. Assault and Battery caused by omission are particularly tricky: in *Fagan v MPC* (1968) and *DPP v Santana-Bermudez* (2003).

Case precedent – *DPP v Santana-Bermudez* [2003] EWHC 2908 (Admin)

Facts: In this case D failed to notify a police officer of the presence of hypodermic needles in his pockets despite having been asked this question prior to the search being carried out. The police office sustained a needle stick injury as a result of the defendant's omission.

Principle: Assault and Battery cannot normally be committed by omission. However, if the defendant creates a dangerous situation liability may arise.

Application: D created the danger by omitting to inform the police officer. D was convicted of ABH.

---

2. With regard to a duty, this could fall under a number of headings and examples.

Common Pitfall

The general rule is that there can be no liability for failing to act, unless at the time of the omission the defendant was under a legal duty to act. It is important not to confuse this legal duty with a moral duty to act.

There are a number of situations defined by case law, which identify when a person has a legal duty to act. They are:

Duty arising from a contract	• Where a person is under a positive duty to act because of his obligations under a contract, a failure to perform the contractual duty in question can form the basis of criminal liability. *Pitwood* [1902]
Public office	• A person holding a public office (such as a Police Officer) may be under a public duty to act. *Dytham* [1979]
Voluntary assumption of responsibility	• A common law duty to act can arise in circumstances where the D has voluntarily assumed responsibility to care for another person. *Stone and Dabinson* [1977]
Creation of a dangerous situation	• If the defendant accidentally commits an act that causes harm, and subsequently becomes aware of the danger he has created, there arises a duty to act reasonably to avert that danger. The D is under a legal duty to avert the danger he has created. *Miller* [1983]
Duty arising from a special relationship	• D may be liable for failing to act where there is a special relationship between V and D – this is generally a relationship of close family proximity. *Gibbins and Proctor* [1918]

Duty arising from contract

Where D is under a contractual obligation to act, a failure to do so can give rise to criminal liability. The key case that you need to remember in relation to this principle of law is the case of *Pitwood* (1902).

Case precedent – *Pittwood* [1902] TLR 37

Facts: D was a level crossing keeper, but one day left the gate open when a train was approaching. The train hit a vehicle and killed the driver. D was charged with manslaughter.

Principle: Omission to act when D is under a contractual duty.

Application: D's employment contract created a duty to act, i.e. closing the gate, a duty which he failed to perform.

Duty arising from public office

In circumstances where the defendant neglects their duty whilst in public office can give rise to criminal liability. In the case of *Dytham* (1979) the defendant who was an on duty police officer stood and watched as a man was attacked and beaten to death. The defendant made no attempt to intervene and he did not call for assistance. He was convicted of wilful misconduct in public office.

Voluntary assumption of responsibility

In the case of *Instan* (1893) the defendant assumed caring responsibility for an elderly aunt. The aunt developed gangrene in her leg and she stopped eating. The defendant neglected to feed the aunt and did not call for assistance when it was clearly needed. The aunt died and the defendant was convicted of the aunt's manslaughter. The principle that voluntary assumption of responsibility can give rise to criminal liability also applied in the case of *Stone and Dobinson* (1977).

Creation of a dangerous situation

In circumstances where a defendant creates a dangerous situation they are under a legal duty to avert further damage/harm. In the case of *Miller* (1983) the defendant fell asleep whilst smoking. He awoke to find that the mattress that he was sleeping on was on fire. Instead of calling the emergency services or attempting to put the fire out, he left the room and went to sleep in another room.

The principle in *Miller* was extended to manslaughter in *Evans* (2009), where the defendant supplied the victim with a controlled substance and failed to summon help the victim when he became unconscious and died.

Duty arising from a special relationship

Where the defendant and the victim are in a relationship of close proximity the law may impose a duty to act. The most obvious relationship that gives rise to such a duty is the relationship between parent and child: *Gibbins and Proctor* (1918). The range of relationships to which this principle applies is not limited only to parent and child.

Causation

In the case of a result crime it must be established that the defendant is the cause of the prohibited result, issues in relation to causation appear frequently in relation to homicide cases. You need to make sure that you understand the rules in relation to causation and how to apply them!

In this section we will consider:

Factual causation → Legal causation → Intervening events

In order to establish causation it must be demonstrated that D is the factual and the legal cause of the prohibited consequences.

Causation requires proof that D's conduct was:

The first step in establishing causation is to establish factual causation.

Cause in fact (factual causation)

To be a cause *in fact* the defendant's conduct must satisfy the **'but for'** test. This means that we must be able to say that the consequence would not have occurred 'but for' the defendant's actions. This test is usually very easy to apply to a problem question; however, it does not adequately deal with situations where there are multiple causes, for example.

Example: Bob dislikes Nigel and wants to kill him. Bob puts rat poison in Nigel's coffee, but before Nigel can drink his coffee, Nigel suffers a heart attack and dies. Is Bob the factual cause of Nigel's death?

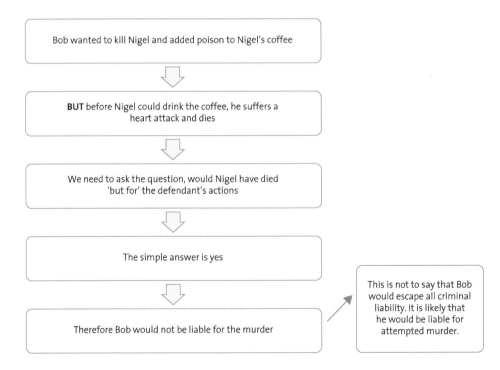

This scenario is drawn from the facts of a real case: *White* (1910).

Common Pitfall

One of the most common mistakes that students make in relation to causation is that they fail to deal with factual and legal causation. More often than not students remember the test for factual causation and fail to discuss causation.

You must remember that factual causation is a necessary but insufficient test for establishing causation. You MUST deal with legal causation. If you do not you have not established a causal link and as a direct result you will limit the award of marks that the examiner can make.

Now consider the following example.

Example: Jody stabs Leon, and Leon is taken in an ambulance to hospital. As the ambulance is approaching the hospital, Laurence, who is driving a car, hits the ambulance and Leon is killed in the impact of the collision. Is Jody liable for the murder of Leon? Would your answer differ if the stab wound was only a minor injury?

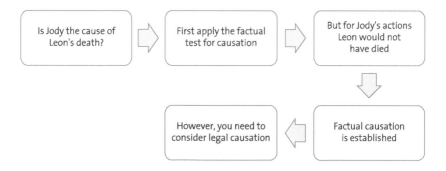

When you are looking at a problem question, it can sometimes be difficult to reach a final conclusion as to the cause of a victim's death – particularly when there are a number of possibilities! So in an exam, do not agonise over the conclusion. Show your working out and impress the examiner with your ability to work your way methodically through the alternatives.

Common Pitfall

Students often form their own opinion about whether D should be held liable for a criminal offence. Do not let this cloud your ability to apply the law. It may be obvious to you that D is the cause of death, but the examiner will need to see your knowledge and application of law in relation to causation. We cannot give many marks at all for the expression of personal opinion alone!

We are now moving on to consider legal causation.

Cause in law (legal causation)

In order to establish legal causation the prosecution must demonstrate that the defendant's actions were a 'substantial and operating' cause of the victim's death: *Smith* (1959). One of the key cases in relation to this principle is the case of Smith.

❖ One of the most important points to note about legal causation is that it does not require the defendant's actions or omissions to be the sole or even the main cause of the victim's death: *Hennigan* (1971).

❖ It is also important to note that D can be an indirect cause of V's death: *McKechnie* (1929).

❖ Another important rule in relation to causation is the 'thin skull' or 'eggshell skull' rule. This rule stipulates that the defendant must take the victim as he finds him. It is no defence to argue that V has a particular weakness rendering him more susceptible to death or injury. The leading case in relation to this rule is *Blaue* (1975). The pyramid below illustrates the operation of the Thin Skull Rule:

Case precedent – *Blaue* [1975] 1 WLR 1411

Facts: D stabbed V, penetrating her lung. She was told at hospital that she needed a blood transfusion and surgery was necessary to save her life. She refused this transfusion as she was a Jehovah's Witness and it was against her religion. Medical evidence indicated that she would not have died had she had the transfusion.

Principle: Thin skull rule

Application: D argued that the victim's refusal of treatment broke the chain of causation. The Court of Appeal rejected this argument and extended the thin skull rule to 'the whole man, not just the physical man' (Lawton LJ p 1415).

But what happens when something happens between the time that the defendant inflicted the injury and the time that defendant dies? We will consider intervening events in the next section.

Intervening events

The legal term for an intervening event is a *novus actus interveniens*. If the defence successfully establishes that there was a *novus actus interveniens* this will break the chain of causation.

Common Pitfall

You must be careful here with your use of language. If you say 'there are a number of intervening events' you are essentially saying the chain of causation has been broken. The correct thing to say is 'we will now consider **WHETHER** there has been an intervening event'.

Intervening events can take several forms:

Naturally occurring events	• see *Environment Agency v Empress Car Co.* [1999] 2 AC 22
Acts of third parties	• see *R v Jordan* (1956) 40 Cr App R 152 and *R v Cheshire* [1991] 1 WLR 844
Acts of the victim	• see *R v Roberts* [1971] 56 Cr App R 95

Act of God

In cases where it is the sole or immediate cause of the prohibited consequence. You can use the following case to support this principle of law: *Southern Water Authority v Pegrum* (1989).

Act of a third party

The act or actions of a third party can only break the chain of causation where their acts or actions are free, deliberate and informed. The acts or actions of the third part must provide the immediate cause of the prohibited consequences in action.

Case precedent – *R v Pagett* [1983] 76 Cr App R 279

Facts: In this case the D used a women as a human shield and fired his gun at the police. The police returned fire and killed V. D was held liable for her death.

Principle: Legal causation – acts of third parties

Application: D shot at the police first, causing the police to act in self-defence. Therefore D's act of shooting at the police and using the girl as a shield caused the death of V.

Case precedent – *R v Jordan* [1956] 40 Cr App R 152

Facts: In this case the D stabbed V, but V's treatment at hospital was poor, and V died as a result of the treatment. The wound was no longer life-threatening.

Principle: Intervening act by a third party

Application: The judge in this case ruled that in order for medical treatment to break the chain of causation the medical treatment must be 'palpably wrong'. In this case the treatment was palpably wrong. However, in *R v Cheshire* [1991] 3 All ER 670 the judge said that the chain of causation would only be broken if D's act was not significantly important, *'so independent of D's acts, and in itself so potent in causing death'* (at 855).

R v Jordan

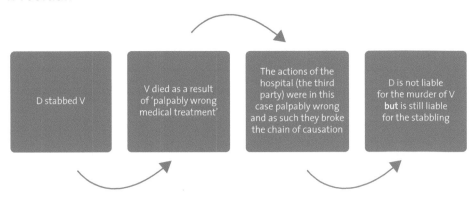

This case can be contrasted with the case of *R v Cheshire* (1991) in which, following an act of violence by the defendant the victim was sent to hospital. Whilst receiving medical treatment there were complications and the victim died as a result of the complications. In this case the complications were the natural consequence of the D's actions.

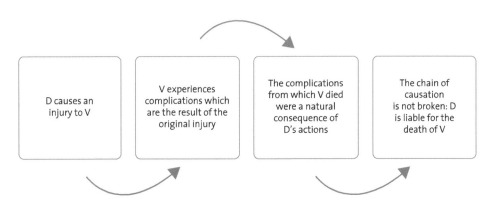

The decision in *Cheshire* was followed in the case of *Mellor* (1996) and the case of *Gowans* (2003). It is therefore safe to assert that it is highly unlikely that negligent medical treatment given which is the result of a D's violent actions will be permitted to break the chain of causation in future cases. The case of *Jordan* appears to be an exceptional case which would be unlikely to have the same outcome were it heard now.

Aim Higher

Read the following cases and look at the language the court uses in identifying the cause in law.

R v Pagett [1983] 76 Cr App R 279
R v White [1910] 2 KB 124
R v Roberts [1971] 56 Cr App R 95

You will notice the different language that the court uses – *substantial, operating and substantial, proximate, imputable, significant contribution* – these concepts are closely related.

The final category of intervening events that we need to consider is the actions or omissions of the victim and the extent to which these may break the chain of causation. The following principles apply in relation to this category:

❖   In circumstances where the V attempts to escape harm and is injured in the process the chain of causation will not normally be broken. Only in cases where the V's actions were 'so daft as to be unforeseeable' will the chain of causation be broken: *Roberts* (1972).
❖   If V's actions are not 'daft' then V will be held liable, and the question as to whether the victims actions are 'daft' is a question of fact for the jury: *Marjoram* (2000).
❖   It is important to note that a victim's wilful neglect or deliberate aggravation of wounds that have been caused by the defendant are unlikely to break the chain of causation: *Dear* (1996).
❖   Where D inflicts harm, physical or psychological, on a victim and the victim goes on to commit suicide, D may be held liable for V's death: *Dhaliwal* (2006).

Problem areas: drug cases

❖   Cases involving the consumption of drugs are particularly problematic. They involve unlawful activity by the drug dealer (the sale of a controlled substance) and aggravating factors on behalf of the victim (the consumption of the drug). Where the victim dies as the result of the consumption of drugs provided by D, liability may arise under the *Miller* principle as extended in *Evans* (2009) where D fails to summon help.
❖   Where D injects the controlled substance into V and V dies, D may be held liable for the death of V: *Cato* (1976).
❖   A drug dealer does not cause a victim to take controlled substances even if the consumption of the substance is foreseeable: *Dalby* (1982).

❖ Where D hands the drugs and or other drug paraphernalia to V, who then voluntarily consumes the drugs and dies, D is not liable for the death of V: *Kennedy* (2007).

Consider the example below:

Example: Refath attacks Phil and as a result of this attack Phil suffers post-traumatic stress disorder (PTSD). Phil commits suicide.

What principles of law and which cases do you feel would be relevant to establishing causation in this case?

Aim Higher

Remember that few scenarios are clear-cut, it is essential that you debate the issues in your paper. As has been mentioned, you are constructing liability; you are not there to deliver a verdict – that is the role of the jury/magistrates. Your role is to consider:

❖ which offences D may be liable for;
❖ whether liability can be constructed from those offences;
❖ what defences if any D may avail himself of;
❖ if there are alternative or lesser charges.

From this we can conclude that intervening acts are an important element within the chain of causation, and therefore in demonstrating the *actus reus*. Any intervening acts must originate from the three sources above, and be significant within the chain.

A summary of the points that we have considered in this section

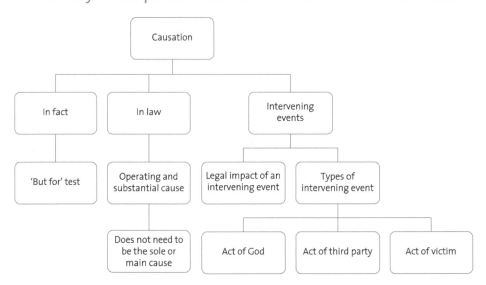

Coincidence of *actus reus* and *mens rea*

In order for liability to exist there must be coincidence of *actus reus* and *mens rea*. We will now consider this requirement in more detail.

This rule requires that the defendant must have had the requisite *mens rea* for the offence at the time the *actus reus* of the offence was committed – some textbooks refer to this as contemporaneity of *actus reus* and *mens rea*. Therefore, let us imagine that Zena plans to murder Bernie on Saturday morning whilst he is asleep. On Friday evening Zena reverses out of the drive and accidently runs Bernie over, and Bernie dies in hospital the next day. Zena cannot be convicted of Bernie's murder because there is no coincidence of *actus reus* and *mens rea*.

Actus reus	→	AR and MR must coincide in time for liability to exist	←	Mens rea

Now consider the following leading case in this area. This case involves a defendant committing the *actus reus* of an offence before forming the *mens rea* for the offence. It explains how the courts have developed mechanisms to deal with such situations to ensure that justice is served.

> ### Case precedent – *Fagan v MPC* [1969] 1 QB 439
>
> **Facts:** D accidentally drove onto a police officer's foot. When he realised what he had done, he refused to move the car, despite the repeated request of the police officer.
>
> **Principle:** Coincidence of *actus reus* and *mens rea*
>
> **Application:** The court agreed that the *actus reus* and *mens rea* must coincide but one could occur before the other. In this case, the *actus reus* took place before the *mens rea* materialised (when D knew that he was actually on the police officer's foot).

The prosecution must also establish that the *actus reus* and *mens rea* coincide. If the prosecution is unable to establish these factors beyond a reasonable doubt the defendant is entitled to an acuital.

In the next case the defendants form the *mens rea* for the offence before they commit the *actus reus* of the offence.

> ### Case precedent – *Thabo Meli and Others* (1954)
>
> **Facts:** The Ds in this case had agreed to kill V. They took V off to a secluded location and beat him. Thinking that they had killed the V, the Ds threw V's body off a cliff. In reality V was still alive, but died some time later from exposure.

Principle: Coincidence of *actus reus* and *mens rea*

Application: In this case the *mens rea* was in existence before the Ds actually committed the *actus reus* of the offence (the death of V). The court held that it was impossible to divide up what was essentially a series of acts.

The two cases above describe the different situations in which coincidence of *actus reus* and *mens rea* can present difficulty for the courts. As a general rule if you are facing a problem question in which there is an issue with coincidence of *actus reus* and *mens rea* you should consider the following:

If AR performed before MR is established
- Apply *Fagan*

If MR is established before AR is committed
- Apply *Thabo Meli*
- Followed in *Church* (1965) and *LeBrun* (1991)

Key Points Checklist

❖ The physical element of a crime is called the **actus reus**	✔
❖ If the **actus reus** cannot be proved, then the defendant cannot be convicted	✔
❖ **Mens rea** describes the mental state of the defendant	✔
❖ If a defendant is to be convicted of a criminal offence then the **actus reus** and **mens rea** MUST coincide	✔

A useful technique that will help you prepare for the examination is to work through scenarios in your course textbook identifying the *actus reus* and *mens rea* of each offence. This will help you to identify both elements clearly within a problem question.

We are now moving on to consider the second element of criminal liability, which is *mens rea*.

Mens rea

Mens rea (Latin for guilty mind) must coincide with the *actus reus* of an offence in order for D to be liable for a criminal offence. Like the term *actus reus* you must be careful when dealing with *mens rea* as the term is frequently misunderstood as motive or premeditation, neither of which are relevant to a consideration of *mens rea*.

In this section we will consider:

It is important to note that you must have a sound understanding of *actus reus* (AR) and *mens rea* (MR) in order to answer any problem question in criminal law. These are the buliding blocks of criminal liability – this is not a area of criminal law that you can afford to have a poor understanding of. A detailed understanding of AR and MR are essential to your success in your criminal law assessments.

As you are working your way through this textbook you will need to refer back to this section on *mens rea* frequently as the concepts we discuss in this section permeate all criminal offences.

Types of *mens rea*
In this chapter we will consider the following types of mens rea:

* intention
* recklessness

It is important to note that these are not the only forms of *mens rea*. Other forms of *mens rea* include:

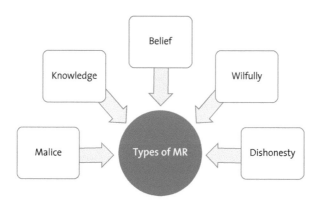

Intention will now be examined in each of these areas, in detail.

Intention

The primary meaning of intention is an aim, purpose or desire to bring about a particular consequence. What is significant in relation to the concept of intention in criminal law is that its meaning has been found by the courts to be a little wider than simply 'aim, purpose or desire'.

Thus a person who embarks on a particular course of conduct in the knowledge that certain consequences are 'virtually certain' to occur is also deemed to have intended the consequences, irrespective as to whether it was their primary aim, purpose or desire.

Thus intention encapsulates two different forms of intention:

❖ direct intention; and
❖ oblique intention, sometimes referred to as an indirect intention.

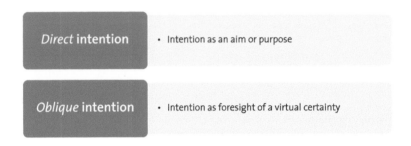

Look at the example below, and consider whether Jodie possesses direct intention or oblique intention.

Example: Jodie owns a taxi firm and is struggling with money, she decides that she can solve her money problems if she makes a claim on her insurance for one of the cars. She decides to cut the brakes on a car with the aim that the car will be badly damaged in an accident. Jodie does not care whether the driver and other people are in the taxi when it crashes. Does Jodie have the *mens rea* for murder?

We could say that Jodie does not aim to hurt people in this case. That is not her purpose. She may in fact hope that everyone is able to jump to safetly! However, she does have foresight of a virtual certainty that the driver/customers/pedestrians may be seriously injured in the process if she cuts the brakes of the car.

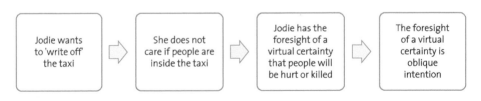

We are now going to consider some of the key cases that have refined the meaning of intention – specifically oblique intention. These cases exclusively involve homicide: murder cases to be more specific. We would recommend that you look at the chapter on murder (Chapter 5) in more detail once you have completed this section on intention.

Refining the meaning of oblique intention

Our starting position is to recognise that there is no statutory definition of intention and that the courts have remained remarkably reluctant to supply students of law and practitioners with a nice, neat definition of the concept! It is also worth noting that the judiciary have tended to consider what does not constitute intention – as opposed to what does constitute intention!

The current approach to the meaning of intention has evolved through a series of cases in which the central argument has always concerned the degree of foresight of probability.

Each case will now be briefly considered, including its importance.

Case law	Circumstances
Hyam [1974] 2 All ER 41	D had caused the death of two of V's children when setting fire to V's house, an action which she insisted was intended merely to frighten V. The House of Lords held that murder could be committed by a person who foresaw the high degree of probability of death or serious injury.
Moloney [1985] AC 905	D shot and killed his stepfather, V. The House of Lords held that the judge had misdirected the jury that intention included foresight of probability. The jury should have been directed that a consequence is intended where it is the natural consequence of D's actions.
Hancock and Shankland [1986] AC 455	Two miners, who were taking part in a national strike, sought to prevent another miner from going to work. They pushed concrete objects from a motorway bridge into the path of a convoy of vehicles taking the miner to work. One of the objects smashed through the windscreen of the taxi and killed the driver. The court held that the greater the degree of probability, the greater the degree of foresight.
Nedrick [1986] 3 ALL ER 1	The defendant had a grudge against Y and set fire to her house in the early hours of the morning. Y's child, V, died in the fire. The defendant said that his only aim was to wake Y up and frighten her. The court held that a virtually certain consequence was sufficient in order for a jury to find that D intended the result.
Woollin [1999] 1 AC 82 HL	In this case the D was frustrated by his baby's continual crying and threw the child against the wall. The child died of head injuries. The court affirmed the decision in *Nedrick* and held that a jury was entitled to infer intention of the basis that the consequences of D's actions were virtually certain.

The case of *Woollin* is therefore the leading case in relation to intention now.

These cases can be summarised in the following timeline:

| *Hyam* [1974] 2 All ER 41 | *Moloney* [1985] AC 905 | *Hancock and Shankland* [1986] AC 455 | *Nedrick* [1986] 3 All ER 1 | *Woollin* [1999] 1 AC 82 |

From these cases we can identify intention as having developed from:

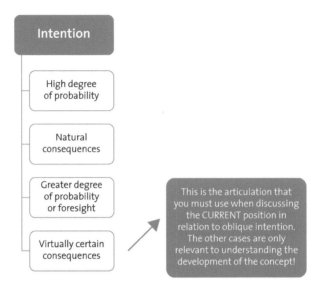

Intention

- High degree of probability
- Natural consequences
- Greater degree of probability or foresight
- Virtually certain consequences

This is the articulation that you must use when discussing the CURRENT position in relation to oblique intention. The other cases are only relevant to understanding the development of the concept!

Case precedent – *R v Woollin* [1998] 3 WLR 382

Facts: D threw his baby in exasperation when it wouldn't stop crying. The baby died from head injuries. It was accepted that the defendant did not intend to cause harm to the child.

Principle: Oblique intention

Application: His conviction for murder was upheld by the Court of Appeal, and his appeal was allowed by the House of Lords. It was found that the appropriate test for oblique intention was that formulated in *Nedrick*, and that this should have been applied to this case.

A jury may find that a defendant intended an outcome if it was a **virtually certain consequence** of his actions and he realised this was the case.

Aim Higher

It is important to note that foresight of a virtual certainty is evidence of intention upon which a jury MAY infer intention. A judge should not equate foresight of a virtual certainty with intention. They are not one and the same.

In *Matthews and Alleyne* [2003] EWCA Crim 192, the Court of Appeal found that foresight of virtual certainty is evidence of intention, in which a jury may infer intention. They are under no obligation to do so.

So we can see the continued further refinement of the meaning of oblique intention here. This is a useful case to use in an assignment relating to intention and the evolution of law.

In the next section we are going to consider recklessness. Given that the meaning of intention clearly includes foresight of a virtual certainty a good starting position for understanding recklessness is to view it as a situation in which D has foresight of harm that falls bellow 'virtual certainty'.

Recklessness

The term recklessness refers to the situation in which a defendant takes a risk which is unjustifiable.

Historically the courts have accepted two species of recklessness:

1. Subjective recklessness
2. Objective recklessness

What is interesting about recklessness is that the courts appear to have gone full circle in terms of which form of recklessness should be applicable in English criminal law.

The recklessness full circle

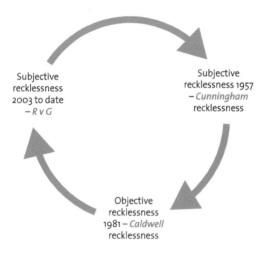

Subjective recklessness 2003 to date – *R v G*

Subjective recklessness 1957 – *Cunningham* recklessness

Objective recklessness 1981 – *Caldwell* recklessness

The two tests which are used to determine subjective and objective recklessness are:

Subjective test	Objective test
• Proof that D is aware of, or foresees the risk of harm	• Proof that the reasonable man would have foreseen the risk of harm
• The taking of the risk is not justifiable	• The taking of the risk is not justifiable

The leading case law with regard to the subjective test for recklessness is the case of *Cunningham*.

Case precedent – *Cunningham* [1957] 2 All ER 412

Facts: Cunningham stole his mother-in-law's gas meter from the basement of the house because it contained cash. However, the gas was still turned on, and she was badly hurt as a result of inhaling the gas. He was charged with maliciously administering a noxious substance so as to endanger life. The *mens rea* for this offence is recklessness.

Principle: Subjective recklessness.

Application: If D had foreseen the risk of harm caused by ripping out the gas meter and gone on to take the risk nonetheless then D was subjectively reckless if the taking of the risk was unjustifiable.

In 1981 the House of Lords introduced an objective form of recklessness in the case of *Caldwell*. It was held that a defendant need not subjectively recognise the risk of harm in order to be reckless. If the reasonably prudent bystander would have foreseen the risk of harm then this was sufficient to establish liability.

The difficulty with this objective test was that it operated particularly harshly in relation to individuals who were unable through age or infirmity to recognise the risk of potential harm. An illustration of the harsh operation of the test can be seen in the case of *Elliot v C (a minor)* (1983).

In *G and another* (2003) the House of Lords overruled *Caldwell* and restored the subjective test for recklessness. You can see the timeline of cases in the diagram below:

Cunningham (1957) 2 QB 396	*Caldwell* [1981] 2 WLR 509	*Lawrence* [1981] AC 510	*R v G & R* [2003] 3 WLR

In *R v G and another* (2003) their Lordships agreed that 'reckless' in criminal damage bears the subjective meaning defined by the Law Commission in its Report, *A Criminal Code for England and Wales Volume 1: Report and Draft Criminal Code Bill* (Law Comm. No 177, 1989). That definition was:

A person acts recklessly within the meaning of section 1 of the Criminal Damage Act 1971 with respect to –

(i)   a circumstance when he is aware of a risk that it exists or will exist;

(ii) a result when he is aware of a risk that it will occur;

and it is, in the circumstances known to him, unreasonable to take the risk.

Transferred malice

In circumstances where a defendant has the *mens rea* to commit a particular crime but the actual victim differs from the intended victim the defendant does not escape liability. The doctrine of transferred malice operates to ensure that a defendant cannot escape liability on the basis that the actual victim differs from the intended victim: *Latimer* (1886).

Example: Sue hates Yusuf and decides to kill him. She tries to shoot Yusuf, but misses and shoots Ralph. Is Sue liable for the death of Ralph?

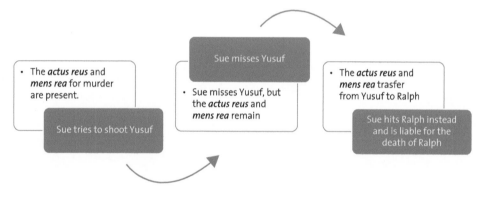

- The *actus reus* and *mens rea* for murder are present.

  Sue tries to shoot Yusuf

- Sue misses Yusuf

- Sue misses Yusuf, but the *actus reus* and *mens rea* remain

- The *actus reus* and *mens rea* trasfer from Yusuf to Ralph

  Sue hits Ralph instead and is liable for the death of Ralph

Case precedent – *Latimer* [1886] 17 QBD 359

Facts: D aimed a blow at another person's head. The blow missed the intended victim and hit another person instead.

Principle: Transferred malice

Application: The *mens rea* of this offence remains the same, transferring from the intended victim to the other person. Therefore the *mens rea* remains as recklessness.

It is important to remember that the *mens rea* transfers exactly in the doctrine of transferred malice. The importance of this can be seen in the case of *Pembliton* (1874). In this case D threw a stone at V, but missed and the stone broke a window instead.

The *mens rea* was intention or recklessness but for an offence against a person, not against property.

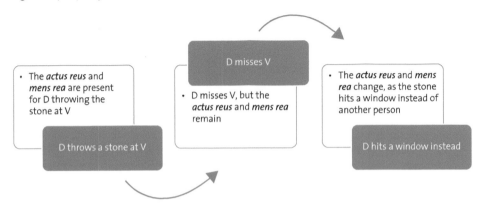

In *Pembliton* (1874) the jury found that the defendant's intention was to hit a person not property and therefore D was not liable.

Look at this case again – what would have happened if a piece of stone flew off and injured B (not the intended victim)? In this case, it *would* constitute transferred malice, as the *actus reus* and *mens rea* are the same, but is transferred from V to B.

Common Pitfall

When applying transferred malice be careful to ensure that the *mens rea* transfers completely and in the same form.

For example, the *mens rea* cannot transfer if the subsequent offence is different from the intended offence.

In the next section we will consider offences for which *mens rea* is not required in respect to at least one aspect of the *actus reus*. These offences are called strict liability offences.

Strict liability

What is key about these strict liability offences is that the defendnt can be convicted even where he or she was unaware of the circumstances. It is important to note that these offences are controversial in nature. As they run counter to the general principle pervading the criminal law that it is the defendant's culpability that justi-fies the imposition of a criminal sanction.

Strict liability offences are normally created by statutes and it is fair to say that they relate to criminal offences which are less serious in nature than the majority of offences that we are considering together in this book. Strict liability offences are most commonly used for regulatory offences, or in relation to health and safety.

In order to be convicted of a strict liability offence the defendant need not have intended, or known about the circumstances or consequence of the act. This means that if the person has committed the act, then they are legally responsible, whatever the circumstances – whatever their mental state. The defendant can then be convicted without the need for the prosecution to demonstrate intention, knowledge, recklessness or negligence.

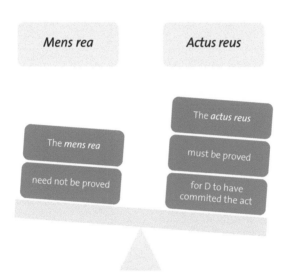

Up for Debate

Strict liability offences are controversial, not least because they are inconsistent with the general ethos of culpability. You will find that there are many articles that focus on this critical debate. Given the nature of strict liability offences and that their focus tends to be regulatory in nature it is more likely that an examiner will set an essay question on this topic. This means that you will need to demonstrate critical understanding of the arguments for and against the use of strict liability offences. Irrespective of your position one thing is for certain: the government are increasing creating strict liability offences. For example HMRC (Her Majesty's Revenue and Customs) in 2014 announced its intention to introduce a strict liability offence of failing to disclose offshore taxable income.

Example: Tony sells cigarettes to Laura, who is 14 years old (under the legal age to buy cigarettes). Strict liability would apply in the following way:

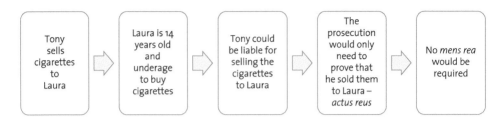

In another example, Zena is late for an appointment and speeds in her car along the motorway. Strict liability would apply in the following way:

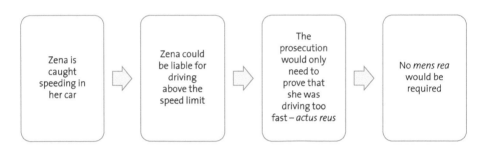

There are a number of useful cases which can be applied when assessing whether an act is classified as strict liability. For example:

Case precedent – *Alphacell v Woodward* [1972] AC 824

Facts: D's factory waste pipe became blocked, and pollutants from the factory entered the local river, polluting the water.

Principle: Strict liability offences do not require proof of *mens rea* or negligence.

Application: D was liable under strict liability because the waste from the factory was the pollutant, despite D not being negligent.

The case of *Gammon v AG* (1985) laid down a set of useful criteria regarding whether or not an offence should be deemed strict. These criteria include:

1. The crime is regulatory as opposed to a true crime; or
2. The crime is one of social concern; or
3. The wording of the Act indicates strict liability; or
4. The offence carries a small penalty.

Strict liability is also often criticised for producing unfair and harsh outcomes. This was highlighted in the case of *Pharmaceutical Society of Great Britain v Storkwain*

(1986). In this case pharmacist provided drugs to a person who had forged the prescription. The pharmacist did not know that the prescription was forged, but was on the basis prosecuted strict liability for providing the drugs to the person. Only the act of providing the drugs had to be established.

Aim Higher

Strict liability offences can be justified as they provide a greater level of protection and safety to the public; and because the *mens rea* does not need to be proved, a conviction may be more likely.

A summary of the points we have covered in this section is:

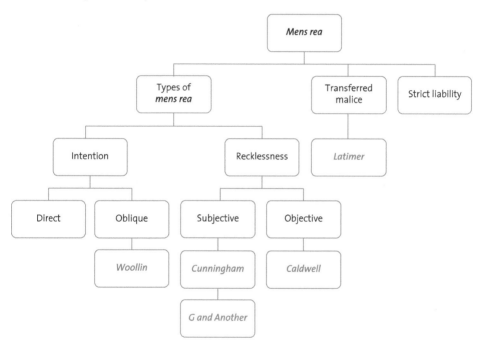

Absence of defence

Chapter 1. That being the formula for constructing criminal liability involves: *actus reus* + *mens rea* + the absence of a defence + criminal liability. Therefore is D commits and criminal offence and is able to demonstrate the existence of a valid defence then D will not be held criminally liable.

On the other hand if the D has the committed the *actus reus* of an offence with the requisite *mens rea* but fails to put forward a defence they will held liable for their conduct.

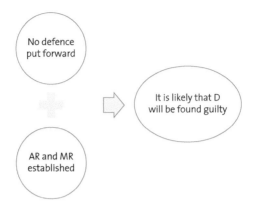

General defences are considered in much more detail later on in this book in Chapter 10 and Chapter 11.

Putting it into practice

To aid your understanding of *mens rea*, and intention in particular, plan how you would answer the following question. Remember to include case law to illustrate your answer.

'Intention must always be proven in the case of serious offences.'

Suggested solution
You should always adopt a structured response to an essay question rather than writing down everything that you know in no particular order!

1. Introduction
2. Main body
3. Conclusion

This question is asking you to consider two separate issues:

1. What is intention – what does it mean?
2. Whether anything less than intention can suffice in the case of serious criminal offences.

In relation to part 1, you will need to explain the following:

❖ that there is no statutory definition of intention;
❖ intention means – aim, purpose desire;
❖ it also has a broader meaning – explain the difference between direct and oblique intention;
❖ you should provide an explanation of the historical development of the concept of oblique intention;
❖ you must explain the leading case of *Woollin* and recent refinements such as the case of *Matthews* and *Alleyne*.

In relation to part 2 you will need to consider:

❖ any historic blurring between the test for oblique intention and recklessness;
❖ where intention ends and recklessness begins;
❖ what is meant by the term recklessness: subjective and objective recklessness;
❖ whether intention should include foresight of a virtual certainty;
❖ the most serious criminal offences require proof of intention – however, there are still some very serious offences that can be committed where there is proof of recklessness – subjective reckless manslaughter, for example.

Table of key cases referred to in this chapter

Key case	Brief facts	Principle
Fagan v MPC [1968] 3 All ER 442	D omitted to act by driving off the policeman's foot	Omissions
DPP v Santana-Bermudez [2003] EWHC 2908 (Admin)	D created danger by failing to tell the policeman about the needle in his pocket	Omissions
Pittwood [1902] TLR 37	Omission under D's duty to act, under his employment contract	Omissions
R v Quick & Paddison [1973] 3 AER 397	Automatism is a possible defence for actions	Voluntariness
Pagett [1983] 76 Cr App R 279	D caused the death of V, even though D did not directly kill V himself	Legal causation
R v Jordan [1956] 40 CR App R 152	D stabbed V, but V died from poor treatment at the hospital, rather than the injuries	Legal causation
R v Cheshire [1991] 3 All ER 670	D shot V. V died of complications from the gunshot wound.	Legal causation
Blaue [1975] 1WLR 1411	D stabbed V, V refused treatment on religious grounds. D liable for the death of V	Thin skull rule
Hyam [1974] 2 ALL ER 41	D set fire to a house, causing the death of two children	Intention
Moloney [1985] AC 905	D shot his father, but was unaware that the gun was pointing at him	Intention
Hancock and Shankland [1986] AC 455	Two miners threw a concrete brick from a bridge. Their intention was to stop the car, not cause injury.	Intention

Key case	Brief facts	Principle
Nedrick [1986] 3 ALL ER 1	D set fire to V's house, killing V. Intention was present.	Intention
Woollin [1998] 3 WLR 382	D threw his crying baby, who died. However, D did not intend to harm the child.	Intention
Cunningham [1957] 2 QB 396	D took a gas meter off the wall, poisoning his mother-in-law	Subjective recklessness
Caldwell [1981] 2 WLR 509	House of Lords refined the meaning of recklessness into objective recklessness	*Caldwell* (objective) recklessness
Lawrence [1981] AC 510	House of Lords refined the meaning of recklessness into objective recklessness	*Caldwell* (objective) recklessness
R v R & G [2003] 3 WLR	Two boys started a fire in a bin, which spread to a shop	Subjective recklessness
Latimer [1886] 17 QBD 359	D tried to hit A, missed and hit B instead	Transferred malice
Pembliton [1874] LR CCR 119	D threw a stone at V, missed and hit a window instead	Transferred malice
Alphacell v Woodward [1972] AC 824	Pollutants from D's factory entered a river course	Strict liability
Sweet v Parsley [1969] AC 132	Landlady not convicted because she did not intend her house to be used for drug taking	Strict liability
Gammon v AG [1985] AC 1	Identified criteria for determining strict liability	Strict liability
Pharmaceutical Society of GB v Storkwain [1986] 2 ALL ER 265	When strict liability can lead to an injustice	Strict liability

---

@ **Visit the book's companion website to test your knowledge**

❖ Resources include a subject map, revision tip podcasts, downloadable diagrams, MCQ quizzes for each chapter, and a flashcard glossary

❖ www.routledge.com/cw/optimizelawrevision

3

Non-fatal Offences Against the Person

Understand the law

- Can you define each of the offences in this chapter?
- Which offences in this chapter are common law offences, and which are statutory offences outlined in the OAPA 1861?

Remember the details

- Can you remember the *actus reus* and *mens rea* of each offence?
- Can you define each element of the *actus reus* and *mens rea* using case law examples?

Reflect critically on areas of debate

- Do you understand how consent may operate as a defence to an offence in this chapter?
- Can you define intention and recklessness accurately and critically discuss them in relation to case law examples?

Contextualise

- Can you relate these offences to other areas of criminal law such as sexual offences and homicide?

Apply your skills and knowledge

- Can you complete the example essay and problem questions provided in each section of this chapter using case law and statutes to support your answer?

Chapter Map

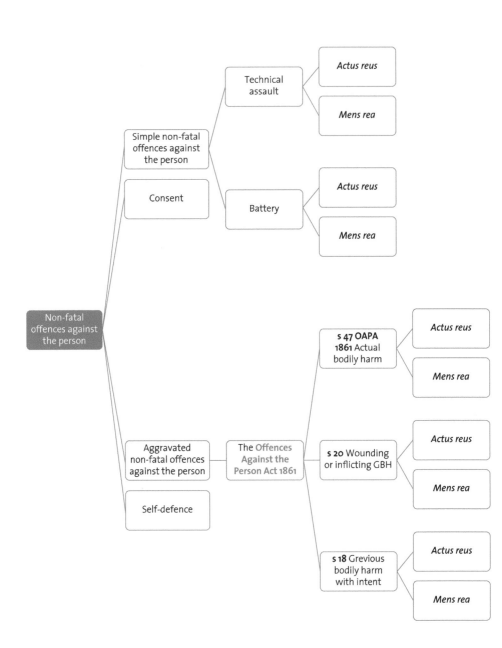

Elements Chart

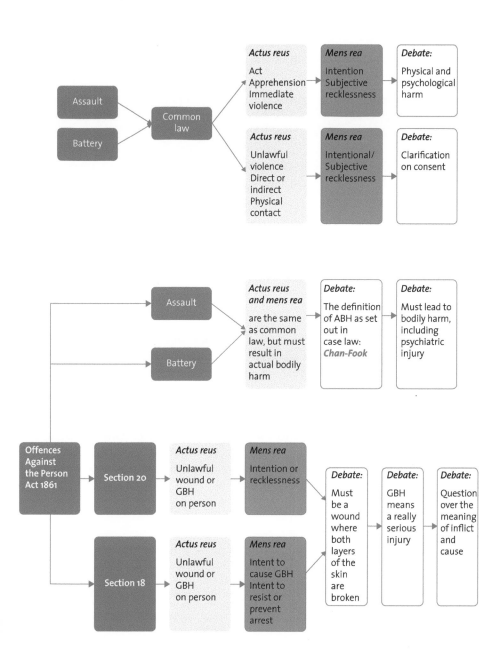

Introduction

In this chapter we are going to consider non-fatal offences against the person. This is a popular examination topic in its own right, but issues in relation to non-fatal offences against the person can overlap with sexual offences, property offences and homicide against the person. This is another area of the criminal law syllabus in which is it vitally important that you have a solid understanding of because this area of law may be related to a significant proportion of your studies.

> ## Aim Higher
>
> As you progress through this chapter, think about how these non-fatal offences relate to other criminal offences, such as homicide, sexual offences or property offences. This will help your understanding of these and other offences, and how they interact.

In this chapter we will start by considering the least serious offences against the person and at the end we will consider the most serious offences against the person. A traditional classification for non-fatal offences against the person is to classify them as 'simple offences' and 'aggravated offences'.

Simple non-fatal offences and aggravated offences against the person

We will start our consideration of non-fatal offences against the person by considering offences created under the common law. These non-fatal offences against the person are common law offences; however, they are charged under s 39 of the Criminal Justice Act (CJA) 1988.

The more serious non-fatal offences against the person are statutory offences and they are provided for in the Offences Against the Person Act (OAPA) 1861. In this section we will consider the following offences: assault occasioning actual bodily harm (ABH) (s 47), malicious wounding or causing GBH (s 20) and finally malicious wounding or causing GBH with intent (s 18), which is the most serious non-fatal offence against the person.

Common law	Offences Against the Person Act 1861
• Technical assault • Battery • Charged under s 39 Criminal Justice Act 1988	• s 47 OAPA 1861 Assault occasioning actual bodily harm • s 20 OAPA 1861 Malicious wounding or causing grievous bodily harm • s 18 OAPA 1861 Malicious wounding or causing grievous bodily harm with intent

We will look at each of the offences in turn. As you read through this chapter, it is important to be clear about the differences between the simple common law offences and the statutory aggravated offences created by the OAPA 1861.

Simple non-fatal offences against the person

Introduction

Before we start this section we need to issue you with words of warnings: criminal law students and the media often use the term 'assault' rather loosely, and it is important that you use language with precision. The term assault is an umbrella term, and it is frequently used to describe:

❖ a technical assault or 'psychic assault'
❖ a battery.

We would encourage you to identify the specific offences – and rather than using the term 'assault', demonstrate to the examiner that you are aware that there are two distinct offences that fall under this umbrella term.

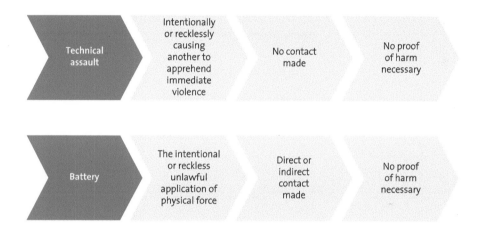

Section 39 Criminal Justice Act 1988

Although the offences of technical assault and battery are common law offences they are charged under s 39 of the CJA 1988. Section 39 provides that these offences are summary offences and upon conviction a person is liable for a level 5 fine and a maximum term of imprisonment of six months.

Technical assault

This offence is a common law offence and as such, the definition of the offence is not located in the statute books. The case of *Collins v Wilcock* (1984) 3 All ER 374 provides a definition for the two offences:

> *The law draws a distinction ... between an assault and battery.* **An assault is an act which causes another person to apprehend the infliction of immediate unlawful force on his person**; *a battery is the actual infliction of unlawful force on another person.*

We will now identify the elements of the *actus reus* (AR) and *mens rea* (MR) for the offence of technical assault.

You must remember that it is vital that you split the definition of each offence into the AR and MR and that you deal with each of these elements individually.

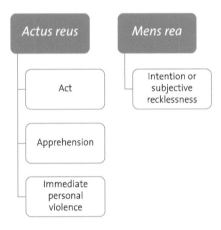

D does an Act

The first element of the AR is that the defendant (D) must do an act. The act can include a physical act such as a gesture, or words.

❖ A technical assault cannot be committed by omission: *Fagan v Metropolitan Police Commissioner* (1968). We considered this case in Chapter 2 on General Principles of Criminal Law. In this case D's refusal to move his car off the police officer's foot was considered a continuing act.

Up for Debate

In order for the offence of technical assault to be made out the D must have done an act. This means an act, rather than an omission: *Fagan v MPC* (1969). However, in *DPP v Santana-Bermudez* (2003), the Divisional Court stated:

> 'where someone (by act or word or a combination of the two) creates a danger and thereby exposes another to a reasonably foreseeable risk of injury which materialises, there is an evidential basis for the actus reus of an assault occasioning actual bodily harm.'

Thus there are situations in which a failure to act will be deemed sufficient – primarily where the D creates a dangerous situation.

❖ An act can also refer to other types of action. This means that the threat does not need to be a purely physical act. It can be committed by words.

Case precedent – *Constanza* [1997] Crim LR 576

Facts: D sent two threatening letters, made numerous silent phone calls, wrote offensive words on Vs front door and regularly followed her home. This led to V suffering clinical depression.

Principle: The Court of Appeal held that letters and words could amount to an act for the purposes of a technical assault.

Application: Use this case to illustrate that words alone, written or verbal, are sufficient to constitute an act for the purposes of a technical assault.

It is important to note that words can also negate a technical assault which may otherwise occur. For example in *Tuberville v Savage* (1669) it was held that words can also indicate that an act will not occur.

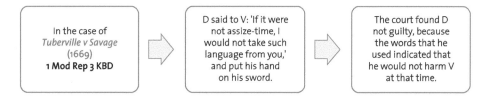

The *actus reus* of the technical assault also requires that V **apprehend immediate unlawful force**.

D causes V to apprehend immediate unlawful force
As in any area of law, whenever you identify what the law is, you need to make sure you break it down into its constituent parts and define it. In this case, the act of common law assault is when V:

But what do each of these mean? Some elements seem obvious, but others need further clarification (such as 'immediate'). The only way that some words can be fully understood is through examining the refinement of the terms through case law.

Aim Higher

You will gain extra marks by using case law to provide authority for your articulation of the law. Using case law demonstrates your level of knowledge to the examiner, and strengthens the point you are making.

The case precedents in this textbook are not the ONLY precedents to illustrate points of law though, and it is possible to have different cases illustrating the same point of law!

Distinguishing apprehension from fear

For the *actus reus* of assault, the requirement is that V must **apprehend** immediate personal violence.

Common Pitfalls

Be careful here, as there is a common mistake that is made by many – this is not about being in fear; instead V must '*apprehend*' the violence immediately.

When looking at a problem question, you must be clear that V has actually **apprehended** the violence.

Example: If D swings a baseball bat towards V, then V will probably see it as it is being swung and apprehend immediate unlawful personal violence. Apprehension is not necessarily the same thing as fear, though!

The apprehension of violence does not need to be apprehension of significant violence: it can be trivial but it does need to be unwanted, and therefore unlawful.

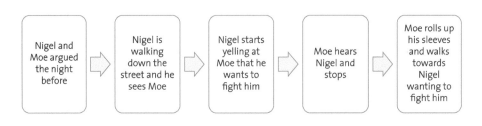

In this example, Nigel shouting at Moe and saying that he wants to fight him is the act that leads Moe to apprehend the violence. Moe rolling up his sleeves and walking towards Nigel further evidences this.

However, if we manipulate the facts of the example and Nigel now sees Moe whilst Nigel is a passenger on a train that is moving, it is obvious that Moe cannot use force against Nigel in this situation. Therefore there is no apprehension of immediate unlawful force and there is no technical assault.

Immediate

The apprehension must be of immediate unlawful force. The immediacy of the force is important, because it is directly related to V apprehending and/or experiencing the force. If the violence is not immediate, then the *actus reus* cannot be made out.

The term immediate does not mean instantaneous; it means imminent: *Smith v Chief Superintendent of Woking Police Station* (1983).

The next question considers how immediate the threat of violence must be. Let us work through an example, which you can then reapply to a problem question.

Sally tells her neighbour, Holly, that if she does not keep her garden tidy, she is going to give her 'a slap' in a fortnight. Has Sally committed a technical assault?

There are various issues arising here:

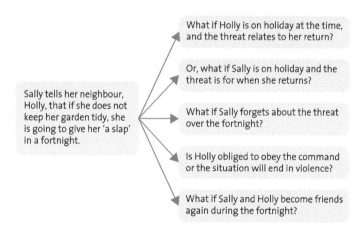

We can see from this diagram that there are many variables, all arising from the lack of immediacy. From these, we can see that immediacy is missing from this scenario.

This is a useful way to analyse a scenario within a problem question or exam, by determining how 'immediate' the unlawful violence would be, and if the period is short enough or imminent enough for apprehension to occur.

Unlawful force

The force which D is threatening must be unlawful. This simply means that the offence of technical assault will not be made out where the threatened force is lawful. We will consider the concept of when force is lawful or unlawful in more detail later in this chapter.

We are now going to move on to consider the *mens rea* for the offence of technical assault.

Intention or subjective recklessness

We considered the concepts of intention and subjective recklessness in Chapter 2. Technical assault is a crime of basic intent. This means that intention or proof of recklessness will suffice.

Intention: This is where it is D's aim, purpose or desire to bring about a particular consequence. A jury or magistrates are also entitled to infer intention on the basis that D foresaw the consequences of his actions as virtually certain.

Subjective recklessness: The test for subjective recklessness was articulated in the case of *Cunningham*. It provides that D is reckless where he foresees the risk of harm and goes on to take that risk. The risk is an unjustifiable risk.

Another relevant case regarding recklessness is *R v Spratt* (1991). In this case, D was shooting an air rifle at a target, but shot a young girl, who he did not know was there. The Court found D not guilty, because he did not act intentionally or recklessly.

Example: Roger and Jane have an argument and Roger walks up and down the road looking for Jane, intending to frighten her into agreeing with his viewpoint by pointing a gun at her.

We can see from this example that the aim, purpose or desire of Roger's actions is to frighten Jane.

If this was a problem question, think about how you would establish that Roger has committed the offence of technical assault.

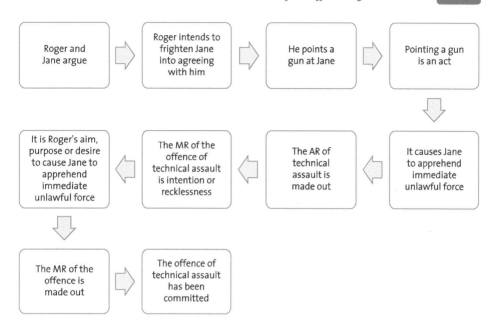

We are now going to consider the second simple non-fatal offence against the person: Battery.

Battery

As you will recall from the introduction to simple non-fatal offences against the person, this offence is a common law offence. As such the definition of the offence is located in the decisions of the courts and not in the statute books.

We return again to the case of *Collins v Wilcock* (1984), which provides a definition for the two offences:

> The law draws a distinction ... between an assault and battery. An assault is an act which causes another person to apprehend the infliction of immediate unlawful force on his person; **a battery is the actual infliction of unlawful force on another person.**

Thus the offence of battery requires the infliction of unlawful force on another person. As with technical assault, make sure that you discuss and define the meaning of the words. For example, a discussion of 'infliction' would be essential when considering the offence and liability.

Reminder – the *actus reus* and *mens rea* for common law battery are:

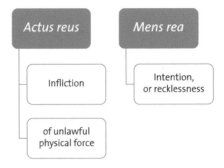

Infliction

The *actus reus* requires the infliction of physical force. We must therefore understand what is meant by the term infliction.

❖   The slightest application of physical force may amount to an infliction.
❖   This includes the touching of a victim's clothing: *Thomas* (1985).
❖   The application of force will often involve direct contact and touching between D and V. However, this is not a requirement because the contact can also be indirect. For example:

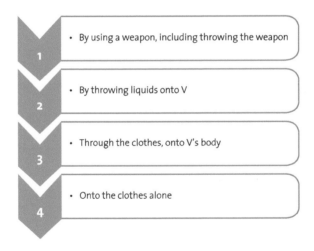

1 • By using a weapon, including throwing the weapon

2 • By throwing liquids onto V

3 • Through the clothes, onto V's body

4 • Onto the clothes alone

The courts have also taken a view, as with technical assault, that the infliction must require some positive action and not an omission. This was highlighted in the case of *Innes v Wylie* (1844), where a policeman blocked the path of a defendant. The judge held that battery should be a positive act, rather than inaction. Therefore the defendant must have done some act in order for it to be constituted as a battery.

Aim Higher

Contrast the cases of *Santana-Bermudez* (2004) and *Miller* (1983) to consider omissions within these cases.

Both cases are particularly important in relation to omissions, and are extremely useful cases when answering a problem question on battery.

Example: Nora pokes Shaun with a sharp pencil. From the discussion above, would you argue that this is direct or indirect force? Why is this? Which cases can you use to support your argument?

❖ There is no requirement that the touching is hostile: *Wilson v Pringle* (1986).
❖ A battery may include a continuing act as per the case of *Fagan*.
❖ The application of physical force need not be a direct application of force; it can be achieved indirectly: *DPP v K* (1990).

Case precedent – *DPP v K* [1997] 1 ALL ER 331

Facts: A young boy put acid from the school science lab into a hand drier in the toilet block. The acid caused harm to another child when he operated the drier.

Principle: D was found guilty, and the judge noted that for battery, force need not be directly applied.

Application: The application of force need not be direct.

The second element of the AR is that the infliction of physical force must be unlawful

The physical force must be unlawful
In order to construct liability for battery the prosecution must be able to establish that the application of physical force was *unlawful*. So, there is no battery where:

V expressly or impliedly consents to the touching and has the capacity to consent	
Consent can be provided throughout everyday life	For example shaking hands, moving past someone or giving someone a hug

D has an excuse for inflicting physical force, or genuinely believes that he has a lawful justification	
For example he acts in self-defence or to prevent a crime from taking place	Action is a parent reasonably chastising a child

This can of course provide problems for the court in terms of when such actions can be classed as unlawful, for example everyday actions where people touch another, such as walking down a busy street or shaking hands with a client.

When answering a problem question on simple offences against the person check the type of unlawful touching which has occurred, and if it can actually constitute everyday activity. If so, it is unlikely that this would constitute unlawful personal violence.

Other factors that you might want to take into consideration include the proximity of the touching and the degree of physical force used. For example:

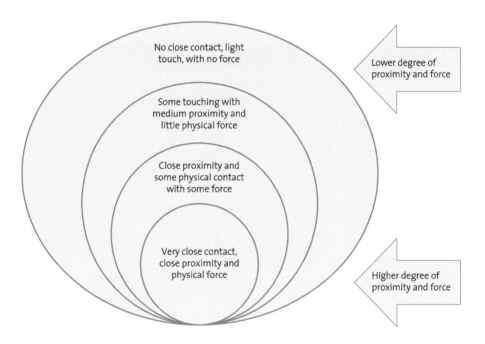

The higher the degree of proximity and the greater the degree of force the more likely it will be unlawful.

As with common law assault, the rule on omissions is the same in relation to battery as it is for technical assault. The offence cannot be committed by omission. It is possible for psychiatric injury to constitute a battery.

Case precedent – *R v Ireland* [1997] 3 WLR 534

Facts: D made a number of silent phone calls to women, who suffered psychological injuries as a result. The issue here was whether silent phone calls can constitute a technical assault and whether the psychological injury caused can constitute a battery.

Principle: Words alone and silent phone calls can amount to a technical assault; psychological injury caused by this can amount to a battery and potentially an aggravated offence.

Application: Use this case to illustrate that the application of force can take many forms.

Intention or recklessness

For the *mens rea* of battery D must intend to apply unlawful force onto V, even if it does not lead to harm or injury. Intention and subjective recklessness are also considered above in relation to technical assault

For example:

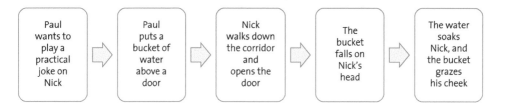

| Paul wants to play a practical joke on Nick | Paul puts a bucket of water above a door | Nick walks down the corridor and opens the door | The bucket falls on Nick's head | The water soaks Nick, and the bucket grazes his cheek |

In this example, the water soaks Nick, and the bucket grazes his cheek. Paul has shown intention as it is his aim, purpose or desire that Nick gets covered in water. He is reckless as to whether force will be applied in other ways (through the bucket hitting Nick).

A useful case to help explain recklessness in relation to battery is *R v Venna* (1975). In this case, D resisted arrest by a policeman, and in so doing broke a bone in the policeman's hand. D argued that he did not intend to harm the policeman. The Court found D guilty as he was subjectively reckles as to whether the police officer would be injured.

| Resisting arrest | Bone is broken | Intentionally/recklessly applied force | *Mens rea* is established |

Activity 1

Using case law to support your answer, attempt the following questions.

(1) Annie throws a rock at Brian, which misses him. Just after it happens, Brian is told that Annie threw the rock at him. Does this constitute an assault?

(2) Nigel and Daphne have an argument at work. Later that evening Nigel phones Daphne and threatens to hit her. Does this constitute assault?

Using the discussion above, consider the circumstances of each question, and identify if an assault has occurred in each question.

A summary of the points we have covered in this section is:

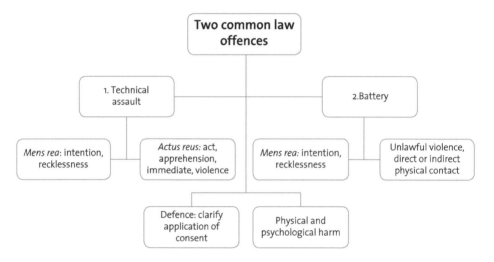

In the next section of this chapter we are going to consider aggravated offences against the person.

Aggravated offences against the person

Introduction
There are three aggravated offences against the person created under the Offences Against the Person Act (OAPA) 1861.

1. Assault occasioning actual bodily harm: s 47.
2. Maliciously wounding or inflicting grievous bodily harm: s 20.
3. Maliciously wounding or inflicting grievous bodily harm with intent: s 18.

In relation to aggravated offences it might help you to remember that the lower the section number the more serious the offence is! These offences are aggravated offences because, unlike technical assault and battery, these offences require proof of some degree of harm.

Aim Higher

The seriousness of the offences is determined by the level and type of harm caused and the *mens rea* of D. These distinctions are important in terms of identifying the right offence in an assessment question on non-fatal offences against the person.

In this book we have considered the least serious offences first, working our way up to the more serious non-fatal offences against the person. The general convention when answering a problem question is to start with the MOST SERIOUS potential offence and work your way towards the LEAST SERIOUS offence.

Section 47: Assault occasioning actual bodily harm
Section 47 provides:

> Whosoever shall be convicted upon an indictment of any assault occasioning actual bodily harm shall be liable to be kept in penal servitude.

As with our discussion of all other substantive offences we must first break down the elements of the offence created by s 47.

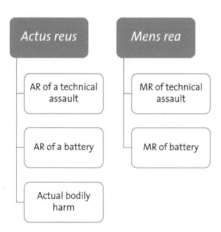

One of the most important points for you to remember (this is something that is very often overlooked) is that in order to establish liability for the s 47 offence you must be able to establish the AR and MR, or technical assault or battery AND actual bodily harm.

Actus reus of technical assault or battery
We have covered these issues in detail earlier in this chapter. You should remind yourself of the constituent elements of both a technical assault and a battery.

Occasioning actual bodily harm

You must additionally be able to demonstrate that the technical assault or battery has 'occasioned' or caused actual bodily harm.

It is important to understand the meaning of the words **actual bodily harm**, to ensure that you do not confuse this offence with the offences of battery or wounding. In this section, we will use the case of *Chan-Fook* (1994) as a basis.

In *Chan-Fook* the words actual bodily harm were defined by the judge, and are now understood as:

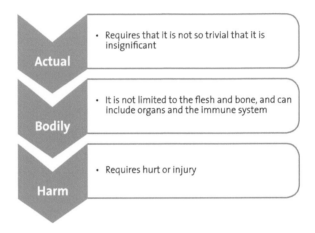

Actual
- Requires that it is not so trivial that it is insignificant

Bodily
- It is not limited to the flesh and bone, and can include organs and the immune system

Harm
- Requires hurt or injury

These meanings were tested in the case of *DPP v Smith* (2006), when D cut off V's ponytail and some hair off the top of her head without her consent. V became very distressed as a result. However, D was acquitted because the judge ruled that hair was above the body and consists of dead follicles. But on appeal, D was found guilty. Sir Igor Judge stated:

> *In my judgment, whether it is alive beneath the surface of the skin or dead tissue above the surface of the skin, the hair is an attribute and part of the human body. It is intrinsic to each individual and to the identity of each individual. Although it is not essential to my decision, I note that an individual's hair is relevant to his or her autonomy. Some regard it as their crowning glory. Admirers may so regard it in the object of their affections.* **Even if, medically and scientifically speaking, the hair above the surface of the scalp is no more than dead tissue, it remains part of the body and is attached to it.** *While it is so attached, in my judgment it falls within the meaning of 'bodily' in the phrase 'actual bodily harm'. It is concerned with the body of the individual victim.*
>
> *In my judgment, the respondent's actions in cutting off a substantial part of the victim's hair in the course of an assault on her – like putting paint on it or some unpleasant substance which marked or damaged it without causing injury elsewhere – is capable of amounting to an assault which occasions actual bodily harm. The justices were wrong in law.*
>
> *(DPP v Smith [2006] EWHC 94 Para 18)*

This case is important because it identifies that hair is considered part of the body, and its unlawful cutting is an offence. The case is summarised below, and is a useful case to remember and apply in an exam:

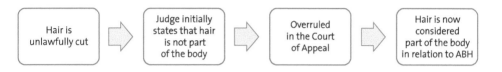

| Hair is unlawfully cut | ⇨ | Judge initially states that hair is not part of the body | ⇨ | Overruled in the Court of Appeal | ⇨ | Hair is now considered part of the body in relation to ABH |

Going back to the case of *Chan-Fook* (1994), this case also highlighted that *bodily* is not limited to 'skin, flesh and bones' since the body includes organs, the nervous system and the brain, and also *psychiatric* injury.

However, 'bodily' does not include:

❖ emotions such as fear, distress or panic;
❖ states of mind which are not evidence of an identifiable clinical condition.

This definition was tested in the case of *R v D* (2006), when clarification was provided by the courts on the nature of psychiatric injury, as in the case precedent below:

Case precedent – *R v D* [2006] EWCA Crim 1139

D's wife committed suicide, and D was charged with manslaughter and GBH. The judge ruled that the case should not proceed, as there was not a reasonable chance of conviction. The Court sought to provide a distinction between a medically diagnosed *psychological* condition and a medically diagnosed *psychiatric* condition. The court stated:

> 'The problem which we have to address is whether psychological injury, not amounting to recognisable psychiatric illness, falls within the ambit of bodily harm for the purposes of the 1861 Act. The Chan-Fook case drew a clear distinction between such identifiable injury and other states of mind. It did so consistently with authority in the civil law. The line identified in Chan-Fook was applied by the House of Lords to the criminal law, and has been consistently applied in claims for damages for personal injury' (Para 31).

Thus following *Chan-Fook* (1994), when V claims psychiatric injury as part of the harm suffered, it is essential to gain expert advice to substantiate that the injury has taken place, and is as a result of D. The *Chan-Fook* case is key in determining the meaning of ABH, and a number of cases have subsequently refined the meaning of ABH. These are described in the case law timeline below.

This timeline is really useful to remember because it tells you the three key cases regarding the definition of ABH, which you can then apply to a problem question or scenario, when discussing the relevant offence.

We are now going to consider the *mens rea* for the **s 47** offence.

Intention or recklessness as to the technical assault or battery

We have already considered the meaning of both intention and recklessness in the context of technical assault and battery. We will not repeat these principles here. What is key, however, is that it is not necessary for the defendant to have had foresight that ABH would be caused: *Savage* (1992).

Activity 2

Look at the scenario below, and then answer the following question:

Ali is out walking in the park with his dog. Bee and his wife Cea walk over to pat the dog. Ali, thinking Bee may be coming to attack him, instructs the dog to attack Bee. The dog bites Bee's hand, and Cea, witnessing the incident from a few yards away, becomes scared and runs off. Cea is now suffering from anxiety (due to the incident) and goes to see her doctor.

Which offences if any have been committed here?

Faced with this scenario, it is important to first break down the information, and then consider each of the non-fatal offences (NFOs) in turn.

Aim Higher

It is not uncommon for a question on non-fatal offences against the person to include a number of different potential offences. The best strategy when you have multiple events and/or multiple parties is to deal with the parties or events in the order in which they appear in the question.

Let's try breaking this scenario down into manageable components. This can be shown diagrammatically, which is a useful way to plan your answers when dealing with a scenario or problem question within an exam:

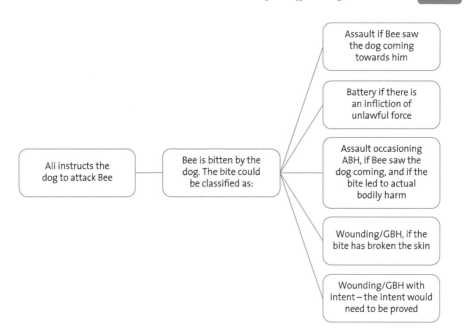

Malicious wounding and causing grievous bodily harm

Introduction

The **Offences Against the Person Act (OAPA) 1861** contains two offences which, on the face of it, appear very similar. They both involve the concept of grievous bodily harm. However, one offence is much more serious and this is the s 18 offence because it is committed with intent to commit grievous bodily harm.

We can see below the scale of seriousness between the two offences, and why s 18 is more serious:

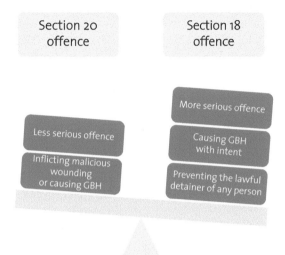

The table below outlines the two different offences. It is important to understand the full differences between them.

Section 20	Section 18
The less serious offence, which is malicious wounding (infliction) or causing grievous bodily harm (GBH) (Offences Against the Person Act 1861 s 20).	The second and more serious offence is causing grievous bodily harm with intent to cause grievous bodily harm or with intent to resist or prevent the lawful apprehension or detainer of any person (Offences Against the Person Act 1861 s 18).

Common Pitfalls

Remember that wounding and GBH relates to **s 20** of the **OAPA 1861**, and that wounding and GBH **with intent** refers to **s 18** of the **OAPA 1861**. **But**, that they are separate offences.

Section 20: wounding or inflicting GBH

Section 20 of the OAPA 1861 provides:

Whosoever shall unlawfully and maliciously wound or inflict any grievous bodily harm upon any other person, either with or without any weapon or instrument, shall be guilty of a misdemeanour, and being convicted thereof shall be liable ... to be kept in penal servitude ...

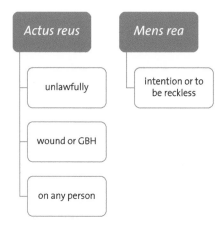

As is now our tradition we will now consider each of the elements of the s 20 offence in detail.

Actus reus – the meaning of unlawful

An act will not be considered unlawful where it was:

To prevent another crime	Reasonable chastisement	In self-defence
• The act may be justified if it was taken to prevent a more serious crime	• For example, a parent using reasonable chastisement on a child	• The act may be justified if D can show that he acted in self-defence

Distinguishing between a wound and GBH

For both the s 20 and s 18 offences, there must be a wound or GBH arising from D's actions.

A wound occurs where both layers of the skin (the dermis and the epidermis) are broken.

Case Quote

For example in the case of *C (A Minor) v Eisenhower* [1983] 3 WLR 537, when an air gun pellet caused a bruise and weeping to the eye, Robert Goff LJ stated that:

> 'In my judgment, having regard to the cases, there is a continuous stream of authority – to which I myself can find no exception at all – which does establish that a wound is, as I have stated, a break in the continuity of the whole skin.'

The outcome of the case was, therefore, that D was found not guilty, because the wound did not break both layers of the skin.

Grevious bodily harm (GBH) is defined as 'a really serious injury', such as a broken bone, severe bruising, missing teeth etc. This meaning was tested in the case of *Bollom* (2003).

Case Quote

In *R v Bollom* [2003] 2 Cr App R6, the defendant injured his partner's young toddler, causing bruising and grazes. He was found guilty of GBH, but appealed on the basis that the injuries were not severe enough to constitute GBH. The Court of Appeal found that the phrase should be given its ordinary and natural meaning of 'really serious bodily harm'. Thus, in the Court's view:

'The ambit of grievous bodily harm is therefore potentially wide, as is demonstrated by the inclusion, for instance, of psychiatric injury ... The prosecution do not have to prove that the harm was life- threatening, danger ous or permanent: R v Ashman (1858) ... Moreover, there is no requirement in law that the victim should require treatment or that the harm should extend beyond soft tissue damage ... or the harm would have lasting consequences.'

The victim in *Bollom* was a young child. This prompted the court to further remark that, when assessing the severity and impact of injuries, other considerations such as age and health should be included.

Examples of wounds and GBH

Wound: Cuts, puncture wounds including those caused by a broken bone piercing through the skin

GBH: Broken bones, internal injuries, pscyhiatric injury

Aim Higher

More detail on the type of injuries that will constitute:

1. battery
2. ABH

3. GBH
4. wounding

can be found in the CPS Charging Standards on the CPS website: www.cps.gov.uk/legal/l_to_o/offences_against_the_person/

Demonstrating an understanding of how the CPS views the severity of different injuries for charging purposes will enhance the quality of an answer on offences against the person (OAP) and attract more marks from the examiner.

It is important to note that GBH can also include psychiatric injury, although this must also be sufficiently serious to be classed as GBH: *Burstow* (1997).

In *Burstow*:

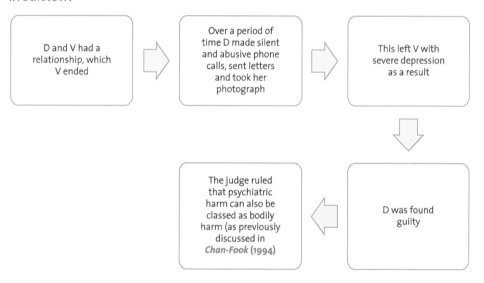

Key Points: Offences Against the Person Act

Offence	The injury	Examples/case law
Assault	There is no physical injury, but there is apprehension of violence	*Constanza* (1997) *Tuberville v Savage* (1669) *Fagan v MPC* (1969) *Cunningham* (1957)
Battery	A trivial injury, such as a poke or push	*R v Ireland* (1997) *DPP v K* (1990) *R v Venna* (1975)
ABH	Is more than trivial, and requires hurt or injury, such as a graze or bruise	*Chan-Fook* (1994) *DPP v Smith* (2006) *R v D* (2006)

Offence	The injury	Examples/case law
A wound	Occurs when both layers of the skin are broken – the dermis and the epidermis	*C v Eisenhower* (1983) *R v Belfon* (1976) *Savage and Parmenter* (1991)
GBH	Is a really serious injury, such as missing teeth or severe bruising	*Burstow* (1997) *Bollom* (2003)

Aim Higher

A really useful exercise when revising for a criminal law assessment is to create your own case tables. Putting examples and case law into columns can serve as a really useful quick reference resource – particularly in the last moments before you go into the examination room!

On any person

The *actus reus* here is very straight forward, and ensures that the offence is committed against **another person**.

Mens rea

The s 20 offence can be committed by proving that D acted intentionally or recklessly. We have considered the *mens rea* of intent and recklessness already within this chapter, and again the same principles apply here.

The defendant need not have foreseen the severity of the harm caused, but should have some foresight of harm: *Mowatt* (1968).

It is worth noting that the wording of s 20 includes the term 'maliciously'. This simply means with intention or subjective recklessness.

Section 18: grievous bodily harm
Section 18 of the OAPA provides:

Whosoever shall unlawfully and maliciously by any means whatsoever wound or cause any grievous bodily harm to any person ... with intent ... to do some ... grievous bodily harm to any person, or with intent to resist or prevent the lawful apprehension or detainer of any person, shall be guilty of felony, and being convicted thereof shall be liable ... to be kept in penal servitude for life ...

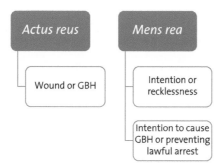

We will now consider the individual elements – although, as you will see, many of the principles that we have discussed in relation to s 20 of the OAPA are applicable here also.

D must cause a wound or cause GBH
The first point worth noting is that s 20 uses the word 'inflict' and s 18 uses the word 'cause'. The following cases confirm that *cause* and *inflict* have the same meaning:

D must have acted recklessly or acted with intention
The same principles in relation to intention and recklessness apply here as applied in relation to our earlier discussion of these *mens rea* elements.

However there is an important difference between the s20 and s18 offences and that is the issue of ulterior.

❖ The s 20 offence requires intention or recklessness as to some level of harm.
❖ The s 18 offence requires ulterior intention to be proved – that is in relation to an intention to cause GBH or intention to resist/prevent a lawful arrest.

We will now consider the last element of the *mens rea* for this offence.

Ulterior intent to cause GBH or to prevent/resist a lawful arrest
In order for these criteria to be made out, D must have:

1. acted with the intent to cause GBH; or
2. intention to prevent or resist a lawful arrest.

If the ulterior intent cannot be satisfied then the s 20 offence will be applicable. A useful case to remember is *R v Belfon* (1976), which is explained below.

Case precedent – R v Belfon [1976] 1 WLR 741

Facts: D pushed a girl to the ground, and then attacked a passer-by who tried to help her. D caused very serious injuries to these people.

Principle: D was cleared of the s 18 offence, because it could not be shown that he had the full intent of causing GBH, and instead he was convicted of the s 20 offence.

Application: If the ulterior intent cannot be established and all that is in existence is an intention to cause general harm then s 20 is the appropriate offence.

Transmission of diseases

The transmission of diseases such as sexually transmitted infections, sometimes referred to as biological injury, has become increasingly important in recent years, as the implications of sexually transmitted infections (STIs) become more apparent. The transmission of an STI can constitute a s 20 offence, where it can be demonstrated that D was reckless or acted with intention to cause some harm to V.

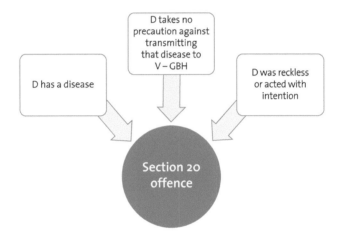

What is intention to resist or prevent the lawful detention of any person?

A quite specific part of the *mens rea* is related to resisting or preventing the lawful detention of any person. So, for example, if D is arrested by a policeman and resists the arrest by using force, then D may have committed an offence. This can be D resisting his own arrest, or D may prevent the lawful arrest of another person.

Aim Higher

The Law Commission is undertaking a consultation process in relation to reforming the law in relation to non-fatal offences against the person. The Act is regarded by many as being archaic and outdated. The first stage is a scoping paper, which is expected to lead to a series of recommendations, and the restructuring of the offences within the Act.

http://lawcommission.justice.gov.uk/areas/offences-against-the-person.htm

Look at the Law Commission's website to find an update on this exercise, and think about the potential impact on non-fatal offences from such an exercise.

Activity 3

Roger and Tariq are in a cafe, eating their lunch. Simon sees them through the window, and storms into the café, shouting, 'I've been looking for you, I'm going to give you a good hiding,' at Tariq. He pulls Tariq up from the chair and punches him three times in the face, breaking his nose, cutting his lip and knocking out two teeth.

Now answer these two questions, giving reasons for your answers:

1. Was the injury to Tariq a wound or GBH?
2. Was this a s 18 or a s 20 offence?

Aim Higher

When you are writing coursework, it is important that you fully reference your work. This includes the sources that you have used – both text and internet sources – and quotations/paraphrasing. Referencing is important for all your coursework, including problem questions and scenarios, and an assessor will check your work to ensure that it is fully and properly referenced.

A summary of the points we have covered in this section is:

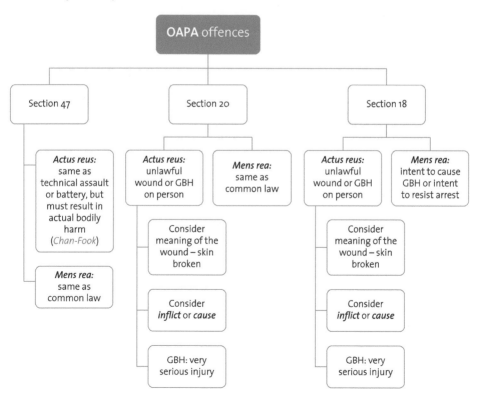

Potential defences to non-fatal offences against the person

In this last section we are going to consider two potential defences to a non-fatal offence against the person. These defences are:

1. Consent
2. Self-defence.

You will need to understand the operation of both of these defences in relation to an allegation that the defendant has committed a non-fatal offence against the person. Once again a complete understanding of this topic necessitates understanding as to when a valid defence will negate liability.

Consent

Consent is an important element of non-fatal offences, as it can negate the unlawfulness of the defendant's actions. Thus there are circumstances in which consent will operate as a defence to such an allegation. There will always be circumstances in which individuals will need to be able to consent to varying levels of physical harm. For example:

❖ tattooing
❖ contact sports
❖ surgical operations.

All of these activities and many more involve the defendant suffering a varying level of harm (in some cases a potentially very serious level of harm). However, these activities are considered 'lawful' activities and as such, irrespective of the severity of the harm inflicted, consent will operate as a valid defence. The law does not, however, deem all activities that an individual can consent to lawful and we will now consider two key cases that underscore the importance of the activity being deemed 'lawful' if the defence is to succeed.

Case precedent – *Brown* [1993] 2 All ER 75

Facts: D undertook sadomasochistic practices at home, in private with the consent of others. The actions included acts of extreme violence, often to V's genitals, to gain pleasure. Brown was charged with assault and ABH, and found guilty. The trial and appeal judges upheld the conviction, dismissing the defence that V consented.

Principle: Sadomasochistic activity was not a lawful activity and as such consent was no defence. The court held that consent could only be a defence to activity that did not cause bodily harm.

Application: This case can be applied to demonstrate that not all consensual activities are lawful ones. It can also be used to illustrate the distinction between offences that cause bodily harm and those that do not.

In the case of *Wilson* (1996) the Court of Appeal held that the case of *Brown* did not apply where a husband branded his name on his wife with a red-hot knife. This created some blurring of the boundaries of the law and some argued that this meant that sadomasochistic activity between a husband and wife would not give rise to prosecution. This question was put to rest in the case of *Emmett* (1999).

Key principles in relation to valid consent

❖ The victim must understand what s/he is consenting to: *Burrell v Harmer* (1967).
❖ We are all deemed to consent to low-level contacts with other people that come about as part of our everyday lives – for example as a result of standing on a crowded underground train or bus: *Wilson v Pringle* (1986).
❖ In the context of a contact sport it is presumed that the participants consent to a normal degree of contact and contact that is clumsy or misjudged. However, where a player deliberately inflicts harm they will not be able to argue the defence of consent: *Barnes* (2005).

Aim Higher

An excellent example of this principle was seen very recently in the 2014 football World Cup in Brazil, where in the midst of a match one player was alleged to have bitten a player on the opposing team. Whilst all participants in the match would be deemed to have consented to a certain level of contact, even those tackles that are the result of a late decision or poor judgement, it is impossible to argue that football players consent to being bitten while on the pitch. Thus were this incident to have occurred in England the player in question would not have been able to argue consent as a defence and could have been charged with a criminal offence – some might argue 'and quite rightly so'!

Aim Higher

Defences against offences, including non-fatal offences, are a basis for academic debate across many areas, particularly consent.

A useful article for further reading on consent in particular is Elliot and de Than, 'The case for a rational reconstruction of consent in criminal law', *Modern Law Review* (2007), pages 229–49.

We are now going to consider self-defence.

Self-defence

Self-defence is a justificatory defence in which D uses force against V in order to protect:

- himself;
- another; OR
- property.

Additionally, D can use reasonable force when attempting to prevent the commission of a crime: s 3(1) **Criminal Law Act 1967**.

The ingredients of the defence are as follows:

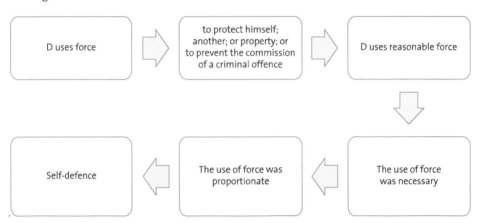

In what circumstances can force be used?

Self-defence originated as a common law defence, but it has been put on a statutory footing under the **Criminal Justice and Immigration Act 2008**. Section 76 leaves the common law framework of the defence intact. It provides that self-defence and use of reasonable force are defences in the following circumstances:

- to protect oneself;
- to protect another;
- to protect property;
- to prevent the commission of a criminal offence;
- to assist in the apprehension of a person at large.

The use of force must be reasonable

There are two separate components to this requirement. The first is that the use of force must be necessary; the second is that the use of force must be proportionate. If D fails to meet one of these criteria, the defence fails. We will now consider each of these elements.

The use of force was necessary (necessity test)

This is evaluated from the defendant's perspective – it is therefore a subjective test. Thus when attempting to apply this test you must ask yourself: did D believe that the use of force was necessary in the circumstances? If the answer is yes then you can proceed to the next question (the proportionality test). If the answer is no, i.e. the defendant did not believe that the use of force was necessary, then the defence fails. It does not matter that a reasonable man would have felt the use of force necessary, as the test is a subjective one.

In the event that the defendant makes a mistake and believes mistakenly that the use of force is necessary, the defence does not automatically fail. The question is: did the defendant honestly believe that force was necessary? If the answer to this question is yes, the defence may still succeed: *Williams* (1987). There is an important limitation to a mistaken belief that the use of force was necessary, and that is where the defendant has voluntarily become intoxicated. In these circumstances, where the mistake is induced by the consumption of drugs or alcohol, the defence will fail: *O'Grady* (1987). There are clearly good policy reasons for this limitation.

The use of force was proportionate (proportionality test)

If it is established that the use of force was necessary, the next test that must be passed is that the degree of force used was in the circumstances proportionate. If the use of force was excessive, the defence will fail. In relation to the proportionality of the force used the following observations can be made:

❖ The test is an objective one. In the circumstances as D believed them to be, was the degree of force used reasonable?
❖ The defendant should do no more than is necessary to address the gravity of the threat.
❖ The defendant can use a pre-emptive strike: *Beckford* (1988).
❖ It is important to consider whether the defendant's actions are in response to the perceived threat, or whether they may be motivated by revenge.

Aim Higher

In the case of *Bird* **(1985)** a failure to retreat was held to be evidence that the defendant wanted to engage in confrontation. Although this is not an established principle of law it is worth considering the point at which the force was used. If force is used against an attacker who is unconscious on the floor this force would be unreasonable and would be evidence of revenge, not reasonable force.

Putting it into practice

Feedback on Activity 1

1. If Brian had no knowledge that a rock was being thrown at him by Annie, then he does not 'apprehend immediate unlawful personal violence'.
2. Yes, based on the case law of *Ireland* and the use of silent phone calls – please note though that it would depend on the proximity between D and V and whether it could be immediate.

Feedback on Activity 2

The issues are that the dog could be classified as a weapon. If Bee sees the dog coming it could be assault (apprehension of immediate unlawful personal violence), battery, and could also be actual bodily harm (it could be more – but ABH is sufficient here). For Cea, if there was psychiatric injury we would need to find the assault or battery that would cause that (which is unlikely here as it does not say that she is apprehending immediate unlawful personal violence).

Feedback on Activity 3

1. GBH is defined as 'really serious injury', which includes a broken nose and knocked-out teeth. This was confirmed in *Bollom* (2003) and *Wilson* (1984). This differentiates the injury from ABH or wounding, as it is very serious.
2. Section 20 requires some intention or recklessness, whereas s 18 requires intent to be proved. The main issue here is the level of intent, as indicated by the words spoken by Simon before the offence. For s 18 it would need to be proved that Simon intended to cause harm – it was his overriding purpose – and that Simon knew the consequences of his actions and the harm/injury caused. From this, we can tell whether it was a s 18 or a s 20 offence.

In both questions, you need to make reference to the *actus reus* and *mens rea* as the guides for liability of an offence – work through each step and apply it to the question.

Table of key cases referred to in this chapter

Case name	Area of law	Principle
Bollom [2003] 2 CR App R 6	Type of injury and GBH	GBH is defined by the judge as 'really serious harm'
Brown [1993] 2 All ER 75	Consent	Under the legal concept of assault and battery, the victim does not consent
Burstow [1997] 1 Cr App R 144	No difference between inflicting and causing GBH	The judge ruled that psychiatric harm can be classed as bodily harm
Chan-Fook [1994] 1 WLR 689	Elements of ABH	The judge defined the words 'actual bodily harm'
Clarence [1888] 22 QBD 23	Defined the term *inflict*	Passing on a sexual disease was not 'inflicted'
Constanza [1997] Crim LR 576	Clarification of immediate personal violence	V apprehends injury at some time, not excluding the immediate future
Cunningham [1957] 2 All ER 412	Precedent on recklessness	D's actions were reckless, and he understood the consequences

R v D [2006] EWCA Crim 1139	Clarification of psychiatric injury	Distinction between psychological and psychiatric condition
Dica [2004] 3 All ER 593	Infliction and cause have the same meaning	Consent was irrelevant, as the women became infected as a result of D's actions
Donovan [1934] 25 Cr App R 1	Consent	V consented to the harmful activity
DPP v K [1990] 1 All ER 331	The use of force within battery	For battery, force need not be directly applied
DPP v Smith [2006] EWHC 94	Definition of bodily	Hair is now regarded as part of the body in regard to 'bodily'
Eisenhower [1983] 3 WLR 537	Definition of a wound	The judge defined the wound as a break in the continuity of the whole skin
Fagan v MPC [1969] 1 QB 439	Act of assault precedent	An act rather than an omission is required
Haystead v Chief Constable of Derbyshire [2000] 3 All ER 890	Common law offences v **OAPA 1861**	The judge defined that assault and battery are common law offences
Ireland [1997] 3 WLR 543	Act of assault	Silent phone calls constitute common law assault
Konzani [2005] All ER D 292	Transmitted diseases	D found guilty, although the Judge agreed that D 'honestly believed' that there was consent
Miller [1954] 2 QB 282	Definition of injury	Definition of ABH from D's actions
Mowatt [1968] 1 QB 421	Use of the word malicious	D's actions were malicious, and this can be seen from the actions themselves
Parmenter [1991] 2 WLR 408	Recklessness	Provides a link between the act and its consequences
Savage [1991] 94 Cr App R 193	Recklessness	Provides a link between the act and its consequences
Spratt [1991] 1 WLR 1073	Recklessness	D was not guilty, because it was not his intention to act recklessly

Case name	Area of law	Principle
Tuberville v Savage [1669] 1 Mod Rep 3 KBD	Use of words in assault	Words indicated that D would not harm V
Venna [1975] 3 All ER 788	Recklessness	The recklessness of Ds actions caused the injury to the policeman
Wilson [1996] Crim LR 573	Consent	Issues regarding V giving explicit consent, by an adult in their own home

@ **Visit the book's companion website to test your knowledge**

❖ Resources include a subject map, revision tip podcasts, downloadable diagrams, MCQ quizzes for each chapter, and a flashcard glossary

❖ www.routledge.com/cw/optimizelawrevision

4

Sexual Offences

Understand the law

- Can you distinguish between the following offences: rape, assault by penetration, sexual assault?

Remember the details

- Can you remember the *actus reus* and *mens rea* for each offence?
- Can you support each element of the *actus reus* and *mens rea* by reference to relevant case law and statutory provisions?

Reflect critically on areas of debate

- Do you understand the distinction between conclusive and evidential presumptions?
- Are you able to articulate the definition for consent under the Sexual Offences Act (SOA) 2003?

Contextualise

- Can you relate the offences to other areas of the law, such as non-fatal offences?

Apply your skills and knowledge

- Can you complete the activities in this chapter, using relevant authority to support your answers?

Chapter Map

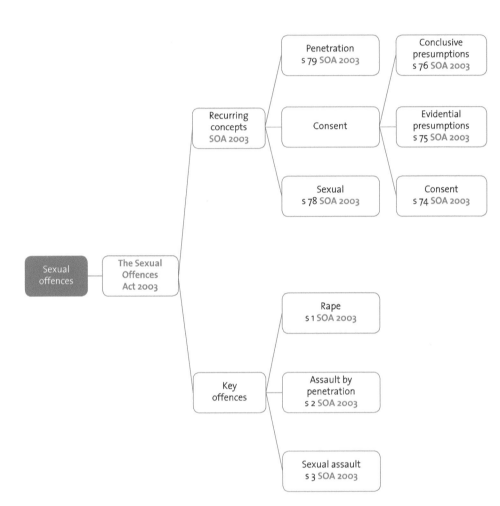

Introduction

In this chapter we are going to consider sexual offences. Sexual offences is a topic that does not appear on all criminal law courses, so you must check the syllabus for your course before revising this topic. If sexual offences are included in your course it is important to check which specific offences are covered, as there can be some variation. The key offences are:

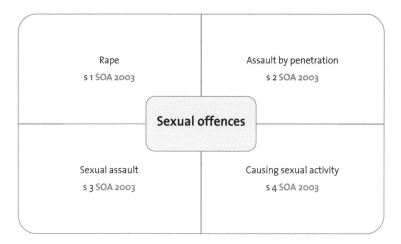

In this chapter we will focus on:

* rape
* assault by penetration
* sexual assault.

This is an area of law that was significantly reformed by the Sexual Offences Act (SOA) 2003. This Act brought together a number of statutory and common law provisions. The SOA 2003 simplified the law, abolishing some offences and introducing a number of others. As we progress through this chapter you will notice that many of the key authorities in this area of law were decided before the SOA 2003 was introduced. Do not let this concern you; it is not unusual for case law to remain 'good law' after significant statutory reform.

We will not consider in any detail offences against young children or people who suffer from a mental disorder, and will not cover preparatory offences (which are offences with the intent of committing a sexual offence, such as grooming).

Recurring concepts in the Sexual Offences Act 2003

There are a number of recurring concepts in the SOA 2003 and before we consider the key offences we are going to examine these concepts, as an understanding of these concepts is critical to understanding the ingredients of the key offences under the SOA 2003. These recurring concepts are:

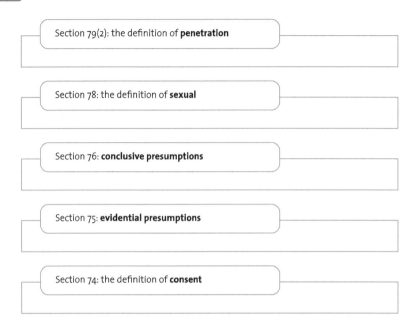

Section 79(2): the definition of **penetration**

Section 78: the definition of **sexual**

Section 76: **conclusive presumptions**

Section 75: **evidential presumptions**

Section 74: the definition of **consent**

We will now examine each of these terms in detail. You will need to be comfortable with these recurring concepts if you are planning on answering a question on sexual offences.

Penetration

Section 79(2) stipulates that penetration is a continuing act from entry to withdrawal. This gives statutory effect to the decision in *Kaitamaki* (1984). Consensual penetration can become unlawful if consent is withdrawn at any point: *Cooper and Schaub* (1994). The slightest penetration will suffice: s 79(9) SOA 2003.

Sexual

Several offences under the SOA 2003 require 'sexual activity'. The term *sexual* is defined in s 78 of the SOA 2003. Section 78 of the SOA 2003 stipulates that an act is sexual if a reasonable person would consider that:

a) Whatever the circumstances or any person's purpose in relation to it, it is because of its nature sexual, or

b) Because of its nature it may be sexual and because of the circumstances or the purpose of any person in relation to it (or both) it is sexual.

From this section of the SOA 2003, it is apparent that an act can be sexual in nature based on the **circumstances** and/or the **nature and purpose** of the act. Therefore s 78 SOA 2003 provides that:

s 78(a)	The act is inherently sexual	Sexual intercourse, oral sex, masturbation	A reasonable person would regard the action as sexual
s 78(b)	The act is potentially sexual	Touching, kissing, penetration	It may be sexual, depending on the circumstances and the nature and purpose of D's motives

In *H* (2005) the court laid down a two-stage test to s 78(b) SOA 2003.

1. The jury must be satisfied that the act is capable of being sexual; and then
2. Would a reasonable person considering the context and the surrounding circumstances and the purpose of D regard the act as actually sexual?

The following cases illustrate forms of behaviour that have been deemed sexual by the courts:

❖ touching the breasts of a victim – *Burns* (2006);
❖ kissing a victim – *W* (2005);
❖ stroking the legs of another is capable of being deemed sexual – *Price* (2004).

Aim Higher

Sexual offences can sit in parallel with other offences, such as non-fatal offences. Where the defendant's actions are not sexual but are not consensual it is possible to construct liability for another non-fatal offence against the person.

When planning your answer to a problem question on sexual offences, work through the *actus reus* and *mens rea* for the possible sexual offences, and then consider whether D may be liable for alternative offences.

Thinking through and mapping out your answer first will really help you do this. Demonstrating the ability to identify alternative/parallel offences will enable the examiner to award more marks.

Consent

In the following sections we are going to consider conclusive and evidential presumptions that relate to consent to sexual activity. We will also consider the general definition of consent. Before we do this it is important to explain these terms.

Conclusive presumptions	A conclusive presumption cannot be rebutted
Evidential presumptions	The defence can rebut an evidential presumption

Aim Higher

When working your way through a question on sexual offences make sure that you deal with the issue of consent in the following order:

1. Is there a conclusive presumption (s 76)?
2. Is there an evidential presumption (s 75)?
3. The general definition of consent (s 74)?

If you find that there is a conclusive presumption (s 76) there is no need to go on to consider s 75 or s 74. If you find that there is an evidential presumption it may not be necessary to go on to consider the general definition of consent.

Conclusive presumptions
Section 76 of the SOA 2003 provides that:

(1) If in proceedings for an offence to which this section applies it is proved that the defendant did the relevant act and that any of the circumstances specified in subsection (2) existed, it is to be conclusively presumed—

    (a) that the complainant *did not consent* to the relevant act, *and*

    (b) that the defendant *did not believe* that the complainant consented to the relevant act.

(2) The circumstances are that—

    (a) the defendant intentionally *deceived* the complainant as to the nature or purpose of the relevant act;

    (b) the defendant intentionally *induced* the complainant to consent to the relevant act by impersonating a person known personally to the complainant.

Up for Debate

Do you feel that these conclusive presumptions encapsulate the most serious situations in which consent is not present? It is interesting that deceit and inducement are high-lighted as conclusive presumptions, whereas violence and being unlawfully detained are rebuttable presumptions.

We will now examine s 76(2)(a) and (b) in more detail.

Deceit
Section 76(2)(a) deals with fraud and deceit. Where a defendant deceives the victim as to the nature of the act that is being performed there will be a conclusive presumption that the victim did not consent **and** that the defendant did not believe that the victim was consenting. Examples of conduct that would fall within the remit of s 76(2)(a) include:

| *Williams* (1923) | The defendant had sex with the victim telling her that the act would improve her breathing |
| *Flattery* (1877) | The defendant had sex with the victim telling her that the act was a medical procedure that would improve her illness |

The following are examples of conduct that will not trigger s 76(2)(a):

Linekar (1995)	The defendant had sex with the victim promising to pay her money. He left without paying.
Jheeta (2007) B (2013)	The deceit must be in relation to the nature not the quality of the act

The nature or purpose of the relevant act is key, and V should be aware of and consent to the act proposed by D, for deceit to be established. This was seen in the case of R v Jheeta (2007), where D sent threatening text messages to V and pretended to be a police officer in order to enable him to continue a sexual relationship with V.

Example
D pretends to be a doctor undertaking a survey on breast cancer. On this basis three women allow D to undertake a breast examination, including touching of their breasts. Would you consider this deceit as to the nature of the part of D?

This is based on the facts of a real case, R v Tabassum (2000), in which D pretended to be a doctor. On appeal, the Judge ruled that the women gave their consent to touching for medical purposes only, and that D had deceived the women as to this purpose.

Induced
Section 76(2)(b) deals with inducement in a very specific form. This is where the defendant impersonates a person known personally to the complainant in order to induce the victim into sexual activity. In these circumstances there will be a conclusive presumption that the victim did not consent **and** that the defendant did not believe that the victim was consenting.

An example of inducement through impersonation can be seen in the following case:

Case precedent – R v Elkekkay [1995] Crim LR 163 (CA)

Facts: D is in a flat with a couple. V goes to bed and her boyfriend falls asleep on the sofa. D climbs into V's bed while she is asleep and, believing D is her boyfriend, V speaks to D and begins to have sexual intercourse with D. When V realises D is not her boyfriend, she screams and manages to escape.

Principle: Inducement

Application: D is convicted of rape, as it is demonstrated that he impersonated V's boyfriend.

The key to the operation of s 76(2)(b) is that the impersonation must be of someone known personally to the victim. Thus impersonating a film star or other celebrity not known personally to the victim will not trigger s 76(2)(b).

Evidential presumptions

Evidential presumptions are rebuttable presumptions. This means that they are accepted as being true, unless the defence is able to rebut them by adducing evidence to the contrary. Section 75 of the SOA 2003 provides that a presumption against valid consent will arise in the following situations.

(1) If in proceedings for an offence to which this section applies it is proved—

    (a) that the defendant did the relevant act,

    (b) that any of the circumstances specified in subsection (2) existed, and

    (c) that the defendant knew that those circumstances existed, the complainant is to be taken not to have consented to the relevant act unless sufficient evidence is adduced to raise an issue as to whether he consented, and the defendant is to be taken not to have reasonably believed that the complainant consented unless sufficient evidence is adduced to raise an issue as to whether he reasonably believed it.

(2) The circumstances are that—

    (a) any person was, at the time of the relevant act or immediately before it began, *using violence against the complainant* or causing the complainant to fear that immediate violence would be used against him;

    (b) any person was, at the time of the relevant act or immediately before it began, *causing the complainant to fear that violence was being used*, or that immediate violence would be used, against another person;

    (c) the complainant was, and the defendant was not, *unlawfully detained* at the time of the relevant act;

    (d) the complainant was *asleep or otherwise unconscious* at the time of the relevant act;

    (e) because of the complainant's *physical disability*, the complainant would not have been able at the time of the relevant act to communicate to the defendant whether the complainant consented;

    (f) any person had administered to or caused to be taken by the complainant, without the complainant's consent, *a substance* which, having regard to when it was administered or taken, was capable of causing or enabling the complainant to be stupefied or overpowered at the time of the relevant act.

(3) In subsection (2)(a) and (b),

the reference to the time *immediately before the relevant act* began is, in the case of an act which is one of a continuous series of sexual activities, a reference to the time immediately before the first sexual activity began.

Common Pitfalls

Be careful if one of the characteristics above is raised as part of the offence for rebuttable presumption. This is because there must be proof that D did the act and that D knew that there was the existence of any of the points set out below.

You cannot simply assume this without proof.

This is particularly important if you are answering a question on rebuttable presumptions. You would need to demonstrate in your argument that D was aware of one or more of the points below in s 75.

It is important to note that the prosecution does not have to prove that the victim did not consent. It is for the defence to rebut the evidential presumption that there was no valid consent by adducing sufficient credible evidence to the contrary: *Larter and Castleton* (1995). If the defendant fails to do so, it will be presumed that the victim did not consent and that the defendant had no reasonable belief in the victim's consent: *Ciccarelli* (2012).

Use the steps below to work through whether an evidential presumption could apply:

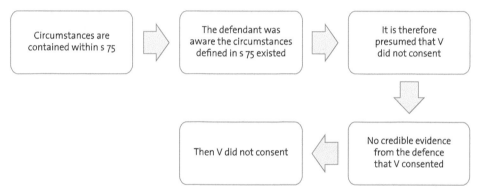

The definition of consent

In the vast majority of cases the issue of consent does not hinge on the existence of conclusive or evidential presumptions. Thus the jury will determine consent on the basis of s 74 of the **Sexual Offences Act (SOA) 2003**, which provides a general definition of consent. Section 74 provides that:

A person consents if he agrees by choice, and has the freedom and capacity to make that choice.

❖ A failure to resist does not equate to consent: *Olugboja* (1982).
❖ Submission is not the same thing as consent: *Doyle* (2010).
❖ For consent to be valid it must be given by free choice: *Jheeta* (2007).

A reasonable belief in consent

Prior to the **Sexual Offences Act 2003**, where a defendant had an honest but mistaken belief that the victim consented he could escape liability. This was the case even if the honest mistaken belief was entirely unreasonable.

Case precedent – *DPP v Morgan* [1976] AC 182

Facts: The case surrounded three appellants who were convicted of rape. They had been drinking with an RAF officer who invited them back to his house to have sexual intercourse with his wife. The appellants highlighted that he had told them that his wife would be consenting, but would protest for enhancement. V did not consent, and sustained physical injuries.

Principle: Honest belief of consent

Application: The Judge directed the jury that the defendants' belief in consent had to be reasonably held and they were found guilty. They appealed, contending there was no requirement that the belief needed to be reasonably held. On appeal the court agreed that there was no requirement that the belief was reasonable, only honest.

The Sexual Offences Act 2003 changed this position. The belief in consent must now be a reasonable one.

Aim Higher

The new legislation altered the law contained in the **SOA 1956**, which provided the accused with a defence where he was found to have an 'honest belief' that V was consenting.

If you are going to use the case of Moran in relation to consent you must remember to explain that it is no longer good law!

There are a number of factors that may impact on a victim's ability to provide valid consent. In addition to those considered in s 76 and s 75 of the SOA 2003 these include:

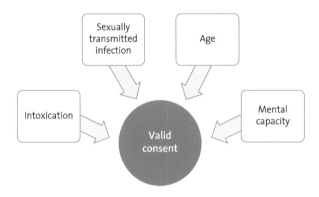

Consent and intoxication

Section 75(2)(f) of the SOA 2003 considers the issue of intoxication in the context of substances administered without the victim's consent. This of course could include drugs and/or alcohol. What happens when the victim has become voluntarily intoxicated?

The issue of intoxication and consent has given rise to much debate over the years. Following the leading case of *Bree* (2007), a drunken consent is valid consent. However, in circumstances where the victim has temporarily lost the capacity to choose whether or not to engage in sexual activity the victim does not consent.

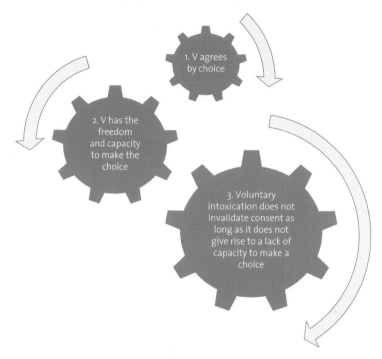

1. V agrees by choice

2. V has the freedom and capacity to make the choice

3. Voluntary intoxication does not invalidate consent as long as it does not give rise to a lack of capacity to make a choice

Consent and capacity

Only a person who has the capacity to consent to sexual activity can give valid consent. Unfortunately the SOA 2003 does not provide a definition of the term capacity. The following points should be borne in mind when dealing with the issue of capacity in relation to consent:

❖ The victim must have sufficient knowledge and understanding in order to provide valid consent: *Howard* (1965).
❖ Issues in relation to capacity can arise in relation to the victim's age, intoxication, physical and/or mental disability.

Informed consent: failure to disclose sexually transmitted infections

Where a defendant has sexual intercourse with an individual and fails to disclose a sexually transmitted infection the failure to disclose does not vitiate the victim's consent: *Dica* (2004).

In *B* (2007) the court held that a defendant's failure to disclose that he was HIV positive did not trigger s 76(a) SOA 2003 where there was no deceit. In *McNally*

(2013) the court left the question unanswered as to whether a defendant who gives a positive assurance that they are not HIV positive when in fact they are HIV positive could potentially vitiate consent.

In *Assange v Swedish Prosecution Authority* (2011) it was suggested that a failure to disclose HIV status is not relevant to the issue of consent under s 74 SOA 2003.

You will find the following flowchart of use when dealing with issues in relation to consent.

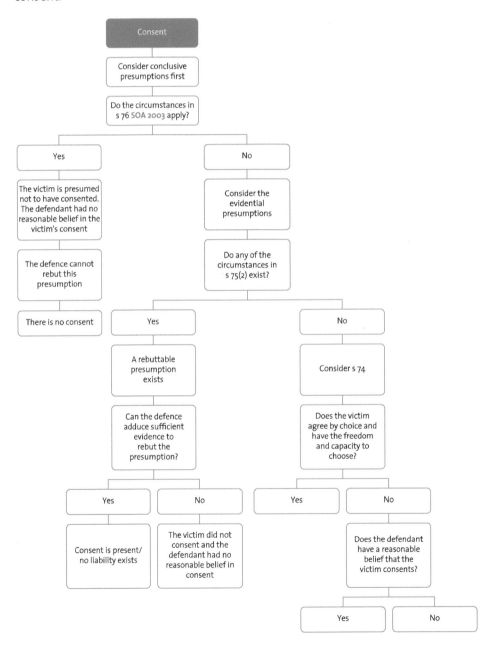

The Key Offences

In the next section of this chapter we will consider the main sexual offences contained in the **Sexual Offences Act (SOA) 2003**. Each will be considered in turn, focusing on how the different offences are defined and the key elements of each offence.

Rape

By s 1 of the **SOA 2003**, the *actus reus* of rape is committed where:

> (1) A person (A) commits an offence if —
>
> > (a) he intentionally penetrates the vagina, anus or mouth of another person (B) with his penis,
> >
> > (b) B does not consent to the penetration, and
> >
> > (c) A does not reasonably believe that B consents.

This can be split into the following *actus reus* and *mens rea* elements:

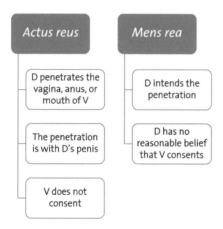

Actus reus: *D penetrates the vagina, anus or mouth of V*

This is an important element, as it recognises that penetration must occur for the offence to be constituted.

Penetration may involve the slightest penetration of the vulva, thus full penetration is not required. It is also important to note that ejaculation does not need to occur for the act to be deemed penetration. This supports the earlier discussion regarding rape as a continuing act.

2 Actus reus: *the penetration is with D's penis*

This element identifies that D must be male (with his penis), although V can be either male or female.

It is useful to note that this is the only offence requiring penetration specifically with the penis. This is not a requirement of other offences in this chapter.

Actus reus: *V does not consent*

We have already discussed the basis of consent above. However, with rape, it is also important to consider the age of V. This is because age can determine whether D is liable for the offence of rape, of for another offence regarding children.

If you are answering a problem question, the age of V may be noted, and this could lead you to a different offence for discussion.

Common Pitfalls

When you are looking at sexual offences, it is important to consider the age of V.

Under s 5 of the **SOA 2003**, rape is committed where V is below the age of 13 regardless of any consent from V. This affects the *actus reus* for consent, as set out above.

Mens rea: *D intended the penetration*

Here it must be demonstrated that D intended to penetrate V with his penis. It is vital that penetration takes place with the penis, and the penetration must be intentional.

For example, if D accidentally penetrates the anus instead of the vagina during consensual sexual intercourse, would this constitute intent? This is more likely to be considered a mistake, particularly if D is inexperienced. Therefore, it is for the prosecution to prove that D intended the penetration.

Mens rea: *D has no reasonable belief that V consents*

An important element of the *mens rea* for rape is that the D must have a reasonable belief in the V's consent.

The law in relation to the marital rape was overturned in 1992 when a landmark case found that a woman does not automatically give consent to her husband, thereby ending the husband's immunity from rape.

Case precedent – *R v R* [1992] 1 AC 599

Facts: D and V were married, but were living separately. V was living at her parents' house. D entered V's parents' house and raped V.

Principle: End of husband's immunity from rape

Application: D was found guilty of rape, because V did not consent. From this point, a wife is not assumed to automatically consent to sexual activity with her husband, and can withdraw consent from her husband.

Assault by penetration

By s 2 of the SOA 2003, the *offence* of assault by penetration is committed where:

(1) A person (A) commits an offence if—

    (a) He intentionally penetrates the vagina or anus of another person (B) with a part of his body or anything else,

    (b) The penetration is sexual,

    (c) B does not consent to the penetration, and

    (d) A does not reasonably believe that B consents.

(2) Whether a belief is reasonable is to be determined having regard to all the circumstances, including any steps A has taken to ascertain whether B consents.

This can be split into the following *actus reus* and *mens rea* elements:

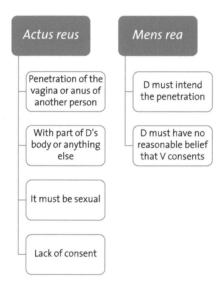

Actus reus
- Penetration of the vagina or anus of another person
- With part of D's body or anything else
- It must be sexual
- Lack of consent

Mens rea
- D must intend the penetration
- D must have no reasonable belief that V consents

Actus reus: *penetration of the vagina or anus of another person*

This offence is similar to rape (as set out above), but there are some important differences:

❖ penetration does not need to have taken place with the penis (considered below);

❖ penetration of the mouth is not included in this offence.

The reason why this offence was included in the SOA 2003 was due to concerns that the gravity of penetration with another object was not fully captured by the offence of sexual assault (discussed below). Hence, the offence of assault by penetration was created, providing a maximum sentence of life imprisonment.

Common Pitfalls

This offence does not extend to penetration of the mouth, as it was felt that penetration of the mouth **was** already fully considered within the offences of rape and sexual assault.

When answering a problem question, do ensure that you are clear about the facts of the offence, as this can lead you to determine whether D is liable for the offence of rape or for assault by penetration.

Actus reus: *with part of D's body or anything else*

Another difference from the offence of rape is that penetration does not have to be by the penis. This means penetration could be by another part of the body, such as fingers, or with an object.

The significance of this element is that D is not, therefore, automatically male – D may be male or female, as can V.

Rape	Assault by penetration
D is always male as penetration must be with his penis	D can be male or female, as penetration can be by part of the body or something else

Actus reus: *it must be sexual*

This element is another difference from the offence of rape – assault by penetration is sexual, whereas rape is not required to be sexual. This gives the offence a broader scope than rape, and widens liability for the offence.

We have briefly considered the meaning of *sexual* already, and will consider this in more depth in the next section. But it is useful to note that there are grey areas between sexual and non-sexual penetration, and you should begin to explore these as part of a discussion on sexual offences.

V does not consent

We have considered the issue of consent earlier in this chapter.

Mens rea: *D must intend the penetration*

This intention is the same as that for the offence of rape, as is the nature of the intention.

Mens rea: *D has no reasonable belief that V consents*

Reasonable belief is also the same as for the offence of rape, and is considered in more detail in the next section.

S 5 of the **SOA 2003** and above, s 6 cover the situation where V is below the age of 13. It provides that the offence of assault by penetration is committed whether or not V consents.

Example
Rachel and Steve are having consensual intercourse when Steve asks Rachel if he can penetrate her vagina with his hand. She says no and tries to move away, but Steve does so anyway.

In this example, the offence of assault by penetration would be applicable – think through the *actus reus* and *mens rea* for this offence, and use the diagram below to check through your working.

How would the diagram be different if Steve did not hear what Rachel said?

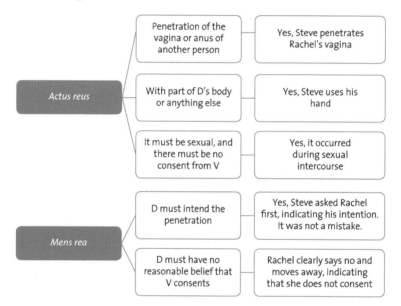

Sexual assault: section 3

Section 3 of the **SOA 2003** covers sexual assault, and provides:

(1) A person (A) commits an offence if—

(a) He intentionally touches another person (B),
(b) The touching is sexual,
(c) B does not consent to the touching, and
(d) A does not reasonably believe that B consents.

(2) Whether a belief is reasonable is to be determined having regard to all the circumstances, including any steps A has taken to ascertain whether B consents.

This can be split into the following *actus reus* and *mens rea* elements:

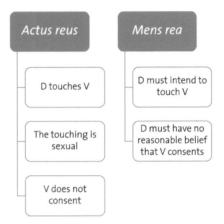

As with the offence of assault by penetration, in sexual assault both D and V can be either male or female.

Common Pitfalls

If you have read the chapter on non-fatal offences, compare the *actus reus* and *mens rea* for sexual assault with the *actus reus* and *mens rea* for assault. You will see that the *actus reus* and *mens rea* for sexual assault are much broader, and involve touching, whereas assault refers to the immediate apprehension of violence.

Do be careful not to confuse the two offences when answering a problem question, as the two offences are quite different.

Actus reus: *D touches V*
Touching can include:

* touching through clothing;
* touching any part of the body;
* with anything else.

To help your understanding of the concept of touching, look at the chapter on non-fatal offences to find further definitions of touching, and what can and cannot be regarded as touching in terms of these offences.

Actus reus: *the touching is sexual*
For sexual assault, it needs to be demonstrated that the touching is of a sexual nature, relating to the intention of D and the circumstances of the offence.

In many cases this touching can be very obvious, but it is not always clear. The case below refined the definition of touching in sexual assault.

Case precedent – R v H [2005] 2 All ER 859

Facts: D approached V, whom he did not know, and tried to pull her towards him using her tracksuit trouser pockets on each side and asked if she wanted to have sexual intercourse.

Principle: Touching through the clothes

Application: It was held that touching through the clothes was enough to commit a sexual offence, even though the touching itself may not constitute a sexual offence but the intention and the circumstances were sexual in nature.

This case identifies that touching through clothes is part of the *actus reus* (above), but the influence of the sexual intention and circumstances constitute the difference between sexual assault and common law assault.

When you are working through a problem question which involves touching, work through these steps to decide if this touching is of a sexual nature and would constitute sexual assault.

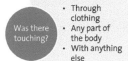  

If the answer to the questions above is yes, then liability for sexual assault may be present. If the answer to these questions is no, then the touching is not sexual and as such liability for sexual assault cannot exist. However, D may have committed another offence; assault and battery, for example.

Actus reus: *V does not consent*
As with the other sexual offences, the consent of V is required as this constitutes an important element of the *actus reus*.

Mens rea: *D must intend to touch V*
As noted above, D must intend to touch V. This is important to the *mens rea*, because it differentiates between intentional touching and a mistake. For example:

❖ not intentionally touching V;
❖ brushing past a person;
❖ shaking their hand.

Again, further information on touching is set out in the chapter on non-fatal offences, and sets out the nature of touching another person.

Mens rea: *D has no reasonable belief that V consents*

We have already touched upon reasonable belief of consent, and this is an important element of sexual assault.

This is particularly relevant here, as consent is not always sought in advance, such as when giving a person a hug or putting your arm around a person.

Up for Debate

The **SOA 2003** was written following concern that the **SOA 1956** was outdated and needed reform, and to respond to changing attitudes in society. There was also concern that the **SOA 1956** did not provide sufficient definition of consent.

Now you have considered liability for the main sexual offences in the **SOA 2003,** do you think that these concerns have been addressed?

There is clearly a view that the range of offences has been widened, and it affords greater protection to children in particular. Given that the legislation is still relatively new, this additional protection will be tested through the courts over the coming years.

Putting it into practice

Question 1

Mike and Alison meet at a party. They have been drinking heavily and return to Mike's flat together, where consensual intercourse takes place. Mike wakes up in the middle of the night and decides to have intercourse with Alison again, even though she is asleep. Alison wakes up to find Mike on top of her, penetrating her. She protests and tries to push him off, but her speech is slurred and Mike cannot make out what she is saying. He continues to penetrate her, and is subsequently charged with rape.

Consider Mike's criminal liability (if any).

Suggested solution

The defence cannot argue that Alison was consenting to sex, since it is well established that a person who is asleep or unconscious cannot consent to intercourse (*R v Fletcher* (1859)). The defence will therefore have to argue that (i) Mike genuinely believed Alison was consenting and (ii) he had reasonable grounds for doing so (s 1(1)(c) **SOA 2003**). Thus, even if the jury are convinced that Mike's belief in consent was genuine, they must also conclude he had reasonable grounds for holding it.

On this point, s 75(2)(d) provides a presumption that D did not hold a reasonable belief since 'the complainant was asleep or otherwise unconscious at the time of the relevant act'. The defence will thus be under an obligation to adduce sufficient evidence of reasonable grounds. Mike may try to argue that the fact Alison had sex with him some hours earlier suggested in his mind that she would consent to having sex again. On the other hand, however, the fact that Alison was making muffled protests at the time may tend to suggest that Mike should have been aware that she was not consenting, and he should have ceased penetration at that point. There may also be an issue here with regard to intoxication. However, even if Mike is drunk, intoxication is no defence to a charge of rape (*R v Woods* (1981) 74 Cr App R 312).

Question 2

Gordon and Eliza meet in a pub, and are drunk. They return to Gordon's house and have sexual intercourse. The next morning Eliza cannot remember if she consented to the intercourse.

Given s 74 of the SOA 2003, do you think Eliza had the freedom and capacity to consent, or could any form of consent be classed as full consent?

Make sure you evidence your thoughts and ideas, to build a strong argument.

Work through s 74 of the SOA 2003, and apply the definitions to the example. You will probably focus on the freedom and capacity to consent, i.e. if Eliza was drunk, did she have the full capacity to make this decision? Or, did Gordon pressure her, but she cannot remember?

These types of situation can be difficult to judge, so you must go back to the legislation and case law, work through each methodically, and use the findings to draw a conclusion. Sometimes, particularly with these types of offence, they are not the answer you wish to hear – but it is still essential.

Key Points Checklist

The law in relation to sexual offences was reformed by the **Sexual Offences Act 2003** – this is the key legislative provision that you must be familiar with in relation to this topic. The key offences are: Rape, s 1 SOA 2003; Assault by Penetration, s 2 SOA 2003; Sexual Assault, s 3 SOA 2003.	✔
The *actus reus* of rape is: penetration; of the anus, vagina or mouth; with the defendant's penis; lack of consent on the victim's behalf. The *mens rea* of rape is: intentional penetration of the anus, vagina or mouth with the penis; D does not reasonably believe that V consents.	✔

The **actus reus** of assault by penetration is: penetration of the anus or vagina; with any part of the D's body or any object; lack of consent on the victim's behalf; the penetration must be sexual. The **mens rea** of the offence is: intentional penetration of the anus or vagina; D does not reasonably believe that V consents.	✔
The **actus reus** of sexual assault is: D touches V; the touching is sexual; V does not consent. The **mens rea** of the offence is: D intends to touch V; D does not reasonably believe that V consents.	✔
The SOA 2003 provides a definition for consent: s 74 SOA 2003. It also creates a number of conclusive and evidential presumptions regarding the existence of consent.	✔
Consent is a feature of the **actus reus** and the **mens rea** of these three offences and you must therefore address consent in relation to BOTH aspects.	✔

Table of key cases referred to in this chapter

Key case	Brief facts	Principle
Katamaki v R [1985] **AC 147**	Not withdrawing when there is no consent	Rape is a continuing act
R v Lineker [1995] **2 Cr App R49**	Non-payment to a prostitute	The form of consent from V
DPP v Morgan [1976] **AC 182**	Three defendants having intercourse with another's wife on his instructions, in the belief she was willing	Honestly held belief in relation to consent
R v R [1992] **IAC 599**	Husband and wife were separated when he raped her	Removal of the marital exemption
R v H [2005] **2 All ER 859**	D touched V through her clothes and requested sexual intercourse	Refines the definition of touching
R v Doyle [2010] **EWCA Crim (CA)**	V submits to intercourse as she is not able to withdraw consent	Submission to sexual intercourse is not consent
R v Bree [2007] **EWCA Crim 804**	D and V had been drinking and were both intoxicated when sexual intercourse occurred	Consent while intoxicated
R v Malone [1998] **2 Cr App R 447**	V did not make D aware of her lack of consent	Evidential presumptions – circumstances
R v Hysa [2007] **EWCA Crim 2056**	V could not recall the events due to intoxication	Evidential presumptions – capacity to consent

R v Jheeta [2007] **EWCA Crim 1699**	D sent threatening text messages, and pretended to be a policeman	Conclusive presumptions – deceit
R v Tabassum [2000] **2 Cr App R 328 (CA)**	D pretended to be a doctor and V let him touch her breasts on this basis	Impact of deceit on consent
R v Elkekkay [1995] **Crim LR 163 (CA)**	D pretended to be V's boyfriend	Conclusive presumptions – inducement

@ **Visit the book's companion website to test your knowledge**

❖ Resources include a subject map, revision tip podcasts, downloadable diagrams, MCQ quizzes for each chapter, and a flashcard glossary

❖ www.routledge.com/cw/optimizelawrevision

5

Homicide – Including Murder and Manslaughter

Understand the law

- Can you identify the difference between murder, voluntary manslaughter and involuntary manslaughter?

Remember the details

- Can you remember the definition for each offence?
- Can you remember the *actus reus* and *mens rea* for each offence?

Reflect critically on areas of debate

- Can you reflect critically on the proposed reforms to the law in relation to homicide?

Contextualise

- Can you relate the offences to other areas of the law, such as non-fatal offences against the person?
- Can you relate this area of law to general defences such as self-defence?

Apply your skills and knowledge

- Can you complete the activities in this chapter, using relevant authorities to support your answers?

Chapter Map

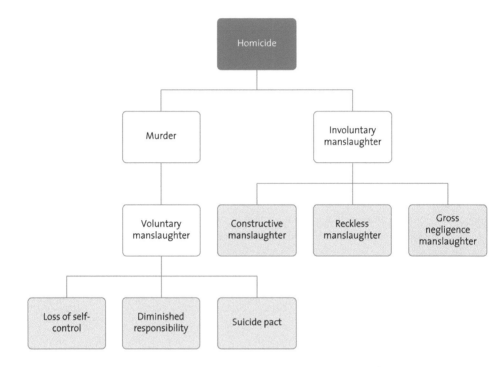

Liability Chart

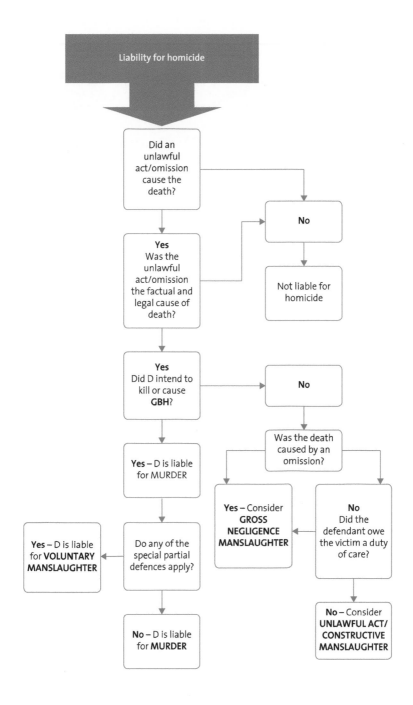

Introduction

In this chapter we will consider homicide. Homicide is an umbrella term for unlawful killings. Most criminal law courses consider a discrete number of homicide offences including murder, voluntary manslaughter and involuntary manslaughter. It is important that you are able to identify the common and unique elements of each of these offences. Homicide is a very popular topic with examiners and as such it frequently features in multiple formats in examination papers.

> **Common Pitfall**
>
> The term homicide is used as an overarching term under which a number of specific offences are grouped. We do not charge suspects with homicide or convict defendants of homicide. Be careful not to make this novice error in your assessments!

The offences that we will consider in this chapter are common law offences. Therefore the definitions of the separate offences are not found in statutes or Acts of Parliament. They are located in the decisions of the superior courts of England and Wales. A common mistake that students make when discussing homicide is to attribute the definitions of these offences to the Homicide Act 1957 (and sometimes to other statutory modifications).

Chapter summary

> **Common Pitfall**
>
> Problem questions on homicide are particularly popular with examiners and, in such a question, the distinction between the different offences of murder and manslaughter can be unclear. This is quite deliberate on the part of examiners, who typically want to provide you with the opportunity to show your knowledge of the case law and apply the legal principles of the different offences.
>
> Remember that you cannot construct criminal liability without working your way through the *actus reus* and *mens rea* for each potential offence.

The common elements of homicide offences

The offences that we will consider in this chapter share some common elements. These elements are:

1. There must be a killing.
2. The killing must be of a human being/person.
3. The killing must be unlawful.

Aim Higher

As you progress through this chapter, you will see reference to a number of legal principles which also apply to non-fatal offences.

These principles can apply to both homicide and non-fatal offences, and are therefore
crucial important for you to fully understand. As you work through these principles,
check that you understand how they can apply to both types of offence, and this will
help your understanding.

We will start our examination of these offences by considering the most serious of
the homicide offences: murder.

Murder

The traditional definition of murder was drawn from the seventeenth-century writ-
ings of the then Chief Justice, Sir Edward Coke (1552–1634). This definition remains
the core or the basis of the modern definition of murder. You will find that many
textbooks on criminal law break this original definition into individual components.

> *Murder is when a man of sound memory, and at the age of discretion, unlaw-
> fully killeth within any country of the realm any reasonable creature in rerum
> natura under the King's peace, with malice aforethought, either expressed by
> the party or implied by law [so as the party wounded, or hurt, died of the wound
> or hurt within a year and a day at the same].*
>
> *(Coke 3 Inst 47)*

Not all of this definition remains good law: for example, the requirement that the
victim must die within a year and a day was reformed by the **Law Reform (Year and
a Day Rule) Act 1996**. As such, students are generally to be encouraged to use the
more modern and user-friendly definition of the offence!

Definition

Murder is the unlawful killing of another human being with malice aforethought
(this simply means intention to kill or cause grievous bodily harm).

As is always the case when dealing with a criminal offence, you must break the
definition down into the constituent elements. The key elements of the offence of
murder are:

1. There must be a killing.
2. The killing must be of a human being (a person).
3. The killing must be unlawful.
4. The killing must be committed with malice aforethought (intention to kill or
    cause GBH).

We now need to divide the different components into the distinct elements that represent the *actus reus* and *mens rea* of the offence of murder.

You can see that we have done this for you here:

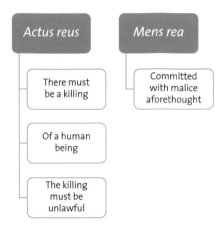

Actus reus

We will now explore the elements that constitute the *actus reus* of murder. If you are answering a question on murder you must methodically work your way through each element.

There must be a killing

The defendant must have caused an acceleration of the victim's death. There are two aspects here to consider: the first is that the victim must be dead and the second is that the defendant's acts or omissions must be the cause of the victim's death.

Death

Although it may seem rather obvious that the victim must be dead it is important to understand the point at which life ceases to exist in law. The common law position is that a person who has suffered brain death is legally dead. The legal consequence of this is that a person who is brain dead in law cannot be killed, whether by a medical practitioner or by anyone else.

In circumstances where the victim is not brain dead but is being sustained by life support, the victim is considered alive. Therefore, if life support is removed it results in the death of the victim. There are circumstances in which life support can be removed lawfully from a person who is not brain dead. Doctors may, for example, remove life support from a patient where it is no longer in the patient's best interests.

Causation

The defendant's acts or omissions must be the cause of the victim's death. Murder is a result crime and as such it must be established that the defendant is the factual and legal cause of death. We have considered causation in Chapter 2.

The act or omission must cause the death of the victim. It is not sufficient that the act causes significant injury.

For example, Billy, intending to kill or cause GBH, hits Simon on the head with a baseball bat, causing a significant head injury to Simon. Simon is in a coma and being kept alive on a life-support machine.

If Simon is not brain dead, then Billy cannot be liable for murder because in law Simon is still alive and as such there has been no killing. Billy may be liable for a non-fatal offence against the person instead.

However, if Simon's life support is withdrawn and as a result of the withdrawal of life support, Simon subsequently dies, then Billy could be held liable for murder.

It can help to remember the steps below:

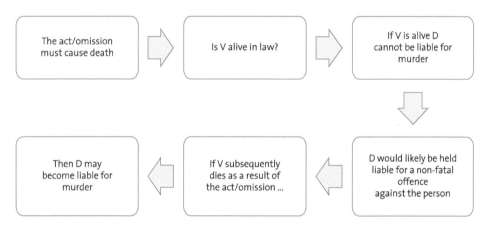

The killing must be of a human being

In Coke's definition of murder a human being is *'any reasonable creature in rerum natura'*. *In rerum natura* means 'in the nature of things' or 'in existence'. For our purposes it is a person. Although this may seem rather obvious, there is an important point that must be understood in relation to this element of the offence.

Crucially at what point does an unborn child/foetus become a human being; or, put another way, at what point does an unborn child acquire the status of a person?

In order to be considered a 'person or human being' the child/foetus must be wholly expelled from the mother. Complete expulsion means that no part of the child remains in the birth canal. It does not, however, require the umbilical cord to have been cut: *Poulton* (1832). Therefore an unborn child is not a person: *AG Ref No 3 1994* (1998).

The final element of the *actus reus* is that the killing must be unlawful.

The killing must be unlawful

One interpretation of this requirement is that it simply means that a killing will not be deemed unlawful where it is justified or excused. This could mean that the defendant has used reasonable force in self-defence, for example. In the case of *Re A (children) (2000)* the Court of Appeal held that an operation which separated conjoined twins would not be an unlawful killing where it was carried out to save the life of one twin, even though separation would inevitably result in the death of the weaker twin.

Case precedent – *A (Children) (Conjoined Twins: Medical Treatment)* [2001] 2 WLR 480

Facts: This case involved conjoined twins. Doctors advised that in order to preserve the life of one twin, the babies needed to be separated. If the twins were not separated both twins would certainly die. However, the separation of the twins would lead to the death of the weaker twin. The doctors sought permission from the courts to separate the twins in the absence of parental consent. They also sought a ruling from the court as to whether the operation would be lawful given that it was virtually certain that the weaker twin would die as a result of the separation.

Principle: Unlawful killing and necessity

Application: The courts allowed the operation to take place. The separation was lawful despite the virtually certain death of the weaker twin on the basis of necessity.

In the next section we will consider the impact that consent has on whether a killing is deemed unlawful.

Consent

It is clear that an individual can consent to certain harmful activity, activity that would in the absence of consent render the activity unlawful and potentially criminal. Good examples of this are contact sports, surgery, body piercing and tattooing. In the context of homicide a victim's consent does not generally affect the unlawfulness of criminal homicide. In other words a victim cannot consent to being murdered!

Whilst an individual has the right to refuse medical treatment, they cannot request that a doctor 'actively kill them'. The outcomes may in this illustration be the same (the patient dies), but individuals do not have the right to implicate another in a positive act that will end their life. This was made clear in the case of *Purdy (2009)* (Art 8(1) **European Convention on Human Rights**).

We have now considered the *actus reus* elements of the offence of murder. In order to establish liability for the offence we must now deal with the *mens rea* for the offence.

Mens rea

There is one *mens rea* element for the offence of murder. In Coke's definition of murder the *mens rea* for the offence is termed 'malice aforethought', and you need to be careful with this term as it is potentially misleading. Malice aforethought simply means intention to kill or cause grievous bodily harm: *Cunningham* (1982).

> Murder is, of course, killing with malice aforethought, but 'malice afore-thought' is a term of art. It has always been defined in English law as either an express intention to kill, as could be inferred when a person, having uttered threats against another, produced a lethal weapon and used it on a victim or implied where, by a voluntary act, the accused intended to cause grievous bodily harm to the victim and the victim died as a result.
>
> *(per Lord Hailsham in* Cunningham *(1982),*
> *citing Lord Goddard CJ in* Vickers *(1957))*

Common Pitfall

Be careful with the term malice aforethought. The term malice aforethought is not the same as premeditation, or motive. It has nothing to do with malice or wickedness either. The term refers to an intention to kill or cause grievous bodily harm.

Key point

It is very important to remember that the *mens rea* is what differentiates the offence of murder from manslaughter. Remember that the *actus reus* elements are the same for these different homicide offences.

We have discussed intention earlier in Chapter 2 and you will recall that intention can take two forms: either direct intention or oblique intention.

Direct intention	• When it is D's aim or purpose to achieve a result. • Therefore D wanted to kill V – it was D's aim to kill V.
Oblique intention	• When it is not D's aim but it is virtually certain to happen as a consequence. • Therefore D may not wish to kill V or to cause GBH, but it is virtually certain to happen as a result.

The *mens rea* for murder is present where there is intent to kill, or intention to cause grievous bodily harm (really serious harm). The leading case is the case of *Woollin*. It is important to note the significance of the decision in *Matthews and Alleyne* as this case established the principle that whilst foresight of a virtual certainty may be evidence of intention the jury is not bound to infer that this is the case. The jury *may* conclude that it is evidence of intention.

Up for Debate

There have been a number of calls for reform of the offence of murder, most recently in 2005 when different degrees of murder were proposed (first and second degree murder and manslaughter).

However, given the political importance of the offence of murder and politicians' commitment to a mandatory life sentence for the offence, these reforms have stalled.

Reform of the law in relation to homicide remains topical and it would be sensible to familiarise yourself with the key reforms. Showing an understanding of areas of law that have been identified as in need of reform is a good way to attract extra marks in an assessment.

A summary of the points we have covered in this section is:

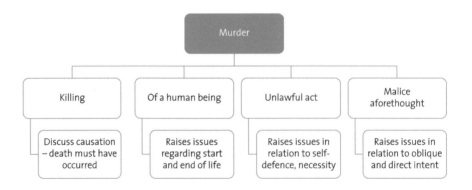

Voluntary manslaughter

Introduction

In this section we are going to consider manslaughter. Like homicide, manslaughter is a generic term. There are two forms of manslaughter: voluntary manslaughter and involuntary manslaughter. Voluntary manslaughter is closely related to murder, in so far as the *actus reus* and *mens rea* for murder are present. However, in the case of voluntary manslaughter there are 'special circumstances' in existence that enable the defendant to avail themselves of one of three special partial defences.

The diagram below illustrates the relationship between the different offences.

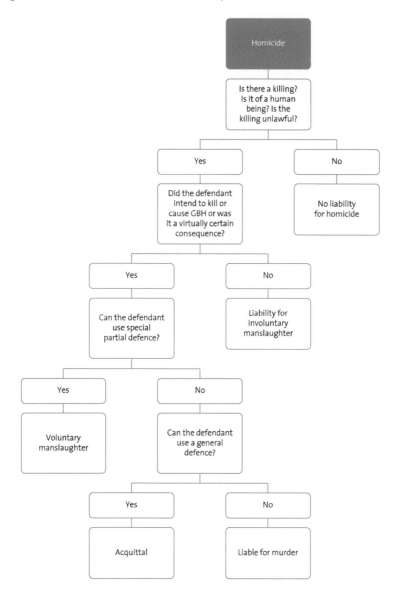

Voluntary manslaughter has exactly the same *mens rea* and *actus reus* as the offence of murder; however, there are circumstances that exist that enable the defendant to run a special partial defence. In successfully running one of these special partial defences the charge of murder is reduced to voluntary manslaughter. This is significant because the only sentence that can be handed down in a murder trial is a mandatory life sentence. In reducing the charge to voluntary manslaughter the judge has discretion in sentencing, although it is important to note that the maximum sentence that can be passed in the case of voluntary manslaughter is a life sentence.

The special partial defences are:

❖ diminished responsibility; or
❖ loss of self-control (previously referred to as provocation); or
❖ suicide pact.

The *actus reus* and *mens rea* for voluntary manslaughter are:

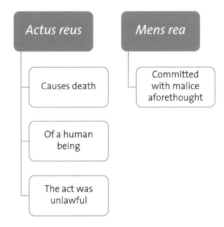

As you can see, the *actus reus* and *mens rea* are identical to those of murder.

Actus reus

The *actus reus* of this offence is the unlawful killing of a human being.

Mens rea

The *mens rea* for the offence of voluntary manslaughter is malice aforethought or intention to kill or cause GBH. It is important to remember that a finding of voluntary manslaughter cannot be made if the *mens rea* for murder is absent. If intention to kill or cause GBH is missing, or if there is a reasonable doubt that it may not be present, you should move on to consider involuntary manslaughter as a lesser or alternative charge.

Special partial defences

What distinguishes voluntary manslaughter from murder is the existence of special circumstances. These special circumstances allow the defendant to run a special partial defence applicable **ONLY** to a murder charge.

Common Pitfall

Remember that these special partial defences are applicable ONLY to a charge of MURDER. It is not uncommon for students to assume that diminished responsibility and loss of control are general defences applicable to any charge. This is a fundamental mistake. These defences cannot be utilised in the case of a non-fatal offence against the person.

Do not use these defences for any offence other than murder!

We will now consider each of the special partial defences which, if established, reduce the offence from murder to voluntary manslaughter.

Diminished responsibility

Diminished responsibility is a statutory defence, found in s 2 of the Homicide Act 1957 as amended by s 52 of the Coroners and Justice Act 2009. The substance of this defence is that at the time of the killing the defendant was suffering from a recognised mental abnormality.

The statutory definition of diminished responsibility was originally laid down in s 2(1) of the Homicide Act 1957, which stated:

> Where a person kills or is a party to the killing of another, he shall not be convicted of murder if he was suffering from such abnormality of mind (whether arising from a condition of arrested or retarded development of mind or any inherent causes or induced by disease or injury) as substantially impaired his mental responsibility for his acts and omissions in doing or being a party to the killing.

In 2009 the provisions in s 2(1) of the Homicide Act were amended by the Coroners and Justice Act (CJA).

Homicide Act 1957 set out the law on diminished responsibility → Coroners and Justice Act 2009 amended the Homicide Act 1957

Section 2 of the Homicide Act 1957 is amended by s 52 of the CJA 2009. The key provision that you should use when considering this partial defence states:

> (1) A person (D) who kills or is a party to the killing of another is not to be convicted of murder if D was suffering from an abnormality of mental functioning which:
>
> (a) arose from a recognised medical condition;
> (b) substantially impaired D's ability to do one or more of the things mentioned in subsection (1A); and
> (c) provides an explanation for D's acts and omissions in doing or being a party to the killing.

In the same way that we break down a criminal offence into constituent elements you should break down a defence into the different ingredients or elements of the defence. You must remember to consider ALL of the different ingredients.

The ingredients of this defence can be identified as follows:

1. D must be suffering from an abnormality of mind.
2. The abnormality of the mind must arise from a recognised medical condition.
3. The abnormality must have impaired D's ability.
4. The abnormality provides an explanation for D's acts or omissions.

We will now consider each of these elements in further detail.

Aim Higher

As you read through the rest of this section, think about how this differs from the **Homicide Act 1957**, and why these changes were made.

This will help you to consider the circumstances of a problem question, but will also help you to discuss the differences in more depth, if you are answering an essay question on reform of homicide or on defences. Given the relatively recent change, this is quite a useful example to cite.

The defendant must be suffering from an abnormality of mental functioning

In the case of *Byrne* (1960), Lord Parker described abnormality of mind as

> a state of mind so different from that of ordinary human beings that the reasonable man would term it abnormal.

The abnormality of mental functioning does not need to be permanent, nor does it need to have existed since birth.

The abnormality must be a recognised medical condition

There are a number of pre-CJA 2009 cases which illustrate a range of conditions that would fall within the definition of an 'abnormality of mental functioning'. The table below illustrates a range of conditions caught by the definition.

Issue/behaviours	Case
Battered woman's syndrome	*Hobson* [1997] Crim LR 759 – V stabbed and killed her abusive husband. Psychiatric reports found she was suffering from battered woman's syndrome.
Paranoid psychosis	*Sanderson* (1993) CR App R 325 – D beat and killed his girlfriend. Psychiatric reports found that D suffered from paranoid psychosis due to a traumatic upbringing.
Depression	*Gittens* (1984) 79 Cr App R 272 – D was suffering from depression and killed his wife when released from hospital.

It is worth noting that in the case of *Dowds* (2012) it was held that the presence of a recognised medical condition is a 'necessary, but not necessarily a sufficient, condition to raise diminished responsibility as a defence'.

The table above only provides a snapshot of conditions. Other conditions that are likely to be captured by the term 'recognised medical condition' include:

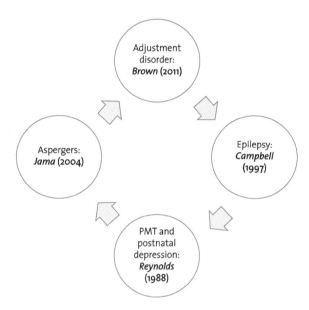

Medical evidence is vital to the success of the defence of diminished responsibility. In *Dix* (1982) it was held that medical evidence was 'a practical necessity'. It is important to note that once medical evidence has been presented it is up to the jury as to whether they accept the evidence. It is important to remember that when you are answering a problem question your role is to construct criminal liability; you are not the jury and therefore you must note when issues are a matter of fact for the jury.

The defendant bears the burden of proof when advancing the defence of diminished responsibility. However, the defence only need establish the existence of diminished responsibility on the balance of probabilities: *Dunbar* (1958).

Case precedent – *Campbell* [1986] 84 Cr App R 255

Facts: D killed V when giving her a lift, after she refused his advances. D was convicted and won an appeal after determining that he suffered from epilepsy and put forward the defence of diminished responsibility due to frontal lobe damage. This information was not available at the time of the trial.

Principle: Diminished responsibility

Application: It is important to note here that if the issue of diminished responsibility emerges through the evidence, then the judge must point this out to D's counsel.

Substantially impaired D's ability to do one or more of the things mentioned in subsection (1A)

It must be demonstrated that the recognised medical condition substantially impaired the defendant's ability to do one or more of the following:

(a) to understand the nature of their own conduct;
(b) to form a rational judgement; and
(c) to exercise self-control.

The question as to whether the defendant's ability was substantially impaired is a question for the jury: *Khan* (2010).

Aim Higher

If you decide to answer a question on diminished responsibility in an exam you need to work through each of the ingredients outlined in this section – you need to remember to then apply the law to the facts of the question!

In short, you must determine whether the illness described in the question is likely to be considered a recognised medical condition, and whether the illness has impaired D's ability. Keep focused on these points, and this will help you reach a conclusion.

The abnormality of mental functioning MUST provide an explanation for D's acts and omissions in doing or being a party to the killing

The abnormality of the mental functioning must be a cause of or a significant contributory factor towards D causing or carrying out the conduct. This is essentially a causal connection between the abnormality of mental functioning and the defendant's action or omission.

Note the emphasis on 'cause' here – it demonstrates the direct relationships required to prove this defence.

The interpretation by the courts has been that diminished responsibility must be an inside cause, without an external influence. For example, intoxication is classed as an external influence and is not therefore considered as diminished responsibility.

However, if long-term alcoholism or addiction has caused long-term internal damage, then this could be taken into consideration.

Case precedent – *Dowds* [2012] EWCA Crim 281

Facts: D and V were frequent binge drinkers and D killed V after one such binge. The Court of Appeal rejected the argument that binge drinking is a recognised medical condition.

Principle: Diminished responsibility

Application: Voluntary intoxication does not give rise to diminished responsibility.

Diminished responsibility and intoxication

Provided that the defendant is not so intoxicated that they are unable to form the *mens rea* for murder they will not be able to avail themselves of diminished responsibility, as voluntary intoxication cannot itself provide an 'abnormality of mental functioning': *Fenton* (1975). The case of *Dowds* (2012) above illustrates this point.

We need, however, to consider the situation in which the defendant is voluntarily intoxicated and also happens to be suffering from another 'abnormality of mental functioning'. In this situation the trial judge should instruct the jury to ignore the effects of intoxication: *Gittens* (1984). The question that should be put to the jury is whether or not the defendant would still have had an 'abnormaility of mind' had he not been drinking: *Dietschmann* (2003).

We can see the timeline of these key cases regarding the relationship between diminished responsibility and intoxication as:

It is important to note that the law differs where the defendant's abnormality of mind is the product of long-term drug or alcohol abuse. This is often referred to as Alcohol Dependency Syndrome (ADS). In *Tandy* (1989) it was held that alcoholism was not on its own sufficient for a plea of diminished responsibility. More recently, in the case of *Woods* (2008) a more lenient approach to ADS has been adopted and it now seems clear that there are certain circumstances in which ADS may give rise to a valid claim of diminished responsibility. These circumstances were later clarified in the case of *Stewart* (2010).

When considering a problem question, work through the following steps to determine whether D is suffering from diminished responsibility:

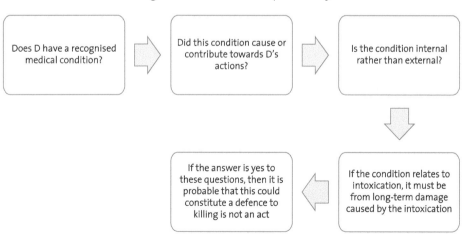

We are now moving on to consider the second special partial defence and that is the defence of loss of self-control. This defence was previously called provocation.

Loss of self-control

Where diminished responsibility considers the internal working of the defendant's mind at the time of the killing, loss of self-control considers the external factors leading up to the killing.

Common Pitfall

Many students make the mistake of discussing provocation in relation to non-fatal offences.

Loss of self-control, like diminished responsibility, is a defence only to MURDER, and you should not therefore discuss this defence in relation to any other offences that have been committed. Countless papers submitted by students have discussed provocation/loss of self-control where the victim has been assaulted following a disagreement. This is incorrect, and you will lose time and possibly marks with this approach in an exam.

The defence of provocation was contained within the Homicide Act 1957. The Coroners and Justice Act (CJA) 2009 abolished the partial defence of provocation, replacing it with the partial defence of loss of self-control.

Provocation within the **Homicide Act 1957**	**CJA 2009** changed this defence	Now called loss of self-control

Before considering the law as it currently stands it is helpful to take a brief overview of the law of provocation before it was reformed. If you answer an essay question on reform of this area of law you will certainly need to understand the position prior to reform. It is also worth noting that the defence of provocation is still applicable in cases where the offence was committed prior to October 2010.

Provocation

Section 3 of the Homicide Act 1957 states:

Where on a charge of murder there is evidence on which the jury can find that the person charged was provoked (whether by things done or by things said or by both together) to lose his self-control, the question whether the provocation was enough to make a reasonable man do as he did shall be left to be determined by the jury; and in determining that question the jury shall take into account everything both done and said according to the effect which, in their opinion, it would have on a reasonable man.

If we deconstruct the definition outlined above we can see that the defence of provocation consists of the following elements:

1. Provocative conduct (things done or said or both).
2. This caused the D to lose their self-control.
3. The reasonable man would have done as D did.

Loss of control

Section 56 of the **Coroners and Justice Act 2009** abolished the defence of provocation, and replaced it with a new defence called 'loss of control'.

Section 54 defines the loss of self-control as follows:

(1)

    (a) D's acts and omissions in doing or being a party to the killing resulted from D's loss of self-control,

    (b) The loss of self-control had a qualifying trigger, and

    (c) A person of D's sex and age, with a normal degree of tolerance and self-restraint and in the circumstances of D, might have reacted in the same or in a similar way to D.

(2) For the purposes of subsection (1)(a), it does not matter whether or not the loss of control was sudden.

(3) In subsection (1)(c) the reference to 'the circumstances of D' is a reference to all of D's circumstances other than those whose only relevance to D's conduct is that they bear on D's general capacity for tolerance or self-restraint.

(4) Subsection (1) does not apply if, in doing or being a party to a killing, D acted in a considered desire for revenge.

We now need to break the defence down into the constituent elements. If you answer a question on loss of self-control you must establish each of these three elements. If you fail to do so the defence will fail.

1. There must be a qualifying trigger.
2. The qualifying trigger must result in the defendant losing self-control.
3. A person of D's sex and age, with a normal degree of tolerance and self-restraint, would have acted as the defendant did.

We will now look at each of these elements in turn.

Qualifying trigger

The meaning of a qualifying trigger is highlighted in s 55:

From this it is important to note that the loss of self-control must have a **qualifying trigger**. This is a fundamental difference from the law on provocation (above).

(3) This subsection applies if D's loss of self-control was attributable to D's fear of serious violence from V against D or another identified person.

(4) This subsection applies if D's loss of control was attributable to a thing or things done or said (or both) which –

(a) constituted circumstance of an extremely grave character, and
(b) caused D to have a justifiable sense of being seriously wronged.

(5) This subsection applies if D's loss of self-control was attributable to a combination of the matters mentioned in subsections (3) and (4).

(6) In determining whether a loss of self-control had a qualifying trigger –

(a) D's fear of serious violence is to be disregarded to the extent that it was caused by a thing which D incited to be done or said for the purposes of providing an excuse to use violence.
(b) A sense of being wronged by a thing done or said is not justifiable if D incited the thing to be done or said for the purpose of providing an excuse to use violence.
(c) The fact that a thing done or said constituted sexual infidelity is to be disregarded.

We can summarise these points as follows:

Qualifying factors	Non-qualifying factors
Fear of serious violence	An excuse to use violence
Circumstances of extremely grave character	Incited by D
Justifiable sense of being seriously wronged	Sexual infidelity
A combination of the above	Revenge

The qualifying trigger(s) must constitute circumstances of an extremely grave character. They must have caused the defendant to have a justifiable sense of being seriously wronged.

If the trigger is not a qualifying one then the defendant cannot utilise the defence of loss of self-control.

What we can see from the above diagram is that there is clear guidance as to what will and what will not constitute a 'qualifying trigger'. The defendant's response must be the result of one or both of the qualifying triggers. The qualifying triggers can be further subdivided into:

Trigger 1: Fear	Trigger 2: Anger	Trigger 3: Both together

Fear
In order to be operative the defendant must fear violence from the victim and not from another person. The fear must also be directed at an 'identified person'.

Anger
The second trigger can be the result of words said, acts done, or both together. However, the 2009 Act requires that the trigger must give rise to:

❖ circumstances of an extremely grave character; and
❖ a justifiable sense of being seriously wronged.

It is clear that these additional requirements render the defence of loss of self-control much narrower than its predecessor of provocation: *Clinton* (2012). The case of *Zebedee* (2012) illustrates that the practical impact of these additional requirements is to ensure that trivial acts or words of provocation cannot give rise to a legitimate claim of loss of self-control.

It is also clear from the diagram on page 122 that certain circumstances/situations can never give rise to a qualifying trigger regardless as to whether the circumstances are of an extremely grave in character and led to the defendant feeling a justifiable sense of being wronged.

Limitations

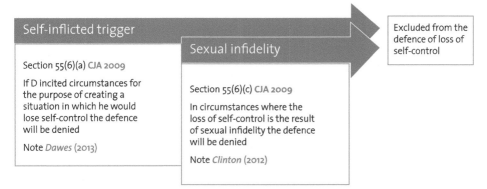

Self-inflicted trigger

Section 55(6)(a) CJA 2009

If D incited circumstances for the purpose of creating a situation in which he would lose self-control the defence will be denied

Note *Dawes* (2013)

Sexual infidelity

Section 55(6)(c) CJA 2009

In circumstances where the loss of self-control is the result of sexual infidelity the defence will be denied

Note *Clinton* (2012)

Excluded from the defence of loss of self-control

In relation to s 55(6)(C) of the **CJA 2009** it is worth noting that in the case of *Clinton* (2012) this provision was interpreted in such a way as to allow evidence in relation to sexual infidelity to be considered in relation to loss of self-control.

D must have suffered a loss of self-control

Once it has been established that the circumstances arose as a result of a qualifying trigger, it must also be established that D suffered a loss of self-control as a result of the qualifying trigger. This is akin to the old subjective test in provocation.

The loss of self-control need not be 'sudden': s 54(2). This is another significant change, as the previous guidance on provocation stipulated that the loss of self-control had to be a 'sudden and temporary' loss of self-control.

Up for Debate

The law on provocation was reformed because it was widely recognised that it failed to operate adequately in relation to people who kill in response to a 'fear of serious violence', in cases where there was a backdrop of continuing domestic violence.

As a relatively recent change in the law, it will be interesting to see how effective the new provisions will be in addressing cases where domestic violence is alleged.

A person of D's sex and age, with a normal degree of tolerance and self-restraint, would have acted as the defendant did

The third and final ingredient for this defence is that a person of the defendant's age and sex, with a normal degree of tolerance and self-restraint, would have acted as the defendant did. This is akin to the objective test in the now-abolished defence of provocation.

A normal person is therefore of the same sex and age as the defendant, which confirms the position under the common law prior to the CJA 2009: *DPP v Camplin* (1978). A normal person has a 'normal degree of tolerance and self-restraint'. What this means in practice is that the following characteristics cannot be attributed to the 'normal person', for the purposes of this test.

| Racism | Homophobia | Alcoholism | Irritability/bad temper | Jealousy |

These characteristics are not attributed to the normal person; or to put it another way, a person with a normal degree of tolerance and self-restraint

Outcome of loss of self-control

The outcome of a successful plea of loss of control is the same as it was for the defence of provocation. The defendant is not acquitted but convicted of the lesser offence of voluntary manslaughter.

Burden and standard of proof

One area that students typically neglect in relation to all defences, is the burden and standard of proof. With respect to the defence of loss of self-control the defence bears the evidential burden:

> Section 54(5): On a charge of murder if sufficient evidence is adduced to raise an issue with respect to the defence under subsection (1), the jury must assume that the defence is satisfied unless the prosecution proves beyond reasonable doubt that it is not.

This means that once the defence has raised evidence in relation to the defence of provocation/loss of control, the legal burden then rests with the prosecution, who must prove beyond all reasonable doubt that the defendant did not suffer a loss of control.

Example

Tom and Ed have a long-running feud. They meet in the street and Tom says, 'I am going to kill you right now, because of what you have done.' Tom reaches into his bag. Ed fears that Tom is taking out a weapon. Ed grabs a glass bottle lying on the ground and stabs Tom 60 times in the face and Tom dies as a result.

Could loss of control be used as a defence for Ed? Work through the following steps to come to a conclusion:

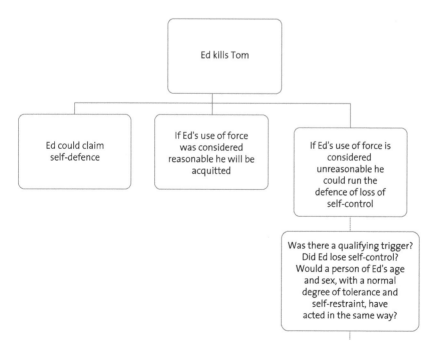

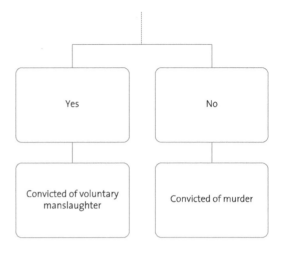

The final special partial defence that we will consider is suicide pact.

Suicide pact

Suicide pact is the third defence which can alter the offence of murder to voluntary manslaughter. It is contained within s 4(1) of the Homicide Act 1957.

> A suicide pact is defined as a common agreement between two or more persons having for its object the death of all of them.

The defence operates in the following way.

If D and V have entered into a suicide pact and D survives, then D can put forward this defence to reduce the offence from murder to voluntary manslaughter. It is important to note that the defence bears the burden of proof.

Remember that it is not an offence for a person to commit suicide, but it is an offence for someone to assist in the suicide, such as enabling V to take pills for an overdose.

Common Pitfall

Be careful not to confuse a suicide pact with assisting a suicide, which is a completely different offence. For the offence of voluntary manslaughter, there must be a **suicide pact** in place, rather than a pact to assist a death.

Example

Sue and Julie make a pact to commit suicide using a shotgun. Sue tries to shoot herself but cannot pull the trigger. Julie shoots Sue and then turns the shotgun on herself. She pulls the trigger but her injury is not fatal and she survives. Julie is charged with Sue's murder.

In this example, it would be for Julie's defence to prove that there was a suicide pact, and the circumstances of this pact. If the jury were convinced that a suicide pact was operative at the time of Sue's death then Julie would be convicted of voluntary manslaughter.

A summary of the points we have covered in this section:

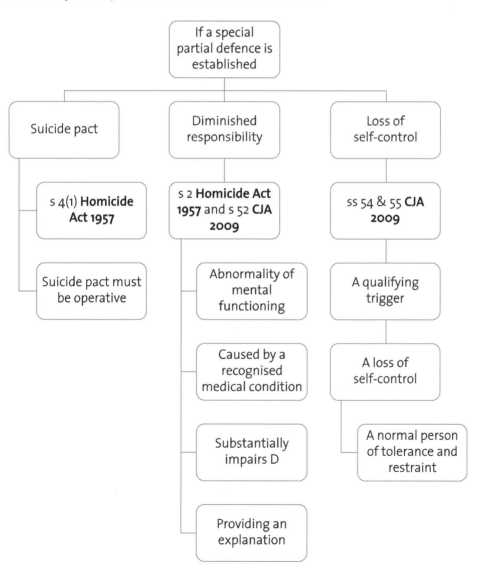

Aim Higher

There are two common types of assessment question in criminal law. These are the essay question and the problem question. The different types of question assess different skills; they therefore require very different approaches.

When initially faced with a problem question many students feel a little overwhelmed and anxious. Problem questions are typically quite long and involve several parties and more than one potential offence. The good news is that, although they can be daunting at first, most students with a little guidance prefer answering problem questions.

The most important thing to remember when answering problem questions is: STRUCTURE, STRUCTURE, STRUCTURE! Your job when answering a criminal law problem question is to identify potential liability and construct liability. You cannot do this if you adopt a haphazard approach. If you use the following structure or method you will demonstrate logical thought and progression in your answer. You will also tick off the key elements required to construct liability.

Answer Structure

1. **Identify and define the offence** – remember to give a source – is it a common law offence or a statutory offence? What is the maximum penalty upon conviction for this offence?
2. **Define the offence** – provide an accurate legal definition – make sure you provide an authority/source for the definition.
3. *Actus reus* – outline the *actus reus* of the offence – if you are dealing with a result crime make sure that you discuss causation.
4. *Mens rea* – explain the *mens rea* for the offence – ensure that you provide relevant authority.
5. **Defences** – consider the existence of relevant defences – make sure that you work your way through the ingredients of each potential defence. Consider the impact of a successful use of specific defences; for example, will running this specific defence result in an acquittal or a special verdict?
6. **Alternate or lesser offences** – consider alternate or lesser offences that may be relevant.
7. **Reform** – a good way to pick up extra marks in a problem question is to note where a particular area of law has been subject to proposals for reform.

Involuntary manslaughter

Involuntary manslaughter is a less culpable form of homicide. It extends to a killing in which D's *mens rea* is less than that required for murder, i.e. there is no malice aforethought (no intent to kill or cause GBH). We will investigate this further later on in this section.

The key differences between murder and voluntary manslaughter (which we have already considered above) and involuntary murder can be summarised as:

Murder	• An unlawful killing of a human being + intention to cause death OR GBH (malice aforethought) = murder
Voluntary manslaughter	• An unlawful killing of a human being + loss of self-control OR diminished responsibility OR killing in a suicide pact = voluntary manslaughter
Involuntary manslaughter	• An unlawful killing of a human being + no intention to cause death (or GBH) + unlawful and dangerous act OR gross negligence OR + recklessness = involuntary manslaughter

As highlighted above, involuntary manslaughter is a form of homicide where the defendant is held responsible for causing the victim's death, even though the defendant did not intend to kill or cause the victim GBH. In this situation the defendant has committed the *actus reus* of homicide but lacks the *mens rea* for a conviction of murder/voluntary manslaughter.

There are three different types of involuntary manslaughter. A defendant can be held liable:

❖ by committing an unlawful and dangerous act (**unlawful act or constructive** manslaughter);
❖ where the defendant owes the victim a duty of care and breaches the duty of care with gross negligence (**gross negligence** manslaughter);
❖ in the course of any conduct, being subjectively reckless as to serious injury (**subjective recklessness** manslaughter).

We will now consider the first two types of voluntary manslaughter, as they are the most likely forms of manslaughter to arise in an exam. You will need to be aware of the key differences, in order to construct liability for the correct offence.

Aim Higher

Involuntary manslaughter is a step between homicide which is intended and accidental homicide; that is, the death is not intended but is the result of an act or conduct. It therefore has a potentially wide span, and circumstances are extremely important here.

Be careful not to confuse involuntary manslaughter with tort or accidental death when considering the circumstances of a death.

Unlawful act (or constructive) manslaughter

Involuntary manslaughter by an unlawful act is also known as *constructive manslaughter*. The Homicide Act 1957 changed the name and meaning of constructive manslaughter, and it is now more widely referred to as unlawful act manslaughter.

In this instance, the death must have occurred from an unlawful act (discussed below), and there must be a risk of some personal injury (not to the extent of GBH, otherwise this would then constitute murder).

There are three *actus reus* elements to unlawful act manslaughter – note that the *mens rea* is the same as for the unlawful act itself.

The *actus reus* and *mens rea* for unlawful act manslaughter are:

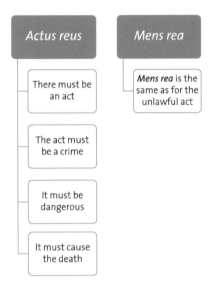

We will now consider these individual elements in more detail.

There must be an act
Unlawful act manslaughter cannot be committed by omission, it requires a positive act: *Lowe* (1973).

The act must be unlawful
The defendant must commit an unlawful act and that act must constitute a criminal offence. A civil wrong will be insufficient grounds on which to construct liability for unlawful act manslaughter: *Lamb* (1967). The unlawful act does not need not be directed at the victim. See *R v Mitchell* (1983).

Common Pitfall

Be careful here, because although the courts insist on using the term 'unlawful act' they actually mean a criminal offence.

> **Case precedent – *R v Franklin* [1883] 15 Cox CC 163**
>
> **Facts:** D threw an item into the sea, hitting and killing a swimmer. It was argued that the act was a civil act, rather than an unlawful act.
>
> **Principle:** Unlawful act
>
> **Application:** This case confirms that the defendant must commit an unlawful act – a criminal offence in the case of unlawful act manslaughter.

The diagram bellow illustrates some of the base level crimes on which the courts have constructed liability for constructive manslaughter.

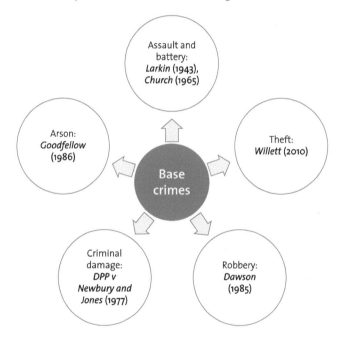

In the case of *Meeking* (2012) a conviction for unlawful act manslaughter was upheld where the base level crime was contrary to s 22A(1)(b) of the **Road Traffic Act 1988**.

The act must be dangerous

The third element of unlawful act manslaughter is that the act must be a dangerous one. In *Church* (1965) it was held that:

> *the unlawful act must be such as all reasonable and sober people would inevitably recognise must subject the other person to, at least, the risk of some harm therefrom, albeit not serious harm.*

The test used to determine whether an act is an objective test: *Ball* (1989). If the defendant has knowledge of the victim or acquires knowledge of the victim whilst committing the crime this knowledge can be ascribed to the 'reasonable man' when applying the objective test: *Watson* (1989).

In *Bristow* (2013) it was held that a burglary, although not normally considered a dangerous crime, could be committed in a dangerous manner. In this case the defendant used a vehicle to commit the offence. A resident at the property was run over and killed in the commission of the offence and the court upheld a conviction for unlawful act manslaughter.

The unlawful act must cause the death of the victim

The defendant's unlawful act must be the cause of the victim's death: *Mitchell* (1983). We discuss the rules of causation in detail in Chapter 2. If you are answering a problem question you must be satisfied that the defendant's actions are a factual and legal cause of death.

Aim Higher

The chapter on the general principles of criminal liability (Chapter 2) considers causation in more detail, and it is recommended that you review this in the context of homicide, so that you are able to apply the same principles to a problem question on homicide.

The mens rea requirement for unlawful act manslaughter

The *mens rea* for unlawful act manslaughter is the same as that required for the unlawful act itself (the base level offence). There is no separate *mens rea* required.

This is an important point to note and you should remember to pull this out and explain the rationale within an answer, so it is clear for the examiner.

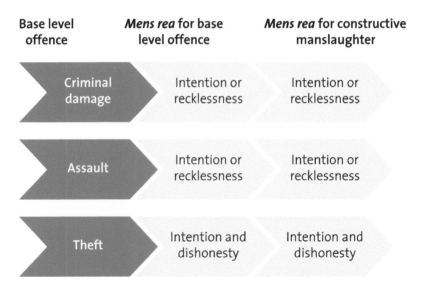

Base level offence	*Mens rea* for base level offence	*Mens rea* for constructive manslaughter
Criminal damage	Intention or recklessness	Intention or recklessness
Assault	Intention or recklessness	Intention or recklessness
Theft	Intention and dishonesty	Intention and dishonesty

Example

Look at this example, and then use the chart below to consider whether this is a case of unlawful act manslaughter:

Chris is short of money, so decides to rob a post office. Chris enters with a gun, and threatens Jill, the postmistress, telling her to hand over the money, or she will be shot. Jill is very frightened and hands the money to Chris. Jill then collapses and dies from a heart attack.

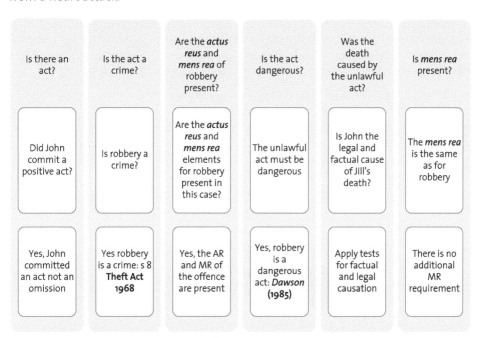

Is there an act?	Is the act a crime?	Are the *actus reus* and *mens rea* of robbery present?	Is the act dangerous?	Was the death caused by the unlawful act?	Is *mens rea* present?
Did John commit a positive act?	Is robbery a crime?	Are the *actus reus* and *mens rea* elements for robbery present in this case?	The unlawful act must be dangerous	Is John the legal and factual cause of Jill's death?	The *mens rea* is the same as for robbery
Yes, John committed an act not an omission	Yes robbery is a crime: s 8 **Theft Act 1968**	Yes, the AR and MR of the offence are present	Yes, robbery is a dangerous act: *Dawson* (1985)	Apply tests for factual and legal causation	There is no additional MR requirement

Summary

Use this checklist to ensure that you understand the requirements for the unlawful act manslaughter.

Unlawful act manslaughter

- There must be an act not an omission.
- The act must be a crime.
- The act must be dangerous.
- The AR and MR of the base-level offence must be present.
- The defendant's actions must be the cause of the victim's death.
- There is no additional MR requirement.

Gross negligence manslaughter

Gross negligence manslaughter is the second type of manslaughter and occurs when D acts unlawfully, but in such a way that D's actions render the defendant criminally negligent.

Therefore the act is not unlawful, but there is a high degree of negligence (gross).

Common Pitfall

Be careful here not to confuse gross negligence manslaughter with tort. You will see similarities in language and principles being discussed, but remember that gross negligence manslaughter is a criminal offence, and negligence is a tort civil wrong.

Introduction

Like the other offences in this chapter gross negligence manslaughter is a common law offence. The leading case is that of *Adomako* (1995). This case laid down the basic elements of the offence. These can be articulated as follows:

1. The defendant must owe the victim a duty of care.
2. The defendant must breach that duty of care.
3. There must be an obvious risk of death.
4. The breach of duty of care must be the cause of the victim's death.
5. The breach must amount to gross negligence and be so serious as to justify the imposition of criminal sanction.

We will look at each of these elements in turn. It is important to remember that each of these elements must exist if liability for gross negligence manslaughter is to be established.

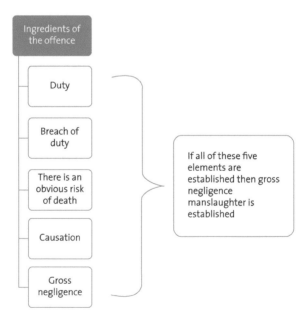

If all of these five elements are established then gross negligence manslaughter is established.

The defendant must owe the victim a duty of care

As with the tort of negligence, there must be a duty of care on the part of D towards V. In Chapter 2 we considered a number of situations in which the criminal law will find the existence of a duty of care. In reality the finding of a duty of care is not limited to these situations. In *Adomako* it was held that the finding of a duty of care is to be determined according to the 'ordinary principles of the law of negligence'.

In the case of *Donoghue v Stephenson* (1932) it was held that in ascertaining whether a duty of care exists:

> You must take reasonable care to avoid acts or omissions which you reasonably foresee would be likely to injure your neighbour. Who then is my neighbour? The answer seems to be – persons who are so closely and directly affected by my act (or omission) that I ought reasonably to have them in my contemplation as being so affected when I am directing my mind to the acts or omissions.

Therefore, the existence of a duty of care is critical to the construction of liability for this offence. The following circumstances, in addition to those established in Chapter 2 have been held by the courts to give rise to a duty of care in relation to gross negligence manslaughter:

❖ By a lorry driver who conceals immigrants in a lorry: *Wacker* (2003).
❖ By firefighters to civilians, even where they have ignored requests to move away: *Winter* (2011).
❖ By a ship's master to crew: *Litchfield* (1998).
❖ By a drug dealer who fails to take adequate steps to summon medical attention for a person to whom they have supplied drugs: *Evans* (2009).

The question as to whether a duty of care exists is a matter of law for the judge to determine: *Evans* (2009).

Therefore:

If a duty of care cannot be established

D cannot be liable for gross negligence manslaughter

Breach of the duty of care

The next element that must be established beyond a reasonable doubt is that the defendant breached the duty of care owed to the victim. This is judged objectively against the standard of the reasonably competent person performing the activity in question: *Andrews v DPP* (1937).

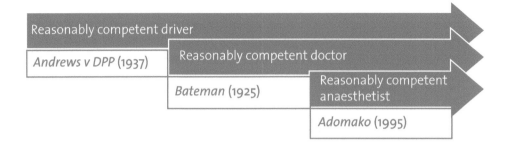

Therefore if the defendant's acts or omissions fall below the standard expected of the reasonably competent person performing that particular activity there is a breach of duty.

There must be an obvious risk of death

In the case of *Singh* (1999) it was established that 'a reasonably prudent person would have foreseen a serious and obvious risk not merely of injury, even serious injury, but of death'. The case of *Misra* (2005) confirmed this requirement. It is not necessary for the prosecution to prove that the defendant actually foresaw the risk of death, only that the act or omission created an 'obvious' risk of death: *Mark* (2004).

The breach of duty must be the cause of the victim's death

It is essential that the breach of duty is the cause of the victim's death. The normal rules of causation apply here. Thus the defendant's actions or omissions must be the factual and legal cause of the victim's death. If a causal link cannot be established then D is not liable.

The jury must be satisfied that the breach of duty is serious enough to constitute gross negligence and as such it should be regarded a crime

Negligence is rarely sufficient fault for criminal liability, so the degree of negligence must be exceptional. It must constitute gross negligence. This is a question for the jury: *Adomako* (1994).

In *Bateman* (1925) it was held that:

> the facts must be such that, in the opinion of the jury, the negligence of the accused went beyond a mere matter of compensation between subjects and showed such disregard for the life and safety of others as to amount to a crime against the state and conduct deserving of punishment.

A key precedent often referred to as the test of gross (a high degree of) negligence is set out below:

Case precedent – *R v Adomako* [1995] 1 AC 171 (HL)

Facts: D was an anaesthetist. During an operation, D did not notice that a breathing tube was not attached properly and the patient died as a result.

Principle: The defendant's conduct fell so far below the standard of care expected of a reasonably competent doctor that it was sufficient to be regarded as grossly negligent and as such criminal.

Application: This case offers a means by which to identify and define negligence. In problem questions, consider how the situation compares with the facts in *Cunningham* to help decide whether a party has been reckless.

Another useful example of grossly negligent conduct is the case of *Reid* (1992), where a diver jumped from a springboard into a pool without considering the danger of hitting anyone who might have been swimming in the pool at the time. D killed another swimmer. It is clear that a very high degree of negligence is required in order to constitute gross negligence: *Andrews v DPP* (1937). It is, however, important to note that the test for gross negligence is rather elastic in nature.

Unlike unlawful act or constructive manslaughter, gross negligence manslaughter can be committed by omission, as well as by a positive act.

Up for Debate

It is for a jury to decide whether the level of negligence is sufficient to be classed as gross negligence, and therefore a criminal act (i.e. what constitutes gross negligence).

There are differing views on whether this uncertainty is actually useful. For example, would it be more useful to be set out clearly, or are the grey areas more useful in terms of evolving law and the range of different circumstances which are covered by this offence?

Mens rea
In *AG's Reference (Number 2 of 1999)* (2000) it was held that proof of the defendant's state of mind is not necessary for a conviction of manslaughter by gross negligence. This does not, however, mean that the offence of manslaughter by gross negligence is a strict liability offence. The fault element required for this offence is negligence that is gross.

Example 1
Consider the following example. Sarah, a nurse, fails to give Zack, a diabetic under her care, his insulin. Zack dies as a result.

In this example you would need to consider:

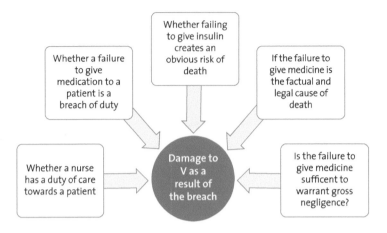

Example 2

Now consider the following example. Use the flow chart below to work through your answer.

A road worker has dug a hole in the pavement to lay a cable, but she forgets to cover it over at night. Paul is walking on the pavement at night, does not see the hole and falls in. Paul fractures his skull and dies.

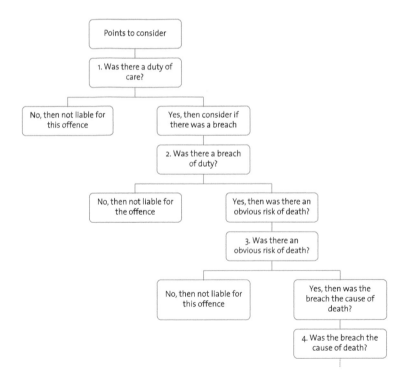

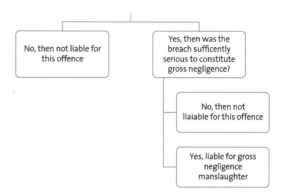

A summary of the points we have covered in this section:

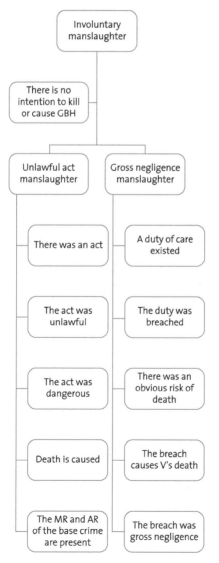

Putting it into practice

Question

Raj suffers from depression and is on medication. He recently lost money to Simon after playing poker. Raj cannot now pay his rent, and his depression has worsened. He sees Simon in the street and, taking a knife, goes outside. Raj says, 'Give me my money back or I will kill you.' Simon refuses, and Raj stabs him with the knife, killing Simon.

Discuss whether Raj would be liable for the offence or murder or voluntary manslaughter.

Suggested solution

To identify whether Raj would be liable for murder or manslaughter, you need to work through the liability for each offence. For the offence of murder you would need to consider:

❖ The definition of murder.
❖ The *actus reus* of the offence.
❖ *Causation*.
❖ The *mens rea* of the offence – malice aforethought – in particular the question makes it clear that the MR for murder is present.

In order to ascertain whether Raj would be liable for voluntary manslaughter you would need to determine whether one of the special partial defences would apply in this case.

You should note that the AR and MR for the offence of voluntary manslaughter are the same as for the offence of murder. You should explain the impact of the successful use of one of these defences. In particular you should note that successfully running one of these defences does not result in an acquittal!

The special partial defences are:

❖ diminished responsibility;
❖ loss of self-control (previously referred to as provocation);
❖ suicide pact.

From these, you could consider both loss of self-control and diminished responsibility. You must define both of these special defences and work your way through each of the ingredients for each defence.

In particular you should focus on diminished responsibility. Consider whether depression is a recognised medical condition and whether Raj could effectively use this as a defence. Remember that this defence is the difference between the offence of murder and voluntary manslaughter, and this would need to emerge from your discussion.

Key Points Checklist

The term homicide is used as an overarching term under which a number of specific offences are grouped. Suspects are not charged with homicide or convicted of homicide.	✓
Murder is a common law offence. As such the definition of murder is not located in the statute books. Rather it is located in the decisions of the courts. Murder is the unlawful killing of a human being with malice aforethought (intention to kill or cause GBH). The sentence upon conviction for murder is a mandatory life sentence.	✓
The *actus reus* for murder is the unlawful killing of a human being. Murder is a result crime and this means that a chain of causation must be established from the defendant's conduct to the resulting death of the victim. The *mens rea* for murder is 'malice aforethought': this simply means intention to kill or cause GBH. Direct or oblique intent will suffice as per *Woollin*.	✓
There are three special partial defences to a charge of murder. If these defences are successfully run they reduce the charge of murder to voluntary manslaughter. This reduction in charge enables the judge to exercise discretion in sentencing. These special partial defences are: loss of self-control; diminished responsibility; and suicide pact. These defences are only applicable to a charge of murder.	✓
Manslaughter is another form of unlawful killing. Like homicide it is a general term. There are two species of manslaughter: voluntary manslaughter as described above; and involuntary manslaughter. What distinguishes these offences is the presence of malice aforethought for voluntary manslaughter and its absence for involuntary manslaughter.	✓
In circumstances where an unlawful killing has taken place and the defendant does not have the requisite *mens rea* for murder an alternative charge would be involuntary manslaughter.	✓
There are three forms of involuntary manslaughter: constructive manslaughter, also known as unlawful act manslaughter; manslaughter by gross negligence; and reckless manslaughter.	✓
Unlawful act manslaughter requires: an unlawful act (not an omission); the act must be a crime; the act must be the cause of the victim's death; the elements of the base level offence must be made out; the *mens rea* for this offence is the *mens rea* for the base offence.	✓
Gross negligence manslaughter: the defendant must owe the victim a duty of care; there must be a breach of the duty of care; the breach must cause the victim's death; the negligence must be gross.	✓

Table of key cases referred to in this chapter

Key case	Brief facts	Principle
R v Jordan [1956] 40 Cr App R 152	V was stabbed, but died from the treatment and not from the stab wound	Causation and intervening acts
A (Children) (Conjoined Twins) [2001] 2 WLR 480	Conjoined twins, one of whom would not survive separation, but was having a detrimental effect on the other twin	Human being and necessity
Martin [2001] EWCA Crim 2245	D shot and killed an intruder entering his home	Murder is an unlawful act and self-defence
Byrne [1960] 2 QB 396	D murdered and mutilated V while experiencing impulses to do so	Diminished responsibility
Hobson [1997] Crim LR 759	Stabbed and killed her abusive husband. Psychiatric reports found she was suffering from battered woman's syndrome.	Diminished responsibility – battered woman's syndrome
Sanderson (1993) CR App R 325	D beat and killed his girlfriend. Psychiatric reports found that he suffered from paranoid psychosis.	Diminished responsibility – paranoid psychosis
Gittens (1984) 79 Cr App R 272	D was suffering from depression, and killed his wife when on a home visit.	Diminished responsibility – depression
Campbell (1986) 84 Cr App R 255	D killed V and was found guilty. On appeal medical evidence of his epilepsy was discovered, and a retrial ordered.	Diminished responsibility
Dowds [2012] EWCA Crim 281	D killed V after a binge drinking session.	Diminished responsibility and intoxication
R v Ahluwalia [1992] 4 All ER 889	D killed V, her husband, after a long period of physical and mental abuse.	Provocation (old law)
R v Doughty [1986] 83 Cr App 319	D killed his baby son when he would not stop crying	Provocation (old law)
DPP v Camplin [1978] 2 All ER 168	D was raped by V, who then laughed at him. D hit V over the head with a pan and killed him.	Characteristics of the reasonable man

Luc Thuet Thuan [1997] AC 131	D said that V, his girlfriend owed him money. Her made her withdraw the money and then stabbed her.	Characteristics of the reasonable man
Smith R v Smith (Morgan) [2000] 3 WLR 654	D suffered from depression, and killed V after an argument	Characteristics of the reasonable man
Attorney General for Jersey v Holley [2005] 3 WLR 29	D and V were separated and both alcoholic. After a day drinking alcohol D killed V after she had slept with another man.	Characteristics of the reasonable man
R v James & Karimi [2006] 2 WLR 887	D killed V, his wife, after she had formed a relationship with another man	Characteristics of the reasonable man and use of provocation
R v Franklin [1883] 15 Cox CC 163	D killed V by throwing an item into the sea	An unlawful act is required
R v Dias [2002] Crim LR 390	D prepared a syringe for V who injected himself and died of an overdose	What constitutes an unlawful act
R v Church [1966] 1 QB 59	V mocked D's sexual ability, and he killed her	A dangerous act
Reid [1992] 1 WLR 793	D dived into a pool and killed a swimmer underneath	Gross negligence
R v Adomako [1995] 1 AC 171 (HL)	D did not attach a tube during an operation, resulting in the death of V	Gross negligence

---

@ Visit the book's companion website to test your knowledge

❖ Resources include a subject map, revision tip podcasts, downloadable diagrams, MCQ quizzes for each chapter, and a flashcard glossary

❖ www.routledge.com/cw/optimizelawrevision

6

Theft and Related Offences

Understand the law
- Can you identify the different sections of the Theft Act 1968, and apply these to the offences of theft, robbery and burglary?

Remember the details
- Can you remember the definitions for each offence?
- Can you remember the *actus reus* and *mens rea* for each offence?
- Can you define these elements using case law?

Reflect critically on areas of debate
- Do you understand the definition of appropriation, and can you critically discuss the meaning of appropriation in relation to consent and the assumption of the rights of an owner?
- Do you understand the test for dishonesty and are you able to critically reflect on the limitations of the definition?

Contextualise
- Can you relate the offences in this chapter to other offences such as non-fatal offences against the person or sexual offences?

Apply your skills and knowledge
- Can you complete the activities in this chapter, using statutes and cases to support your answer?

Chapter Map

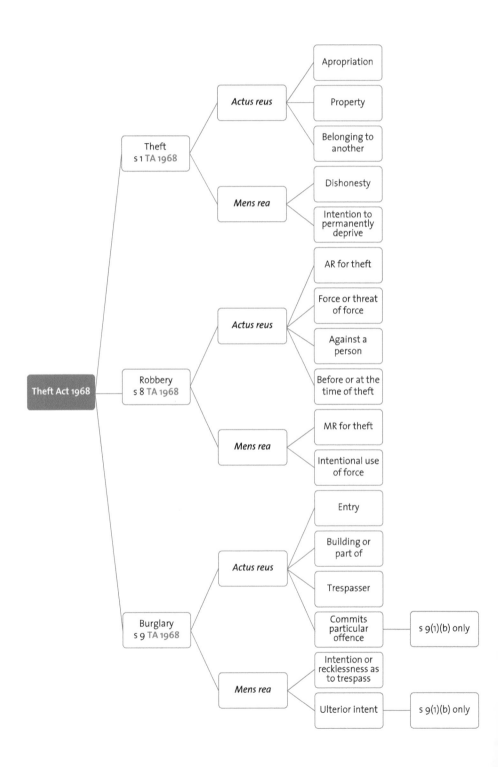

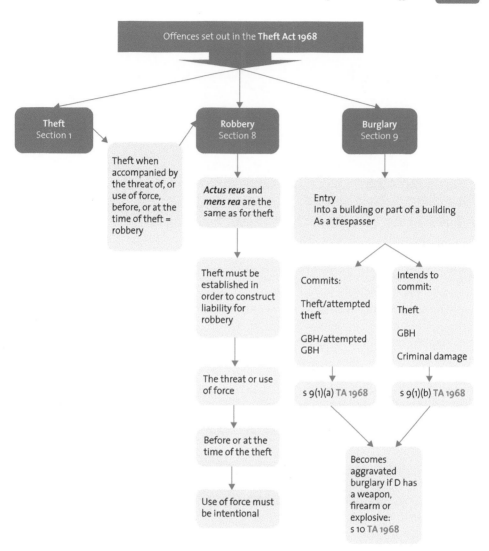

Relationship between the different offences

Introduction

In this chapter we will consider theft and related offences. You can see in the diagram above that we have illustrated the connection between the different offences. It is important that you do not revise theft in isolation as examiners frequently seek to test students' knowledge of the connectivity between these offences. The offences in this chapter are statutory in nature, and this means that all you need do when faced with a problem question, or an essay question is work your way methodically through the different statutory provisions using relevant case law to illustrate your answer.

Aim Higher

Examiners may sometimes set a theft scenario which draws on other areas of law, such as property law, contract law or tort law.

It is important to remember to stay focused on the subject you are being examined on (theft and criminal law), try not to stray into other areas of law, as these can distract from the central issues. That is not to say that you should not note the overlap – and this will demonstrate a rounded understanding of all the issues for the examiner – but do ensure that the vast majority of your answer is in relation to the criminal law! If you wander too far off on a tangent you will limit the award of marks that the examiner can make.

This chapter will focus on defining a number of key terms such as 'property', 'dishonesty' and 'belonging to another'. These terms are vital to fully understanding and applying the law in this area and you need to have a solid understanding of these terms in order to apply them accurately in a problem question. As you work through the chapter, keep focused on these terms, and then test your understanding in the activities at the end.

In this chapter we will focus on the Theft Act 1968, and the subsequent Theft Act 1978, which refined the 1968 Theft Act.

Theft Act 1968

Theft Act 1978 – refines the 1968 Act

The Theft Act 1968 brought together the main theft offences for the first time, clarifying the *actus reus* and *mens rea* for each.

The offences in the Theft Act 1968 that we will consider in this chapter are:

❖ theft
❖ robbery
❖ burglary – including aggravated burglary
❖ trespass with intent to commit a sexual offence – an overview.

Theft

The definition of theft is set out in s 1 of the Theft Act 1968:

(1) A person is guilty of theft if he dishonestly appropriates property belonging to another with the intention of permanently depriving the other of it . . .
(2) It is immaterial whether the appropriation is made with a view to gain, or for the thief's own benefit.

The *actus reus* and *mens rea* for theft are:

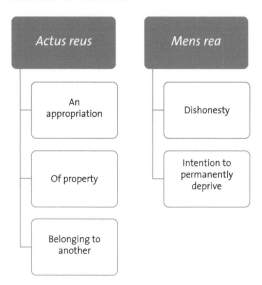

We will now consider each of these five elements in detail.

Appropriation

It is this element of theft that causes the most difficulty for students. At first glance, it might be assumed that the term means the physical removal of property, such as physically removing a purse from a handbag. However, appropriation actually has a much broader meaning.

Section 3(1) of the 1968 Act defines appropriation as:

> Any assumption by a person of the rights of an owner amounts to an appropriation, and this includes, where he has come by the property (innocently or not) without stealing it, any later assumption of a right to it by keeping or dealing with it as owner.

The discussion focuses in relation to appropriation around the phrase 'any assumption by a person of the rights of an owner', that is, dealing with the property in a way which only the owner has a right to.

Appropriation is seen as a continuing act, as confirmed in the case of *R v Hale* (1978) (when revising, you might find it helpful to remind yourself of this concept in relation to the case of *Fagan* and the concept of a 'continuous act' in this case in relation to appropriation).

It is not easy to articulate precisely what behaviour, or acts will constitute an appropriation. The courts have discussed this concept in great detail in a number of different cases. We will consider a number of cases where the issue of appropriation has been considered in cases where there is consent.

Consent

A common issue that has arisen in relation to the concept of appropriation is what happens when the owner of the property has consented to the appropriation? Does the existence of consent invalidate the appropriation in some way?

Case precedent – *Lawrence v Metropolitan Police Commissioner* [1972] AC 626

Facts: V opened his wallet to allow D, a taxi driver, to take the fare from the wallet. D took more money than he was entitled to. In his defence, D highlighted that V gave him the money voluntarily.

Principle: The impact of consent on appropriation

Application: It was held by the House of Lords that appropriation can occur even where V consented.

As a consequence of the decisions in *Lawrence v Metropolitan Police Commissioner* (1972), *Morris* (1984), *Gomez* (1993) and *Hinks* (2001), the meaning of consent has been expanded significantly. Therefore in the following circumstances appropriation may have occurred:

- Where there is no misappropriation
- With or without the consent of the owner
- With or without the property being physically taken or removed
- Where a valid gift has been made by the property owner
- Where there has been an assumption of any one right of the owner

Therefore, the significant factor that turns a lawful appropriation into an unlawful appropriation is the *mens rea* of the defendant. You should highlight this in any assessment question on theft when discussing appropriation.

The three key points to remember on consent are:

1. Appropriation can take place even if there is consent ⇨ 2. Consent is therefore irrelevant to appropriation ⇨ 3. It is the *mens rea* of D at the time of the appropriation, not the existence of consent, that is significant

Appropriation and suffered a loss

It is also important to note that V does not have to suffer a loss in order for an appropriation to take place. This was confirmed in *Corcoran v Anderton* (1980), where D grabbed V's handbag and dropped it then ran off. The Court held that by grabbing the handbag, D did assume the rights of the owner (and a conviction for robbery was upheld). In this case V had not suffered a loss as the defendant quickly abandoned the bag.

This principle was later applied in *Ex parte Osman* (1990), which established that even if the victim does not suffer any loss there may still be an appropriation.

Appropriation and assuming the rights of the owner

The essence of an appropriation is the assumption of any one (or more) of the owner's rights. In *R v Morris* (1983) the two defendants were convicted when they switched the price tags on items in a shop. One was arrested before paying for the goods, the other after paying for the goods.

Switching the labels was something that only the owner had the authority to do, therefore the defendants assumed the rights of the owner (and an appropriation had taken place) the moment the labels were switched.

It was highlighted that there only needs to be any one right of the owner that is assumed.

R v Morris (1983): D switches the labels ⇨ D assumes any one of the rights of the owner ⇨ Appropriation has taken place

Appropriation and gifts

An appropriation can also occur in circumstances where the owner has made a gift of the property to the defendant. This will occur in circumstances where the defendant has acted dishonestly in relation to the transaction.

For example, in the case of *R v Hinks* (2000), D persuaded V, a person of limited intelligence, to give them monetary gifts. The court held that an appropriation could still occur where property has been gifted, even when indefeasible gifts are given.

In the next section we will consider the *actus reus* element of theft, which is that the appropriation must be of property.

Property

According to s 4 of the Theft Act 1968, property is:

Section 4(1) 'Property' includes money and all other property, real or personal, including things in action and other intangible property.

(2) A person cannot steal land, or things forming part of land and severed from it by him or by his directions, except in the following cases, that it to say—

(a) When he is a trustee or personal representative, or is authorised by power of attorney, or as liquidator of a company, or otherwise, to sell or dispose of land belonging to another, and he appropriates the land or anything forming part of it by dealing with it in breach of the confidence reposed in him; or

(b) When he is not in possession of the land and appropriates anything forming part of the land by severing it or causing it to be severed, or after it has been severed; or

(c) When, being in possession of the land under a tenancy, he appropriates the whole or part of any fixture or structure let to be used with the land.

(3) A person who picks mushrooms growing wild on any land, or who picks flowers, fruit or foliage from a plant growing wild on any land, does not (although not in possession of the land) steal what he picks, unless he does it for reward or for sale or other commercial purpose.

For purposes of this subsection 'mushroom' includes any fungus, and 'plant' includes any shrub or tree.

(4) Wild creatures, tamed or untamed, shall be regarded as property; but a person cannot steal a wild creature not tamed nor ordinarily kept in captivity, or the carcase of any such creature, unless either it has been reduced into possession by or on behalf of another person and possession of it has not since been lost or abandoned, or another person is in course of reducing it into possession.

This can be summarised as:

Property is:	Property is not:
Tangible and intangible items	Land, in relation to stealing, with exceptions
Wild and tamed animals reduced into the possession of others	Picking wild flowers or fruit, except for a financial reward

It is clear from s 4 that there are a number of detailed stipulations regarding what does and does not constitute property for the purposes of this offence. It is important to note that the meaning of property can differ between different offences. A number of cases have refined our understanding of what constitutes property for the purposes of theft. These are set out in the table below:

Item	Position in relation to the Theft Act 1968 with refinements
Personal property	Personal property can be classified as movable property, and can therefore be tangible and intangible
Tangible property	Includes movable and non-movable property
Intangible property	Exists as a right, and can be enforced by law
Money	Includes notes and coins. There is an intention to permanently deprive unless the exact same money (the exact notes and coins that had been taken) as the same ones were going to be returned, as set out in *R v Velumyl* [1989] Crim LR 299.
Unlawful possession of property	Property can amount to something that is in unlawful possession, such as stealing illegal drugs. Demonstrated in *R v Smith & Ors* [2011] 1 Cr App R 30.
Body parts	Body parts are also regarded as property of the person whose parts they are, confirmed in *R v Kelly* [1998] 3 All ER 741. There was previous debate regarding classification of a corpse, and this is also now regarded as property.

If you need help understanding the difference between tangible and intangible property, consider the example below.

Example: think about a banker's cheque: as a piece of paper it is tangible property because you can touch it and see it; however, it also represents something else. It represents more than a tangible piece of paper, because it also represents the transfer of money between two people. That representation is an example of a 'thing in action', which is intangible.

It is important to highlight the following case that also concerned intangible property.

For example, in the case of *Oxford v Moss* (1979), it was held that confidential information cannot be stolen. In this case a student accessed a forthcoming exam paper. There was no intention of permanently depriving the university of the paper (the tangible property); it was the information on the paper that was of interest, and this was intangible property. Therefore, the offence of theft could be made out in this case.

Common Pitfall

Aside from checking your understanding of the law relating to property, a common question asked can relate to s 4(3) of the **Theft Act 1968**. An examiner may pose a question asking you to consider whether is it theft to pick mushrooms growing wild on land, or whether a person who picks flowers, fruit or foliage from a plant growing wild on any land, commits theft. The key to remember here is that the above are not considered property for the purposes of the **TA 1968** UNLESS D does it for reward, sale or other commercial purpose.

We are now moving on to consider the third element of the *actus reus* for the offence of theft, and that is the requirement that the appropriated property belongs to another.

Belonging to another

This element of the *actus reus* relates to the property that has been appropriated belonging to another person. The emphasis here is on the word 'belonging'. We will see in this section that the meaning of 'belonging' has a different meaning to the meaning that we would normally attribute to this word. That is because in the context of theft the meaning of 'belonging' is much broader, as it encompasses a person who is in **possession** or in **control** of the appropriated property.

Section 5 of the 1968 Act states:

(1) Property shall be regarded as belonging to any person having possession or control of it, or having in it any proprietary right or interest (not being an equitable interest arising only from an agreement to transfer or grant an interest).

(2) Where property is subject to a trust, the persons to whom it belongs shall be regarded as including any person having a right to enforce the trust, and an intention to defeat the trust shall be regarded accordingly as an intention to deprive of the property any person having that right.

(3) Where a person receives property from or on account of another, and is under an obligation to the other to retain and deal with that property or its proceeds in a particular way, the property or proceeds shall be regarded (as against him) as belonging to the other.

(4) Where a person gets property by another's mistake, and is under an obligation to make restoration (in whole or in part) of the property or its proceeds or of the value thereof, then to the extent of that obligation the property or proceeds shall be regarded (as against him) as belonging to the person entitled to restoration, and an intention not to make restoration shall be regarded accordingly as an intention to deprive that person of the property or proceeds.

(5) Property of a corporation sole shall be regarded as belonging to the corporation notwithstanding a vacancy in the corporation.

Belonging can mean in possession or control

This effectively means that a person does not have to own the property for it to belong to him (s 5(1)), for the purpose of theft. It can be enough that V has possession or control of the property. Thus it is possible for a defendant to be convicted of stealing his own property!

Example: Nihal asks Peter to look after his mobile phone while he is at the gym. Surya steals the phone from Peter's bag when he is not looking. In this example, Peter is in possession of the mobile phone for Nihal, and Surya steals the phone while it is in the possession of Peter, even though it is not his phone.

| Theft can occur if: | the property is in the possession of V | V has control of the property |

Many criminal law students are surprised by the revelation that a defendant can be convicted of stealing their own property from a person that is looking after it. An example of this situation can be seen in the case of *Turner (No 2)* (1971).

> ### Case precedent – *R v Turner (No 2)* [1971] 1 WLR
>
> **Facts:** D left his car at a garage for repairs. The defendant did not want to pay for the repairs so simply collected his car without paying or notifying the owners of the garage.
>
> **Principle:** D can steal his own property if it is in the possession or under the legal control of another.
>
> **Application:** D was guilty of theft as he was interfering with the garage owners' right of possession over the car, until payment for the repairs is made by the owner.

Instructions

Section 5(3) of the **Theft Act 1968** highlights that where a person has specific instructions to deal with the appropriated property in a certain way, any deviation from these instructions can amount to theft. The central issue is whether the instructions are clear. This was decided in *R v Hall* (1973).

If you are answering a question which includes a set of instructions, you will need to identify that:

❖ the instructions were clear;
❖ they were understood;
❖ D did not follow these instructions.

Property received by mistake

Section 5(4) of the Theft Act 1968 states that where a person receives property by mistake and they are under an obligation to return the property, a failure to do so can amount to theft. This principle is outlined in *A-G's Ref (No 1 of 1983) (1985)*.

For example, Rita's bank pays money into her account in error. They actually intend to pay the money into Paul's account. Rita goes to a cash machine and discovers that she has £15,000 more than she expected in her account. Rita knows that this must be an error, but she decides to buy a new car with the money.

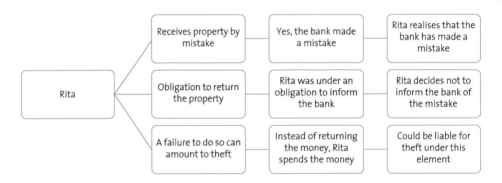

Section 5(4) operates only in circumstances where the giver of the property has made a mistake. It is also important to note that s 5(4) does not apply unless the obligation to return the property is a legal obligation: *Gilks (1972)*.

Abandoned property

The *actus reus* of theft stipulates that the appropriated property must belong to another. Abandoned property does not 'belong to another' and therefore property that is abandoned cannot be stolen for the purposes of s 1 of the Theft Act 1968. In the case of *Ricketts v Basildon Magistrates (2011)* the court dealt with the issue of abandoned property. In this instance the defendant took donation bags left outside a charity shop. The court held that the donor of the bags intended the charity shop to take ownership of the items. As such the bags had not been abandoned.

It is important to note that lost property is not abandoned property: *Hibbert v McKiernan (1948)*.

For example, Sam accidentally leaves her iPhone on the train. Kyle, who has been sitting opposite her, sees the phone and takes it. In this situation Sam has not abandoned her phone, therefore the phone still belongs to her, even though it is not in her possession.

Abandonment of property suggests that the owner no longer has an interest in the property: it does not matter to the owner what happens next to the property or who appropriates it.

For example, DJ purchases a magazine at the train station. He reads the magazine on the train and once he has finished reading it he deliberately leaves the magazine on the train seat in order that someone else can read it. Sarah sits in DJ's seat and picks up the magazine; she takes the magazine home with her. In this situation DJ has abandoned the magazine – he does not care what happens to it next, whether it is disposed of or whether someone else appropriates it. In this case Sarah could not be liable for theft because the property does not 'belong to another': it has been abandoned.

So, when you are determining whether the property belongs to another, remember to consider:

If V is in possession of the property ⇨ If V is in control of the property ⇨ If instructions were not followed ⇨ If D should return the property ⇨ If the property was abandoned

Having considered the three elements of the *actus reus* of theft, we must now consider the two *mens rea* requirements for the offence.

Dishonesty

The first *mens rea* requirement for the offence of theft is that the appropriation of property must be dishonest. Dishonesty is therefore a key concept not only in relation to theft but also in relation to other 'dishonesty offences'. It is therefore very important that you understand the concept of dishonesty and that you are able to apply it to a range of situations.

The **Theft Act (TA) 1968** does not provide a definition of theft. It does however, set out a number of situations in which a defendant will **NOT** be considered dishonest. Section 2 sets out:

(1) A person's appropriation of property belonging to another is not to be regarded as dishonest–

    (a) if he appropriates the property in the belief that he has in law the right to deprive the other of it, on behalf of himself or a third person; or

    (b) if he appropriates the property in the belief that he would have the other's consent if the other knew of the appropriation and the circumstances of it; or

    (c) (except where the property came to him as trustee or personal representative) if he appropriates the property in the belief that the person to whom the property belongs cannot be discovered by taking reasonable steps.

(2) A person's appropriation of property belonging to another may be dishonest notwithstanding that he is willing to pay for the property.

It is important to note that these situations are not the only situations in which a defendant would not be considered dishonest. When discussing whether an appropriation is dishonest you should start with s 2 TA 1968: if the D held any of these beliefs then he would not have acted dishonestly.

Section 2(2) also establishes that D may be dishonest, even if he is willing to pay for or replace the property which he has appropriated. For example, Ryan takes Jo's Kindle without asking, he accidentally breaks the Kindle, and Jo discovers that Ryan has taken and broken his Kindle. Ryan then offers to pay for another Kindle. Ryan could still be liable for theft even though he is willing to pay for it.

What is dishonesty?

What does dishonesty actually mean? The Court of Appeal insists that dishonesty is an ordinary word in everyday use. It is a word that can be understood by the average person without a need for a definition: *R v Feely* (1973).

In the case of *Ghosh* (1982) a two-stage test for dishonesty was established. This test for dishonesty applies to other dishonesty offences.

Case precedent – *R v Ghosh* [1982] QB 1053

Facts: D was a doctor, and claimed fees from patients for surgical operations that he had not carried out.

Principle: Two-stage test for dishonesty

Application: The Court of Appeal held that the jury should be directed towards answering the following questions:

(1) Was D's conduct dishonest according to the current standards of ordinary decent people? and

(2) Did D realise that his conduct was dishonest by the current standards of ordinary decent people?

If D answers yes to both questions then D has been dishonest; but if D answers NO to EITHER question then D is not dishonest.

You will see that this is a twofold test, which contains subjective and objective elements. It is commonly called the '**Ghosh Test**', and you will see this test applied to other areas of law where dishonesty is part of the *mens rea*.

Example: Danny regularly borrows money from his manager's shop till to buy his lunch. He repays all of the money at the end of the week. This has been going on for many months. The manager discovers this and accuses Danny of theft. Look at the two-part test above, and think about whether Danny would be dishonest according to the **Ghosh Test**.

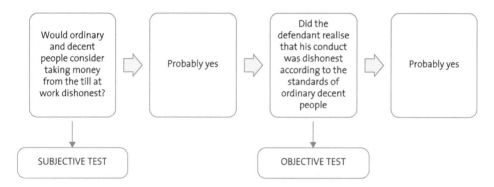

It is for the jury to decide whether the test has been met.

Common Pitfall

When applying the Ghosh Test make sure that you fully work through the subjective and objective elements of the Test as well as s 2 of the **Theft Act 1968**. Some students conclude that D is dishonest in relation to one stage of the Ghosh Test but not dishonest in relation to the other element. They then go on to conclude that D is to be deemed dishonest.

This is incorrect: D must pass BOTH elements of the Ghosh Test in order to be dishonest.

Having considered the first *mens rea* element for theft we will now consider the second element of the *mens rea*, which is the intention to permanently deprive.

Intention to permanently deprive
The intention to permanently deprive the owner of the goods is an essential element of theft. It is a unique element of the *mens rea* for theft offences, so it is important that you pay particular attention to this element in any answer, to differentiate the offence of theft from other offences.

Intention
It is important to note that it is not necessary to show actual deprivation of the property – just an intention to bring about such deprivation.

Common Pitfall

The key element is 'if his intention is to treat the thing as his own to dispose of'.

But be aware, this is not the same as D intending to keep the property for themselves – it effectively means an intention to deprive V of their property.

Intention is outlined in s 6 of the 1968 Act, which states:

6(1) A person appropriating property belonging to another without meaning the other permanently to lose the thing itself is nevertheless to be regarded as having the intention of permanently depriving the other of it if his intention is to treat the thing as his own to dispose of regardless of the other's rights; and a borrowing or lending of it may amount to so treating it if, but only if, the borrowing or lending is for a period and in circumstances making it equivalent to an outright taking or disposal.

(3) Without prejudice to the generality of subsection (1) above, where a person, having possession or control (lawfully or not) of property belonging to another, parts with the property under a condition as to its return which he may not be able to perform, this (if done for purposes of his own and without the other's authority) amounts to treating the property as his own to dispose of regardless of the other's rights.

Case precedent – *DPP v Lavender* [1994] Crim LR 297

Facts: D removed some doors from a council property and put them in his girlfriend's house (which was also owned by the council).

Principle: Intention to permanently deprive

Application: D treated the doors as his own to dispose of (as set out in s 6(1)), regardless of the council's (owner's) rights, therefore he was guilty of theft.

In this case, D intentionally treats the property as his own, regardless of the rights of the owner.

Borrowing

It is important that you are able to draw a distinction between *borrowing* and *depriving*, as this is a popular examination issue. The defendant must have an intention to permanently deprive the owner of their property; it is no defence that the defendant had a change of heart and returned the property: *McHugh* (1993).

It can sometimes be difficult to determine the difference between the intention to permanently deprive and borrowing.

Example: Dean steals a car as a getaway vehicle for a robbery. Dean uses the car and then abandons it.

In this case we can see that the defendant has no intention to permanently deprive the owner of the car. Dean simply intends to use the car in order to escape. In this case liability for theft cannot be made out (that is not to say that liability for other offences does not exist). Can you differentiate between borrowing and intention to permanently deprive here?

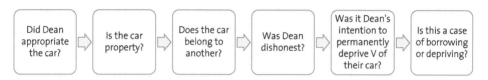

To help you clarify your understanding, look at the case of *R v Mitchell* (2008). You will see that the facts of the case are very similar. In *Mitchell* D was found not guilty. This is because D intended to use the car as a getaway vehicle, so there was no intention to permanently deprive.

In order to constitute borrowing there must be an intention to return the exact property in the same state/condition and the property must retain the same value.

❖ Borrowing money with the intention of replacing it at a later date meets the criteria for intention to permanently deprive unless the defendant intends to replace the exact same notes/coins: *Velumyl* (1989).
❖ Borrowing a ticket and returning it after the event to which it applies has taken place, will constitute an intention to permanently deprive: *Coffey* (1987).
❖ Borrowing a device and draining its goodness/value can amount to an intention to permanently deprive.

Permanently

The concept of intention to permanently deprive will also require you to consider what 'permanently' means for the purposes of the **Theft Act 1968**.

Broadly speaking, it does not need to be established that the deprivation is permanent, as it can also be temporary: for example, stealing a chainsaw from a building site and returning it three years later. Would this be considered permanent or temporary deprivation?

Consider the case below.

Case precedent – *R v Lloyd* [1985] QB 829 (CA)

Facts: V was taking films from his employer, a cinema, giving them to a friend to copy and then returning them in the same condition to the cinema.

Principle: Intention to permanently deprive

Application: D was found guilty, but this was overturned on appeal, as the films were returned in the same condition, so there was no intention to permanently deprive the owner of the property in question.

In reality the concept of intention to permanently deprive is quite broad. Section 6 creates the possibility that something less than permanent deprivation can suffice.

Conditional intention to permanently deprive

Before concluding this section it is important to briefly address the situation where a defendant has a conditional intention to permanently deprive. For example, imagine that Leigh looks through Monique's bag with the intention of ascertaining whether there is anything in the bag worth stealing. In this case Leigh has a conditional intention to permanently deprive Monique of property in the event that he finds anything of value. In *Eason* (1971) and *Husseyn* (1977) it was held that a conditional intent was insufficient. The correct charge here would be attempted theft.

Common Pitfall

It is not uncommon for criminal law students to reach the wrong conclusion not because their understanding of the law is flawed, but because they feel that the defendant should be held responsible. In this situation the application of law is often good, but at the last moment, despite having already established that a key element of liability is missing, a student will conclude that the defendant is liable.

Remember that your conclusion should always flow from your working out. If all the indicators suggest no liability then there is in all likelihood no liability – BUT that is in relation to the specific offence that you have been considering. It DOES NOT mean that the defendant would escape all criminal liability. It is often the case that liability exists for a lesser or alternative offence.

In many ways constructing criminal liability is a little like solving a mathematical problem.

- ❖ You should always show your working out – this is where the examiner awards the majority of the marks.
- ❖ Your answer/conclusion should always flow from your working out.
- ❖ Worst case scenario – if you come to the wrong conclusion you will still have been awarded marks for your working out!

A summary of the points we have covered in this section is:

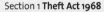

Section 1 Theft Act 1968

Theft is the dishonest appropriation of property belonging to another with the intention of depriving the owner of it.

1. Appropriation	2. Property	3. Belonging to another	4. Dishonesty	5. Intention to permanently deprive
• Consent • Suffered a loss • Assuming the rights of the owner • Gifts	• What constitutes property	• In possession or control • Instructions • Returning property • Abandoned property	• s2 **TA 1968** negative definition • Dishonesty • Ghosh test	• Intention • Borrowing • Permanently

We are now moving on to consider a theft-related offence, the offence of robbery.

Robbery

The offence of robbery is also contained in the **Theft Act 1968**. Section 8 states:

(1) A person is guilty of robbery if he steals, and immediately before or at the time of doing so, and in order to do so, he uses force on any person or puts or seeks to put any person in fear of being then and there subjected to force.

In order to understand the components of robbery you must understand the *actus reus* and *mens rea* of theft. Once you understand the elements of theft, the offence of robbery is easily understood. Essentially, robbery comprises the following elements:

What distinguishes the offence of robbery from theft is the threat of, or the use of, force in order to steal. You will sometimes see robbery referred to as an aggravated form of theft. It is a more serious offence than theft, and one which attracts a more significant sentence upon conviction.

The elements of the offence are:

Actus reus of theft

In order to construct liability for robbery the prosecution must be able to establish the *actus reus* (AR) for theft. In a problem question you will need to outline the AR elements of theft, which are:

❖ appropriation
❖ of property
❖ belonging to another.

Case precedent – *R v Robinson* [1977] Crim LR 173

Facts: D had a genuine belief that he had a right to the property, and he used force to obtain the property from the victim.

Principle: Liability for robbery can only arise where liability for theft is established.

Application: The defendant's genuine belief in his right to the property meant that D was not dishonest (as under s 2(1)(a)). As theft was not committed, the offence of robbery could not be made out.

If the offence of theft cannot be made out, liability for robbery will not exist. If you face this situation in a problem question you can consider a non-fatal offence against the person as an alternative charge (for the threat/use of force).

Try to remember this as:

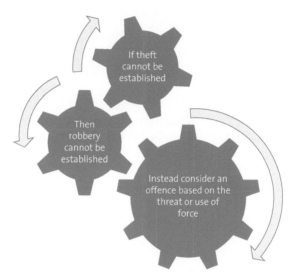

The authority for the principle that liability for robbery flows from liability for theft is *Corcoran v Anderton* (1980).

Aim Higher

Make sure that as you work through the offence of theft methodically, these elements must be satisfied. Frequently students discuss the use of force rather than the offence of theft itself. The examiner will be able to award marks where a student demonstrates knowledge of the ingredients of theft. Avoid being vague when discussing these elements.

Force or threat of force to any person

The second element of the *actus reus* of theft is that D must threaten or use force. The term *force* is an ordinary word that does not require definition. It is a question of fact for the jury: *Dawson* (1976). It is irrelevant whether the victim actually feels threatened; it is the intention of D that is important here: *B v DPP* (2007).

In the case of *R v Dawson & James* (1976), V was nudged off balance by D in order for the second defendant to steal his wallet. This amounted to an offence of robbery. From this case it can be seen that a relatively low level of force was all that was needed.

Up for Debate

if we consider that it is the role of the jury to determine whether force has been used or the threat of it, is it possible that different juries could come to different conclusions in cases involving the same facts?

Do you think that there should be some guidance given to the jury in order to obtain some form of consistency?

The force may also be directed somewhere else, in order to steal. For example, in *R v Clouden* (1987), D wrenched a handbag from V's hands. Although the force used was on the handbag, in order to pull it away from the victim, the court held that this could amount to robbery.

We can see these cases in the following timeline:

The threat of force

There is no need for D actually to use force against the victim; the threat of force is sufficient. The threat of force may be express (a verbal threat, actual force) or implied (threatening, or menacing behaviour).

It is useful to refer back to the chapter on non-fatal offences (Chapter 3), in particular the offence of technical assault. In a technical assault V apprehends immediate unlawful violence. If the other elements of the offence of robbery are not made out it is possible that liability for an offence against the person (technical assault, battery or an aggravated offence) may be made out.

The force can be against 'any person'

It is not necessary for the force to be directed against the owner of the property itself. It can be directed against 'any person'.

Immediately before or at the time of the theft

The use of force or threat of force must be immediately before, or at the time of the theft. If a defendant uses force after the theft this will not amount to robbery.

Case precedent – *R v Hale* [1978] Cr App R 415 D1

Facts: D1 went upstairs and appropriated jewellery, whilst D2 was downstairs with V. D1 rejoined D2 downstairs, where they tied up V.

Principle: Appropriation is a continuing act. Force or threat of force immediately before or at the time of the theft.

Application: The issue related to whether this was a use of force immediately before or at the time of the theft.

Thus, in the above case, the theft of the jewellery was a continuing act: D1 had appropriated the jewellery, and still had the jewellery when the victim was tied up. As a result D1 and D2 were convicted of robbery.

Another useful case is *R v Lockley* (1995), where it was held that, as in *Hale*, there was a continuing act where the defendant used force to escape. Therefore force can be used in order to steal AND in order to escape once the theft has been committed.

We can summarise this as:

The mens rea *for theft*

The *mens rea* for theft must be made out. The elements that need to be established are:

* dishonesty;
* intention to permanently deprive.

The force or threat of force is intentional

In addition to the *mens rea* requirements for theft it must be established that the use of force or the threat of force by D is intentional. Thus accidental force will not suffice. The use of force must be in order to steal.

A summary of the points we have covered in this section is:

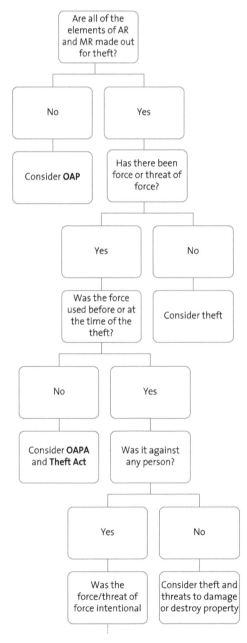

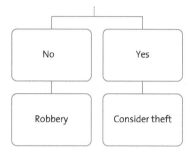

Burglary

In this next section we are going to consider another offence in the Theft Act 1968: the offence of burglary. This is an offence under s 9 of the Theft Act 1968. It is not uncommon for students to think that burglary is simply breaking into a property in order to steal. This is an oversimplification of the offence of burglary. In reality the offence is more sophisticated than this.

Section 9 of the Theft Act 1968 provides:

> (1) A person is guilty of burglary if –
>
>   (a) he enters any building or part of a building as a trespasser and with intent to commit any such offence as is mentioned in subsection (2) below; or
>   (b) having entered into any building or part of a building as a trespasser he steals or attempts to steal anything in the building or that part of it or inflicts or attempts to inflict on any person therein any grievous bodily harm.
>
> (2) The offences referred to in subsection (1)(a) above are offences of stealing anything in the building or part of a building in question, of inflicting on any person therein any grievous bodily harm, and of doing unlawful damage to the building or anything therein.

Common Pitfall

Note: this section used to include the offence of rape, but this has now been repealed by the Sexual Offences Act 2003.

> (3) A person guilty of burglary shall on conviction on indictment be liable to imprisonment for a term not exceeding –
>
>   (a) where the offence was committed in respect of a building or part of a building which was a dwelling, fourteen years;
>   (b) in any other case, ten years.

Aim Higher

In subsections (1), (2) and (3) you will see references to buildings and dwellings. The offence can be committed in an inhabited vehicle or vessel (such as a camper van or a canal barge). This can include when the person living in the vehicle or vessel is there, and when they are not.

The types of burglary
There are two different ways in which burglary can be committed. These are:

The Common Elements

- enters a building or part of
- as a trespasser

Section 9(1)(a) Burglary	Section 9(1)(b) Burglary
• Intent to commit any one or more of the three offences; theft, criminal damage, GBH	• Commits theft or attempted theft, or inflicting or attempting to inflict GBH

In the case of s 9(1)(a) the offence is committed upon 'entry' to the building, as a trespasser, where D has the ulterior intent to commit one of the following offences: theft, GBH or criminal damage. In the case of s 9(1)(b) the offence is committed when one of the specific offences is actually committed (i.e. theft/attempted theft, GBH/attempted GBH). Either way D must have entered the building or part of a building as a trespasser and must have intended or have been reckless as to the trespass.

Example: Carlo and David enter a building site as trespassers to skateboard on the site. While they are there, they decide to take some building materials home in order to construct jumps and ramps to practise on. They have therefore committed a s 9(1)(b) offence, as they trespassed first, and then decided to steal the pipe.

However, if Carlo and David entered the building site with the intention of stealing the pipe, this would be a s 9(1)(a) offence.

We will now look at the individual elements of the offence of burglary.

Entry
The defendant must make a 'substantial and effective entry' into a building or part of a building: *Collins* (1973). There are two critical issues in this context:

❖ How much of the defendant must have entered the building or part of the building in order for entry to occur? It is sufficient for only part of D's body to have entered the building or part of it.

❖ What if the defendant uses an object or innocent agent to enter the building: is this sufficient? Entry can be substantial and effective where it is achieved through an innocent agent or a device.

Case precedent – *R v Ryan* [1996] Crim LR 320

Facts: D tried to burgle a house, and was found wedged in the open window where he was stuck. Part of his body was in the house.

Principle: Effective entry

Application: D was convicted of burglary and appealed on the basis that he was stuck, therefore entry was not effective. The conviction was upheld, as part of his body was inside the house.

Building or part of a building

The entry must be into a building or part of a building. Therefore it is important to understand what constitutes a building or part of a building.

The definition of a building is broad: it includes a house, a flat, a caravan, an office block, etc. An immobile container can also be considered a building, as illustrated in the following case.

Case precedent – *B and S v Leathley* [1979] Crim LR 314

Facts: D stole from a container, which had been in the same position for a number of years.

Principle: Definition of a building

Application: That an immobile container can be classed as a building.

There are a number of other cases which have refined the term *building*, and it is important to remember the key rule is:

A building is a permanent structure

In order to constitute a building, part of the structure must be a permanent structure. This explains why the container in the above case was considered a permanent structure: because it had been there for many years. The diagram below identifies permanent and temporary structures:

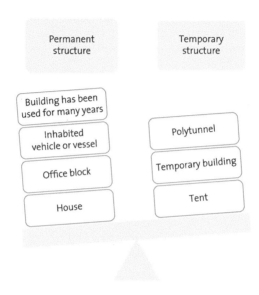

Part of a building

It is also possible to commit this offence by entering part of a building. For example, a trespasser may have permission to enter a particular building because it is open to the public. However, that permission does not extend to all parts of the building. It may not apply to:

❖ the staff room
❖ the stock room
❖ behind the till/cashiers.

The notion of a private area was clarified in *R v Walkington* (1979), which found that there does not need to be a physical separation of part of a building: a counter or a line will suffice: for example, walking behind the counter of a shop to steal from the till, or entering a room marked private, which they have not been given permission to go into.

Example: JJ is shopping for a new TV, when he walks past a window through which he can see a table set up with lots of cupcakes. JJ is hungry and decides that he wants to take some of the cakes with him. He enters a door marked 'Private Staff Only'. JJ fills his backpack with the cupcakes and walks back into the shop and continues shopping for a TV. Eventually JJ leaves the shop.

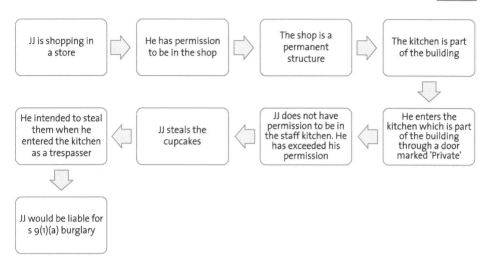

Trespasser

In civil law, a person is a trespasser when they are on land/property without permission. Clearly someone breaking into a property is a trespasser, but what if someone enters the building legally? We have touched on this point briefly under the previous heading.

For example, it may be that a defendant enters one part of the building with the permission of the owner, but then proceeds to an area where they do not have permission. Or it may be that they have permission to enter the building generally, but they then go on to do something that they do not have permission to do. In these situations the response of the courts has been to treat the defendants as having **exceeded their licence or permission**.

Case precedent – *R v Jones and Smith* [1976] 2 All ER 412

Facts: D1 and D2 were at their parents' house with their permission, and stole a television.

Principle: Trespass and exceeding permission

Application: The permission to be in the dwelling was exceeded when D1 and D2 stole the television. Therefore they were classed as trespassers.

Based on the case law that we have discussed this for, look at the example below to work through the concept of trespass:

Example: Karen works in a hotel as a beauty therapist. Unknown to the management, Karen frequently goes into the kitchen and takes food, which she eats when she gets home. Would this be classed as trespass? Work your way through the following steps to determine whether Karen is a trespasser:

Intentional or reckless as to trespass

The *mens rea* requirement for burglary is that the defendant is intentional or reckless as to the trespass; as mentioned above, this rules out accidental trespass. It is therefore essential that D knows that he or she does not have permission, or that they are at least reckless as to whether permission exists: *Walkington* (1979).

We are now going to consider the offence of aggravated burglary.

Aggravated burglary

Section 10 of the Theft Act 1968 creates an offence of 'aggravated burglary'. It provides that an offence of aggravated burglary is committed where a person commits burglary and **has with him at the time**:

* a firearm;
* an imitation firearm;
* any other 'weapon of offence'; or
* an explosive.

A weapon of offence means an object that can be construed as a weapon, if the accused intended it to be used for that purpose. This could be a knife, screwdriver etc.

This is a common mistake, so in a problem question check where the weapon is, and who is in possession of it.

In order to construct liability for this offence it must first be established that a burglary has taken place, under either s 9(1)(a) or s 9(1)(b). If liability for burglary cannot be demonstrated, then D would not be liable for aggravated burglary. The key additional factor differentiating burglary from aggravated burglary is the possession of the firearm/weapon/explosive.

| D must be liable for the offence of burglary | for the offence of aggravated burglary to be considered |

Remember that D only needs to be in possession of the weapon. It does not need to be proven that D intended to use it, only that D had it at the time of the burglary.

For example, Harold sees a house window open so climbs inside. Pearl is inside, and Harold grabs a knife from the kitchen table and tells Pearl to give him her money, which she does. Do you think this would constitute 'at the time has with him'?

According to case law this would be sufficient. There is in fact a very similar case, the case of *R v O'Leary* (1986), which held that as stealing is a continuous offence, when D picked up the knife, the offence changed from burglary to aggravated burglary.

A summary of the points we have covered in this section is:

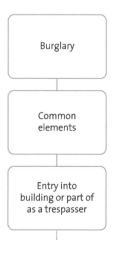

Burglary

Common elements

Entry into building or part of as a trespasser

Trespass with intent to commit a sexual offence

This offence spans the areas of theft and also sexual offences. More information on sexual offences and the different types of offence can be found in the chapter on sexual offences (Chapter 4). Below we will consider a very specific offence linked to trespass.

Section 63 of the Sexual Offences Act 2003 provides:

(1) A person commits an offence if –

    (a) he is a trespasser on any premises,
    (b) he intends to commit a relevant sexual offence on the premises, and
    (c) he knows that, or is reckless as to whether, he is a trespasser.

(2) In this section –

    'premises' includes a structure or part of a structure;
    'relevant sexual offence' has the same meaning as in section 62;
    'structure' includes a tent, vehicle or vessel or other temporary or movable structure.

This offence replaces the offence of burglary under s9(1)(a) of the Theft Act 1968, where D entered as a trespasser with intent to rape. The Sexual Offences Act 2003 widened the definition to 'relevant sexual offence' to mean that all the sexual offences would be included within this one offence.

Putting it into practice

Question

Consider the case of *R v Gomez* [1993] AC 442 – research the facts of the case and the case summary:

❖ **Which aspect of theft does this case focus upon?**
❖ **Explain why this case is important in the offence of theft.**

Suggested solution

D was an assistant manager at a retail store. He accepted cheques from X, knowing that they were worthless. He told the manager that the cheques were as good as cash. As the manager handed over the property with consent D argued that no appropriation could have been found. On appeal to the House of Lords, they stated that consent is not relevant to appropriation (following *Lawrence*).

This case focuses on when appropriation takes place, i.e. when goods are transferred from the owner with the owner's consent. In this case, this was when the owner was led to believe that the cheques were sound. The fact that the cheques were dishonest then calls into question the appropriation of the goods from the owner, and the time that this occurred.

Prior to the *Gomez* case, the law was that if D used deceit in obtaining the goods from the owner, then they were not liable for theft because they were the owner of the goods. However, the judge in the case of *Gomez* turned this on its head, and argued that the act led to appropriation of the goods by D. This is because the judge ruled that appropriation can take place if the owner consents.

As a result of this case, the law on appropriation was clearer to interpret and apply in case of appropriation occurring at different times.

Problem question

George sees that his local museum is hosting an art exhibition by his favourite painter. George decides that he wants to take his favourite painting to hang on his wall. So, in the evening when the museum is closed he sneaks into the museum through a back door marked 'Staff Only', and takes the painting off the wall. As he is walking back, a guard confronts George, telling him to put the painting back. George looks around and picks up an ancient dagger from a cabinet, points it at the guard and runs out of the museum with the picture and dagger.

Identify what offence George would be liable for and why.

Remember to follow the structure that we have practised in earlier chapters:

1. **Identify the crime.**
2. **Define the crime.**
3. **Address all elements of the *actus reus*.**
4. **Address all elements of the *mens rea*.**
5. **Deal with potential defences.**
6. **Deal with alternative/lesser charges.**

As a general rule you should always start with the most serious potential offence. In this case the most serious offence would seem to be aggravated burglary. However, in order to establish aggravated burglary we must first establish that George is liable for the offence of burglary, so we need to work through the elements to ensure that they are satisfied.

Following the above structure, work your way through each element of the AR and MR of the offence. In this case, it would be the s 9(1)(a) burglary offence, as George had the intention to steal the painting before he went to the museum – it was his intent before he entered the museum. The elements we then need to focus on are:

❖ **entry;**
❖ **into a building or part of a building;**
❖ **as a trespasser;**
❖ **intention or recklessness as to the trespass.**

Trespass – George trespassed into the museum because he entered the museum when it was closed in the evening, and he should not have been there.

The building – the museum is a building and is a permanent structure. George enters through a door marked 'Staff Only', and he crosses the line, so not only should he not be in the building, but he should definitely not be in the 'staff only' part of the building.

Entry – George's entrance is effective as he enters the building and removes the picture.

Therefore George fulfils the elements of burglary, which are required before the offence of aggravated burglary can be considered. The offence changes from burglary to aggravated burglary (s 10 **TA 1968**) when George picks up the dagger in response to the guard. A dagger is classed as a weapon of offence, so meets the criteria. Remember that George does not need to show intent to use the dagger, but it must be in his possession, as seen in *R v O'Leary* (1986).

Key Points Checklist

❖ Theft is defined in s 1 of the Theft Act (TA) 1968. Theft is the dishonest appropriation of property belonging to another with the intention to permanently deprive the owner of it.	✓
❖ Section 2 of the TA 1968 provides a negative definition of dishonesty. In essence it outlines a number of situations in which a defendant will not be deemed to have been dishonest.	✓
❖ In the event that the defendant's situation is not captured by s 2 of the TA 1968 the Ghosh test will apply. The Ghosh test is a two-stage test with a subjective and objective element. The defendant must pass through both stages of the test.	✓

❖ Robbery is closely related to the offence of theft. It is defined in s 8 of the TA 1968. In order to establish liability for robbery you must first establish liability for theft. What differentiates robbery from theft is the threat or use of force in order to steal. Thus once the *actus reus* and *mens rea* of theft have been established it must additionally be shown that D: threatened or used force; before or at the time of the theft; against any person; and that the threat of force or force was intentional.	✓
❖ Burglary is defined in s 9(1)(a) and s 9(1)(b) of the TA 1968. The common elements of the offence are: that D enters; property or part of; as a trespasser, intending or being reckless as to the trespass. In order to make out s 9(1)(a) the defendant must have an ulterior intent to commit: theft, GBH or criminal damage. In relation to s 9(1)(b), having entered the property or part of as a trespasser D must go on to commit: theft/attempted theft or GBH/attempted GBH.	✓
❖ An aggravated species of burglary is contained in s 10 of the TA 1968. It provides that D commits an offence when they commit burglary whilst in possession of one or more of the following: firearm; imitation firearm; explosive; or weapon.	✓

Table of key cases referred to in this chapter

Key case	Brief facts	Principle
R v Lawrence [1972] AC 626	V gave D his purse to take a taxi fare, and D took more money than he was entitled to	Consent in theft
R v Gomez [1993] AC 442	D informed V that the cheques were good, when he knew that they were worthless	Consent in theft
R v Hale [1978] 68 Cr App R 415	D burgled V's house, stealing jewellery and tying up V	Appropriation is a continuing act
R v Hinks [2000] 3 WLR 1590	D persuaded V to give out gifts of money	Gifts can be classed as appropriation
Oxford v Moss [1979] 68 Cr App Rep 183	D accessed an exam paper due to be set by the university	Classification of tangible and intangible property
R v Turner (No 2) [1971] 1 WLR	D removed his car from a garage, without paying for the repairs	Possession of property

Key case	Brief facts	Principle
Ricketts v Basildon Magistrates [2011] 1 Cr App Rep 15	D took bags left outside a charity shop	Abandoned property – belonging to another
DPP v Lavender [1994] Crim LR 297	D took doors from his council property and put them in his girlfriend's house	Intention to permanently deprive
R v Lloyd [1985] QB 829 (CA)	D took films from the cinema where he worked to copy, and then returned them	Intention to permanently deprive
R v Robinson [1977] Crim LR 173	D believed he had a right to the property, and used force	Theft must be proved for the offence of robbery
R v Dawson & James [1976] 64 App R 150	D nudged V, while another stole V's purse	The level of force required for robbery
R v Clouden [1987] Crim LR 56	D pulled on V's handbag to pull it away	Use of force can be applied to the handbag
R v Hale [1978] Cr App R 415 D1	D1 stole jewellery while D2 was with V. D1 & D2 tied up V afterwards	Immediately before or at the time
R v Lockley [1995] Crim LR 656	D used force to escape after stealing V's property	Force used to escape after the property is stolen
R v Jones and Smith [1976] 2 All ER 412	D1 and D2 stole a television from a dwelling they had permission to be in	Definition of trespass
B and S v Leathley [1979] Crim LR	D stole from a container, which had been in the same position for many years	Definition of a building
R v Walkington [1979] 1WLR 1169	D stole from within a private area	Definition of a private area
R v Ryan [1996] Crim LR 320	D tried to burgle a house, and was found stuck in the window, halfway into the house	Effective entry

---

@ Visit the book's companion website to test your knowledge

❖ Resources include a subject map, revision tip podcasts, downloadable diagrams, MCQ quizzes for each chapter, and a flashcard glossary

❖ www.routledge.com/cw/optimizelawrevision

7 Criminal Damage

Understand the law

- Do you understand the definition for criminal damage and aggravated criminal damage in the Criminal Damage Act 1971?

Remember the details

- Can you remember the *actus reus* and *mens rea* for criminal damage?
- Can you remember the *actus reus* and *mens rea* for aggravated criminal damage?

Reflect critically on areas of debate

- Do you understand the definition of arson, and can you critically discuss the difference between arson and the basic offence of criminal damage?

Contextualise

- Can you relate criminal damage to other property offences?

Apply your skills and knowledge

- Can you complete the activities in this chapter, using statutes and case law to support your answer?

Chapter Map

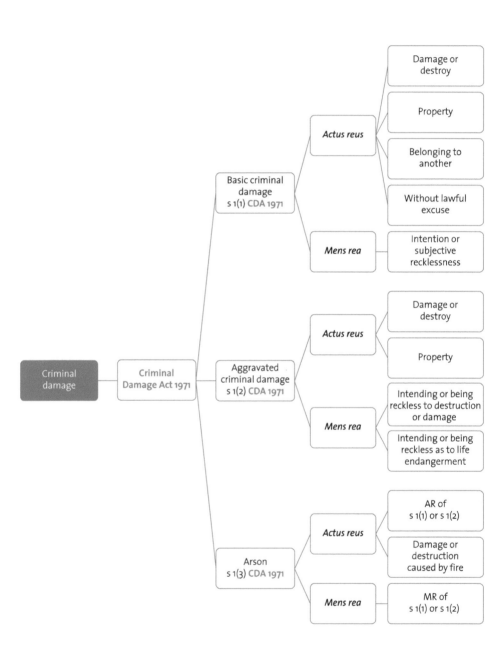

Introduction

In this chapter we are going to consider criminal damage. This offence can take several forms, and these different offences are all set out in s 1 of the Criminal Damage Act 1971. The Act sets out three types of offence, which are:

❖ basic (s 1(1))
❖ aggravated (s 1(2))
❖ arson (s 1(3))

We will consider each of these offences in turn. As is our normal practice we will break the definitions of each offence down into the *actus reus* and *mens rea* and consider how each offence can be applied, particularly in the context of a problem question.

As you consider the different offences, you will find it helpful to reflect on other property offences such as theft, as these offences can sometimes be linked together in a problem question. It is also worth noting that there are similarities between the definitions of the different property offences. Think about the circumstances in which different property offences may be linked, and how you would approach this in an exam or assessment.

Aim Higher

As you progress through this chapter, consider the **Theft Act 1968**, and the similarities between the different property offences. Make sure that you are clear as to the similarities and differences.

The key legislation that you must be familiar with is the Criminal Damage Act (CDA) 1971.

Simple criminal damage

Section 1(1) of the Criminal Damage Act 1971 creates an offence of 'simple' criminal damage. It provides:

> *A person who without lawful excuse destroys or damages any property belonging to another intending to destroy or damage any such property or being reckless as to whether any such property would be destroyed or damaged shall be guilty of an offence.*

The basic offence is a triable-either-way offence with a maximum sentence of ten years' imprisonment: s 4(2) CDA 1971.

Aim Higher

A good way of picking up additional marks in an assessment question is to demonstrate knowledge of the following:

1. Whether the offence is a common law or statutory offence.
2. Whether the offence is a summary offence, a triable-either-way offence or an indictable offence.
3. The maximum sentence upon conviction for the offence.

It is worth noting that s 30(1) of the **Crime and Disorder Act 1998** creates a racially aggravated form of criminal damage, which is also a triable-either-way offence and has a maximum sentence of 14 years' imprisonment. Although we will not consider the racially aggravated form of criminal damage, it is worth noting this offence, particularly in an essay question, or where the facts of the question give rise to the possibility that the criminal damage has been racially aggravated.

Section 1(1) can be split into the following *actus reus* and *mens rea* elements:

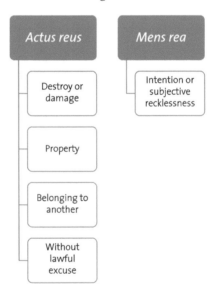

In order for a defendant to have committed the *actus reus* for the offence of simple criminal damage the defendant must have:

1. Damaged or destroyed
2. Property
3. Belonging to another
4. Without lawful excuse.

We will now look at each of these elements in turn.

Destroy or damage

The question as to whether property has been destroyed or damaged is a question of fact for the jury/magistrates. This element of the *actus reus* allows for:

❖ the destruction, or
❖ damage of property.

The term destruction is self-explanatory in so far as it indicates a sense of finality and irreparable repair. The term damage requires further explanation.

❖ Damage does not need to be permanent: *Roe v Kingerlee* (1986).
❖ Damage can be temporary: *Roper v Knott* (1898).
❖ The damage does not have to be tangible or visible provided that the value of the property is affected: *Cox v Riley* (1986).

You can remember these points as:

The key points to remember in relation to the term *damage* is that as a result of the defendant's actions, the property must suffer from:

❖ a reduction in value, or
❖ a reduction in its usefulness.

Example: Lucy and Lee have just got married and go on honeymoon. When they come back, they find that the best man has painted their house windows pink as a welcome home joke. Lucy and Lee are very unhappy – would this constitute criminal damage? Look at the list above, and see whether damage or destruction has occurred.

If you are working through a problem question and you are considering whether damage or destruction has taken place, working through the above list will help you to determine if it has taken place, and whether it would be considered damage or destruction.

Up for Debate

Contrast the following cases relating to damage. In *A (A Juvenile) v R* (1978) spit was not regarded as damage, whereas in *Samuels v Stubbs* (1972) jumping up and down on a policeman's cap was held to be damage.

Does this provide enough guidance on what constitutes damage, or should there be greater guidance on the definition of damage? This is a useful critical point to refer to in an essay question.

We are now moving on to consider the second element of the *actus reus* of simple criminal damage which is property.

Property
The defendant must destroy or damage *property*. The meaning of property for criminal damage is set out in s 10(1) of the **Criminal Damage Act (CDA) 1971**, and it is similar, *but not identical*, to the definition of property for theft contained in s 4 of the **Theft Act 1968**. The definition of property in the CDA 1971 is broader than the definition of property in the **Theft Act 1968**.

For the purposes of criminal damage property, does not include the following:

❖ mushrooms and fungi growing wild on any land;
❖ flowers, fruit, foliage, plants, shrubs or trees growing wild on any land;
❖ intangible property such as copyright.

We will now consider the next *actus reus* element of the offence of simple criminal damage which is that the property must belong to another (this AR element is exclusive to the offence of simple criminal damage).

Belonging to another
The meaning of 'belonging to another' is set out in s 10(2) of the **Criminal Damage Act 1971**, which states that property belongs to another person if that person:

❖ has custody or control of it;
❖ has in it any proprietary right or interest (such as a lessee but not an equitable right);
❖ has a charge on it.

It is important to note that it is possible for a person to be convicted of criminal damage if it is owned, at the same time, by someone else, e.g. joint ownership or shared ownership. It is also worth noting that, under s 10(3), trust property belongs to anyone who has a right to enforce the trust.

Example: Sam asks Layla to look after his iPad while he is swimming. Mollie swipes the iPad from Layla and stamps on it with her foot, damaging the device. Would Mollie be liable for criminal damage in this example? Work through the steps below in relation to property:

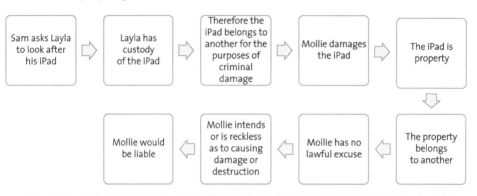

Sam asks Layla to look after his iPad ➡ Layla has custody of the iPad ➡ Therefore the iPad belongs to another for the purposes of criminal damage ➡ Mollie damages the iPad ➡ The iPad is property ⬇

Mollie would be liable ⬅ Mollie intends or is reckless as to causing damage or destruction ⬅ Mollie has no lawful excuse ⬅ The property belongs to another

We are now going to consider the final element of the *actus reus* for criminal damage and that is that the damage or destruction of property belonging to another must have taken place without lawful excuse.

We have included this as an element of the *actus reus* of the offence for the sake of simplicity. However, it is perhaps more accurate to describe this requirement as a defence as opposed to an element of the AR of the offence.

Lawful excuse

The phrase *lawful excuse* is set out in s 5(2) of the **Criminal Damage Act 1971**, and provides for two specific defences to criminal damage. These are now considered below:

Section 5(2) of the **Criminal Damage Act 1971** provides that a person charged with an offence to which the section applies will be treated as having a lawful excuse if:

Section 5(2)(a): D believed that the person or persons entitled to consent to the damage or destruction either had consented, or would have consented to the damage or destruction of the property.

Section 5(2)(a) stipulates that D must honestly believe that a certain person (or persons) would have consented to the damage or destruction (set out in s 5(3)). You will see here that the words centre on D's belief.

The case of *Jaggard v Dickinson* (1980) focuses on D's belief that the owner had or would have consented to cause the damage. In this case, D was out late at night and lost her keys. She broke into her friend's house, believing that her friend would agree to this action and the damage caused. She had in fact broken into the wrong house. Thus the belief in consent is a subjective one. The key question here is: did D have an honest belief in the owner's consent, or an honest belief that the owner would have consented?

Therefore D need only show a valid belief of consent.

Another useful case to use here is *Denton* (1982), where D1 asked D2 to burn down his factory, so he could make a claim against the insurance. In this case, D2 was found not guilty, as it was proven that D1 (the owner of the factory) had indeed asked D2 to set fire to the factory, thereby giving his consent.

Up for Debate

The interesting aspect of this case is that D2 was found not guilty of criminal damage, as it was found that he believed he had the consent of D1, who was the owner of the factory.

Therefore D1, as the owner of the factory, was also acquitted of criminal damage because he was the owner of the building, and could therefore damage the building if he wished – it is his property to do as he wished with (i.e. not belonging to another).

What do you feel about this decision? It is worth noting that although the defendants were not liable for criminal damage that is not to say that they were not liable for any criminal offences! We will consider the issues raised here later in the chapter.

We will now consider s 5(2)(b) of the CDA 1971. This provides that the defendant should be treated as having a lawful excuse where:

Section 5(2)(b) – D believed that property belonging to himself or another was in immediate need of protection, and so D damaged or destroyed other property in order to protect it, where D believed that the means of protection used were reasonable.

What is significant in relation to s 5(2)(b) is that the test in relation to the above section is a subjective test. The question is not whether the actions of D were reasonable but whether believed those actions to be reasonable: *Hunt* (1977).

This defence is broad, due to the range of circumstances which could apply – it is key that D must have had a genuine belief that the property was at risk, the requirement for protection was immediate, and D believed that his actions were reasonable. You can remember these four key parts as:

It may not always be clear whether all four elements are contained within D's lawful excuse. Look at the example below and see if you can identify them:

Example: Tom and Abbey are neighbours, but the vehicular access across Tom's land to Abbey's house is disputed. Tom builds a wall across the land, blocking in Abbey's car. Abbey knocks down the wall, arguing that this was to protect her vehicular rights without delay.

❖ Can you identify the four elements here?
❖ What would you argue would be the outcome from this example?

This is in fact a real case, and is *Chamberlain v Lindon* (1998).

But – be careful how broadly you apply these four elements, as seen in the case below:

Case precedent – *Hill and Hall* (1989) 89 Cr App R 74

Facts: D1 and D2 intended to cut wires around the perimeter of a nuclear base. They argued that if the base was bombed, their homes could be damaged. By cutting the fence, they could persuade the base to move elsewhere. D1 and D2 used lawful excuse because they were concerned about the potential damage to their homes.

Principle: Lawful excuse

Application: D1 and D2 were found guilty of criminal damage, as the claim was spurious and the potential for damage too remote (i.e. not immediate).

We will now consider the two tests used in lawful excuse in a little more detail.

D damaged or destroyed (other) property in order to protect property

For example, consider the case of *Hunt* (1977). In this case set fire to bedding in order to draw attention to a defective fire alarm at an old people's home. The defendant in this case was held not to have reasonably believed that setting fire to bedding would have protected property. He was therefore not protecting the property, he was demonstrating that the fire alarm was not working, and hence was found guilty.

D believed that the means used were reasonable

As we have already discussed this test is subjective: D must honestly believe that the means of protection adopted was reasonable.

Look at the example below, and work through whether the subjective test (for reasonableness) would apply here.

Example: Julie is sitting having a glass of lemonade when she notices that her next door neighbour's car is rolling backwards out of the drive. The car is travelling towards two cars parked on the opposite side of the road. Julie rushes out of her house, catches up with the car and pulls on the handbrake sharply, stopping the car but damaging its electronic braking system.

Work through the steps below to see if Julie could use lawful excuse in this case:

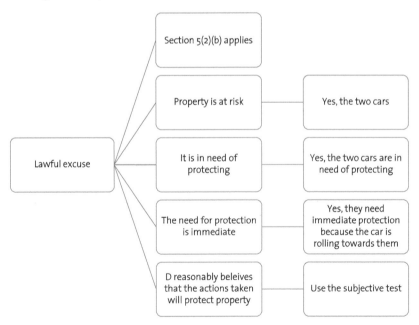

Having discussed the four elements of the *actus reus* we will now move on to consider the *mens rea* for the basic offence of criminal damage. Remember that both AR and MR must be present to successfully construct liability for the offence.

Mens rea: intention or being reckless as to the damage

Simple criminal damage is a crime of basic intent. That means that either intention on behalf of the defendant or recklessness will suffice. The *mens rea* required for the simple offence of criminal damage is set out within s 1(1) of the **Criminal Damage Act 1971**. It is:

| Intention or recklessness | • **intention** to destroy or damage property belonging to another, or
• being **reckless** as to whether any such property would be destroyed or damaged |

We will now consider the meaning of these two key terms in more detail.

Intention

Intention is an important concept here, and it is covered more fully within the section on *mens rea* in Chapter 2. For criminal damage, it must be proved beyond a reasonable doubt that the D intended to cause the criminal damage. You will remember from our earlier discussion on intention that the meaning of intention encapsulates both direct and oblique intention. Remember the definition of direct and oblique intention as:

| *direct* intention | • intention as an aim, purpose or desire |
| *oblique* intention | • foresight of a virtual certainty |

Recklessness

A defendant can cause criminal damage intentionally *or* by being reckless. Again, the principles of recklessness are discussed in more detail in the section on *mens rea* in Chapter 2, and these principles would also apply to criminal damage.

You will recall that there are two types of recklessness – subjective and objective. These mean:

Subjective test	Objective test
• Proof that D is aware of, or foresees the risk of harm and nevertheless goes on to take that risk. The risk is an unjustifiable risk.	• The reasonable man would have foreseen the risk of harm.

For a significant period of time the courts determined that test for recklessness in the case of criminal damage was an objective one: *Caldwell* (1982). This meant that the risk of harm needed only to be obvious to the reasonable man. Thus if the accused through lack of age/experience or infirmity lacked the ability to foresee the obvious risk he or she would still be held liable: *Elliot v C* (1983).

However, in the case of *G* (2004) the objective test for recklessness was overruled and the subjective test for recklessness was reinstated. It is worth noting that D does not need to:

❖ foresee the extent of the damage: *G* (2004); or
❖ realise that what they are doing to the property constitutes damage: *Seray-Wurie v DPP* (2012).

The House of Lords in *G* (2004) set out the meaning of subjective recklessness in relation to criminal damage as:

❖ a circumstance when he is aware of a risk that exists or will exist;
❖ a result where he is aware of a risk that it will occur; and
❖ it is, in the circumstances known to him, unreasonable to take the risk.

The following illustration outlines the timeline for recklessness in relation to criminal damage:

The more recent case of *Seray-Wurie v DPP* (2012) mentioned above is a useful and recent case to consider when considering the *mens rea* requirement for criminal damage.

Case precedent – *Seray-Wurie v DPP* [2012] EWHC 208 (Admin)

Facts: D wrote on parking tickets with a black pen, which could not be erased.

Principle: D need not appreciate that his actions constitute damage for the purpose of criminal damage.

Application: The judge ruled that the prosecution must prove D intended or was reckless (subjectively) in causing the damage to the property in question. However, the prosecution does not need to prove that D *knew* that his actions constituted damage for the purpose of criminal damage.

Example: Ashley, aged 11, used a can of spray paint to write the name of Liverpool FC onto a bridge over a railway track, showing off to his friends. Ashley claims that he honestly believed that when his friends had gone home, he would be able to remove the paint with water from his drink bottle. He had seen his dad remove paint from a wall at their house with water. Being only 11, Ashley did not understand that when his dad cleaned the paint off the wall at home the paint had been water-based paint and not oil-based, as was the case with the spray paint. The paint on the bridge had to be removed by the rail authorities with a special solvent. Decide whether or not Ashley has committed criminal damage contrary to s 1 CDA 1971.

Work through the following steps to help you come to your conclusion. These are based on the elements of the *actus reus* and *mens rea*, to determine liability, as you would be expected to discuss when considering liability for criminal damage in a problem question:

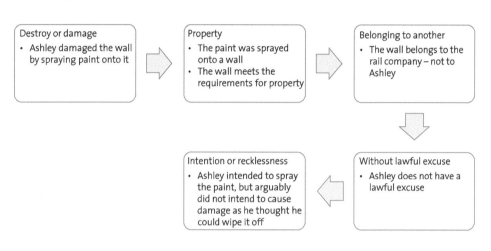

Destroy or damage
- Ashley damaged the wall by spraying paint onto it

Property
- The paint was sprayed onto a wall
- The wall meets the requirements for property

Belonging to another
- The wall belongs to the rail company – not to Ashley

Intention or recklessness
- Ashley intended to spray the paint, but arguably did not intend to cause damage as he thought he could wipe it off

Without lawful excuse
- Ashley does not have a lawful excuse

We are now moving on to consider aggravated criminal damage.

Aggravated criminal damage

Section 1(2) of the Criminal Damage Act 1971 provides for an aggravated form of criminal damage. It stipulates that:

> A person who without lawful excuse destroys or damages any property, whether belonging to himself or another –
>
> (a) intending to destroy or damage any property or being reckless as to whether any property would be destroyed or damaged; and
> (b) intending by the destruction or damage to endanger the life of another or being reckless as to whether the life of another would be endangered,

commits an aggravated form of criminal damage.

The difference from the simple offence of criminal damage is an aggravating factor. That factor is the ulterior *mens rea* (an intention or recklessness as to whether life is endangered).

Common Pitfall

Note that this offence does not require proof that the property damaged or destroyed belonged to another, i.e. D can damage his own property, and still be liable for the offence.

The offence of aggravated criminal damage is an indictable offence subject to a maximum term of life imprisonment.

Aim Higher

The case history relating to this offence has evolved, particularly over the last thirty years in an effort to refine the issue of the damage endangering life. To aid your understanding, research the case of *Steer* **(1987)**, and then compare this to the case of *Warwick* **(1995)**.

The case of *Steer* was recently re-applied in *Luke Wenton* **(2010)**.

Another useful example is the case of *Webster* **(1995)**, where D pushed heavy coping stones onto a moving train, which showered passengers with debris. In this case D was reckless to endangering the lives of the passengers from the roof material hitting them.

Aim Higher

This offence is often linked in assessments with homicide, and in particular the offence of murder. Look at the chapter on homicide, and re-read the section on murder. This will help you to put both offences in context, and also to link them should this arise in a problem question.

Liability for aggravated criminal damage

The *actus reus* and *mens rea* for the aggravated offence are similar to the basic offence, but there are number of important differences. It is important that you are aware of these distinctions.

The main difference is that, in contrast to the basic offence, the aggravated offence can be committed where D destroys or damages his own property (in other words the requirement that the property belongs to another is not present in the aggravated form of criminal damage).

Example: Dan owns a manufacturing business, and is in financial difficulty. He decides to damage some of the very expensive machinery in order to make a fraudulent insurance claim. Under the basic offence, Dan would not be liable as he is the owner of the property. However if Dan damages machinery in such a way that the damage presents a danger to human life. And he intentionally endangers life or is reckless as to whether it is endangered he will be liable for the aggravated offence.

Now we will consider the individual elements of the aggravated form of criminal damage.

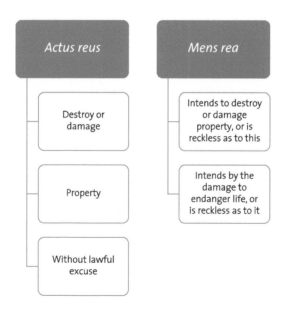

We will now consider each of the individual AR and MR elements.

Actus reus

Destroy or damage
The elements of *destroy* and *damage* are the same as for the simple offence of criminal damage, and their meanings are the same.

Property
The meaning of property is the same as for the simple offence of criminal damage.

Without lawful excuse

You need to exercise particular caution here because in the context of the aggravated offence the defence of lawful excuse does not apply. This is because a lawful excuse (as defined in s 5(2) of the CDA 1971 cannot be justification for endangering life.

In the context of the aggravated offence, 'without lawful excuse' refers to the operation of other general defences such as self-defence, for example – this requirement applies to all criminal offences even where it is not explicitly mentioned in the definition of an offence.

Now we will consider the *mens rea* elements of the aggravated form of criminal damage.

Mens rea

We can see here that the *mens rea* requirement for the aggravated offence differs from that of the simple offence of criminal damage. In essence there are two elements to the MR for aggravated criminal damage.

Intention or recklessness as to the damage or destruction of property

The aggravated form of criminal damage requires intention or subjective recklessness as discussed in relation to the simple offence of criminal damage.

D intends by the destruction or damage of property to endanger the life of another or is reckless as to whether the life of another is endangered

This component of the *mens rea* is key. It is what transforms basic criminal damage into the aggravated form of criminal damage. It is what justifies the imposition of a much more severe sentence. The defendant must at least have been reckless as to whether life would be endangered by the damage or destruction: *Steer* (1988). The endangerment of life must be a result of the damage or destruction and not merely the danger itself: *Webster* (1995) and *Dudley* (1989).

Aim Higher

Life does not actually have to be endangered by the damage or destruction – it is D's intention or recklessness as to endangerment of life which is important here (D's guilty mind).

For example, in the case of *Sangha* (1998), D set fire to furniture in an unoccupied house. D was found guilty of the aggravated offence, despite the fact that the building was constructed in a way that prevented the spread of fire to adjoining properties.

We can see that it was D's intention or that D was reckless as to whether life would be endangered by setting fire to the house. It is this factor that is relevant here – not the construction of the house or that no one was actually hurt.

Now let us look at the case of *Dudley* (1989), and trace the steps in the diagram below:

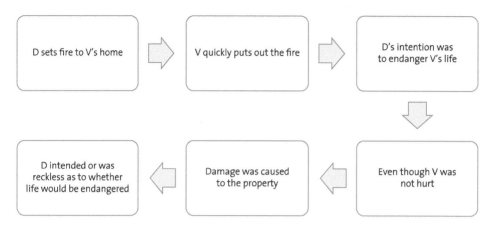

A summary of the points we have covered in this section is:

Section 1(2) of the Criminal Damage Act 1971

Destroy or damage	Property	Intending to destroy or damage property or being reckless to this	Intending by criminal damage to endanger life, or being reckless as to this

Arson

We are now going to consider the offence of arson. According to s 1(3) of the **Criminal Damage Act 1971**:

> *An offence committed under this section by destroying or damaging property by fire shall be charged with arson.*

It is important to note that arson under s 1(3) is not a separate offence in its own right, but simply refers to where D commits an offence under s 1(1) or s 1(2) by means of fire (i.e. damaging the property by fire).

Simple arson is a triable-either-way offence punishable with a maximum sentence of life imprisonment. Aggravated arson is an indictable offence also punishable with a maximum term of life imprisonment.

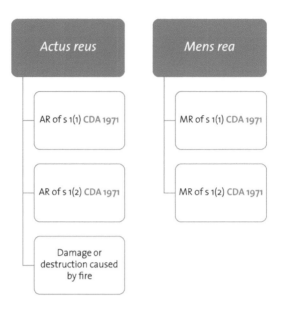

Actus reus

The *actus reus* for the offence of arson will depend on whether it is a simple or aggravated form of criminal damage.

The added requirement here is that D must destroy or damage the property by fire. It is worth noting that in *Miller* (1954) the House of Lords held that arson was capable of being committed by omission in cases where the fire had initially started accidently and the defendant had taken the decision to do nothing about the fire (such as by failing to call the emergency services).

Mens rea

If D is charged with simple criminal damage by fire, it must be shown that D intended to damage or destroy or was reckless as to destruction or damage.

If D is charged with an aggravated offence by fire, it must be proved that D intended to endanger the life of another, or was reckless as to whether life would be endangered.

Aim Higher

Remember that arson applies to all types of property, so could include a house, a garden fence, a handbag, a car or even somebody's rubbish. So consider what we have discussed earlier in the chapter in relation to the definition of property, and apply this to the offence of arson.

Establishing offences under the CDA 1971

When answering a problem question, adopt the following structure, which is not necessarily the order of the elements in the statutory wording.

AR

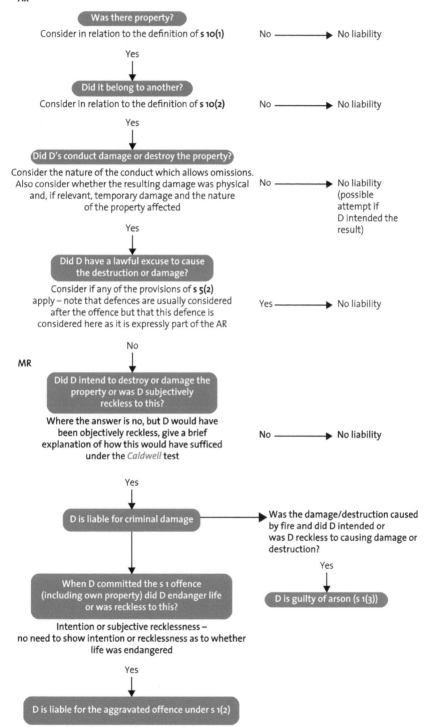

Was there property?

Consider in relation to the definition of **s 10(1)** No ──────▶ No liability

Yes ↓

Did it belong to another?

Consider in relation to the definition of **s 10(2)** No ──────▶ No liability

Yes ↓

Did D's conduct damage or destroy the property?

Consider the nature of the conduct which allows omissions.
Also consider whether the resulting damage was physical No ──────▶ No liability
and, if relevant, temporary damage and the nature (possible
of the property affected attempt if
D intended the
result)

Yes ↓

Did D have a lawful excuse to cause
the destruction or damage?

Consider if any of the provisions of **s 5(2)**
apply – note that defences are usually considered Yes ──────▶ No liability
after the offence but that this defence is
considered here as it is expressly part of the AR

No

MR ↓

Did D intend to destroy or damage the
property or was D subjectively
reckless to this?

Where the answer is no, but D would have
been objectively reckless, give a brief No ──────▶ No liability
explanation of how this would have sufficed
under the *Caldwell* test

Yes ↓

D is liable for criminal damage ──────▶ Was the damage/destruction caused
by fire and did D intended or
was D reckless to causing damage or
destruction?

Yes ↓

↓ D is guilty of arson (s 1(3))

When D committed the s 1 offence
(including own property) did D endanger life
or was reckless to this?

Intention or subjective recklessness –
no need to show intention or recklessness as to whether
life was endangered

Yes ↓

D is liable for the aggravated offence under s 1(2)

Putting it into practice

Question

Joe lives in a terraced house, and hears odd noises coming from his neighbour's house. Joe goes into the road, and sees that his neighbour's house is on fire in the kitchen. Worried that the fire will spread to his own house, Joe gets his hosepipe from the garden, opens his neighbour's window and sprays water into the house, and puts out the fire. The water causes significant damage, and more than the fire did.

Would Joe be liable for a criminal damage offence?

Suggested solution

To determine liability, you must first provide a definition of the offence that you are considering. Then divide the definition into the *actus reus* and *mens rea* elements of the offence. You need to work your way through each element in turn as shown in the above diagram:

Section 1(1) of the Criminal Damage Act 1971

❖ Destroy or damage – yes, Joe damages his neighbour's house with the water putting out the fire.
❖ Property – yes, the building itself and the contents inside the kitchen which have not been damaged by the fire.
❖ Belonging to another – yes, belonging to his neighbour.
❖ Intention to being reckless – this may be more of a grey area, as Joe could have waited for the fire brigade.
❖ Without a lawful excuse – this is the focus of the question, because Joe acted out of concern that the fire would spread and damage his own property.
❖ Did Joe intend to destroy or damage property or was he reckless as to whether it would be destroyed or damaged?

Under s 5(2)(b), a lawful excuse will be present where D believed that the property was in immediate need of protection. The four elements an answer should consider are:

1. Immediate – Yes, the fire could take hold and spread quickly, within minutes.
2. Did Joe reasonably believe that there was a risk to property? – Yes, Joe did not break in, but used a window and a hosepipe.
3. Property is at risk – Yes, particularly as a terraced house is at greater risk of a fire spreading.
4. In need of protection – Yes, Joe acted to protect his property from the fire.

You could consider the case of *Chamberlain v Lindon* (1998) here, as this is a useful case for comparison.

Key Points Checklist

The offence of criminal damage is governed by the Criminal Damage Act 1971. This Act creates two distinct offences: simple criminal damage s 1(1) and aggravated criminal damage s 1(2). Section 1(3) provides that criminal damage caused by fire should be charged as arson.	✔
The *actus reus* for simple criminal damage is: the damage or destruction of property belonging to another. The *mens rea* for the offence is intention or recklessness. Section 5(2) of the CDA creates a defence of lawful excuse.	✔
The *actus reus* for aggravated criminal damage is: the damage or destruction of property. The *mens rea* for the offence is intention or recklessness AND intention or recklessness as to whether life would be endangered by the damage or destruction of property.	✔
Arson s 1(3) can be simple arson (AR + MR for s 1(1)) with the damage or destruction caused by fire; or aggravated arson (AR + MR for s 1(2)) with the damage or destruction caused by fire.	✔

Table of key cases referred to in this chapter

Key case	Brief facts	Principle
Cresswell v DPP Curry v DPP [2006] EWHC 3379	D damaged badger traps to stop the badgers being hurt	Definition of property
R v Smith [1974] QB 354	D made home improvements to a rented home, and removed them when he left	Intention and own property
Seray-Wurie v DPP [2012] EWHC 208 (Admin)	D wrote on parking tickets with a permanent pen	Recklessness
Jaggard v Dickenson [1980] 3 All ER 716	D forcibly entered V's house late at night, after losing her keys	Consent to cause criminal damage
Chamberlain v Lindon [1998]	V built a wall across land blocking in D's car. D knocked down the wall for his vehicular access.	Protecting property – lawful excuse
Hill and Hall (1989) 89 Cr App R 74	D1 and D2 intended to cut wires in fencing around an army site, as they were concerned a bomb could damage their homes	Protecting property – lawful excuse
Sangha [1998] 2 All ER 325	D set fire to V's house, causing damage and endangering lives	Aggravated offence
Dudley [1989] Crim LR 57	D sets light to V's home	Aggravated offence – intent

> **@ Visit the book's companion website to test your knowledge**
>
> ❖ Resources include a subject map, revision tip podcasts, downloadable diagrams, MCQ quizzes for each chapter, and a flashcard glossary
>
> ❖ www.routledge.com/cw/optimizelawrevision

8   Fraud and Blackmail

Understand the law
- Can you identify which sections of the Fraud Act 2006 relate to the principal fraud offences in this chapter?
- Can you identify which section of the Theft Act 1968 refers to the offence of blackmail?

Remember the details
- Can you remember the *actus reus* and *mens rea* for each offence?
- Can you define the *actus reus* and *mens rea* using case law?

Reflect critically on areas of debate
- Do you understand the definition of dishonesty in relation to fraud, and how dishonesty is tested?

Contextualise
- Can you relate the *actus reus* and *mens rea* to other areas of law, particularly theft offences?

Apply your skills and knowledge
- Can you complete the activities in this chapter, using liability and case law?

Chapter Map

Elements Chart

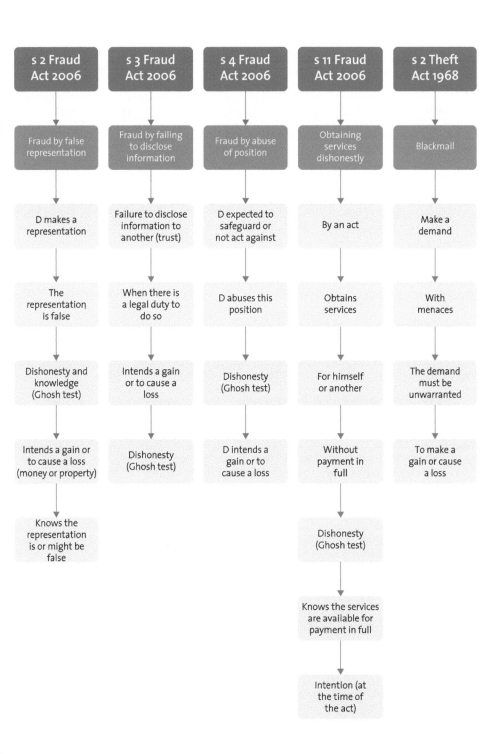

s 2 Fraud Act 2006	s 3 Fraud Act 2006	s 4 Fraud Act 2006	s 11 Fraud Act 2006	s 2 Theft Act 1968
Fraud by false representation	Fraud by failing to disclose information	Fraud by abuse of position	Obtaining services dishonestly	Blackmail
D makes a representation	Failure to disclose information to another (trust)	D expected to safeguard or not act against	By an act	Make a demand
The representation is false	When there is a legal duty to do so	D abuses this position	Obtains services	With menaces
Dishonesty and knowledge (Ghosh test)	Intends a gain or to cause a loss	Dishonesty (Ghosh test)	For himself or another	The demand must be unwarranted
Intends a gain or to cause a loss (money or property)	Dishonesty (Ghosh test)	D intends a gain or to cause a loss	Without payment in full	To make a gain or cause a loss
Knows the representation is or might be false			Dishonesty (Ghosh test)	
			Knows the services are available for payment in full	
			Intention (at the time of the act)	

Introduction

The offence of fraud is contained in the Fraud Act 2006 [FA 2006]. The FA 2006 came into force on the 15th of January 2007, abolishing the following offences under the Theft Act 1968:

* obtaining property by deception (s 15);
* obtaining a pecuniary advantage by deception (s 16);
* obtaining execution of a valuable security by deception (s 20); and
* obtaining a money transfer by deception (s 15(A)).

The FA 2006 also abolished the following offences under the Theft Act 1978:

* obtaining services by deception (s 1); and
* evasion of liability (s 2).

Section 1 of the FA 2006 created a new general offence of fraud and ss 2, 3 and 4 introduce three offences:

1. false representation (s 2);
2. failure to disclose information where there is a legal duty to do so (s 3); and
3. abuse of position (s 4).

Fraud introduction

Section 1 of the Fraud Act (FA) 2006 creates a single offence of fraud which can be committed in a number of different ways. Section 1 provides:

(1) A person is guilty of fraud if he is in breach of any of the sections listed in subsection (2) (which provide for different ways of committing the offence).
(2) The sections are –

    (a) section 2 (fraud by false representation),
    (b) section 3 (fraud by failing to disclose information), and
    (c) section 4 (fraud by abuse of position).

(3) A person who is guilty of fraud is liable –

    (a) on summary conviction, to imprisonment for a term not exceeding 12 months or to a fine not exceeding the statutory maximum (or to both);
    (b) on conviction on indictment, to imprisonment for a term not exceeding 10 years or to a fine (or to both).

(4) Subsection (3)(a) applies in relation to Northern Ireland as if the reference to 12 months were a reference to 6 months.

Fraud by false representation

Introduction

Fraud by false representation is set out in s 2 of the Fraud Act (FA) 2006, and as you work through the chapter, you will see that the concept of dishonesty, and an intention by the defendant to make a gain (or cause a loss) are key to this offence.

Section 2 FA 2006 stipulates:

(1) A person is in breach of this section if he –

    (a) dishonestly makes a false representation, and
    (b) intends, by making the representation—

        (i) to make a gain for himself or another, or
        (ii) to cause loss to another or to expose another to a risk of loss.

(2) A representation is false if –

    (a) it is untrue or misleading, and
    (b) the person making it knows that it is, or might be, untrue or misleading.

(3) 'Representation' means any representation as to fact or law, including a representation as to the state of mind of –

    (a) the person making the representation, or
    (b) any other person.

(4) A representation may be express or implied.

(5) For the purposes of this section a representation may be regarded as made if it (or anything implying it) is submitted in any form to any system or device designed to receive, convey or respond to communications (with or without human intervention).

The *actus reus* and *mens rea* for false representation are:

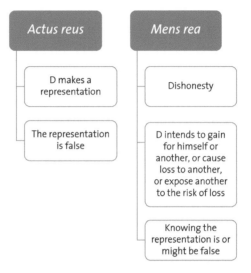

We will now consider the different elements of fraud by representation in detail.

D makes a representation

The first element of the *actus reus* is that the defendant must have made a representation. The representation can be made in a number of different ways. For example, the defendant can make a representation orally, by conduct, or by silence.

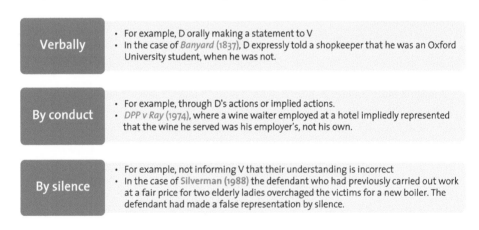

This is a useful checklist for an exam, and you should try to identify the type of representation made by D to strengthen your arguments in a paper – using the case law above to evidence your argument. An examiner will expect you to identify the nature of the representation. You should support your work by reference to relevant cases.

Aim Higher

You will note in the above diagram the reference to 'implied representation', and it is useful to remember that D's representation can be either implied or express; both are a sufficient form of representation for this offence. Identifying the form of representation will enable the examiner to award more marks.

Aim Higher

Case law has established that when D uses a credit/debit card, or gives a cheque, D effectively makes an implied representation to the other person that there are sufficient funds available for the payment to go through, and that D has the authority to use the card or cheque.

Providing a credit/debit card or cheque knowing that the payment will not go through, or using a stolen card, can be regarded as a false representation.

Test your understanding of representation with this example:

Example: Marco wants to buy a necklace for his girlfriend and sees a gold necklace and pendant. The shop assistant tells Marco that it is 18 carat gold. In fact the necklace is only 9 carat gold, and worth half the price. What type of representation has the shop assistant made?

The shopkeeper made a verbal express representation in this case, by stating the quality (carat) of the necklace.

Case precedent – *Harris* [1975] 62 Cr App R28

Facts: D booked a hotel room, but did not pay the bill.

Principle: Representation

Application: A person who books a hotel room impliedly represents that they intend to pay for the room. This applies to other such services, such as paying for a meal or using a taxi.

Now look at the case of *Darwin and Darwin* (2008). Can you determine the type of representations which were made and when they are made?

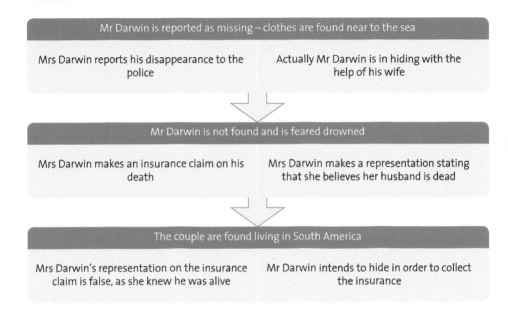

There are two more issues that we must address before moving on to consider the second element of the *actus reus* of this offence.

Who is the representation made to?

The representation can be made to a person, or to a 'system or device': s 2(5) FA 2006. Sometimes an examiner will pose a problem question involving a machine or system. This might involve a:

❖ vending machine;
❖ cash machine;
❖ computer system.

It is clear from s 2(5) of the FA 2006 that representations to any of the above are included by this section.

What must the representation contain?

A representation can include a statement of fact, a statement of the law, or a representation as to the state of mind of the person making the representation or any other person (s 2(3)).

The terms *statement of fact* and *statement of law* are fairly straightforward, but it will be helpful to elaborate on the term *state of mind*.

Example: Phil is selling DVDs at a car boot sale and he tells prospective buyers that he is saving up for a Christmas present for his daughter, when actually Phil plans to spend the money on alcohol.

In this example, Phil's state of mind (i.e. what D intends to do with the money) is different from the representation he makes to the buyer. Therefore he is making a false representation to the buyer.

Test your knowledge

We have considered a number of examples of representation above. Now apply your understanding of s 2 FA 2006 to the following scenarios:

a. Martina enters a shop and takes a dress she wants to buy up to the counter. Martina gives her debit card to the shop assistant knowing that she has insufficient funds to pay for the dress.
b. Ivor wants some chocolate from a vending machine. He only has foreign coins in his pocket. He inserts some of the foreign coins into the machine in the hope that they will work.
c. Gillian applies for a children's bus pass. This discounted bus pass is only available if the applicant is under is under 16 years of age. Gillian sent the form off two days after her 16th birthday.

We are now moving on to consider the second element of the *actus reus* and that is that the representation must be false.

The representation is false

Under s 2(2) of the FA 2006, a representation is false if:

a) it is untrue or misleading; and
b) the person making it knows that it is, or might be, untrue or misleading.

Think about the case of *Darwin and Darwin* (2008) that we considered earlier. At what point were the false representations made? In this case, it was when Mrs Darwin informed the police that her husband was missing (because she knew he was not missing), and when she made the claim on life insurance (because she knew that he was still alive). These clearly relate to s 2(b), as Mrs Darwin knew her husband was still alive, and therefore she knew that the representations were false or misleading.

We are now moving on to consider the *mens rea* elements of the offence. It is important to remember that *all three* elements of the MR must be present in order for liability to be constructed. It is the mental state of the defendant that differentiates what would otherwise be lawful conduct from unlawful conduct. The *mens rea* requirements for this offence are:

Knowing the representation is, or might be false

The first *mens rea* requirement is that D must have known that the representation is, or might be false. In circumstances where the defendant does not know that the representation is false, or may be untrue/ misleading, liability cannot be constructed for this offence. Therefore the following situations would not constitute knowledge for the purposes of this offence:

- ❖ a defendant who has made a mistake;
- ❖ a defendant who is confused;
- ❖ a defendant who makes a statement in good faith believing that his/her representation is accurate.

D dishonestly makes the false representation

The second element of the *mens rea* is that D must have been dishonest. We considered the test for dishonesty in the previous chapter. The test for dishonesty is the same as that used for the offence of theft – the two-stage Ghosh test. This test includes an objective and a subjective element. The jury will be required to determine the following:

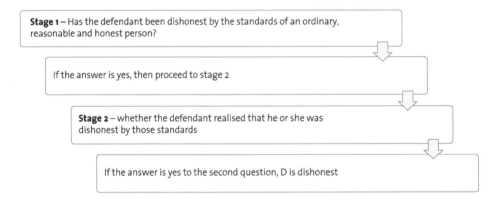

Look at the example below, and then apply the Ghosh test:

Example: D is a market trader selling cakes and business has been slow today. V, a diabetic, comes to the stall and asks D if there is sugar in the cakes. Eager to make a sale, D says there is no sugar in the cakes, even though D knows that the cakes contain sugar. V purchases one of the cakes.

Here, in order to establish dishonesty we would need to demonstrate that according to standards of ordinary, reasonable and honest people the defendant was dishonest. If the answer to this stage is yes then we proceed to the second stage and ask: did the defendant realise that he was dishonest according to those standards?

D intends, by the false representation, to gain for himself or another, or cause loss to another, or expose another to the risk of loss

The definition of gain and loss is set out in s 5 of the **FA 2006**. This is:

(2) 'Gain' and 'loss' –

  (a) extend only to gain or loss in money or other property;
  (b) include any such gain or loss whether temporary or permanent;
  and 'property' means any property whether real or personal (including things in action and other intangible property).

(3) 'Gain' includes a gain by keeping what one has, as well as a gain by getting what one does not have.

(4) 'Loss' includes a loss by not getting what one might get, as well as a loss by parting with what one has.

Note here that the emphasis is on D's intent to make a gain from the false representation – but that you do not need to demonstrate that a gain has actually been made.

This broadens the scope of the offence, so that it includes instances where a false representation was made which did not result in a gain or a loss. It is important to note that the gain or loss can be:

❖ permanent
❖ temporary
❖ retaining property that D already has in their possession.

Case precedent – *R v Wai Yu-tsang* [1991] 4 All ER 664

Facts: D was employed by a bank and agreed with other employees that he would not inform the bank that cheques purchased were dishonoured. The defendant in this case agreed with others to not enter information about dishonoured cheques into the bank records.

Principle: False representation (intent)

Application: In this case D would not make a gain or a loss personally, but his employer would. Under the FA 2006, the intention of the D is considered not whether the D actually caused a gain or loss.

Now look back over the *actus reus* and *mens rea* of this offence and then apply your knowledge to the example below:

Example: A charity collector knocked on Diane's door and asked Diane if she had any clothes she could give away. Diane said that she did. Diane ran into her neighbour's back garden and took the clothes off the washing line. Diane did this because she had a grudge against her neighbour, who kept playing loud music.

Applying your knowledge of the FA 2006, determine whether Diane has committed an offence?

Work through the steps below to come to an answer:

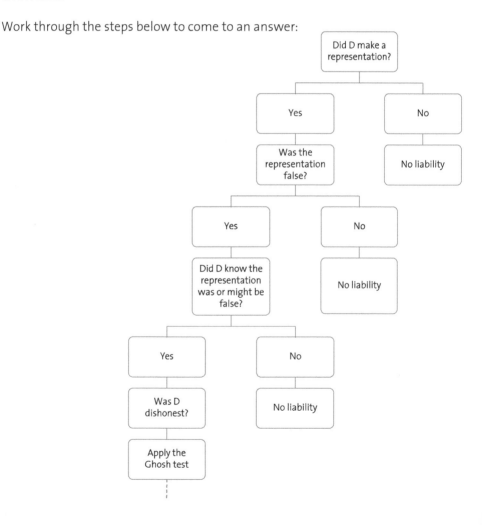

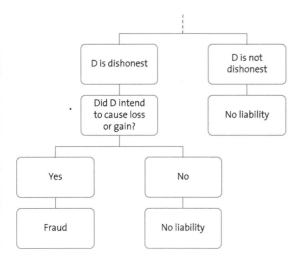

A summary of the points we have covered in this section is:

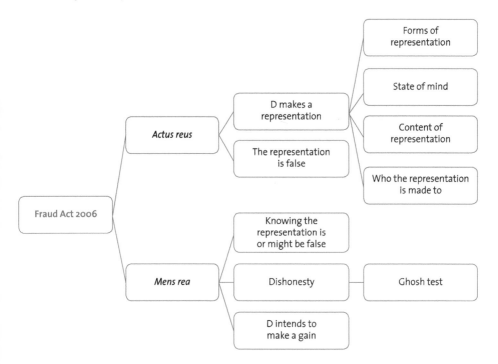

Fraud by failing to disclose information

The offence of fraud by failing to disclose information is contained in s 3 of the Fraud Act 2006. It provided that a person commits an offence where he:

❖ dishonestly fails to disclose to another person information which he is under a legal duty to disclose, and
❖ intends by failing to disclose the information:

    i.   to make a gain for himself or another, or
    ii. to cause loss to another or to expose another to risk of loss.

The *actus reus* and *mens rea* for this offence are:

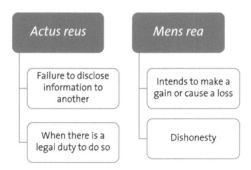

Failure to disclose information to another

The first element of the *actus reus* of this offence is a failure to disclose information. However, this only applies in circumstances where D is under a legal obligation to disclose.

Case precedent – *R v Frith* [1990] 91 Cr App 217

Facts: D was a consultant who failed to inform the hospital he was working for that a number of patients he was caring for were private patients.

Principle: Failure to disclose information

Application: The defendant in this case was under a legal duty to disclose this information.

Legal duty to disclose

Whether a duty to disclose information exist, is a question of law for the judge to determine. In a problem question you would need to establish the legal duty for D to inform V. The following situations are likely to give rise to such a duty.

❖ an employment contract;
❖ another type of legal contract;
❖ related to D's work or position;
❖ insurance or financial agreements;
❖ relating to trade or markets;
❖ being a trustee.

It is not necessary for the defendant to know that such a legal duty exists.

Intends to make a gain or loss

We considered the concept of intention in the section on false representation.

Dishonesty

We have considered the concept of dishonesty earlier in this chapter and the principles in relation to dishonesty apply here.

A summary of the points we have covered in this section is:

Failure to disclose information to another	Where there is a legal duty to do so	D intends to make a gain or cause a loss	Dishonesty
• from D to V	• a legal relationship	• permanent • temporary • D retains what D already has	• Ghosh test

Fraud by abuse of position

This is a narrower offence in so far as it is limited to circumstances in which a defendant occupies a particular position. For example:

❖ an accountant and their client;
❖ a solicitor and their client; or
❖ an employer and employee.

Within this relationship, D uses his position, trust and power in order to commit fraud.

The offence is set out in s4 of the **FA 2006** as:

a) D occupies a position in which he is expected to safeguard or not act against the financial interest of another;
b) where D dishonestly
c) abuses their position

    i. intending by this to gain for himself or another, cause loss to another, or
    ii. expose another to the risk of loss.

The *actus reus* and *mens rea* of the offence are:

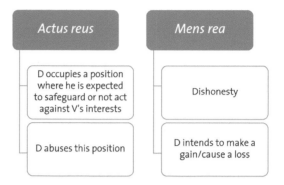

D occupies a position where he is expected to safeguard, or not act against V's interests

D occupies a privileged position, and because of this D is expected to safeguard another's financial interests, or not act against the financial interests of another. Positions that might give rise to such expectations include: trustee and beneficiary, director and company, professional person and client, agent and principal, employee and employer etc.

If there is any doubt as to whether this relationship exists, the judge will determine this as a matter of law.

D abuses the position

There is no definition of abuse of power, and it can depend on the individual circumstances of the case, and the nature of the relationship between D and V.

A useful case relating to an omission is the case of *Gale* (2008). In this case D was a baggage handler who accepted a bribe to put cargo in an aeroplane hold, without checking the contents. The cargo was illegal drugs. As D held a position of trust, the court found that he abused this trust.

D occupies a position of trust with V	This relationship can be determined as a point of law	D abuses this position	By an act or omission

It is not however, necessary to prove that D knew he occupied a position of trust in which he was expected to safeguard V's interests or not act against them – this should be determined as part of the *actus reus* (the act) from the type of relationship between D and V, as already discussed.

Dishonesty

Dishonesty is once again a vital part of this offence. The Ghosh test is applicable here also.

D intends to make a gain / cause a loss

Again, the discussion in relation to gain/loss in relation to fraud by false representation is applicable here.

A summary of the points we have covered in this section is:

D occupies a position where he is expected to safeguard or not act against V	D abuses his position	Dishonesty	D intends to make a gain/cause a loss
• Point of law on the type of relationship	• Can be an act or omission	• Ghosh test	• From his position in the relationship with V

Obtaining services dishonestly

This offence is outlined within s 11 of the FA 2006, replacing the offence of 'obtaining services by deception'. One of the reasons for this change was to cover offences carried out by using machines, such as chip and PIN machines, or those carried out on a computer and/or on the internet.

Up for Debate

Note here that the name of the offence focuses on obtaining services, therefore D must obtain the service as part of the *actus reus*.

This is different from the other offences we have considered – think about why this is different as you work through this section.

The *actus reus* and *mens rea* for this offence are:

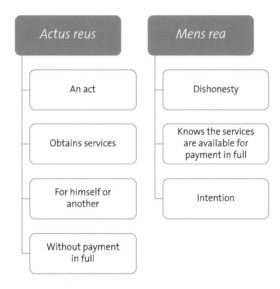

D performs an act

The first element of the *actus reus* of this offence requires D to perform an act. There must be a causal link between the act and the obtaining of the service. This is because the statutory wording requires that D, by his *dishonest* act, obtains the service. This means that if D honestly obtains the service and then decides to leave without paying, the service is not obtained by the dishonest act. The correct offence in this example would be making off without payment, a separate offence (which is described in the next section).

You can summarise this as:

Obtains services

The term *services* includes:

* the provision of board and lodgings;
* entertainment;
* social and sporting amenities;
* repair and decorating;
* letting goods on hire and the provision of transport.

These are quite wide definitions, and have been tested and refined through case law over the years.

Common Pitfall

Be careful here, as D must not have actually obtained the service yet – D would not be liable if he had not watched the festival, or not travelled on the train.

For example, consider the case of *Nabina* (2002), where D dishonestly lied about his personal details to obtain a credit card. This dishonest act allowed him to obtain the card *and* the continued use of the card to purchase services would both amount to a s 11 offence.

But be careful – there are instances which do not constitute a dishonest act. These can include:

> If another person makes a mistake

> Services that do not require payment

For himself or another

Here D can undertake the dishonest act to gain/use services for himself or another person.

Example: Nathan books a holiday for his mother with a card he obtained under a false name. Look at the following steps to work through this case:

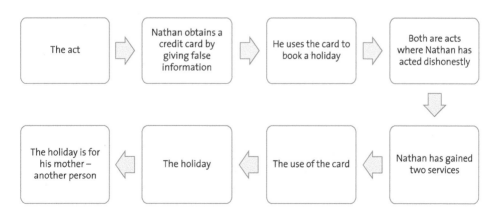

Without payment in full

This is covered by s 11(2)(b) of the FA 2006, which sets out that D must obtain the service without making payment in full.

When you are applying this element to a problem question, remember to check that the services do require payment in full – i.e. that they are not provided free. Otherwise, payment will not be required and this element of the *actus reus* will not be made out.

We are now moving on to consider the *mens rea* for the s 11 offence.

Dishonesty

Once again, as per the previous offences, it must be shown that D acted dishonestly, and this is established through the use of the Ghosh test.

D knows the services are available for payment in full

The next element of the *mens rea* for this offence is that D must know that the services are made available, on the basis that payment has been, is being or will be made. Therefore D knows that the service requires payment in full (s 2(a)).

This is usually obvious given the circumstances or the type of service.

Intention

It must be shown that D did not intend to pay for the service – in full or in part. The intention must be present when the act is committed by D.

Therefore, not only does D avoid payment, but D *intends* to avoid payment, i.e. D does not fail to make payment by mistake, or by thinking he had already paid.

Aim Higher

What if D changes his mind at the last minute and does make the payment? Or if D changes his mind part way through the act and originally intended to make payment and then changes his mind?

What you need to remember is D's intent to make payment in full, at the time of the act. This should give you the basis to make a decision, and to clearly argue this decision in your answer.

A summary of the points we have covered in this section:

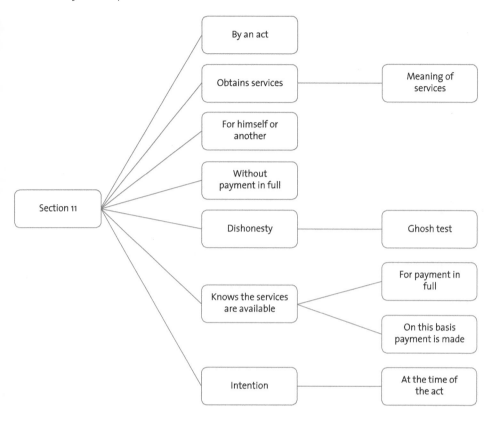

Blackmail

The offence of blackmail is contained within s 21 of the **Theft Act 1968**. Section 21 of the **Theft Act** states:

(1) A person is guilty of blackmail if, with a view to gain for himself or another or with intent to cause loss to another, he makes any unwarranted demand with menaces; and for this purpose a demand with menaces is unwarranted unless the person making it does so in the belief –

    (a) that he has reasonable grounds for making the demand; and
    (b) that the use of the menaces is a proper means of reinforcing the demand.

(2) The nature of the act or omission demanded is immaterial, and it is also immaterial whether the menaces relate to action to be taken by the person making the demand.

(3) A person guilty of blackmail shall on conviction on indictment be liable to imprisonment for a term not exceeding fourteen years.

To be liable for blackmail the defendant must:

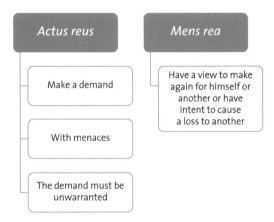

We will now consider each element of the offence of blackmail in more detail.

D must make a demand

Making a demand is the first essential element for blackmail – without the demand, there can be no blackmail. The demand must require V to do something, or it must require V not to do something. Blackmail is a conduct crime and it is therefore irrelevant whether D's demands are effective.

The demand can include a number of different actions, and the demand can be express or implied: *Collister & Warhurst* (1955).

The way in which the demand is made can be important. For example:

❖ The demand does not need to have been read by or communicated to V, but there must be proof of the demand.
❖ Where a demand is made by post, as soon as the letter is posted, the demand has been made.
❖ The demand can be made in a number of different ways. It can be oral and in a letter, a fax such as a text message, email, on the internet etc.

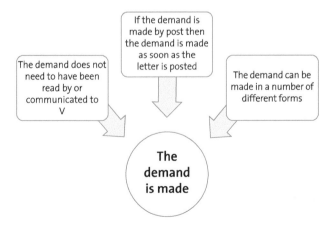

This places the emphasis on D making the demand (which is sufficient), rather than V being aware that the demand has been made.

Case precedent – *R v Hester* [2007] EWCA Crim 2127

Facts: D became involved in a gang. He was instructed by the gang to obtain money by blackmailing the victim. D was convicted of blackmail.

Principle: The demand for blackmail

Application: The defendant appealed against his conviction on the basis that at the time he joined the gang the demand had already been made by other members of the gang. As such he argued that his conviction was unsound. The defendant's appeal was unsuccessful. The court ruled that the demand was a continuing act.

The demand is a continuing act and continues until the demand is withdrawn.

With menaces

The demand must be accompanied by menaces and similar to the demand, these can also be express or implied. Menaces are serious, or significant threats.

The word *menace* and its meaning are important here. Clearly it extends beyond physical violence (*Tomlinson* (1895)), and D must be aware of the likely effect on V. 'The threat must be of such a nature and extent that the mind of an ordinary person of normal stability and courage might be influenced or made apprehensive, so as to give way unwillingly to the demand' (*R v Clear* (1968), LJ Seller).

Up for Debate

Do you think there is an issue here in terms of the subjectivity of the threat/demand?

A person that is confident and outgoing may not give way as quickly as a timid person? Do you think that the circumstances in which the threat are made may also have an impact? For example: a demand made in a letter may have less impact than a demand made face to face?

For example, if the menace was contained within a letter, it may prompt a different response from V than if they were face to face with D.

Consider the case of *R v Lawrence and Pomroy* (1971). Here the menace was implied, but delivered face-to-face by a large intimidating man. The phrase or test used to describe the level of security required to amount to blackmail.

In the case of *R v Garwood* (1987), the victim was of a timid nature, and if D is aware of the impact of his actions on D, this could also be classed as menaces.

When you are working through a problem question there are a few points you will need to consider:

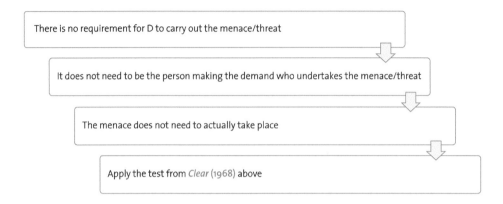

Consider these points as you work through a problem question, and this should help you to determine whether or not the demand is accompanied with menaces.

The demand must be unwarranted
Section 21(1) of the Theft Act 1968 outlines that in order for a demand to be warranted the person making the demand believes both:

(a) that they had reasonable grounds for making the demand; and
(b) that the use of menaces is a proper means of reinforcing the demand.

Therefore, if there are no reasonable grounds for making the demand and the menaces are not a proper means of reinforcing the demand, the demand is unwarranted. It is important to note that this is based on the defendant's belief. In other words what D believes to be true. The test is subjective.

This is decided on a subjective basis, and a court would consider both parts of s 21(1).

Reasonable grounds for making the demand
Remember that this is based on the D's belief. D must believe that there were reasonable grounds. It does not matter whether those grounds were reasonable.

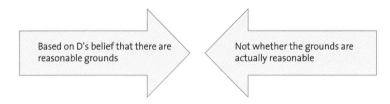

The use of menaces is a proper means of reinforcing the demand
This part of the test asks whether D's actions were an appropriate means for re-inforcing the demand.

Common Pitfall

What D threatens amounts to a criminal offence. It is therefore automatically classed as an unwarranted demand.

A useful case to demonstrate this is *R v Harvey* (1981), where the Ds threatened to harm V's family unless he returned money. The judge ruled that the demand and menace were criminal actions and were not reasonable or proper.

With a view to make a gain or intent to cause loss

Section 34(2)(a) of the Theft Act 1968 defines a 'gain' and 'loss' as only a gain or loss of money or other property. This would therefore exclude other types of benefits, such as those of a sexual nature (e.g. where D threatens to tell V's employer that V has stolen money from the company unless V has sexual intercourse with D).

In a problem question, double check what the gain or loss for D could be, as this can be included by examiners to check a student's knowledge! For example, consider the case of *R v Bevans* (1988), where D's gain was an injection of morphine. At first you may think that this is not a gain or money or property, but the judge found that D did in fact gain property – the morphine – and as such was liable for blackmail. It is important to note that the gain or loss can also be temporary.

A summary of the points we have covered in this section is:

Make a demand	With menaces	Demand must be unwarranted	Intend to make a gain or cause a loss
• Type of demand • Communication	• Can be an act or omission	• Reasonable grounds for making the demand • Menaces is a proper means	• Of money or other property

Putting it into practice
Question 1

Ian is a doctor and makes house calls most days. He visits Jane, an elderly woman who collects antique china. While at the house, Ian realises that Jane's vase is very old and valuable, and tells Jane that he really likes it but it is not worth much, if anything. On this basis, Jane tells Ian that he can have the vase, as he has helped her recover from her illness. Ian takes the vase to the local auction house, who sell it at auction for £10,000.

Would Ian be liable for a fraud offences?

Suggested solution

When approaching this case you should follow the structure that we have practised:

1. **Identify the crime**
2. **Define the crime**
3. **Deal with all elements of the *actus reus***
4. **Deal with all elements of the *mens rea***
5. **Deal with potential defences**
6. **Address lesser or alternative offences**

When looking at this case, you would first need to identify which fraud offence has occurred. Here we can see a relationship between two people, one of whom is a doctor who makes a gain, so the offence of fraud by the abuse of position would be the offence to consider.

Work through the *actus reus* and *mens rea* to define whether Ian would be liable for this offence. D occupies a position of trust – here we can see that Ian is a doctor and Jane is the patient, implying a privileged relationship between the two people. Ian's role as a doctor means that Jane would be likely to believe his views, as he is there to help improve her health and safeguard her interests – not to act against her. Remember that if there is a question over D occupying a position of trust, this would become a point of law.

D abuses that position – the question shows that Ian knew the true cost of the vase, but knowingly gave Jane false information. Remember that there is no formal description of 'abuse' as it depends on the circumstances, but you could argue that Ian abused this position of trust by providing false information which Jane believed.

Dishonesty – in this situation you would be referencing and working through the Ghosh test, and applying this to the scenario to demonstrate whether Ian had acted dishonestly.

D intends to make a gain or cause a loss – here Ian makes a clear gain of £10,000, from the abuse of position. Not only this but Jane loses the vase (property), which would constitute a loss for her.

As you argue through your answer, remember to refer to the legislation and how it would be applied to the facts of this question.

Question 2

Anna and Meera are artists and Meera is very well known. Meera sees a painting by Anna and takes it to her studio, adds her own name to the bottom and sells it in her gallery. James knows that Anna actually painted the picture, and as a friend of Anna is very cross. He confronts Meera and says: 'Pay me £1,000 or I will beat you up for what you did to Anna.' Meera is very scared of James, so agrees quickly and gives him the money.

Would James be liable for any offences?

Suggested solution

Remember to follow the structure that we have practised:

1. **Identify the crime**
2. **Define the crime**
3. **Deal with all elements of the *actus reus***
4. **Deal with all elements of the *mens rea***
5. **Deal with potential defences**
6. **Address lesser or alternative offences**

The offence you would be focusing on here is blackmail, under the Theft Act 1968. Remember to work through the elements of blackmail, to identify whether James is liable. Provide a full definition for the offence and the source of the offence.

Make a demand – we can see from the question that James made an oral demand from Meera, and that the demand was explicit and specific: 'Pay me £1,000 or I will beat you up for what you did to Anna'. Remember that a demand can take a number of forms, and can also be implied.

With menaces – taken from the position of V (Meera), she is scared of James and quickly agrees, which is how it can be argued that the demand was with menaces. You can also refer to and apply the test established in *Clear* (1968).

The demand must be unwarranted – the examiner would expect to see you discuss the two main parts of this element – reasonable grounds for making the demand, and it is unwarranted if it is a criminal offence. In the question James threatens to beat up Meera, i.e. cause her unlawful harm, which could constitute a criminal act (non-fatal offences), hence this would be the area that you would expect to pull out within the answer.

There must be a gain by D or the victim suffers a loss – clearly within the question James would make a gain of £1,000, which he does not appear to pass on to Anna either. The gain is monetary and passed the test.

Remember to refer to appropriate case law and legislation throughout your answer.

Key Points Checklist

Section 1 of the Fraud Act 2006 creates a single offence of fraud. This offence can be committed in three ways: s 2 fraud by false representation s 3 fraud by failing to disclose information s 4 fraud by abuse of position	✔
The *actus reus* of fraud by false representation (s 2 of the Fraud Act 2006) is the making of a false representation. The *mens rea* of the offence is that D was dishonest, that D knew that the representation was false and that D's intention was to make a gain or cause financial loss.	✔
The *actus reus* of fraud by failing to disclose (s 3 of the Fraud Act 2006) is a failure to disclose information to another, where there is a legal duty to disclose information. The *mens rea* of the offence is that D intends to make a gain or cause loss and that D does so dishonestly.	✔
The *actus reus* of fraud by abuse of position (s 4 of the Fraud Act 2006) is that D occupies a position of trust where he is expected to safeguard the interests of V, and D abuses that position of trust. The *mens rea* for the offence is that D does so with the intention to make a financial gain or cause loss.	✔
Blackmail is defined in s 21 of the Theft Act 1968. The *actus reus* of the offence is that D makes a demand with menaces and the demand is unwarranted. The *mens rea* of the offence is D intends to make a gain for himself or another, or cause loss to another.	✔

Table of key cases referred to in this chapter

Key case	Brief facts	Principle
DPP v Ray [1974] AC 370	D ate a meal in a restaurant, then realised he could not pay – remained silent and ran out	Type of representation
Harris [1975] 62 Cr App R28	D booked into a hotel room, but had no intention of paying	Representation
Metropolitan Police Commissioner v Charles [1976] AC 177 (HL)	D writes a cheque to V, knowing there are insufficient funds available and the cheque will not go through	Representation
R v Wai Yu-tsang [1991] 4 All ER 664	D agreed not to tell his employer about dishonoured cheques	Intent within false representation
Gale [2008] All ER 130	D was a baggage handler at an airport, and accepted a bribe to put cargo on an aeroplane	Abuse of position of trust
Nabina [2002] All ER 733	D used false information about himself to gain a credit card	Obtaining services dishonestly

R v Collister & Warhurst [1955] 39 Cr App R100	D implied his demand to V by asking what he had in his possession	Implied demand in blackmail

@ Visit the book's companion website to test your knowledge

❖ Resources include a subject map, revision tip podcasts, downloadable diagrams, MCQ quizzes for each chapter, and a flashcard glossary

❖ www.routledge.com/cw/optimizelawrevision

9 Inchoate Offences

Understand the law
- Can you identify which sections of the Criminal Law Act 1977 relates to conspiracy?
- Can you identify which section of the Criminal Attempts Act 1981 refers to the offence of attempt?

Remember the details
- Can you remember the *actus reus* and *mens rea* for conspiracy and attempt?
- Can you define the *actus reus* and *mens rea* of these offences using case law?

Reflect critically on areas of debate
- Do you understand the definition of intention in relation to conspiracy, and how intention is established?

Contextualise
- Are you able to contextualise the different inchoate offences and relate them to other substantive offences?

Apply your skills and knowledge
- Can you complete the activities in this chapter, using case law and legislation to support your work?

Chapter Map

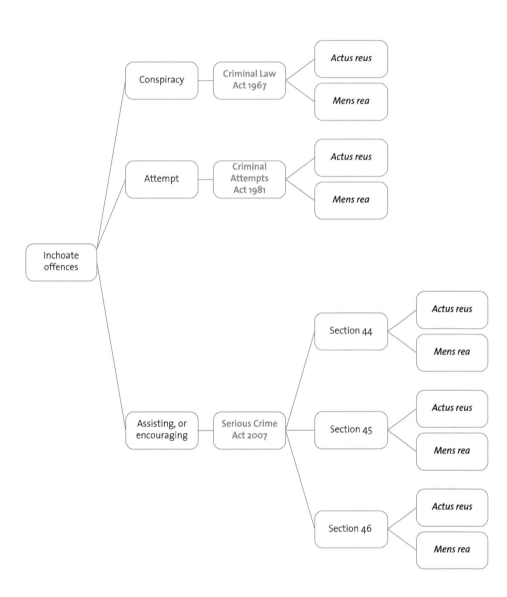

Inchoate elements

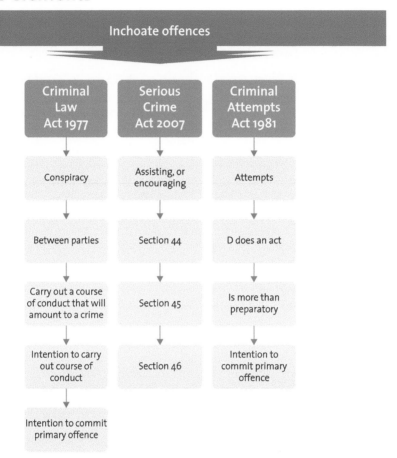

Inchoate offences

As you work through this chapter, you will notice that inchoate offences are differ-ent from the offences that we have discussed in other chapters, largely because they are committed before the primary criminal act takes place. They cover the time when D progresses his thoughts or plans to commit a criminal offence into a reality, i.e. the preparatory stages in committing an offence.

The focus of inchoate offences is on the activity that takes place before the crime if committed. Therefore, the primary offence is incomplete (inchoate). Conspiracy charges have been used against terrorist suspects in the UK who have been apprehended before carrying out their terrorist objectives.

In this chapter we will consider:

❖ conspiracy;
❖ attempt;
❖ encouraging, or assisting.

We will start our coverage of inchoate offences by considering the offence of conspiracy.

Conspiracy

Conspiracy is an agreement between parties to commit a crime, and this can be punished even where no positive steps have been taken to commit the intended offence. Conspiracy is set out in the Criminal Law Act (CLA) 1977.

The CLA 1977 effectively abolished previous conspiracy offences under common law, except for in the following cases:

❖ conspiracy to defraud;
❖ conspiracy to corrupt public morals;
❖ conspiracy to outrage public decency.

The above are common law offences.

Aim Higher

Although the main conspiracy offences are contained within the **CLA 1997**, there are also separate conspiracy offences contained within other Acts; for example, the **Fraud Act 2006**.

Section 1 of the Criminal Law Act 1977 stipulates:

(1) Subject to the following provisions of this Part of this Act, if a person agrees with any other person or persons that a course of conduct shall be pursued which, if the agreement is carried out in accordance with their intentions, either –

   (a) will necessarily amount to or involve the commission of any offence or offences by one or more of the parties to the agreement, or
   (b) would do so but for the existence of facts which render the commission of the offence or any of the offences impossible,

he is guilty of conspiracy to commit the offence or offences in question.

The *actus reus* and *mens rea* for conspiracy are:

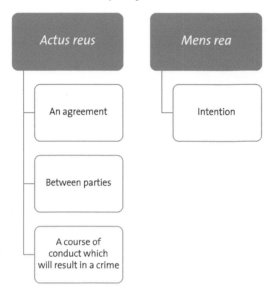

Aim Higher

Students often discuss statutory conspiracy as if it were a crime in itself, for example, by stating that 'D is therefore guilty of conspiracy'.

You must remember that conspiracy always attaches to an offence, and you must not forget to state which crime it is that the parties are conspiring to commit; for example, stating that 'D is guilty of conspiracy to commit murder'.

D may be liable for conspiracy to commit murder, or conspiracy to commit blackmail.

We will now consider these elements in more detail.

An agreement

The first conduct element in the *actus reus* is the agreement. An agreement can be oral as well as written down. The agreement must be to commit a criminal offence. The parties to conspiracy need not go on to commit that offence. It is sufficient that a general agreement has been reached.

Between parties

There must be at least two parties to an agreement. This means that in the following situation, there will be no agreement:

❖ When a company director conspires in the company name – this is because the company does not have a separate mind. Therefore the director conspires with himself.
❖ Where the defendant conspires with a person who is mentally disordered and unable to understand the nature and purpose of the proposed course of conduct.

In addition, s 2(2) of the CLA 1977 stipulates:

D is not liable if the only person he agrees with is his spouse	• However, marriage after a conspiracy, or during its continuance, is no defence. A spouse can commit conspiracy where there is an agreement between spouses to conspire with others.
D will not commit conspiracy where the agreement is made with an individual under the age of criminal responsibility.	• Section 2(2)(c)
A defendant is not liable for conspiracy where they are the intended victim of the offence in question.	• Section 2(1)

Aim Higher

When the facts of a problem question involve more than one potential defendant you must remember to consider conspiracy. Look for key words such as 'agreed', 'planned', 'decided'. It is possible that the examiner is asking you to consider conspiracy.

We are now moving on to consider the third element of the *actus reus*, which is that the parties to the agreement must have agreed on a course of conduct that will result in a criminal offence.

A course of conduct that will result in a crime

The parties must agree that at least one of them pursues a course of action that will result in a criminal offence.

There is no 'result' element within the *actus reus*, so it does not need to be shown that the intended crime was actually committed. In circumstances where the Ds go on to commit the substantive offence it is the substantive offence, not the conspiracy to commit the substantive offence, that should be charged. This is illustrated in the case of *Wright* (1995).

Common Pitfall

It is important to remember that the offence committed must be linked to the offence that the D conspired to commit. Exercise caution where the offence committed differs significantly from the offence committed. It is not unusual for students to become confused considering the act committed not the act agreed.

But note – conspiracy should only be discussed if the agreed offence is **not** committed. If the offence agreed upon **is** actually committed, then both Ds will be joint principals to the offence, or one will be the principal and the other will be the secondary participant.

Remember these key points as:

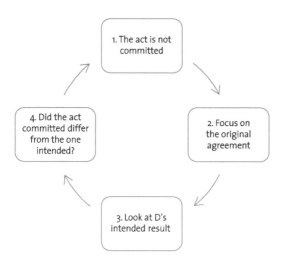

1. The act is not committed
2. Focus on the original agreement
3. Look at D's intended result
4. Did the act committed differ from the one intended?

Example: George and Eve agree to traffic heroin from one country to another. However, Eve actually puts cannabis in the bags instead and cannabis is trafficked from one country to another.

Would George be liable for conspiracy to traffic illegal drugs?

Facts very similar to this occurred in the case of *Siracusa* (1989). In this case the defendant was convicted. The court held that the agreement was the essence of the crime of conspiracy – the agreement between the parties must be as to the specific offence. The court held that this could include a lesser offence (in this case trafficking a Class B drug instead of a class A drug.

We are now moving on to consider the *mens rea* for conspiracy.

Intention

❖ Intention relates to an intention to commit an offence; and
❖ an intention that their agreement will lead to a course of conduct that will lead to the offence.

It is vital that the Ds intend to carry out a course of conduct that amounts to a criminal offence. Recklessness or negligence is insufficient. Intention and intention alone will suffice. The case of *Saik* (2006) identifies and confirms this principle. D must also intend that the offence will occur.

> **Case precedent – *McPhillips* [1990] 6 BNIL**
>
> **Facts:** D was guilty of conspiracy to plant a bomb, but was not a party to the conspiracy to murder, because, unknown to his accomplices, he did not intend the result (the evidence being that he intended to give a warning so the area could be evacuated).
>
> **Principle:** Intention
>
> **Application:** This is the correct position, and D was found not guilty of conspiracy to murder.

Now that we have considered the main elements of conspiracy, we will look at other aspects of conspiracy which you would need to consider in an essay question, we will consider in detail the specific conspiracy offences contained in the CLA 1977.

When does the conspiracy actually occur?

As already noted, the conspiracy 'crystallises' at the point that the parties agree. The conspiracy is a continuing offence, so it continues until it is terminated by the commission of the act, abandonment or frustration. As it is a continuing offence other parties can also join an existing conspiracy. This was established in *Leigh* (1775).

> **Aim Higher**
>
> A single agreement can involve more than one conspiracy. For example, in the case of *Cooke* (1986), an agreement by rail stewards to sell personal food on a train was a conspiracy to defraud British Rail, *and* also a conspiracy to defraud passengers.

Where there is an agreement to commit offences of a certain type, agreements to commit the particular offences of that type are evidence of a general conspiracy.

For example, in *Hammersley* (1958), police officers in Brighton conspired with suspected criminals by alerting the criminals about police intentions to prosecute or investigate them. The purpose of this was to solicit and obtain reward for these favours. It was held that, although the conspiracy involved a number of illegal agreements over a number of years, there was only one conspiracy (to obstruct the course of public justice), not a series of conspiracies.

Example: friends Cho and Harriet talk about defrauding Albert of some valuable paintings he has in his home. They both agree that it is a good plan. However, they are overheard by Bert, who reports their conversation.

Have Harriet and Cho committed a conspiracy?

Work through the steps below to decide.

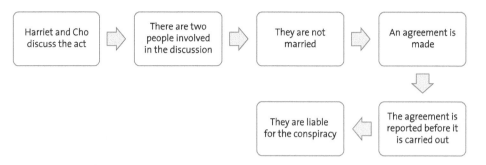

Conspiracy and impossibility

As seen above, there is no result element in the *actus reus* of conspiracy. The *actus reus* of conspiracy does not require that the offence actually occurs. But what if the crime could never have occurred because the facts render it impossible?

Case precedent – *DPP v Nock* [1978] AC 979

Facts: D conspired, with others, to produce cocaine from a powder containing the drug. However, there was no actual cocaine in the powder.

Principle: Conspiracy and impossibility

Application: An agreement to do the impossible can be used as a defence in conspiracy.

The **CLA 1977** was amended by s 5 **Criminal Attempts Act 1981**. This amendment was necessary to deal with the decision in *DPP v Nock* (1978).

Section 5 of the **Criminal Attempts Act 1981** provides that:

(1) Subject to the following provisions of this Part of this Act, if a person agrees with any other person or persons that a course of conduct shall be pursued which, if the agreement is carried out in accordance with their intentions, either –

   (a) will necessarily amount to or involve the commission of any offence or offences by one or more of the parties to the agreement, or
   (b) would do so but for the existence of facts which render the commission of the offence or any of the offences impossible,

   he is guilty of conspiracy to commit the offence or offences in question.

A summary of the points we have covered in this section is:

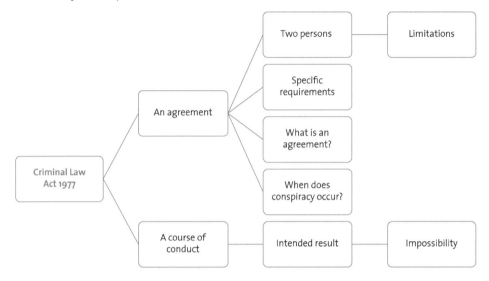

Attempts

The law on attempts is set out in s 1 of the **Criminal Attempts Act (CAA) 1981**. It provides:

(1) If, with intent to commit an offence to which this section applies, a person does an act which is more than merely preparatory to the commission of the offence, he is guilty of attempting to commit the offence.

Aim Higher

The **CAA 1981** effectively turned the previous common law offence of attempt into a statutory offence. This was in response to a report by the Law Commission on the law on attempts, which made a number of recommendations.

The *actus reus* and *mens rea* are:

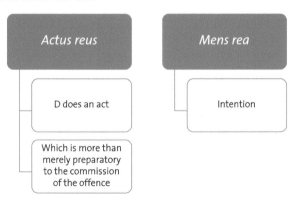

The **CAA (1981)** stipulates that:

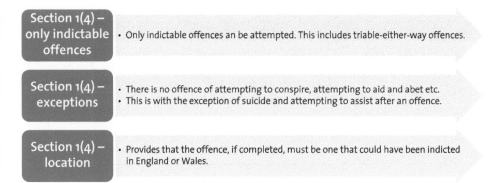

Section 1(4) – only indictable offences	• Only indictable offences an be attempted. This includes triable-either-way offences.
Section 1(4) – exceptions	• There is no offence of attempting to conspire, attempting to aid and abet etc. • This is with the exception of suicide and attempting to assist after an offence.
Section 1(4) – location	• Provides that the offence, if completed, must be one that could have been indicted in England or Wales.

It is clear that there are strict rules regarding the type of offence that can be attempted. It is therefore important that you remember the following checklist when dealing with attempts.

| Must be an indictable or triable either way offence. | ⇨ | Not a participation offence | ⇨ | Indicted in England or Wales |

We are now going to consider the second element of the *actus reus*.

The act is more than merely preparatory to the commission of an offence

In order to establish liability for attempt the D must have done something which is 'more than *merely* preparatory'. Thus the D must have moved from the planning and preparation stages to the active commission of the offence in question. The difficulty here is that the line between preparation and acts which are more than 'merely preparatory' is not all that clear.

Before the **CAA 1981** the courts had developed a series of tests to determine at what stage D was actually 'attempting to commit a crime' – i.e. the difference between preparatory acts and those which are more than 'merely preparatory'.

The following three cases illustrated the distinction between the two:

| *Eagleton* (1885) | *Davey & Lee* (1967) | *Jones* (1990) |

Look at the cases in the table below and see if you can identify any principles emerging from them

Case	Facts
Boyle and Boyle (1987)	The Ds in this case damaged a door whilst attempting to gain entry into a property that they intended to burgle. The court held that this was sufficient to amount to acts that were more than merely preparatory.
Tosti and White (1997)	The Ds in this case drove to the scene of the intended offence with oxyacetylene equipment, which they hid in a hedge, and then they examined a heavy padlock on a barn door. These were *'essentially the first steps in the commission of the offence'*.
Dagnall (2003)	Despite not having touched V in any sexual way, the defendant in this case was convicted of attempted rape because he had virtually succeeded in what he was intending to do and had overcome V's resistance. He was only prevented from committing the rape by the arrival of the police.
Campbell (1991)	In this case police believed D was going to rob a post office. The defendant was observed in close proximity to the post office. He then left the area and returned half an hour later. He was arrested by the police outside the post office. He had in his possession an imitation gun. He admitted when questioned that his intention was to rob the post office but said he had changed his mind and was arrested before he could leave. This was 'merely preparatory' (not 'more than').

From these cases, we can see that the point at which acts make the transition from preparatory acts to acts which are more than merely prepartory depends on the circumstances of the case, and the offence in question. What is clear is that the D must be at the beginning of the commission of the offence.

After looking at these cases, consider the example below, and whether an attempt was made.

Example: Ed is a burglar. He carefully selects the houses that he burgles, trying to ensure as best as he can that the properties he selects will render a high yield in terms of the items that he steals. Ed has been watching Paul's house for several days in an attempt to establish the owner's daily routine. On Tuesday morning Ed is lurking outside Paul's house waiting for him to leave for work. Amber, Paul's elderly and nosy neighbour, sees Ed and is suspicious and she calls the police. PC Caesar arrests Ed, who has in his possession specialist tools for gaining entry into properties, gloves and an instruction manual for disabling alarm systems and CCTV.

Would Ed be liable for the offence of attempted burglary?

Up for Debate

Case law is gradually refining the meaning of 'attempt', and as this refinement continues, the line between preparatory actions and attempt will become clearer. Is this an indication that the Act is unclear?.

Intention

Section 1(1) refers to the defendant acting 'with intent to commit an offence'. Therefore, only intention to commit the offence in question is sufficient. It is worth noting that intention to commit a different offence is insufficient.

Case precedent – *Fallon* [1994] Crim LR 519

Facts: D shot a police officer and the court needed to decide if it was accidental or deliberate.

Principle: Intention

Application: The Court of Appeal cautioned against the provision of a complicated direction on the meaning of intention.

In order to establish liability for attempt, the prosecution must establish that D possessed intention with reference to the consequences specified in the *actus reus* of the offence. There can be occasions when this does not sit neatly with the *mens rea* for the primary offence. Look at the examples in the diagram below, and think about situations in which this can occur:

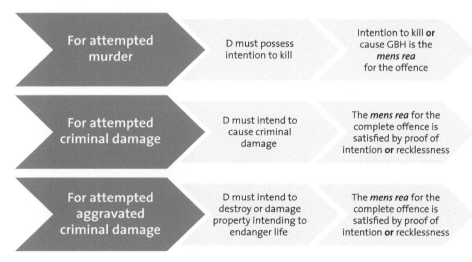

Attempt and impossibility

It is possible that a defendant may embark on a course of conduct in which they attempt the impossible. Section 1(2) of the **CAA 1981** stipulates that in these a defendant may be still be liable for attempt:

> . . . even though the facts are such that the commission of the offence is impossible.

In the case of *Jones* (2007), a police officer pretended to be a 12-year-old and sent text messages to the defendant D as part of an undercover operation to catch the author of graffiti in a toilet seeking young girls for sex. D replied to the text messages sent by the police officer and was charged and convicted of attempting to intentionally incite a child under the age of 13 to engage in sexual activity contrary to s 8 of the **Sexual Offences Act 2003**. In reality it would have been impossible for the defendant to commit this offence in relation to the 'victim' as the intended victim was not under the age of 13.

A summary of the points we have covered in this section is:

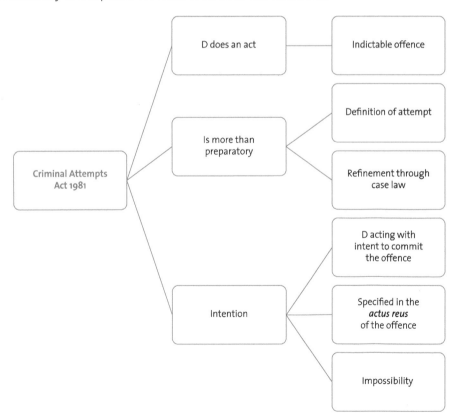

Encouraging or assisting

Prior to the implementation of the **Serious Crime Act (SCA) 2007** there was a common law offence of incitement. Section 59 of the **SCA 2007** abolished the common law offences. Sections 44, 45 and 46 of the **SCA 2007** create three inchoate offences.

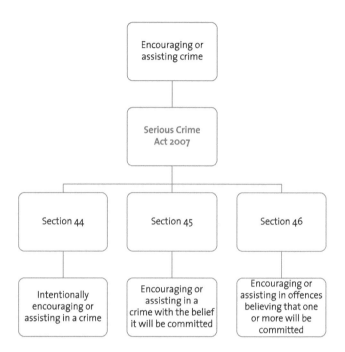

We will consider each of these sections in order.

Section 44: intentionally encouraging or assisting an offence

(1) A person commits an offence if –

    (a) he does an act capable of encouraging or assisting the commission of an offence; and

    (b) he intends to encourage or assist its commission.

(2) But he is not to be taken to have intended to encourage or assist the commission of an offence merely because such encouragement or assistance was a foreseeable consequence of his act.

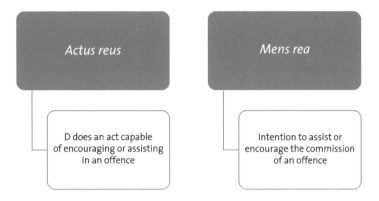

We will now consider each of these elements separately.

D does an act capable of assisting or encouraging in the commission of an offence

The defendant must do an act which is 'capable' of assisting or encouraging in the commission of an offence. Section 65(2) provides that this offence can be committed by omission where D fails to discharge a duty. The act does not actually have to assist or encourage in the commission of an offence; it is sufficient that it is capable of doing so.

Intention to assist or encourage in the commission of an offence

Thus a defendant that foresees that their behaviour may encourage or assist in the commission of an offence does not have the requisite *mens rea* for the offence. This does not include where D foresees encouragement or assistance as a likely consequence of his actions.

We will now consider s 45 of the SCA 2007.

Section 45: encouraging or assisting an offence believing it will be committed

Section 45 of the SCA 2007 provides that:

A person commits an offence if –

(a) he does an act capable of encouraging or assisting the commission of an offence; and

(b) he believes –

    (i) that the offence will be committed; and

    (ii) that his act will encourage or assist its commission.

The *actus reus* and the *mens rea* for this offence are illustrated in the diagram below:

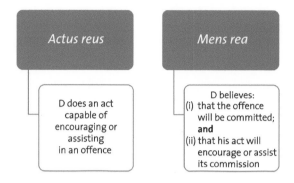

We will now consider each of these elements separately.

D does an act capable of encouraging or assisting in an offence

As per the s 44 offence, D must do an act which is 'capable' of assisting or encouraging in the commission of an offence. Section 65(2) provides that this offence can be committed by omission where D fails to discharge a duty. The act does not actually have to assist or encourage in the commission of an offence; it is sufficient that it is capable of doing so.

D must believe that the offence will be committed AND that his act will encourage or assist in the commission of an offence

Thus there are two elements to the *mens rea* requirement for the s 45 offence. In the first place D must believe that the offence will be committed. D must also believe that his act will encourage or assist in the commission of an offence. It is not necessary that his actions actually accomplish this; only that D believes that they will.

It is not therefore, an offence for D to do something that he fears or suspects will assist in the commission of an offence. Nor is it an offence to do something that D fears or suspects will encourage the commission of an offence. D must have a belief that it will encourage or assist in the commission of the offence.

It is irrelevant whether D's belief is a mistaken one; an honest belief is all that is required to construct liability.

We will now consider the s 46 offence.

Section 46: encouraging or assisting offences believing one or more will be committed

(1) A person commits an offence if –

   (a) he does an act capable of encouraging or assisting the commission of one or more of a number of offences; and

(b) he believes–
   (i) that one or more of those offences will be committed (but has no belief as to which); and
   (ii) that his act will encourage or assist the commission of one or more of them.

(2) It is immaterial for the purposes of subsection (1)(b)(ii) whether the person has any belief as to which offence will be encouraged or assisted.

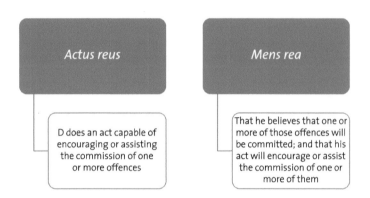

Actus reus

D does an act capable of encouraging or assisting the commission of one or more offences

Mens rea

That he believes that one or more of those offences will be committed; and that his act will encourage or assist the commission of one or more of them

We will now look at the different elements necessary to construct liability for this offence.

D does an act capable of encouraging or assisting the commission of one or more offence

We have considered this *actus reus* requirement in part under ss 44 and 45, although clearly in this case there is reference to one or more offences. This provision is intended to capture the situation where D anticipates that their actions will assist or encourage in the commission of one or more of a range of offences: *Sadique* (2013).

That D believes that one or more offences will be committed and D believes that his action will encourage or assist the commission of one or more of them

As with the s 46 offence there are two elements to the *mens rea* requirement for the s 45 offence. In the first place D must believe that the offence or offences will be committed. D must also believe that his act will encourage or assist in the commission of an offence or offences. It is not necessary that his actions actually accomplish this; only that D believes that they will.

Therefore if D does something that he fears or suspects will assist or encourage in the commission of an offence or offences, this will not be sufficient to satisfy the MR requirement for this offence.

Reform of inchoate offences

There have been calls for further reform of this area of law. The Law Commission considered the question of reform and how the law could be developed in this area. Conspiracy and Attempts (Law Com No. 318, December 2009).

The area of inchoate offences offers a useful case study in the evolution of the law, as in a relatively short space of time it has progressed from:

A common law offence

with further reforms recommended

to a statutory offence

Conspiracy

The Law Commission in *Conspiracy and Attempts* (Law Com No. 318, December 2009) recommends replacing the offence of conspiracy under the CLA 1977 with the following:

1. Conspiracy would involve an agreement by two or more persons to engage in the conduct element of an offence and (where relevant) to bring about the consequence of the offence (the result required by the offence).

At present the law requires an agreement to pursue a course of conduct, but there is no mention of the required results (although the case law has implied this).

2. D must have intended to engage in the conduct and intended to bring about the consequences (result).

Direct and oblique intention would suffice in these situations; however, recklessness would not.

Case precedent – *Anderson* [1986] AC 27

Facts: D provided supplies to a prisoner to help his escape from the prison, not believing that it would actually work.

Principle: Reform of intention in conspiracy

Application: It was held that there need be no intention to bring about the result, only an intention to pursue a course of conduct. This case was criticised because it meant that a conspiracy could exist where no party intended the crime to result. Although this case was largely ignored, the proposed law makes it clear that such a situation would not give rise to conspiracy. D may instead be convicted of assisting or encouraging crime.

---

3. Spouses would no longer be immune from liability.
4. D could be found guilty even though the person with whom he conspires is a victim of the offence (abolishing the current rules).

5. There would also be a defence of acting reasonably in order to prevent crime or harm. This would be along the same lines as the defence in relation to ss 44–46 Serious Crime Act 2007.

Attempt

The Law Commission in *Conspiracy and Attempts: a consultation paper* (Law Com CP No.183, 2007) recommended two new offences.

❖ An offence of attempt that operates only where D has reached the last acts necessary to complete the offence.
❖ An offence of criminal preparation.

It would need to be shown that D intended to commit the crime, meaning intention (direct or oblique) would suffice as would a conditional intent.

Up for Debate

These offences were eventually abandoned. Do you agree that this was the right course of action, or is further reform of attempts still required?

Putting it into practice

Question

Look at the scenario below and then answer the following question:

Shirley, Debra and Linda are part of a gang at school. Shirley and Linda have been bullying April. Debra did not agree with this, but was too scared to confront the other girls. Shirley sent a text to Linda saying that they should trap April in the toilets at lunchtime and give her a 'good slapping'. Linda agreed and sent a text to Debra telling her of the plan. Debra agreed to keep watch, but then decided that she would disclose the plans to a teacher.

At lunchtime Shirley and Linda trapped April and took her inside the toilets. Debra kept watch outside but immediately told the first teacher that she met what was about to happen. The teacher arrived on the scene just in time.

Both Shirley and Linda were convicted of conspiracy to commit ABH – is Debra also guilty of this offence?

Suggested solution

Remember to apply the structure that we have practised throughout this book:

1. **Identify the offence**
2. **Define the offence**
3. **Deal with all aspects of the AR**
4. **Deal with all aspects of the MR**
5. **Deal with potential defences**
6. **Address lesser alternative charges**

Remember in relation to inchoate offences that you need to discuss the primary substantive offences too! This should include an accurate legal definition with sources. It should also include brief discussion of the AR and MR.

This case clearly considers conspiracy. You need to work through the *actus reus* and *mens rea* to determine liability regarding Debra. Remember to refer to the correct legislation, noting the evolution of the offence from a common law offence into an Act.

An agreement – first go through the checks: the agreement is made between two or more people, and they do not fall within the exemptions, i.e. they are not married. Further, we can see that a written agreement has been made, i.e. a text message, setting out the agreement, which is then passed onto Debra from another, again indicating that an agreement is in place and is made between two or more people.

A course of conduct – here you first need to check that the agreement relates to the same offence as that attempted, i.e. the offence has not changed. In this case it refers to ABH, and you would need to demonstrate that this is consistent throughout. For example, if the agreement was ABH but the offence attempted was murder, this may affect liability.

The *mens rea* is the key point here – particularly whether Debra intends to reach a decision with the others. Look at the sequence of text and other messages, and see if you can determine whether Debra's intention to make an agreement is clear.

In particular look at her knowledge that the surrounding circumstances are present. Two useful cases to refer to here are *R v McPhillips* (1990) and *Yip Chiu-Cheung* (1994), where D exhibits similar circumstances to D. Consider both cases and their similarities, and apply this to the question.

Key points checklist

Inchoate offences include: Conspiracy; attempt; encouraging or assisting in the commission of a criminal offence.	✔
There are two types of conspiracy: (1) common law conspiracy; and (2) statutory conspiracy. Statutory conspiracy is governed by s 1 of the Criminal Law Act 1971. The *actus reus* for the offence is: an agreement; between parties; to carry out a course of conduct that will lead to the commission of an offence. The *mens rea* for the offence is: an intention to carry out agreed course of conduct; intention to commit the substantive offence.	✔
Attempt is covered by s 1 Criminal Attempts Act 1981. The *actus reus* of the offence is: an act not an omission; the act must be more than merely preparatory to the commission of the primary offence. The *mens rea* for the offence is that the defendant must have had the intention to commit the substantive offence.	✔
The final inchoate offence is encouraging or assisting in the commission of a criminal offence. Section 59 of the Serious Crime Act abolished the common law offence of incitement, replacing it with three separate offences in ss 44, 45 and 46 of the SCA 2007.	✔

Table of key cases referred to in this chapter

Key case	Brief facts	Principle
Griffiths [1966] 60 Cr App R14	D ignored the fact that the goods were stolen	Conspiracy – the agreement
Cooke [1986] 1 AC 909	D and other conspired to sell their own food on a British Rail train	A case can involve more than one conspiracy
Siracusa [1989] 90 Cr App R 340	D agreed to import heroin, but it was actually cannabis that was imported	The agreement must be the same as the result in conspiracy
Yip Chiu-Cheung v R [1994] 2 All ER 924	D, an undercover policeman, conspired with another man to traffic heroin	Intention in conspiracy
Saik [2006] UKHL 18	D was convicted of laundering money, and appeal was held.	D must intend or know that a fact or circumstance necessary for the commission of the crime will exist
Tree [2008]	D sold a speedboat which he thought was from the proceeds of crime, but was from tax evasion	D must intend or know that a fact or circumstance necessary for the commission of the crime will exist
DPP v Nock [1978] AC 979	D conspired to produce cocaine from a powder, but there was no cocaine in the powder	An agreement to do the impossible

Fallon [1994] Crim LR 519	D shot a police officer – the court had to decide if D intended to kill V	Attempts – intention
Haughton v Smith [1975] AC 476	D agreed to meet a van with stolen goods inside, but the police had already intercepted the van	Attempt and impossibility
Anderson [1986] AC 27	D supplied goods to a prisoner, not expecting him to escape	Reform of intention in conspiracy

---

@ **Visit the book's companion website to test your knowledge**

❖ Resources include a subject map, revision tip podcasts, downloadable diagrams, MCQ quizzes for each chapter, and a flashcard glossary

❖ www.routledge.com/cw/optimizelawrevision

10

Defences 1

Understand the law

- Do you understand the definitions of non-insane automatism, insane automatism and intoxication?
- Can you identify how the defences have evolved and have been refined through case law?
- Do you understand the difference between general and specific defences?

Remember the details

- Can you remember the different elements of non-insane automatism, insane automatism and intoxication?
- Can you remember the key cases law in relation to each of these defences?

Reflect critically on areas of debate

- Do you understand the distinguishing features of insanity when compared to diminished responsibility and automatism?
- Do you understand the significance of whether a crime is one of basic or specific intent in relation to the defence of intoxication?

Contextualise

- Can you apply the different defences in this chapters to other areas of the law?
- Can you identify the limitations of these defences?

Apply your skills and knowledge

- Can you complete the activities in this chapter using the liability charts and relevant case law?

Chapter Map

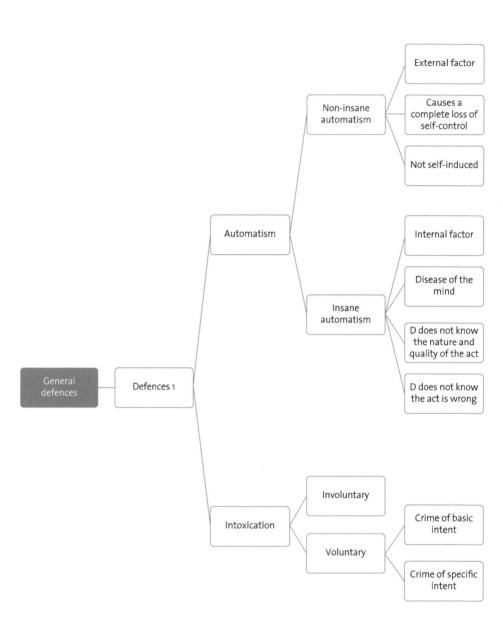

Defences

In the next two chapters we will consider general defences. Defences form an important aspect of criminal law and when you are constructing liability in a problem question you must always consider whether the defendant will be able to avail themselves of a defence. Defences may be specific or general in nature.

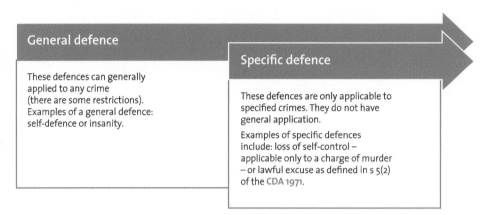

General defence

These defences can generally applied to any crime
(there are some restrictions).
Examples of a general defence:
self-defence or insanity.

Specific defence

These defences are only applicable to specified crimes. They do not have general application.

Examples of specific defences include: loss of self-control – applicable only to a charge of murder – or lawful excuse as defined in s 5(2) of the CDA 1971.

Defences are important because they can determine whether the defendant should be excused from an offence due to surrounding circumstances, or whether D's actions can be justified. Therefore there are two types of defence: justificatory defences and excusatory defences.

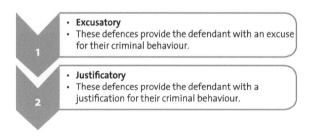

1
- **Excusatory**
- These defences provide the defendant with an excuse for their criminal behaviour.

2
- **Justificatory**
- These defences provide the defendant with a justification for their criminal behaviour.

In this chapter, we will focus on the following defences:

❖ automatism
❖ insanity
❖ intoxication.

When you are dealing with a problem question and you have finished constructing liability for a criminal offence, you should next consider the availability of a potential defence. The key to remember is that in a problem question you must first construct liability for an offence, **THEN** move on to consider defences.

Aim Higher

It is not uncommon for students to start their analysis of a problem question with a consideration of available defences for the defendant. You must remember that liability for an offence must always be constructed first. If the defendant is not liable for a criminal offence they have no need for a defence! Therefore defences – by which we mean specific and general defences – should always come after liability has been constructed.

In the event that the defendant may avail themselves of a specific and a general defence we would suggest that you deal with the specific defence before general defences. Therefore the correct order should be:

1. Construct criminal liability.
2. Discuss the availability of specific defences.
3. Discuss the availability of general defences.

We will start our consideration of defences by outlining the definition of the defence. The we will move on to consider the ingredients of each defence before finally examining the legal effect of successfully running the specific defence.

Aim Higher

When discussing defences it is important in the first instance that you provide an accurate legal definition of the defence. You should also note whether the defence is a common law defence or a statutory defence. You must then remember to consider the elements required to make out the offence. Once you have considered the distinct elements of the defence you can then go on to consider the legal effect of successfully running the defence in question. The consideration of defences in a problem question is as follows:

1. Definition of the defence (with authority).
2. Is the defence a common law or statutory definition (give the source)?
3. Explain each element of the defence (with authorities).
4. Explain the legal effect of successfully running the defence in question.

Automatism

The first defence that we are going to consider is the defence of automatism. There are in effect two types of automatism: non-insane automatism and insane automatism. Automatism is a claim that the defendant was unable to control their actions, or behaviour as a result of an internal, or external factor. It is important that you understand what differentiates non-insane automatism from insane automatism.

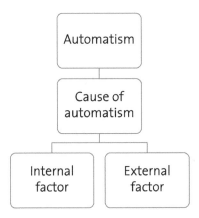

Non-insane automatism is the result of some external factor, whereas insane automatism (often referred to simply as insanity) is the result of an internal factor. Therefore when considering automatism a critical question will be: is the defendant's loss of control the result of an internal or an external factor? This question is crucial because the outcome of successfully running the defence of non-insane automatism is quite different from the outcome of successfully running the defence of insane automatism (insanity). You can see the different outcomes in the diagram below:

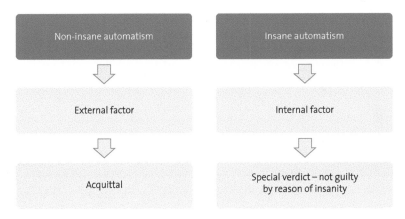

We are now going to consider the defences of non-insane automatism and insane automatism separately.

Non-insane automatism

In the case of non-insane automatism the defendant is claiming to have been acting involuntarily as a result of some external factor. The defendant is said to have been acting in a state of automatism. In *Bratty v AG for Northern Ireland* (1963) Lord Denning defined automatism as:

> An act which is done by the muscles without any control by the mind, such as a spasm, a reflex action or a convulsion or an act done by a person who is not conscious of what he is doing, such as an act done when suffering from concussion . . .

The key ingredients of this defence are:

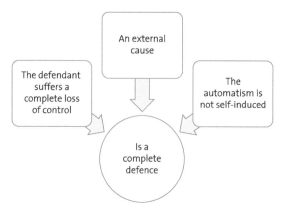

We will now look at each of these ingredients separately.

The defendant suffers a complete loss of control

In order for the defence of non-insane automatism to succeed the defendant must have suffered a complete loss of self-control. If the defendant has not suffered a complete loss of self-control and has retained some ability, albeit limited ability, to control his or her actions then the claim of non-insane automatism will fail: *Broome v Perkins* (1987).

We will now consider a number of different scenarios which may arise within a problem question, in which you would need to consider whether non-insane automatism can be used as a defence.

The defendant is conscious
Where D is conscious he must lack complete control over his actions.

Case precedent – *Broome v Perkins* [1987] Crim LR 271

Facts: D was driving his car in a hypoglycaemic state, but from time to time he exercised control over the vehicle by braking violently.

Principle: Automatism and consciousness

Application: D was found guilty, because he exercised partial control.

This precedent was then followed in *A-G's Reference (No 2 of 1992)* (1993), where driving without awareness was held to be no answer to a charge of causing death by reckless driving, as the defendant in this case had retained some control over his driving.

This is because the defence of automatism requires a complete loss of control. This is a very strict rule which means where a D retains partial control over their actions, they will not be able to use the defence of non-insane automatism as a defence.

Common Pitfall

Where D acts in a way that he would not normally act but still retains control, he cannot rely on this defence.

In *Isitt* (1978), D argued that his dangerous driving was due to a previous accident that had led to memory loss. At the time of the offence he could not remember what he had done as his subconscious mind had taken over. The Court of Appeal dismissed D's appeal, as he had control over his bodily actions.

Examiners can often test a student's knowledge with examples of this type, so keep focused on the main elements of the defence and remember to support your answer by reference to authority.

The defence of non-insane automatism will also fail if D's initial voluntary conduct leads up to an involuntary act. Look at the case precedent below, and identify the voluntary conduct and how this conduct led to the act.

Case precedent – *Ryan v R* [1967] HCA 2

Facts: D with one hand pointed a loaded shotgun at V, whom he had robbed, and with the other hand he tried to tie V up. V moved and D argued that he involuntarily pressed the trigger because of a reflex action.

Principle: Automatism and voluntary conduct

Application: The pointing of the gun and the placing of the finger on the trigger were voluntary acts, so D was responsible whether the pressing of the trigger was involuntary or not.

Remember these key points as:

- Non-insane automatism requires a complete loss of control
- If D retains full or part control, they cannot rely on non-automatism as a defence
- Examples such as cravings do not constitute automatism
- D is guilty where voluntary conduct leads to an involuntary act

Where D is unconscious or in a state of impaired consciousness

If the defendant is unconscious, then he lacks control over his actions. Expert medical opinion is normally required to establish the facts, particularly as the argument of a full 'blackout' is usually considered with suspicion: *Cooper v McKenna* (1960).

Total or impaired consciousness may result from the use of drugs, hypnosis or alcohol. But whether D can rely on the defence of non-insane automatism in these circumstances depends on whether the final element of the defence is established.

Example: Andy is walking down a busy street when a large shop sign comes loose and falls, hitting Andy on the head. He is in a semi-conscious state and stumbles into Tai, who falls over and severely cuts his head.

Could Andy use the defence of non-insane automatism here?

In this situation, Andy is hit on the head by an object. This is an unexpected external factor, which causes a state of semi-consciousness in which Andy is arguably unable to exercise voluntary control over his actions. As a result of the semi-conscious state Andy bumps into Tai, who cuts his head:

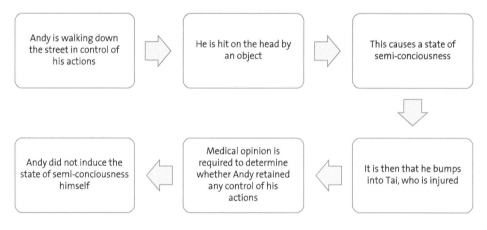

The cause of the automatism/loss of control must be external

The factor that causes the defendant to suffer a complete loss of self-control must be an external factor. This might include a blow to the head or a reflex action caused by a swarm of bees. Look at the case precedent below.

Case precedent – *Hill v Baxter* [1958] 1 QB 277

Facts: D was driving when he was attacked by a swarm of bees, causing involuntary movement to his arms and legs. As a result of the involuntary movements he crashed the car.

Principle: The automatism must be the result of an external factor.

> **Application:** Automatism was a complete defence to the offence of driving without due care and attention.

Examples of external factors include:

❖ the consumption of alcohol;
❖ an insulin injection;
❖ concussion from a blow;
❖ the administration of an anaesthetic or other drug; and
❖ hypnosis.

It is important to note that a hypoglycaemic state that is caused by the intake of insulin is considered to be an external factor. Thus the appropriate defence in the case of hypoglycaemia (low blood sugar levels) is automatism: *Quick* (1973).

In contrast hyperglycaemia, is often the result of an internal factor such as diabetes. Where it is the result of a disease or another internal factor the correct defence would be insanity: *Hennessy* (1989).

Aim Higher

The treatment of diabetics in relation to the operation of this defence is a useful way of illustrating the distinction between internal and external factors.

Sleepwalking is also considered to be the result of an internal cause, as held in the case of *Burgess* (1991).

However, in *T* (1990), D's defence of automatism was successful in relation to a charge of robbery where the D was suffering from post-traumatic stress disorder (she had been raped). The rape was held to be an extraordinary event and as such the post-traumatic stress disorder was an external factor.

The defendant must not have caused the loss of self-control

The final element of the defence is that the automatism must not be self induced. In circumstances where the automatism is self-induced the defence will fail.

The defence will apply only if the defendant is not at fault. The defendant will be at fault if he has induced the state of automatism through the misuse of alcohol or drugs. However, sometimes the distinction is not always as clear as this.

D voluntarily consumes alcohol or dangerous drugs

Self-induced automatism is no defence to crimes of basic intent (i.e. a crime that can be committed recklessly or intentionally). The reason for this is that a person who has self-induced a state of automatism is considered by the courts to be a person that has been reckless in getting into this condition in the first place. In these circumstances a person should not be able to plead the defence of non-insane automatism.

However, where D is voluntarily intoxicated but has committed a crime of specific intent (one for which intention and intention alone will suffice), provided that they lacked the ability to form the *mens rea* for the offence they may be able to avail themselves of the defence. It will depend on whether they formed a drunken intent and whether the other elements of the defence are present.

Remember this as:

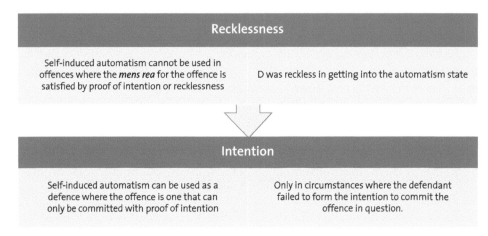

Recklessness

Self-induced automatism cannot be used in offences where the *mens rea* for the offence is satisfied by proof of intention or recklessness	D was reckless in getting into the automatism state

Intention

Self-induced automatism can be used as a defence where the offence is one that can only be committed with proof of intention	Only in circumstances where the defendant failed to form the intention to commit the offence in question.

Therefore, when answering a problem question where the defendant is voluntarily intoxicated and is claiming non-insane automatism, you will need to consider the offence that D is alleged to have committed, and you will need to consider the *mens rea* for the offence to determine whether D can be held liable for the offence.

Aim Higher

There is some overlap here between automatism and intoxication. Voluntary intoxication is a defence to crimes of specific intent provided the intoxication has prevented the formation of the necessary intent.

This point was confirmed in the case of *Bailey* (1983), which concerned the commission of a crime of specific intent by D, who was diabetic and had attacked a man with an iron bar. D had taken insulin and consumed alcohol but he had not eaten. These combined factors can lead to an unconscious and aggressive state. The Court of Appeal held that if the state of automatism was self-induced it can provide a complete defence to a crime of specific intent provided the prosecution cannot prove the necessary intention.

However, if D's state of automatism was brought about by the voluntary consumption of alcohol or illegal drugs, it would be no defence to a crime of basic intent.

Another useful example of this principle can be seen in the case of *Lipman* (1970).

Case precedent – *Lipman* [1970] 1 QB 152

Facts: D killed his girlfriend by stuffing a bed sheet down her throat whilst under the influence of LSD (an illegal drug).

Principle: Subjective recklessness

Application: It was accepted that D could not have formed the specific intent required for murder (intention to kill or cause GBH), because of his drug-induced state. D was, however, liable for reckless manslaughter, because he was reckless in voluntarily taking the LSD in the first place.

D voluntarily consumes prescription drugs

If the defendant takes prescription drugs and this produces unexpected or unforeseen behaviour that leads to the commission of a crime then D may be able to rely on the defence of automatism or intoxication. This is summarised as:

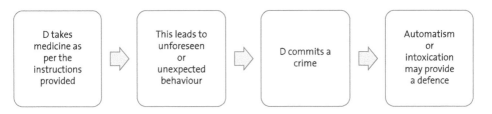

Thus in these circumstances a defendant has a defence to a crime of basic intent and to a crime of specific intent. This was confirmed in the following case.

Case precedent – *Hardie* [1984] 1 WLR 64

Facts: D was depressed about having to move home. He took a non-prescribed drug (some of his girlfriend's Valium) to calm his nerves and then started a fire in a wardrobe. He was convicted of damaging property with intent to endanger the life of another or being reckless as to the endangerment of life contrary to s 1(2) **Criminal Damage Act 1971**.

Principle: Automatism and medicinal drugs

Application: The Court of Appeal quashed the conviction. D had not been reckless because he did not know the Valium would make him unpredictable or aggressive.

Now test your understanding of automatism with this example.

Example: Sheila is driving her car when she feels a sharp pain in her neck. A rare poisonous spider has bitten her neck and Sheila momentarily loses control of the car, the car veers off the road and kills two people waiting at a bus stop.

Could Sheila use the defence of non-insane automatism here?

In the first instance you would provide a definition of non-insane automatism. Then you should ask:

1. Did Sheila suffer a complete loss of self-control?
2. Was this the result of some external factor?
3. Did D induce the state of automatism?

If the defence of non-insane automatism is established Sheila will have a complete defence.

We are now moving on to consider the second form of automatism, insane automatism. This is often referred to as the defence of insanity.

Insanity

It is crucial to note that in the context of this defence, that the definition of insanity is concerned with criminal insanity, and that the definition of criminal insanity does not correspond with the medical definition of inanity. The justification for this distinction is that insanity in this context is a legal, not a medical term and involves considerations of public protection as well as individual responsibility. It is worth noting that many academics have called for reform of this area of law and as such the defence of insane automatism or insanity is a popular topic with examiners.

> ## Common Pitfall
>
> Insanity is sometimes referred to as 'insane automatism' and automatism is sometimes referred to as 'non-insane automatism'. Make sure that your use of these terms is accurate!

There are essentially two different ways in which the defendant's alleged insanity may be relevant to his or her criminal liability for an offence. These are:

1. Where the defendant's mental state renders them unfit to stand trial. In reality this may have nothing to do with the commission of the offence itself (e.g. the illness/condition may have developed after the commission of the offence).
2. Where the defendant was legally insane at the commission of the offence. In such circumstances this may give rise to the defence of insane automatism/ insanity. If the defendant successfully runs the defence of insanity this gives rise to a special verdict of not guilty by reason of insanity.

Special verdict

It is important to remember that the successful use of the defence of insanity does not result in an acquittal as is the case in non-insane automatism. The legal effect of successfully running the defence of insanity is a finding of 'not guilty by reason of insanity'. This in many cases means that the defendant is not free to leave court. In reality the defendant may be subject to detention in a mental health facility. As a result this defence is very rarely utilised by defendants, as they are understandably anxious about the consequences of a finding of not guilty by reason of insanity.

It is vital to remember that insanity will be the appropriate defence where D's mind is affected by an **internal** factor, for example diabetes or epilepsy. Non-insane automatism will be the correct plea where the malfunctioning of D's mind is caused by an **external** factor.

In a problem question where liability for murder has been established and the defendant is suffering from mental health issues you should consider the special partial defence of diminished responsibility. You may also want to consider the defence of insanity. It should be remembered that diminished responsibility is only available where D is charged with murder, whereas insanity is available as a defence to all offences.

The test for insanity – the M'Naghten rules

Insanity is a common law defence and as such the definition of insanity is not located within a statute – the definition derives from the M'Naghten rules, and in their interpretation by the courts. The rules are derived from the case of *M'Naghten* in 1843. The rules state: Every man is presumed sane, but this can be rebutted by evidence that he was

> *'labouring under such a defect of reason, from disease of the mind, as not to know the nature and the quality of the act he was doing, or, if he did know it, or that he did not know he was doing wrong.'*

In the case of this defence the burden of proof rests with the defence to prove on the balance of probabilities. The prosecution may of course attempt to disprove the defence once it has been raised.

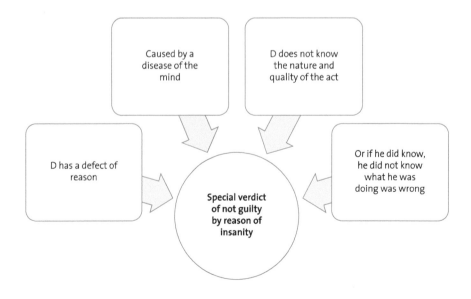

The elements of the defence of insanity are:

1. D has a defect of reason
2. Caused by a disease of the mind
3. Which in turn means that D does not know the nature and quality of his act. Or?
4. If he does know the nature and the quality of the act, he does not know that it is wrong.

We will now consider these elements in more detail.

The defendant has a defect of reason

The defence of insanity will only apply to defendants whose cognitive powers of memory, reason and understanding are defective. Thus a defendant must be incapable of exercising normal powers of reasoning. A defect of reason will not be established in circumstances where D simply fails to use his powers of reasoning: *Clarke* (1972).

Caused by a disease of the mind

The defect of reason must be caused by a disease of the mind – this is a legal question, not a medical one, and it is established where an internal factor causes a defect of reason. A defect of reason will be established in circumstances where *Kemp* (1957). It is the internal nature of the source of the defect of reason which separates insanity from the defence of non-insane automatism.

Internal factors

The defence of insanity tends to be used by defendants suffering from serious mental health issues, but it can also be utilised by individuals who are suffering from a change in the physical state of the brain. For example in *Sullivan* (1984), the defendant committed ABH while suffering from an epileptic seizure. Insanity was the appropriate defence, because the defect of reason had been caused by an internal factor, amounting to a disease of the mind.

A degeneration of the brain is not always required.

Case precedent – *Kemp* [1957] 1 QB 399

Facts: D attacked his wife with a hammer. It appeared he suffered from arteriosclerosis, which caused a congestion of blood in his brain. As a result, he suffered a temporary lapse of consciousness, during which he made the attack.

Principle: Insanity and internal factors

Application: The judge held that the disease must affect the cognitive or intellectual capacities of the mind in the sense of reason, memory and understanding.

In the next section we are going to consider a range of factors and whether or not they are deemed internal or external in nature. We will consider:

* sleepwalking
* diabetes
* normal stress and strain.

Sleepwalking

One issue that the courts have had to consider is whether acts done while sleeping are the result of an internal factor and as such captured by the defence of insanity, or whether they are the result of an external factor and captured by the defence of non-insane automatism. For example, the cases of *Tolson* (1889) and *Lillienfield* (1985) both deal with situations where the defendant was alleged to have committed a crime whilst sleepwalking.

The case of *Burgess* in 1991 confirmed that sleepwalking is the result of an internal factor and therefore the appropriate defence to a crime that has been committed whilst sleepwalking is insanity. The timeline for these important cases is:

Tolson (1889)   *Lillienfield* (1985)   *Burgess* (1991)

From this, we can see that in a problem question, you should first consider whether the cause is internal (insanity) or external (automatism), and this will lead you in the right direction, even if the outcome is not as you might have expected!

Diabetes

Earlier in this chapter we considered the application of law in relation to individuals who commit criminal offences whilst suffering from a diabetic episode.

Whether or not a diabetic episode is considered an internal or external factor will depend on whether the episode was caused by the condition itself, or the use of insulin. In the case of *Quick* (1973), the defendant, who had diabetes, inflicted ABH. The defendant submitted that at the time of his conduct he was suffering from hypoglycaemia (low blood sugar) and was unaware of what he was doing. The Court of Appeal held that this was caused by his use of insulin, not by his diabetes. Therefore the cause was an external factor (insulin) and the defence of non-insane automatism should have been left to the jury.

Remember that:

Too much insulin (external) causes low sugar level → Hypoglycaemia (defence = automatism)

Too little insulin (internal) causes high sugar level → Hyperglycaemia (defence = insanity)

The ordinary stresses and strains of life

It could be argued that the daily stress of life, particularly for a person experiencing problems, could be an internal factor.

For example, in the case of *Rabey* (1977), the defendant, who had become infatuated with a girl, found out that the object of his infatuation did not feel the same way. The defendant hit the victim on the head with a rock. The defendant submitted that where a person's defect of reason results from a 'dissociative state' caused by an stress resulting from a rejection, this should give rise to the defence of automatism. The judge at first instance accepted the argument and allowed the defence of non-insane automatism. On appeal it was held that it did not constitute an external cause, and insanity was the appropriate defence.

The defect of reason means that D does not know the nature and quality of his act
and/or

He did not know that what he was doing was wrong
Either the defect of reason must be responsible for the defendant failing to appreciate the nature and quality of his act, or the defect of reason must result in the defendant not knowing what he was doing was wrong.

Thus there are two important aspects to this element, which are set out in the diagram below:

Not knowing the nature and quality of his act or its consequences	• The concern here is with the physical nature and quality of the act, not its legal or moral quality • e.g. D cuts a woman's throat thinking that he is cutting a loaf of bread • In relation to consequences, D knows that he has cut off a person's head but does not realise the consequences of this
And/or not knowing the act is wrong	• Whether D is able to appreciate the legal as opposed to the moral wrongness of the act he does at the time

Therefore a defendant may know the nature and quality of the act that he is doing but he may still avail himself of the defence of insanity if he does not know what he is doing is legally wrong. Wrong in this context means legally wrong as opposed to morally wrong, as illustrated in the case of *Windle* (1952).

Let us consider the following example: Tim is told by voices in his head to shoot his mother. Would Tim be able to use insanity as a defence?

If Tim is suffering from a defect of reason that is caused by a disease of the mind but he knows that shooting his mother is a crime, then the defence of insanity would not apply. However, if Tim has a defect of reason caused by a disease of the mind and does not appreciate that shooting his mother is a crime, then insanity may be a suitable defence.

A summary of the ingredients for the defence of insane automatism:

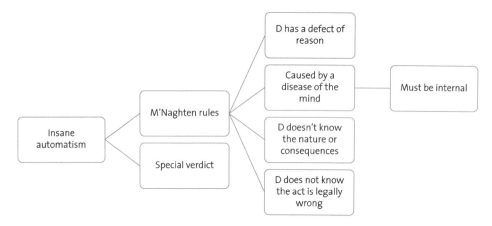

In the next section we are going to consider the defence of intoxication.

Intoxication

Intoxication can occur when a defendant consumes drugs or alcohol. Where intoxication is used as a defence, it is important to understand how far D is impaired by the intoxicant, and how this may impact upon their conduct. The defence is far more complex than simply acknowledging that the defendant was drunk and therefore did not know what he/she was doing.

Common Pitfall

Intoxication rarely provides a defence, as it is limited in nature and is only available where the intoxication prevents the *mens rea* of the offence from being established. It is never a defence where D knows what he is doing but is simply less inhibited or more aggressive because of the intoxicant.

The basic principles with regard to intoxication are as follows:

1. In crimes of specific intent, voluntary intoxication may provide a partial defence where the *mens rea* is not formed.
2. In crimes of basic intent, voluntary intoxication does not provide a defence.
3. **Involuntary intoxication** (i.e. this includes the unforeseen consequences of medication and where V's orange juice has been laced with vodka or drugs by another person) may provide a complete defence to crimes of specific intent and crimes of basic intent provided that the *mens rea* for the offence has not been formed.

4. **A drunken intent is sufficient** – where a defendant is involuntarily intoxicated but still forms the *mens rea* for the offence in question this is sufficient to establish liability.

The first two principles derive from the case of *DPP v Majewski* (1976) and are known as the rule in *Majewski*. The third and fourth principles derive from the case of *Kingston* (1994).

We will now consider these rules in more detail.

Voluntary intoxication: the rule in Majewski

Intoxication will be classed as voluntary where D knowingly consumes intoxicating substances, provided of course that they are generally known to be intoxicating; this includes alcohol and drugs.

D is voluntarily intoxicated if he knows he is ingesting a drug or alcohol, even though he may underestimate its strength. In *Allen* (1989), D intentionally drank wine and was voluntarily intoxicated even though he had not been aware of its high alcoholic content.

Remember this summary as:

Voluntary intoxication ⇨ If D knew what he was ingesting ⇨ It is an intoxicating substance

D must lack the mens rea of the offence

The 'defence' of intoxication will only succeed where D failed to form the *mens rea* for the offence because of the intoxication. For example, if Leah intentionally stabbed Rosia in a pub, could Leah argue that she was intoxicated and therefore have a defence?

The answer to this is no. Leah will not be able to plead the defence of intoxication even to an offence of specific intent. The reason for this is that the example clearly states that she intended to stab Rosia. A drunken intent is still intent: *Kingston* (1995); *DPP v Beard* (1920).

Therefore D must lack the *mens rea* for the offence. He does not have a defence where he took the intoxicant (usually alcohol) in order to give himself 'Dutch courage' so that he could commit the crime. This is because D did have the *mens rea*, albeit at an earlier time. This principle was confirmed in *A-G for Northern Ireland v Gallagher* (1963).

Case precedent – *McKnight* [2000]

Facts: D killed V and claimed she was drunk, but not 'legless'.

Principle: Intoxication and 'Dutch courage'

Application: The Court of Appeal held that where a defendant claims to have been so intoxicated that he lacked the intention to commit a specific intent crime, there has to be some evidential (factual) basis for saying that he was too drunk to form the intent, before it becomes appropriate for the judge to even consider putting intoxication to the jury.

The key principle here is that the intoxication (through drink, drugs or other intoxicating substance) must prevent the defendant forming the *mens rea* for the offence.

Try to remember these key points as:

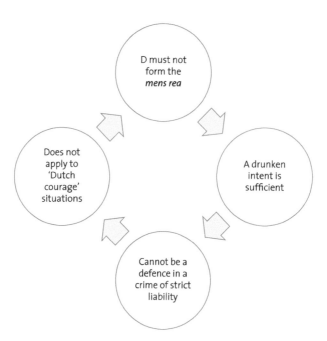

Intoxication and crimes of basic and specific intent

As has been noted previously, where D is charged with a crime of specific intent, voluntary intoxication may provide a defence, provided that the intoxication prevented the D from forming the *mens rea* for the crime in question. However, it should be remembered that where the defendant does escape liability for a specific intent crime, he may be liable for a lesser offence that can be made out by proof of recklessness. For example:

| D is intoxicated and kills V. Murder is a crime of specific intent. | D may be liable for reckless manslaughter or constructive manslaughter (basic intent) |

| D is charged with s 18 **OAPA 1861** (specific intent) | D may be convicted under s 20 **OAPA 1861** (basic intent) |

In a problem question, you will therefore need to consider related offences when dealing with a defendant who is claiming intoxication as a defence. It may be that the defendant is liable for an offence to which there is no appropriate lesser charge – such as theft. In such cases, intoxication would provide a complete defence.

It is important to differentiate between crimes of basic and specific intent when applying this defence, and discussing the distinction between these different types of crime demonstrates a good level of knowledge to the reader.

Crimes of specific intent

Where the defendant is charged with a crime of specific intent, such as murder, voluntary intoxication may provide him with a defence. However, as already noted, this will only be the case where D, because of his intoxicated state, is unable to form the necessary intention: *Majewski* (1976).

Remember this key point:

There mere fact that D is drunk will not necessarily mean that he is unable to form the intention

For example, consider the case below and you can see that, despite being drunk, D still had the *mens rea* – 'a drunken intent is still intent'.

Case precedent – *Kingston* [1995] 99 Cr App R 286

Facts: D had his drinks spiked and was then put in a room with a boy (who was also drugged). D then sexually assaulted the boy.

Principle: Intoxication and specific intent

Application: D admitted that he had paedophilic tendencies, which he could normally resist and that, during the assault, he knew what he was doing. The effect of the drugs was merely to reduce his ability to resist such temptations. It was held that D should not be permitted the defence of intoxication.

Crimes of basic intent

Voluntary intoxication will not provide a defence to a crime of basic intent (one for which recklessness will suffice: *DPP v Majewski* (1976).

The rule in *Majewski* (1976) does not, however, apply to all basic intent crimes. If D commits a crime of negligence such as gross negligence manslaughter, *DPP v Majewski* (1976) will not apply because there is no requirement of recklessness. The prosecution is likely to argue that D is still liable because his getting drunk was negligent, given that a reasonable person is not an inebriated person and that the negligence was gross. Conversely, the defence could argue that if the reasonable sober person would have acted as such, then D is not guilty despite his drunkenness.

Involuntary intoxication

The basic principle is very similar to voluntary intoxication: if D has the *mens rea* for the crime, he will be liable. However, if he lacks the *mens rea* because of involuntary intoxication, he may have a complete defence regardless of the type of crime, whether basic or specific intent. See the illustration below:

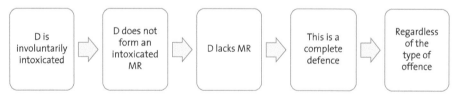

Example: Harry's food is spiked with drugs without his knowledge, and while intoxicated Harry strikes William. Could Harry use intoxication as a defence? Harry will have a defence to all offences provided that he has not formed a drunken intent, because he lacks the *mens rea* and his state has been induced by involuntary intoxication.

In such circumstances, there is no need to draw a distinction between basic intent and specific intent crimes, as intoxication will form a complete defence.

present before the involuntary intoxication. As the *mens rea* was present before, D may then be liable for the offence, despite the involuntary intoxication.

Note here that criminal law is not concerned with moral blame – it is concerned with the *actus reus* and *mens rea*, and if both can be proved, D has no defence. Do you think this is the correct approach to take in these circumstances?

In a problem question ensure that you consider the facts of the case, including:

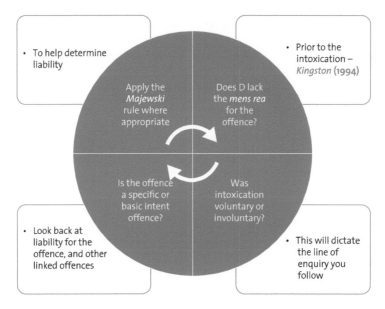

A summary of the points we have covered in this section is:

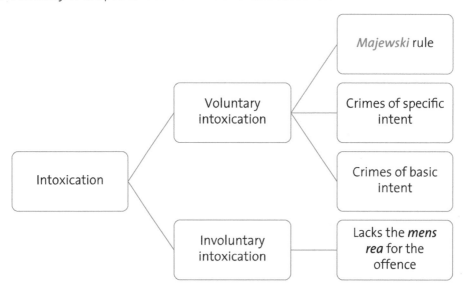

Putting it into practice

Question 1

Andrew is in hospital, and the nurse gives him an antibiotic that Andrew has never had before. Andrew suffers a fit, and his arms and legs move uncontrollably, hitting the nurse in the face. Assess whether Andrew could use the defence of automatism against the offence of battery.

Suggested solution

Remember that it is crucial that you construct liability for an offence before moving on to consider the availability of any defence!

Follow the normal process for constructing liability:

1. **Identify the crime**
2. **Define the crime**
3. **Explain the AR of the offence**
4. **Explain the MR of the offence**
5. **Consider relevant defences**

When examining this scenario, it is reasonably clear that automatism is a potential defence. However, it is key that you identify the right species of automatism. Remember that automatism can be broken down into:

❖ non-insane automatism; and
❖ insane automatism.

Non-insane automatism requires the following:

1. An external factor
2. That causes the defendant to suffer loss of control
3. The loss of control is not self-induced.

By contrast insane automatism requires the following:

1. A defect of reason
2. Caused by a disease of the mind
3. Which results in the defendant not knowing the nature and quality of the act he is performing and/or
4. The defendant did not realise that what he was doing was wrong.

The critical issue in relation to non-insane automatism and insane automatism is whether the cause is an internal or external factor. In this case Andrew's fit is caused by a drug, which is administered by a nurse. The drug is an external factor and it causes the fit, which causes the uncontrollable movements by Andrew: *Hill v Baxter* (1958).

Question 2

Lydia has had an argument with Paula about her boyfriend, and decides to seek revenge. She follows Paula to the pub, where Paula is meeting her friends. Lydia has three strong alcoholic drinks for courage, and then stabs Paula with a broken bottle, killing Paula.

Could Lydia use the defence of intoxication against the offence of murder?

Suggested solution

Once again you will need to establish liability for an offence before considering the availability of any defence. You should follow the normal structure:

1. **Identify the crime**
2. **Define the crime**
3. **Explain the AR of the offence**
4. **Murder is a result crime so you must address causation**
5. **Explain the MR of the offence**
6. **Possible defences**

Intoxication is a defence which can be quite difficult to demonstrate. To do so, you would work through the main elements of the defence, noting that this is voluntary intoxication, as opposed to involuntary intoxication. The general rule laid down in *Majewski* is that voluntary intoxication is a defence to a crime of specific intent.

However, intent is crucial here. Remember that a drunken intent is still intent: *Kingston* (1995). It is also clear that intoxication cannot be used where the defendant became intoxicated for 'Dutch courage'. In this case it would seem that Lydia possessed the *mens rea* for murder prior to the intoxication: *McKnight* (2000).

Key Points Checklist

When dealing with defences in the context of a problem question, you must ensure that you have constructed potential liability for an offence first!	✔
Automatism can be divided into two forms of automatism: non-insane automatism and insane automatism. The outcome of successfully running these defences differs significantly and you must acknowledge this in any answer that you produce. Non-insane automatism can lead to a complete acquittal, whereas insane automatism (also known as insanity) results in a special verdict of not guilty by reason of insanity.	✔
Another key distinguishing feature of the defences of non-insane automatism and insane automatism is the cause. In the case of non-insane automatism the cause is an external factor. In the case of insane automatism the cause is an internal factor.	✔
There are two stages in the criminal proceeding process at which the defendant's mental state may be of relevance. The first is the point at which the defendant stands trial. The defendant must have the capacity to enter a plea and participate/understand the trial process. The second point at which the defendant's mental capacity is relevant is where the defendant was criminally insane at the commission of the crime.	✔
The M'Naghten rules lay down the test for criminal insanity. It is important to note that the definition of criminal insanity differs considerably from the medical definition of insanity.	✔

For the purposes of criminal law, intoxication as a defence can be broken into: (1) voluntary intoxication; and (2) involuntary intoxication. As a general rule individuals voluntarily intoxicated cannot use intoxication as a defence to a crime of basic intent, although it may be a defence to a crime of specific intent provided that the defendant has not formed a drunken intent. In the case of involuntary intoxication the general rule is that this form of intoxication can constitute a defence to any crime, provided that the defendant has not formed a drunken intent or used alcohol for 'Dutch courage'.	✔

Table of key cases referred to in this chapter

Key case	Brief facts	Principle
Hill v Baxter [1958] 1 QB 277	D was driving a car, and was attacked by bees, causing him to crash the car	Automatism as a defence
Broome v Perkins [1987] Crim LR 271	D was driving his car when in a hypoglycaemic state, but exercised some control	Automatism and conscious state
Ryan v R [1967] HCA 2	D pointed a gun at V and tied up V. V moved and D pulled the trigger	Automatism and voluntary conduct
Lipman [1970] 1 QB 152	D killed his girlfriend when high on drugs	Automatism – intention and recklessness
M'Naghten [1834] 10 Cl	D murdered Sir Robert Peel's secretary, but was acquitted due to insanity.	M'Naghten rules
Kemp [1957] 1 QB 399	D attacked his wife with a hammer, and was suffering from a disease which affected his mind	Insanity and internal factors
DPP v Majewski [1976] AC 443	Set out the rules for voluntary intoxication as a defence	Rules of intoxication as a defence
McKnight [2000]	D killed V and claimed she was drunk, but not 'legless'	Intoxication and *mens rea*
DPP v Morgan [1975] AC 182	V was raped by two of her husband's friends, whom he had invited home to have sex with his wife. He said her protests were a sign of her pleasure.	Mistaken belief

@ Visit the book's companion website to test your knowledge

❖ Resources include a subject map, revision tip podcasts, downloadable diagrams, MCQ quizzes for each chapter, and a flashcard glossary

❖ www.routledge.com/cw/optimizelawrevision

11

Defences 2

Understand the law

- Do you understand the similarities and differences between duress by threats, duress of circumstances and necessity?
- Do you understand how the defences in this chapter have evolved, and how they have been refined through case law?

Remember the details

- Can you remember the different elements of duress by threats and duress of circumstances?
- Can you remember the different elements of necessity?
- Can you remember in what circumstances mistake can operate as a defence to criminal liability?

Reflect critically on areas of debate

- Do you understand the distinguishing features of these defences when compared to the defences in the last chapter?

Contextualise

- Can you apply the defences in this chapter to other areas of the law, and provide examples for these?

Apply your skills and knowledge

- Can you complete the activities in this chapter using authorities to support your answers?

Chapter Map

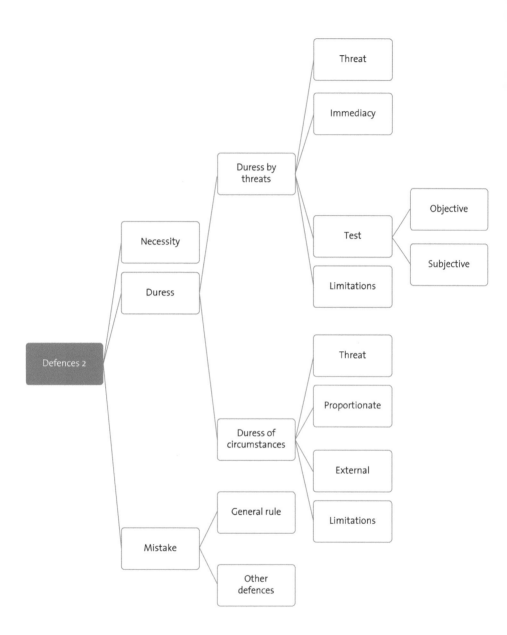

Introduction

In this chapter we are continuing our consideration of defences. In this chapter we are going to consider:

❖ necessity
❖ duress
❖ mistake.

Necessity

The defence of necessity is based on the notion that, in some situations, it may be justifiable for a defendant to engage in criminal conduct in order to avoid a greater harm.

One of the difficulties with the defence of necessity is that it is somewhat unclear as to whether it exists as a distinct defence, or whether it is, in reality, simply a form of duress. This uncertainty causes problems for law students because this defence lacks a widely accepted definition and clear boundaries.

The concept of necessity operates extensively in medicine, where it is used as a justification for medical treatment that takes place without a patient's consent. It is not unusual for the medical profession to be presented with a patient that is unconscious or unable for other reasons to agree to medical treatment that is necessary to save the patient's life. It is unsurprising therefore that many of the leading authorities in relation to this defence have their origins in the practice of medicine. For example, in *Re F (Mental Patient: Sterilisation)* (1990), the judge granted doctors permission to sterilise a patient who lacked the mental capacity to understand the consequences of unprotected sexual activity.

Aim Higher

There are many examples of a defence of necessity being successfully utilised, although the courts have tended to avoid using the term 'necessity', preferring instead to declare that D's conduct was 'not unlawful'. For example, in *Bourne* (1939), it was not an offence under the OAPA 1861 to perform an abortion on a 14-year-old girl who had been raped. It is important to note that at the time in question abortion was unlawful in England and Wales.

In this case the court held that the defendant, who was a doctor, had acted lawfully given that he had acted in good faith and in the best interests of the patient.

One of the most memorable cases in English criminal law is the case of *R v Dudley and Stephens* (1884). In this case the defendants were shipwrecked and adrift in a lifeboat for several days. Before long their supply of food and fresh water ran out and Dudley and Stephens agreed to kill the cabin boy in order to eat his flesh. This would ensure that they did not starve to death. Shortly after they had committed the murder they were consequently put on trial for the murder of the cabin boy. They claimed 'necessity': that the murder of the cabin boy was a necessity if they were both to survive. The court rejected the defence of necessity and the defendants were convicted of murder.

Over the passage of time there have been a number of unsuccessful attempts to run the defence of necessity for example *London Borough of Southwark v Williams* (1971). Thus many commentators have suggested that the defence of necessity is rarely acknowledged in English Law. Although it is important to note that does not mean that the circumstances surrounding the commission of an offence are not considered at all, but in most cases these arguments feed into arguments that mitigate the defendant's sentence. In the case of *Re A* (2000), however, the court appear to have clearly accepted the existence of a defence of necessity.

Case precedent – *Re A [Children] (Conjoined Twins: Surgical Separation)* [2001] 2 WLR 480

Facts: Twins Mary and Jodie were conjoined, and their parents' religion opposed the doctors' advice that the twins should undergo an operation to separate the two children. The hospital applied to the courts for permission to perform the operation without the parents consent. The case was very controversial because the doctors know that if the operation to separate the children took place the weaker twin would certainly die. However, if the operation was not performed both twins would certainly die.

Principle: Necessity and homicide

Application: The Court of Appeal ruled that it would be lawful for the hospital to perform the operation in the absence of the parents consent. The doctors in this case would be afforded the defence of necessity.

Following the case of **Re A** it would appear that the defence of necessity consists of the following elements:

❖ D commits the offence in order to avoid inevitable and irreparable evil;
❖ no more is done than is necessary to avoid the evil;
❖ the evil inflicted is proportionate to the evil avoided;
❖ the offence is one that attracts the defence.

It is helpful to know that the defence of duress (which we will consider next), has expanded to such an extent that the development of the defence of necessity is to all intents and purposes restricted to cases which are extreme or extraordinary in nature. In reality, the development of the defence of duress of circumstances has reduced the scope of necessity. Any future development of the defence is likely to be restricted to extreme or extraordinary cases.

In the next section of this chapter we are going to consider a related defence, the defence of duress. A key distinction between these two related defences is illustrated in the diagram below.

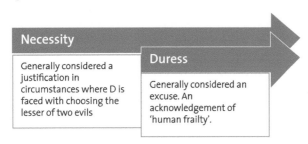

Duress

There are two types of duress: duress by threats and duress of circumstances. When answering a question in which consideration of duress is necessary you must distinguish between the two species and not simply use the term duress. The examiner will need to see that you understand the defence in detail in order to award high marks.

Duress by threats

The defence of duress applies in situations where the defendant is overborne by threats to himself, or another person. The defendant commits a criminal offence to avoid those threats being carried out.

In the case of duress by threats the defendant is admitting that he committed the *actus reus* of the offence with the requisite *mens rea* for the offence. However, the defendant is claiming that at the commission of the offence there were circumstances in existence that excuse the defendant's actions. In essence this defence is a recognition of human frailty. In the case of *Hasan* (2005) Lord Bingham said that a defendant acting under duress is 'morally innocent'. This defence is one which recognises human frailty.

Common Pitfall

Whilst duress by threats and duress of circumstances are general defences neither form of duress is available to a charge of murder or attempted murder – so watch out for this in an exam question.

In the case of *Hasan* (2005) the House of Lords confirmed that the defence operates on the basis of excuse rather than justification. In order for the defence to succeed the following elements need to be present.

A threat

The threat must be one of serious bodily harm or death: *Dao* (2012). A threat of serious psychological injury will not suffice: *Baker* (1997). The threats may be directed at the defendant or the defendant's family. The D can rely on this defence even if he is not in the presence of those making the threats; for example, if D's partner is being held hostage and has been threatened. This was established in the case of *Hurley and Murray* (1967).

The threat must be immediate

The defendant must believe that the threat of death or serious physical harm will occur immediately, or almost immediately, unless he commits the offence: *Quayle* (2005). It is important to exercise caution here, because duress does not provide a defence to a person who unreasonably fails to escape or avoid the threat. The key question here is what is reasonable in the circumstances. This will depend on the nature of the threat and the D's reasons for not going to the police, for example. The opportunity to escape, or go to the police must be assessed at the time at which the threat is made.

Case precedent – *R v A* [2003]

Facts: D was charged with possession of heroin and crack cocaine with intent to supply. She was caught with her boyfriend, and said that she had acted under duress by threats from J, a gang member, who had threatened to kill her in the past.

Principle: Duress by threats – immediacy

Application: On appeal, it was held that whether there was an opportunity to escape was a question that arose when the defendant committed the crime. Whether she had an earlier opportunity to escape.

Test

It is important to note that in order for the defence to succeed the defendant must have believed that the threat will be carried out. This in itself is not sufficient and a person of reasonable firmness sharing the same characteristics as the D would have also given in to the threat: *Howe* (1987).

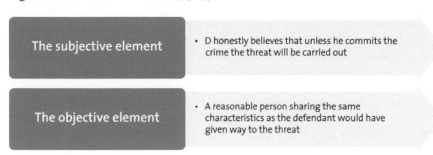

The subjective element — • D honestly believes that unless he commits the crime the threat will be carried out

The objective element — • A reasonable person sharing the same characteristics as the defendant would have given way to the threat

A person of reasonable firmness would have responded as the defendant did

A defendant can only rely on the defence if he meets an external, objective standard, which is that person of reasonable firmness sharing the defendant's characteristics would have acted as the defendant did: *Graham* (1982).

❖ Evidence that D was unusually pliable or vulnerable is irrelevant: *Horne* (1994); *Hegarty* (1984).
❖ Age, sex, pregnancy, disability and serious mental illness are relevant characteristics: *Bowen* (1997).
❖ Post-traumatic stress disorder was accepted as a relevant characteristic in *Sewell* (2004).

Don't forget – that the reasonable person is sober and possesses reasonable fortitude. If a D cannot reach the standard of reasonable fortitude because of alcohol or drugs, the defence will not be available: *Flatt* (1996).

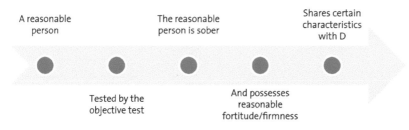

A reasonable person

Tested by the objective test

The reasonable person is sober

And possesses reasonable fortitude/firmness

Shares certain characteristics with D

Limitations

The defence of duress is limited in certain situations. We will now explore these limitations. It is important that you are able to articulate the limitations of this defence in a problem or essay question.

Voluntary association with known criminals or criminal gangs

D cannot rely on this defence if he voluntarily assumed the risk of being compelled to do something against his will, by associating with criminals or criminal gangs.

In *Fitzpatrick* (1977), duress by threats was not a defence to a charge of robbery committed as a result of threats from the IRA, because D had voluntarily joined that organisation.

In the case of *Sharp* (1987), D was party to a conspiracy to commit robbery. He said that he wanted to pull out when he saw that the others had guns. E threatened to 'blow his head off' if he did not carry on with the plan. In the course of the robbery, E killed V. It was held that where a person has voluntarily and with knowledge of its nature, a criminal organisation or gang which he knew might bring pressure on him to commit an offence, and was an active member when he was put under pressure, he cannot avail himself of the defence of duress by threats. D's conviction for manslaughter in this case was upheld.

Murder and attempted murder

The defence of duress is not available to a charge of murder: *Howe* (1987). Similarly, it is not available to a charge of attempted murder: *Gotts* (1992). Following the case of *Ness* (2011), it would seem that a claim of duress is available to a defendant charged with conspiracy to murder.

A summary of the points we have covered in this section is:

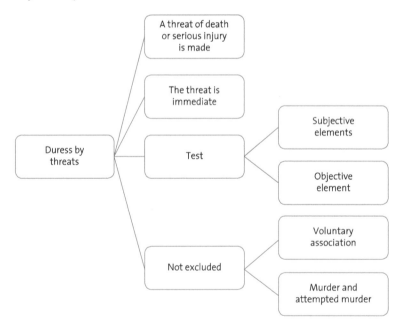

Duress of circumstances

The defence of duress of circumstances arises when a defendant commits an offence as a result of a threat of death or serious injury from the existing circumstances. The threat may come from others, or as a result of the circumstances. What is significant about duress of circumstances is that although there may be threats from others the defendant in this case has not been threatened to comply with a threat.

Duress by threats	• Threats come from a person or persons • There is a threat to comply

Duress of circumstances	• Threat from person(s) or circumstances • No threat to comply

Aim Higher

In recent years there has been some discussion about the relationship between necessity and duress of circumstances. It was decided in *Pommell* (1995) that duress of circumstances is governed by the same principles as duress by threats. This means that the harm sought to be avoided must be death or serious injury. Significantly, it was held that duress of circumstances should be a general defence to all crimes except murder, attempted murder and treason.

Case precedent – *Martin* [1989] 1 All ER 652

Facts: D, who was disqualified from driving, drove his stepson, who had overslept to work. He said that he did so because his wife feared that the son would lose his job, and she threatened to commit suicide if D did not drive him.

Principle: Duress of circumstances

Application: The defence of duress of circumstances should have been left to the jury, although this is actually a case of duress by threats: *'drive or else'*.

The elements of the defence are as follows:

A threat ⇨ By person or circumstances ⇨ Threat must be external ⇨ Test ⇨ Proportionate ⇨ Limitations

In the next illustration you can see a case law timeline through which the parameters of the defence have been refined.

Willer (1986)	*Conway* (1988)	*Martin* (1989)	*Pommell* (1995)

We will now consider the different elements of the defence.

There must be a threat
The threat posed to the defendant must be one of death or serious injury: *Martin* (1989). The threat can be to the accused or to others.

The threat is caused by the circumstances, or posed by others
In the case of duress of circumstances the duress is a result of the circumstances the defendant finds himself in, or as a result of a threat posed by other persons. It is not, however, the result of a direct threat to comply: *Cole* (1994).

The threats must be external
In order for the defence of duress of circumstances to succeed the threats must be external to the defendant. So the suicidal thoughts of the defendant cannot amount to duress of circumstances: *Rodger* (1998).

D must only do what is reasonably necessary to avoid the threat
There is an expectation that the D would do everything possible to avoid the threat or circumstances which put D under duress. If D does not act on these, then this could impact on the success of the defence.

The defendant must meet the requirements of the test
In the case of duress of circumstances the test is whether the defendant acted as he did because of what he reasonably believed to be the situation. The defendant must have had good reason to fear that death or serious injury would result, and a sober person of reasonable firmness would have acted as the defendant did. Once again there is an objective and subjective element to the test.

The response of the defendant is proportionate
In the case of *DPP v Bell* (1992), D escaped a threat of serious harm by driving, despite having consumed alcohol. It was held that if D drives off in fear of his life when he has consumed alcohol, he does not commit an offence if he stops driving after the threat has ceased. This was the case here. Thus the defendant's response must be proportionate to the risk posed.

Limitations to the defence
The defence of duress of circumstances is not available to a charge of murder or attempted murder: *Pommell* (1995). In *S(C)* (2012) the defence was unavailable to a charge of removing a child from England and Wales contrary to the **Child Abduction Act 1984**.

Now look at the example below, and consider how this would apply:

Example: Archie has a party at his house. Three men he has not met before turn up, and one starts flirting with Archie's girlfriend. Archie is upset and asks them to leave. Later that evening, Archie receives a phone call to say that the three men are coming back to the house 'to get him'. Archie fears that the men will kill him or cause him serious harm, so he gets into his car and drives to his grandmother's house, seven miles away, passing the men on the road. They are walking away from the house and do not try to chase him. Further up the road Archie is stopped by the police and found to be drink driving.

Could Archie use duress of circumstances as a defence? Work through the steps below:

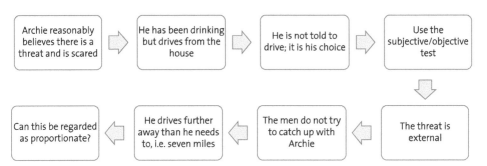

This case situation arose in *Crown Prosecution Service v Brown* (2007). The court found that when the police stopped D, he was not acting under a threat from the men, as he knew they were not pursuing him. The threat had passed, the defendant's response was not proportionate as the threat had passed, and the defendant no longer had reasonable grounds for suspecting the threat still existed. D could have stopped the car as soon as the threat passed.

A summary of the points we have covered in this section is:

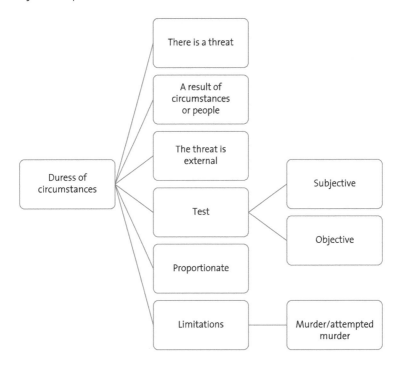

Mistake

In this section we are going to consider the impact that mistake can have on a defendant's criminal liability. In essence this is an argument that D has made a mistake and that the mistake should either excuse or justify D's actions.

The following points should be borne in mind in relation to this defence.

❖ The vast majority of mistakes do not impact on criminal liability.
❖ A mistake as to the law is no defence.

Generally, the plea of mistake is either a denial of the *mens rea*, or an assertion that, had the facts been as the defendant believed them to be, he would have had a defence to the crime with which he is charged.

This defence is unlike the other defences that we have considered in this chapter and the previous one, as there are no particular elements of the 'defence'. Put simply, it depends on the type of mistake and the circumstances.

Mistake of fact negating *mens rea*

Think about the offence of theft – suppose the defendant mistakes another's property for his own when he appropriates it. This would affect liability for the offence. In this situation the defendant has made a mistake in relation to the *actus reus* for the offence of theft (in this case D believes that the property belongs to him). This mistake of fact in relation to the *actus reus* invalidates D's *mens rea*. In other words, the defendant in this case does not make a dishonest appropriation of property belonging to another and there is no intention to permanently deprive the owner of it.

The authority on this defence is *DPP v Morgan* (1975), which is considered below.

Case precedent – *DPP v Morgan* [1975] AC 182

Facts: V was raped by two of her husband's friends, whom he had invited home to have sex with his wife. He said her protests were a sign of her pleasure.

Principle: Mistake

Application: D claimed mistaken belief in consent, and the House of Lords held that D would not be guilty of rape if he honestly, albeit mistakenly, believed that V consented to sexual intercourse.

It is important to note that this case is no longer good law in relation to sexual offences and consent.

Mistake and self-defence

It is settled law that a defendant who mistakenly believes that he is under attack may still rely on the defence of self-defence. In these circumstances the defendant is judged on the facts as he believed them to be: *Williams (Gladstone)* (1987).

Now look at the two cases of *Williams (Gladstone)* (1987) and *Beckford v R* (1987). In both cases it was held that D is to be judged on the facts as he believed them to be, thus emphasising the subjective nature of the test. In both of these cases the defendants made honest mistakes as to whether force was necessary.

According to Lord Lane in *Williams*, the reasonableness of a defendant's belief is only relevant in deciding whether he actually held that belief. The more unreasonable a belief, the less likely it is that D would have held it.

Mistake induced by alcohol or drugs

We have already discussed intoxication in the previous chapter. If a defendant makes a mistake as a result of voluntary intoxication, he cannot rely on the defence of mistake: *O'Grady* (1987); *O'Connor* (1991).

A summary of the points we have covered in this section is:

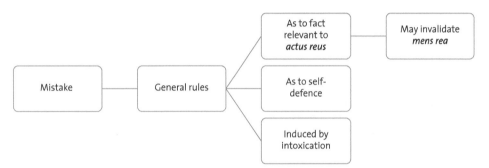

Putting it into practice

Question 1

Tamar is frightened of Emily, who regularly bullies and abuses Tamar. One evening Emily tells Tamar that she will kill Tamar if she doesn't drive to the shop to buy Emily more vodka. Tamar, who has been drinking, fears that Emily will carry out her threat if she does not comply. Tamar gets in her car and drives to the local shop to buy more alcohol. Tamar loses control of the car and hits a pedestrian, who is killed instantly.

Suggested solution

Remember that it is crucial that you construct liability for an offence before moving on to consider the availability of any defence!

Follow the normal process for constructing liability:

1. **Identify the crime**
2. **Define the crime**
3. **Explain the AR of the offence**
4. **Explain the MR of the offence**
5. **Consider relevant defences**

In this question there are two primary offences: one which relates to driving under the influence of alcohol and one that relates to the death of the pedestrian. In a case like this we would suggest that you start with the most serious offence. This is a homicide offence. You can discount murder because Tamar does not have an intention to kill or cause GBH. This factor also rules out voluntary manslaughter because that is a charge of murder reduced to voluntary manslaughter through the existence of a special partial defence. This leaves involuntary manslaughter. You can consider both constructive manslaughter and gross negligence manslaughter. You will need to work your way through the elements of each offence, applying the principles of law to the question. Once you have constructed liability for one of the offences you can then consider the existence of a defence.

You could start by explaining that duress can take two forms: duress by threats and duress of circumstances. In this case we have a threat to comply, therefore duress by threats would seem to be the appropriate species of duress. The elements that you will need to consider are:

1. Is there a threat – is it of death or serious injury?
2. Is the threat one of immediate harm – did Tamar have an opportunity to escape the threat?
3. Did the threat cause Tamar to commit the offence?
4. Test – she will need to satisfy the subjective and objective elements of the test for duress.
5. Does the scenario fall into one of the exceptions/limitations?

Key Points Checklist

There is a lack of clarity regarding whether the defence of necessity exists and, if it does, what its parameters are. The key cases in relation to necessity are *Dudley v Stephens* and *Re A*. Following *Re A* it would appear that a defence of necessity does exist but only in extreme circumstances.	✔
The defence of necessity involves a claim by the defendant that they were forced to act as they did to avert a greater harm occurring.	✔
Duress may be as a result of threats or circumstances. These are general defences although they are limited in applicability. Duress of either type is not available to a charge of murder or attempted murder.	✔
Duress by threats requires: a threat of death or serious injury; the threat is immediate and provides little opportunity for the defendant to alert the authorities or escape the threats; D must reasonably believe that the threat will be carried out (subjective); it must also be demonstrated that a man of reasonable firmness sharing the characteristics of D would have been unable to resist the threats; D must not fall into one of the excluded categories or be charged with committing an excluded offence.	✔

Duress of circumstances requires: a threat of death or serious injury; from a person or circumstances; the threat must be external; D must meet the subjective and objective test; D's response must have been proportionate; it must not be an excluded offence.	✔
In relation to mistake, the general rule is that mistake does not affect liability and mistake as to the law is no defence. Mistake as to fact where it impacts on *actus reus* may invalidate *mens rea*. Mistake as to self-defence may operate as a defence. Mistake induced by intoxication is no defence.	✔

Table of key cases referred to in this chapter

Key case	Brief facts	Principle
DPP v Morgan [1975] AC 182	V was raped by two of her husband's friends, whom he had invited home to have sex with his wife. He said her protests were a sign of her pleasure.	Mistaken belief as to AR
Re A [Children] (Conjoined Twins: Surgical Separation) [2001] 2 WLR 480	Doctors requested permission from the court to separate twins who may otherwise die	Necessity and homicide
R v A [2003]	D was found in possession of illegal drugs, and said she was scared of J, who had threatened to kill her some time ago	Duress by threats – immediacy
Martin [1989] 1 All ER 652	D was disqualified from driving, but drove his stepson to work after his wife threatened to kill herself	Duress of circumstances

---

@ Visit the book's companion website to test your knowledge

❖ Resources include a subject map, revision tip podcasts, downloadable diagrams, MCQ quizzes for each chapter, and a flashcard glossary

❖ www.routledge.com/cw/optimizelawrevision

Index

and aware of his presence, before finally drifting off herself.

Ann was up and about, long before Vince awoke the next morning. She spent all day running errands and settling in while he did little but rest. Just for once, he put aside his driving obsession to make *them* pay and he just enjoyed the moment. The rest of his life might well be akin to hell but Ann was his Guardian Angel.

Vincent insisted their first day in the unit together should be treated as special. He ordered Ann to go buy a bottle of cheap, fizzy plonk with which to toast the event. Spaghetti bolognaise was washed down with the poor quality wine after tumblers had been duly raised as the meal began.

Vince measured his intake carefully, making sure Ann had much more than her share. At eight-thirty they put him to bed, but tonight he was wide-awake and demanded she go shower and return in her sexiest night attire. Poor Ann only had her knitted cotton nighties, so he said to make do with just a towel.

Twenty minutes later, she walked coyly into the bedroom with the white hospital towel around her in the style of a sarong. He beckoned her around to his side of the bed. As she got within range, he reached out around her and slid his hand from the back of her knee up to her buttocks.

He felt her flinch, but just as quickly lean a little weight onto the palm of his hand. As she stood there with arms by her sides, he reached over with his other hand and gently tugged at the towel until it fell away.

Now it was his turn to gasp. Never before had he seen such sheer beauty of form. The ivory-white skin shimmered and the odd few drops of water, left behind from the shower, reflected in the light and stood out like pearls on satin. Thighs, hips, waist, navel and neck were perfect and the breasts stood as tight and proud as spinnakers in a force ten gale.

Through the beauty of those breasts, Vincent could see Ann's face looking down at him. She was no longer timid or embarrassed. It wasn't so much a smile on her face as a look of both desire and exaltation.

She reached out her hand and gently touched his hair. The movement caused him to lower his gaze. A massive jet-black downy triangle lurked invitingly under the perfect curve of that pure white belly.

He drew her closer to the edge of the bed and then licked and kissed the beautiful white area above the forbidden forest whilst his hand slid between her legs. Even though it was a warm evening, her whole body was shaking. She gently cradled his head to her.

This was what Ann had been saving herself for all her life. She started to climb up onto the high bed but Vincent gently bade her go and get the baby oil from the bathroom.

For the next two hours, Vincent put on a virtuoso performance. He examined every inch of that body with eyes, hands, lips and tongue. Sometimes he had her squealing and heaving. In quieter moments, he applied oil and massage. During all this time, the light was on and Ann stayed on top of the sheets.

Only Vincent's torso was uncovered early on, as far as his waist. Ann kissed, nibbled, caressed and fondled his upper body. She understood his limited movement and was happy to put herself over him in any position he required. Nothing needed to be said. Just a gentle pressure from him, this way or that, was enough for her to understand what he was trying to do. She also rearranged herself now and then to her own best advantage.

Not for the first time that night she finally whispered 'enough' and Vincent, aching and sore in every muscle he could feel, finally decided his duty was done. As he lay on his back sweating and panting, Ann put her head in the crook between his chest and shoulder, draped her arm across his chest and was asleep within a minute.

This night it was Vincent's turn to lie there, wide-awake, until the small hours. He loved his girl. But he still hated the world.

Next morning Ann woke up glowing like the setting sun. She kissed Vincent tenderly, bounced out of bed, full of vitality, and buzzed around all day just like a Duracell toy. Vincent could only sit there marvelling at her energy.

She had registered with the local private nursing agency, who had promised her all the work she could handle.

Today she telephoned to confirm that, as from tomorrow, she would be 'on call'. By the time she had put the phone down she was booked to do two five-hour shifts on her first day.

There was never going to be a shortage of well-paid work, and because she was willing and able to make herself available at any time of the day or night, most of the pay was loaded with unsocial hours rates.

The pair lived like misers. No takeaway or ready meals in that home. Just honest to goodness, straightforward cooking. Not only was it cheap, it was also wholesome. When Ann was out working, Vince pored over his books and organised his case against the hospital.

He minimised his legal costs by doing as much work as he was able himself but money to pay solicitors was always going to be a problem. He was clearly aware just how much a full-scale court case against the hospital authorities, with their unlimited defence resources, would cost.

The advice he had been given all along was to arbitrate and settle but he wanted his day in court. He wanted to tell the world how the system had let him down.

When Ann wasn't at work, she was always busy. Vincent was the centre of her world. No, he *was* her world. The unit was spotless, the housework always done on time, meals prepared and Vincent's medical and practical needs tended to. Any spare time after that was spent discussing the case, working on strategies, and planning how they would spend their eventual payout.

Once in bed, the roles were reversed. Vincent took over as the provider. Such was Ann's libido that it was a case of him lighting the blue touch-paper and hanging on however he could. He was forever trying to come up with different initiatives to keep things fresh. This was his way of rewarding her for being his whole life, his love and his reason for living.

Sadly for him, though, these encounters were just a labour of love. Not that he didn't enjoy his work, but somehow he was like a diabetic with a sweet tooth working in a chocolate factory. The sexual athletics left him cold, but his life had become dogged by the one big fear. Like Ruby in the classic Kenny Rogers song, would Ann ever feel the need to take her love to town?

Chapter 6

It took just three months for the first offer to come from the hospital's defence team. It was a ten thousand pounds *ex-gratia* payment with no liability to be admitted and with a secrecy clause.

Not even when the offer was upgraded to include repayment of his legal fees did Vincent do anything but scoff and reject it out of hand. How could ten thousand pounds be considered as compensation for the destruction of his life?

Of course, the hospital had a different view. They were of the attitude that, far from destroying Vincent's life, they had saved it. They also argued that the nerve damage had occurred either during the crash or as a result of Vincent having not been more carefully dealt with at the scene of the accident. The offer of any payment at all was very much, according to them, a goodwill gesture.

Vincent would have liked to have isolated a single culprit at the hospital. He wanted a name to focus on. He wanted the person responsible for his condition. The angry young man would dearly like to pin the blame onto somebody. He wanted justice but he also wanted vengeance. Someone had destroyed his life. He felt he needed to return the favour.

Trying to piece together the events of the night of the injury was not easy. The track doctor was keeping his head down. Everyone knew he was drunk and useless on the night but proving such a thing would be almost impossible, and going the next step and proving the permanent damage was a direct result of his inaction, out of the question.

It was neither fair nor reasonable to place blame on the St. John Ambulance staff. They were fine for picking up and dusting down those riders who had simply tumbled, but were out of their depth with serious injury.

Even Vincent recognised the other riders and helpers had done the best thing in shovelling him into the ambulance as fast as they could and not worrying about possible further damage. You don't have time to deal with the niceties when faced with a dying man.

Full marks, too, for the ambulance driver and St John Sergeant, standing in for the absent doctor, who had administered mouth to mouth on the way to the hospital. Vincent made a note to find and thank them.

Moving on to the hospital, the junior registrar had hit the panic button straight away and the emergency team had done their bit.

Who should have taken responsibility from there? The duty neurosurgeon was on the scene within a couple of hours but by the time he had arrived, the rider had been fully wired and tubed up. There, at that stage, the negligence had taken place. Vincent's physical condition should have been fully checked out, but who should have arranged for it?

Should it have been the junior registrar in casualty? Effectively he had passed responsibility to the emergency response team. They had done their bit, as had the senior duty registrar. In the intensive care unit, the staff had stabilised the lad and set him up on the machines.

The consultant neurosurgeon, rightly or wrongly, assumed the other injuries had been looked at and all necessary steps taken. No, he hadn't checked to make sure. Even at that stage, the reason was obvious.

To all intent and purpose, the boy had been dead. Fortunately for him, the consultant had never actually put his thoughts into writing.

From then on, the interest the surgeon had shown had been cursory at best. As far as he was concerned, this had now become a case for the nursing staff and the administration. Yes, he had glanced at the notes on his rounds but scarcely laid a hand on the patient. There had been no point. Hadn't the junior registrar in ICU performed all the routine tests the day after admission, and hadn't there been auto response in the lad's limbs then?

There was nothing at that time to suggest a spinal problem. And in any case, what was the point in going through the whole gambit of tests on a man who was effectively dead?

The irony was, it had been Ann, and the other duty nurses whom, in carrying out their routine nursing duties of bathing and turning Vincent regularly, had sawn through the spinal nerves.

What had saved Vincent's life was also the reason why he had become paraplegic. It was the 'spare parts' attitude of the senior hospital staff and the chance to get their hands on fresh meat. Without that, Vincent would have been buried, along with his broken back, weeks before his eventual recovery.

The derisory ten thousand pound offer was to prove to be the next huge stepping stone in the lives of Ann and the wheelchair-bound ex-rider. The offer had been a pittance but was enough for his legal team to get together and agree to continue with the action against the hospital without pre-payment of their fees and costs.

American lawyers called such arrangements 'pro bono' or for free. Technically, this was not the case here. The lawyers simply decided to do their work 'on account', although knowing full well, should the case be lost, there would be no chance of them ever receiving payment.

There was a condition attached though. The lawyers were aware Vincent was after more than compensation. He was on a crusade, and legal people know there is little profit in crusades.

They needed to take final decision-making out of the hands of this highly-strung young man and put it under the control of more objective people. Specialist people, who made their not inconsiderable wealth from knowing when to hold 'em and when to fold 'em in the poker game called litigation.

Vincent was reluctant to relinquish his decision-making authority but Ann was able to talk him round. She had no complaints about the couple's lifestyle or all the hours she was working but she listened carefully to the legal team when they explained their reasoning.

Not least in her thoughts was that, should the matter end up in court, and then there be an appeal, no amount of extra hours she might be able to work was going to cover the costs involved. She also accepted that once the hospital's legal team were aware the couple had legal backing and couldn't simply be starved into submission, the scales would be tipped significantly in the plaintiff's direction.

And so, in one of the their many discussions on the subject, Vincent and Ann made another round of decisions. They would accept their legal team's offer of help but would carry on living the life they had set up. All of Ann's income that had accrued so far, and all she earned in future would go into an investment fund. Vincent would set his legal books to one side and let the professionals deal with those things from there on. Instead, he would go down an entirely different track and learn all about investing.

After careful examination, Vincent decided that there was money to be made in the markets for someone with a little common sense, a little knowledge and a lot of guts. Most important for him, not having the use of the bottom part of the body was not a hindrance. In fact, it crystallised the mind and helped to replace hope with determination.

The pair set themselves no goals and no targets at this stage. With 'business' meetings between them happening every day, they didn't need to.

Vincent, however, declared they would spend just a little each month on small indulgences. Not a night on the town or a bottle of French champagne, but a sex toy. His life still revolved around only two things: revenge and making Ann happy.

First month a vibrator, second a couple of hardcore porn videos, followed by a set of dildos. Next, a pair of handcuffs and a soft leather whip was purchased. They combined well with the gantry and hoist over his bed. These toys gave Vincent no sexual satisfaction. His only concern was to see Ann content enough not to want to take her love to town.

Vincent at first stuck all of Ann's accumulated wages into blue chip stocks, even though there was a double-figure interest rate to be had on cash. He reasoned that as the interest rates dropped, which surely they must, the stocks would rise. He didn't feel he was experienced enough to be able to time the turn precisely and reckoned he would be better to go early rather than late.

In searching for a stockbroker to take him on, he was lucky enough to hit upon a bright, young spark who had just become a junior broker in the Midlands office of a large national stockbroking company.

Mark Breeze had always enjoyed playing with figures. Even at school he had enjoyed share market games and had never come out behind. His sheer enthusiasm and knowledge of the markets had seen the branch take him on as an office boy straight after he had left school and it had been only three years before he had been given his chance as a broker.

He and Vincent hit it off from their very first telephone call. Mark quickly recognised Vincent as someone of great determination who had done his homework. Vincent identified in Mark the enthusiasm and swashbuckling approach he was looking for, backed by a great amount of knowledge in how markets worked, for one so young.

A portfolio of less than £10,000 held no interest to the more established brokers in Mark's office anyway. They would normally have simply recommended the client put his money into a unit trust but Mark was aware that, for him, just starting out, it was commission on orders that counted, not amounts invested.

Vincent was happy to keep his money turning over. The two young men spoke on the phone every working day, exchanging ideas and considering opportunities. Mark had a similar amount of money to Vincent and he came up with an idea. He would run mirror accounts for the pair of them. Whatever the one bought or sold, so the other would match it.

This way, Vincent could be confident Mark was not simply turning his money over for the commission, and Mark recognised that Vincent was not only good at assessing his 'tips' but followed the markets closely enough to come up with some good ideas of his own.

Rarely a week went by when they didn't turn their whole capital over at least once. Sometimes they made just a couple of per cent and sometimes five per cent. Rarely, they lost the trading costs on a deal, but they never actually lost any of the capital.

Mark had offered to take Vincent out for lunch after their first month of working together. Vincent turned him down and it was only when Vincent explained why he could not go that the broker found out about the paraplegia.

After discussing things with Ann, Vincent invited Mark round to their unit for lunch instead. Ann was on nights that week and so was able to cook the meal.

It was more than a small shock for Mark to see how the couple lived. Mark was prepared for the wheelchair, but he was not ready to find it occupied by someone as young as Vincent.

Vince had opened the door, showing complete dexterity with his chair. Mark's reaction was one of amazement at just how well the fellow coped. He noted the blond locks and the fresh face, but he also noticed the eyes. Those eyes seemed to miss nothing. He felt he should have checked his zip and straightened his tie before knocking.

The handshake was firm, open, and genuine though. Mark's first impression was not pity, but respect.

Ann had been at the stove. She came forward to meet Mark straight away and Vince introduced them. Mark was again struck with the youthfulness of the pair. Ann had absolutely no airs or graces. Like all 20-year-old males, Mark quickly ran her through his built-in sexometer. In the moment it took for her to smile demurely and explain she would be available in a minute, the read-out was in place.

She was good-looking but did not like to admit it, issuing absolutely no flirt signals at all, but she seemed a genuinely nice person. Isn't it amazing how quickly the human senses can assess things?

It took all of another two minutes for Mark to understand why there had been no flirtatious signals. Her love and devotion to Vincent was obviously complete and absolute.

Since having become 'an item' with Vincent, Ann had adopted a far more comfortable demeanour in the company of other men. She no longer felt challenged by them and was able to be more relaxed, as she was with Mark.

It would be difficult for her not to pick up on the stature of the man. Over 6ft tall, she decided, and well built with it. Good-looking, no doubt, and well manicured, especially for someone not yet 21.

She didn't take in the individual features, just accepting the whole was a very well put together package. 'I bet he doesn't struggle for girlfriends,' was her immediate thought.

It would be difficult not to notice just how frugally the couple lived. For them, the simple meal Ann had prepared was a banquet but for Mark it was, at best, plain. He desperately wished now he had brought flowers instead of the expensive bottle of wine, which he realised was out of place and looked ostentatious with the Shepherd's Pie and in that setting.

The young broker understood the situation even more now, and realised the responsibility he had taken on in looking out for the couple's hard-earned money. Mark could see and understand the bitterness in Vince and, alongside this, his love for Ann. He vowed he would never let them down.

Chapter 7

It took a tick over six months for the two young men to double their money, with Ann's weekly contribution pushing Vincent's capital sum up even more than Mark's. If he had a free evening, Mark had taken to telephoning Vince as he was leaving the office and dropping in with a take-away meal. The three young people became firm friends.

Settling Vincent's claim against the hospital took well over a year of bluff and counter-bluff, but finally the two litigant sides came up with a deal. The figure they agreed on would see Vincent receive a net sum of £195,000.

It came as no surprise to his legal team that Vince still wanted his day in court and hated the idea of the secrecy clause, but that was what the lawyers thought was a good deal, and when Ann agreed with them, Vincent finally accepted it with good grace.

What would the couple do with their money? Ann decided to let Vincent make the decision. She would back him in whatever he wanted to do, but she made him go through the whole pitch before letting him decide how best to use their payout.

'One more year.' he said. 'Twelve months in this same place doing the same things.'

Well, not quite. Ann would cut down from her current working average of 10 hours a day, sometimes six days a week and at all hours of the day and night. Vincent even suggested she could give up completely if she wanted but she wisely pointed out this would not be good. She needed to keep her hand in, whilst he needed time during the day to work and study. Both were fed up with cheap cuts and no frills.

So the new deal between them was this: Twelve more months in which to invest all of their accrued capital plus the payout from the hospital so as to increase their capital to a greater amount, but they could use Ann's income to spend in the meantime. They would also each treat themselves to a little something out of the lump-sum payment.

Vincent decided on a multi-gym in place of his old fashioned weights. Ann, for the first time since they had got together, was a little coy, but what she ended up with was the bedroom being covered with mirrors, mood lighting, from subtle deep colours to bright halogen spots and strobes, and a multi-channel, multi-speaker, wall-to-wall hi-fi system.

The wall at the bottom of the bed was the only one not mirrored. It was painted off-white and used as a huge screen for a video projector.

Much of Ann's now freed up income went on personal items. Working so hard and leading such an inventive private life, along with the plain but wholesome cooking, had kept her in the peak of condition.

Now though, she could discard the baby oil in favour of expensive aromatherapy and massage oils. Nestle's milk and liquid honey was replaced with a variety of body chocolate and delicately flavoured sauces. Cheap soap and water made way for all kinds of skin cleansing and toning products.

Only half way through his second year in the position, Mark was already beginning to become noticed as an outstanding broker. His client list had grown and his success rate was excellent. He came round to the unit with a bottle of Dom Perignon champagne and Belgian chocolates to celebrate the couple's settlement with the hospital authorities.

Vincent explained to Mark what he and Ann wanted to do. The payout would be used to carry on investing the way they had been. Yes, the method had been aggressive and a touch risky here and there, but it had worked.

This was no time to get cold feet and back away just because the figures were greater. Well, maybe they would be a touch more conservative, but the aim was to double the payout money within 12 months. In a rising market, neither felt that an unreasonable aim.

Ann's salary-driven investments now topped £28,000. Not bad for well inside of 18 months dabbling in shares. Vince and Mark had often toyed with the idea of playing the options market. It cut out a lot of the smaller stocks but the leverage to be gained was enormous if you could afford to gamble a bit. Once again Vincent got as many books from the library as he could find and learned all about how the business worked.

Mark was happy to go down the options path as well and, again, agreed to match Vincent's portfolio with a mirror one of his own. This time, though, amounts would be slightly different. Originally, Mark had matched the £10,000 put in by Vince pound for pound. Because his portfolio had not been constantly added to with Ann's weekly income, Mark's was now worth a little over £18,000. He decided to take some of his 'winnings' out so as to upgrade his car, but still matched Vincent's remaining 25 grand (after taking out money to pay for their 'treats') with £10,000 of his own. They were still in it together though.

Soon after this, Mark was offered a position in his firm's London office. This was a huge step up and one he could not refuse. It meant leaving a good deal of his client list behind him, but it represented a massive leap up the ladder and one he certainly could not miss.

As soon as Mark was made aware of the promotion to the Head Office in the City of London, he once again popped into the unit with another bottle of bubbly. He told his friends he was off to London, like Dick Whittington, to make his fortune but, if Vincent wanted, they could carry on with their arrangements. The daily conference calls would continue and would simply need to be a little earlier each day, but that was the only downside.

On the upside, being in London would give Mark quicker access to breaking news and to reports, he would be closer to the options markets and, even more important, to the whispering gallery that makes up the inner sanctum of the broking industry.

Life carried on much the same for Vincent and Ann for another 12 months. Satin sheets and sex games at night, and hard work all round during the day. Mark was true to his word. Every morning he arrived into work at least a half-an-hour before needed and phoned Vince.

The 'conservative' portfolio they had set up using the injury payout money more than doubled in value, with Mark's ability now to get his hands on new stock issues and the hottest of hot stocks.

Vincent kept his eye on things, but had now turned his attention to the tax implications involved with making decent money.

He learned all about trust funds and offshore accounts and how to minimise the payment of taxes and he was happy to spend money setting up the various accounts and systems required.

Ann was now finding these things difficult to follow but was just pleased Vince was so upbeat and positive. He had long since learned to hide his own sexual frustrations and becoming the major breadwinner helped boost his ego significantly.

Mark, however, although a shooting star in the Midlands office, was small fry in the ocean of cut-throat sharks in London EC1. Many times, the money in the options portfolio began piling up, only to get reduced again by a bad loss. He was learning with each mistake, but could the two friends hang in long enough to survive his learning curve?

Most importantly, though, Mark was gaining a reputation as a Player, making lots of contacts along the way.

Vincent's deal with Ann, for them to have one year playing the markets, was almost up. True, the main portfolio had all but doubled, meaning they could buy a nice house and still keep some money in the market, but Vincent had so nearly become very rich many times with the options deals and he had got a taste for it.

One Tuesday, early in the New Year of 1981, the telephone in the sheltered unit rang mid-morning. It was Mark, and Vincent could tell from his voice just how excited he was.

'Vince, don't ask me how I know, but there is a big deal going down. United Press are about to make a take-over bid for Dominion Holdings. You and I are aware these things are never certain until they are done, particularly because the deal will need government approval, but I am putting every penny I can lay my hands on into Dominion options.

'Of course, that's easy for me. If I lose the lot, I still have a job and a life. For you, these are the alternatives: You can put your blue chip portfolio into Dominion Shares. Your risk will be minimal and your potential profit, anything up to up to 30 per cent. We can use your options-trading money to buy Dominion options and hopefully make a small killing there.

'Or you can put the whole lot into the options, in which case you stand to see a huge gain – but you risk your whole future if things go wrong.

'Alternatively, you can put up any amount in whatever ratio between options and shares you feel comfortable with. It's your call, Vincent, but I need an answer now.'

'What are *you* doing?' asked Vincent.

'I told you, it's shit or bust for me, but I can afford to lose, can you?'

Ann wasn't there. Vincent had to make an instant decision.

'All in,' he said.

'I'll have to lay it off as best I can,' Mark pointed out. 'This is insider trading in a big way so I am going to have to duck and dive. I might not be able to get it all on in time. Just leave it with me, I'll do what I can.'

When Ann got home, Vincent told her there was the possibility of a big deal going down.

'That's your department, darling. Whatever you decide, I'll go along with.'

'What happens if I lose the lot?'

'Then I increase my hours again, my love. It really is no big deal.'

Vincent got no sleep that night. Mark had managed to lay off all the money. The one o'clock BBC radio news next day led with the breaking story of a takeover bid of one City giant by another. Mark telephoned shortly afterwards.

'Keep your fingers crossed nobody digs too deep, Vince, because you are currently worth a little over six million pounds. You can either close it out now, or sit. The options should continue to increase but there is always a danger of government intervention ruining the deal.'

'Half out now, let the other half run until you think it should come out,' advised Vincent.

'Good call,' said Mark, who was far happier gambling with winnings than with people's lives.

By the time the Competition Commission had cleared the merger, the valuation of Vince and Ann's portfolios totalled over eight million pounds. Mark, who had left all of his own monies fully invested in the options, was now worth in excess of three million. In one single deal, both Mark and Vincent had become substantially rich.

Even so, they continued to invest their monies in the markets, mostly in blue chip companies now, but they still kept a million pounds between them as 'gambling money'.

Chapter 8

Mark quickly became the darling of the broking world. He accumulated the Porsche, the serviced, top floor pad in the City, the wardrobe full of designer suits and the queue of dolly birds.

The first Sunday of every month, though, he hopped into his car with a bottle of Dom and a hamper of goodies, and drove up to spend lunchtime and the afternoon with his friend in the wheelchair. Not only was Vince his talisman, he was also the catalyst behind Mark's phenomenal success.

It wasn't merely a pilgrimage or a labour of love either. Vincent's ability to read and learn meant he could still help Mark when it came to things like tax minimisation.

Vincent and Ann waited for a couple of months just in case there were any problems from the illegal dealings but Mark had covered their tracks well. The delay hadn't stopped them from dreaming and planning, though.

The regular 'board meetings' between the two devoted lovers decreed that, provided there was no come-back from the insider trading, they would take a million out of the pot and use it to build or buy a grand place to live, and the trappings to go with it.

They also needed to decide on where to pitch their social life as well. Vince had deliberately turned his back on the speedway scene. Deep down, he was still very bitter about what had happened. He did not want to know about the continuing success of Jeff Harding who had remained at Shelford to become the undisputed number one.

Vincent had wanted neither pity nor charity from anyone within the sport. In any case, most of those he had considered friends before the crash had stayed away during those first desperate months.

Winning his case against the hospital had enabled him to reward Ann for her love and loyalty, but the secrecy clause had meant the only loser had been the hospital's insurer. Neither the hospital itself, nor any individual who worked there, had been punished at all. Not yet, anyway.

Being an agency nurse, Ann was constantly meeting new people. She got on well with everyone but did not cultivate anyone in particular.

She loved her work, and helping others, but had no interest in the other nurses' small-talk or the petty intrigues of the various hospitals and clinics she worked in. She laughed off advances from young doctors. She had all she wanted in Vincent.

Ann suggested Vincent should consider taking an active role with other wheelchair people. Apart from the obvious handicap, he was otherwise in fantastic shape and could no doubt 'walk' into any wheelchair team in just about all sports, from archery to basketball.

He couldn't do it, though. That would mean admitting he was handicapped – and this he would never do.

They would just have to build or find a property and then sort out their social scene afterwards.

Logically, the couple did not expect to find a suitable house. They had visions of finding a few acres and building a bungalow to their own design and Ann contacted a dozen estate agents in the South Midlands area they wanted to move to, asking about suitable sites for building their dream home. Some agents sent a variety of papers, whilst others simply said they had nothing suitable.

Dave Scott was only 23-years-old but he had been in the house-selling business since he had left school at 16. He had studied at night school and passed all the surveyors exams. Bright and ambitious, as soon as he had scraped enough money together, he had opened his own agency, Scott Homes.

His wife, Heather, had been a beauty queen in her teens and was barely out of them now. She was a stunningly beautiful, blue-eyed blonde bombshell. She had been a champion swimmer and retained a natural athlete's body. With curly, ash-blonde hair and eyes as big as bush babies', no man could refuse a second look. Wherever she went, Heather Scott turned heads.

Heather and Dave had met because her father, Charles Sturton, was also an estate agent. In fact, he owned one of the biggest agencies in the Warwickshire area. Heather was one of those bubbly, friendly people who could mix in all company. She was an unmerciful flirt, but was so open about it, nobody could decide if she was aware of the effect she had on men.

In fact, because she had had lived with her eye-catching looks all her life, she had learned to not merely cope with the attentions of men but also to use those looks to her advantage. She was tactile, a 'toucher'. She couldn't chat to a man without touching his arm or the lapel of his jacket.

The stunner was just as open with the fairer sex, but even so, one or two resented the fact that she was plainly more comfortable with men and an out and out threat to all other females.

Her and Dave had met whilst he had been working for Heather's dad. Heather had initially been amused by the young man's attitude to her. She was well used to getting a reaction from men. Some just seemed to hang their tongues out and pant like a dog; others tried to become all macho.

Dave did neither. He simply made her laugh. From the couple's first meeting onwards, he had been open and funny, with none of the bravado of the others. This is what had first attracted her.

Then her father's objections had caused her to dig her heels in long enough for her to discover just how nice a bloke he really was.

When Scott Homes was launched, Heather acted as its receptionist and secretary. She knew the industry well, although she had not worked for a couple of years. Her father had preferred to see her enjoying herself in local 'society' and she was well into the social scene of the South Midlands.

Dave and Heather had laughed their way all through their romance as Heather's dad had let it be known from the start that he regarded Dave as a wimp, and certainly not good enough for his daughter.

The wedding had been bad enough. Sturton hadn't bargained on his objections to the match bringing out his daughter's own stubborn streak. Now, having his daughter working as a receptionist in a one-man, 'tin-pot' agency, was really too far below the belt for him to stomach.

Heather had taken Ann's telephone enquiry and had put the note out for Dave. He was intrigued. 'Plot of land between two and 20 acres with outline planning, or likely approval for a single storey dwelling'.

There had to be a story here, he decided. He and Heather had plenty of contacts in the building trade, and maybe there was a chance for some ongoing business, or perhaps this was a call from a rich Arab wanting a local pad?

The enquiry just didn't fit with the Kreswick phone number or address, though. This was not an area he would have expected such an interest to come from. The name, Ann Brown, meant nothing to him.

Dave picked up the phone, spoke with Ms Brown and arranged to call round and discuss the enquiry further.

Dave checked and rechecked the address he had been given. It *was* correct. He was sitting outside a tiny unit on a local council sheltered housing development.

Putting his thoughts to one side, he knocked on the door. Vincent answered it. The young estate agent had been a speedway follower for years when he was younger and recognised the man in the wheelchair instantly. His heart skipped a couple of beats. Vincent had been the subject of his hero worship, and now he had a chance to meet the man in person. Never mind the wheelchair, Dave still regarded meeting Vincent Hansing, the former Shelford Racers No.1, as a great honour.

Dave decided to keep his thoughts, and the fact that he had recognised Vincent, to himself for the moment. He had been at the track the night Vincent had been injured and, like Vincent, had not been to the speedway since. He had been sickened by what he had seen.

That was at the time Heather and him had been planning and saving to get married. After the wedding, seeing Jeff Harding's career blossom, a disillusioned Dave had decided he really didn't want to go back to watching speedway again.

He guessed that Vincent must have felt the same about the sport they once both loved, because there was certainly no evidence of Vincent's once promising racing career in their unit. No photographs and no mementoes.

When they first moved into the unit, Ann had surprised Vincent by proudly displaying his collection of speedway trophies on the mantelpiece, including the coveted British Junior Championship he won in 1976, his first season. But an angry Vincent demanded that she remove them all immediately and they were never on show again. As far as he was concerned, he was finished with speedway.

Vincent studied the young estate agent. He was aware the principal of Scott Homes was coming over and had expected someone older.

What he saw was a barely twenty-something young man with boyish features and a ready grin. Dave wasn't tall – maybe five-nine – but he was quite solid in build. Vincent decided that within the current chunky shape there was a fat man waiting to escape.

Being friendly and disarming is the stock-in-trade of an estate agent. After all, whilst expertise is important, being able to sell oneself is crucial in the business. In this regard, he could see Dave Scott being successful. Maybe almost too successful; Vincent was sure that had Dave possessed a tail, he would be wagging it fiercely.

'That's it,' Vincent thought to himself, 'the man's a bloody spaniel!'

Over a cup of tea in the sparse living room, Vincent related to Dave some of his story. He told the agent about the eventual compensation payout and the fact that they had invested the money wisely and wanted to enjoy their success. Vincent admitted Ann and him had deliberately cut themselves off from the outside world but now felt they were ready to become involved again.

Dave remained businesslike but was inwardly delighted to have got to meet the former rider who had been his idol. That part he would remain quiet about but he was determined to do whatever he could to help the pair.

Both Vincent and Ann had warmed to the likeable young man and told him far more than they had intended. His questions were sensible. How big had they planned for the house to be? How isolated did they want the property? Dave had realised why the desire had been for a single storey residence as soon as he had seen Vincent in his wheelchair.

One of the routine questions the agent asked was, approximately how much had the couple budgeted for spending on the final finished product? This would affect the kind of plot he would be searching for.

Vincent's deadpan answer was: 'About three quarters of a million,' causing Dave to blink hard, before returning quickly to businesslike mode.

Back in the office, Dave told Heather where he had been and the identity of the mystery enquirer. She knew the name, Hansing, but that was all. Together they telephoned around every contact they knew and trawled in half-a-dozen possible sites.

Dave collected together the locations and details, before popping back to the unit with his findings. He wasn't convinced about any of the places he had come up with, but wanted to demonstrate he was on top of the job.

Sure enough, four of the six sites were rejected without even a look. Next morning, he made an appointment to take Ann and Vincent out and look at the remaining possible sites, with Heather deciding to go along for the ride.

On their being introduced, Heather's natural beauty didn't faze Ann, as it did most women. Ann had none of the defensive baggage Heather normally encountered. The two girls chatted happily in the rear of the car whilst Dave and Vincent had their own conversation in the front.

From her own cosseted upbringing, Heather could not conceive of the strength of character Ann must had needed to cope with what life had thrown at her up until now. Like her husband, Heather became determined they would do the right thing by this couple.

The group didn't even get out of the car when they arrived at the first site. It was next to a battery chicken farm. If the noise didn't get you, the smell would. The second place was a little more interesting but, again, didn't ring any excitement bells.

The four stopped at a pub for a quick ploughman's lunch on the way back. They were sitting around a table in the pub garden, enjoying the sunshine, when Heather suddenly sat up straight in her chair.

'Does it have to be a purpose-built bungalow?' she asked.

The three others looked at her as she continued.

'What you need is a place with wide doors and passageways. Is that right?'

'Don't forget the stairs and the heights in the kitchen and the specialised bathroom set-up,' said Ann.

'Well, I'm no expert,' Heather responded, 'but I'm sure what I have in mind would work with a bit of imagination and lateral thinking.'

Heather and Dave looked at each other and both said in unison: 'Foxglove Manor!'

As they drove along, Heather explained to Vincent and Ann that the place had been owned by one of the leading old families in the area. It was an 18th century manor house, now sitting in 20 acres of mainly pastureland but with a spectacular walled kitchen garden. It was approached by a superb driveway and had formal gardens to the front and sides of the house.

Over the years, the owners had fallen on hard times and the last major upgrade on the place had been some 30 or 40 years ago. Since then, it had become something of a Dickensian-style retreat for the last elderly couple in the family line.

They had been forced to sell off some of the family silver and had taken out the odd loan, using the house as surety, in order to be able to pay basic staff and running expenses. The husband had finally died and the widow was taken into care. The house had remained empty and locked up for the last couple of years. Recently the widow had died and the executors were trying to wind up the affairs.

Heather and Dave had discovered the place when it first became empty a couple of years ago. It could just be seen against the skyline from the road, through the imposing driveway entrance, with its magnificent gatekeeper's lodge, now sadly derelict. She and Dave had driven up to the Manor House and taken a look around the place. For both of them it had been love at first sight.

Dave and Heather had desperately wanted the place for themselves but it was way above what they could afford at this stage, and possibly forever. It would be nice if they could find the Manor some good owners, and they agreed that this couple deserved such a place.

What Heather had envisaged was for a smallish specialised retreat, with state of the art facilities for Vincent, to be built onto the back of the property, and for a lift to be installed alongside the magnificent winding staircase in the main entrance hall. With its huge rooms, big, wide doorways and spacious corridors, the house needed very little by way of other major works to become wheelchair-friendly.

OK, so the third floor attic servants' rooms would be out of bounds to Vincent but they were really just an extra bonus anyway.

Ann and Vincent were immediately caught up with the other couple's enthusiasm. Dave pushed the big driveway gates open enough to squeeze the car through. As soon as they saw the house on the skyline they understood why. This was *The Place*.

They were able to look beyond the sad, overgrown driveway and gardens, and the pastureland, unkempt from two years of lying fallow. The house was just magnificent. Even before they got out of the car, their minds were made up. Peeping through windows confirmed all that Heather had said about the size of doors and walkways. She had failed to mention the oak panelling, the chandeliers, the spectacular carved oak sweeping staircase and the minstrel's gallery above. This was a place where Douglas Fairbanks and Errol Flynn would have been at home.

At that stage, the house wasn't technically on the market but it no doubt soon would be. Tired of waiting for their money, the deceased couple's creditors had called in receivers.

Heather was despatched to the receiver's office. The man in charge of the case quickly fell for the young stunner's charms and loaned her the keys to The Manor.

Dave wandered around, dictaphone in one hand and tape measure in the other. This was not a run-of-the-mill property but he decided the principle involved in drawing up a list of features and working out a value was much the same. In any case, it gave him the opportunity to inspect everywhere.

Yes, there was the odd bit of peeling wallpaper here and there, and it was not surprising the place smelled damp and musty, but he could find no major structural problems. The biggest surprise was to find a huge cellar, not common in houses of this period. The cellar was in excellent condition, despite being absolutely full of junk. If anything, it was drier than the rest of the house. Great for a nice wine stock, he mused.

Meantime, the other three were wandering around, wide-eyed and amazed at the splendour of the old place. Each of them could see past the odd bits of peeling paper and the damaged plaster here and there. In this threadbare state, the place looked sad but this was a house built to last more than five minutes, and nothing had been spared in either its original construction or the various upgrades since.

Vincent even got himself up the stairs. One step at a time, he hoisted himself up backwards, whilst Dave carried the chair. He took a look around and he was pleased he had made the effort.

Whereas downstairs had shown real signs of wear and tear, only two of the six huge bedrooms on that second floor looked as if they had been used since the last major renovations.

There, still under dustsheets, was all the original furniture. Beautiful old-fashioned beds, including four posters in three of the rooms, were still made up ready to sleep in. Admittedly, the smell of stale damp still hung everywhere, and they all agreed just about all the soft furnishings would need to be replaced, but the building structure itself was in fine shape.

Dave nipped up to the third floor, where five servants' bedrooms and a bathroom were to be found. All needed decorating but there were no major structural problems.

Under instruction from Vince, Dave visited the liquidator.

'What did he think was going to happen,' Dave asked the middle-aged man?

'A country-house auction,' came the reply.

First, the house itself would be auctioned, and then the contents separately. Dave asked the man to put his idea of a valuation on the place, pointing out that not many buyers would be able to pay for the renovations and with fuel heating prices spiralling, nobody would want such a huge, draughty old shell.

The liquidator agreed that it would cost up to £200,000 to put the house and gardens right, and the chances of getting a mortgage on the place in its current state were remote.

'I suppose we will be lucky to clear £100,000 on the place as it stands,' he mused.

'And what about the internal effects?' asked Dave. 'You know they are also in a terrible state and only really good for a bonfire.'

In his excitement, Dave was beginning to get a hard on. Now was the time to strike.

'I'll tell you what,' Dave added, after a brief pause. 'I've someone who might be interested. He's a cash buyer and ready to deal now. It will cost you at least 20 grand in fees and costs if you decide to auction the place and the thing will drag on for ever. Just give me an overall cash price for the lot as it stands . . .'

The liquidator looked up his books. The outstanding debts amounted to just over £50,000, plus the costs of the paperwork and settling the estate.

'£140,000 would do it,' he said casually.

'Have you a phone?' asked Dave?

Once left in private, he got on to Vince.

'It's yours, all up, for one-forty,' he said, 'plus, of course, a drink for me.'

Vincent's answer took him by surprise but he called the liquidator back into the room.

'My client is prepared to pay £100,000 for the house and contents, plus an additional 10 thousand pounds in notes to you personally when the deal goes through.

The liquidator thought for a minute or so.

At least I've not been thrown out on my ear, Dave mused to himself.

Finally, the silence was broken.

'Ninety-five and fifteen, with seven-and-a-half up front,' said the liquidator.

Dave did not shake hands. He just nodded and said he would return in an hour with the up-front money.

The deal was concluded within three weeks. With no mortgage to negotiate, no surveys, and with solicitors on both sides keen to minimise work and maximise return, the whole thing rolled through unhindered.

'I don't think an agent's fee of five thousand quid is being greedy,' said Dave as he handed over the keys and the deeds. 'After all, I've just sold you a part of my own dreams.' Vincent nodded and wrote out a cheque for that amount.

Three days later, a brand new £15,000 Mercedes pulled up outside Dave's small estate agency. The car sales rep who had been driving it, walked into the Scott Homes office, dropped the keys into Dave's hand, and simply said:

'Courtesy of Mr Hansing.'

Vincent was sitting by the phone waiting for it to ring. He picked it up and hardly allowed Dave to launch into his thank-you speech before interrupting:

'Why don't you and Heather come round for tea tonight? There's something I want to discuss with the pair of you. Oh, and by the way, you'd better bring the food with you. We've nothing in at the moment.' Dave agreed and was about to put the phone down when Vince added quietly.

'You know I only drink Dom Perignon, don't you?'

Two bottles of the best champagne in the world and four cold pheasants, along with still warm crusty bread and butter, set Dave back a smidge over £120. He begrudged not a penny as the four friends sat down at the formica table drinking the fizz from tumblers, whilst pulling the pheasants apart and eating them with their fingers. Heather had baked an apple pie and she made custard to go with it on the small stove while the four of them chatted merrily.

As they finished their meal, Vincent took centre-stage.

'Look here,' he said, 'I know I've stolen your baby with that house and I know it's asking a lot, but do you think you would both work with the pair of us in turning it into the place of our dreams? After all, you both have the local contacts, and from the way she dresses and presents herself, we are aware that Heather has impeccable taste.

'We don't want to buy you and we recognise you want to make

54

your own way in life, so we would expect you to put your own business first, but we would really love it if you were to remain a part of our adventure.'

No discussion between the two was necessary. Dave and Heather were already nodding vigorously as their eyes met. Fees were not mentioned on either side. It was just something the four of them wanted to do.

As the girls cleared away, Vincent asked Dave to follow him into the bedroom. Dave's eyes bulged as he saw the mirrors, erotic video collection and gadgets in the room.

'Close the door behind you and come sit on the bed,' said Vince.

'You are the first person, other than Ann and myself, who has ever seen inside this room.'

As the two of them sat there, Vincent told Dave the full story of how Ann and him had met, and that his one and only disappointment in life was that he could not have normal sex with her.

He explained that in order to try and compensate for this he had resorted to sex toys and what other people might consider strange, or even a little unnatural, behaviour. He confided in Dave his biggest fear in life – that Ann might one day decide to seek elsewhere, what he could not give her.

Vincent went to some lengths to explain why he was telling all this to Dave. The new house would need to have a similar room to this one; or at least, a room to perform the same function. However, it would be as similar to this room as Dom Perignon is to lemonade.

If Dave and Heather were to help with the work on the new place, they would have to know and understand some of the secrets it would hold.

Once he recovered from his surprise, Dave leaned over towards Vincent in a conspiratorial manner.

'I'd never given that side of things a thought,' he said. 'It must be a nightmare for you. Having said that, I kind of understand about your fears maybe even more than you think. You might believe it's great to have such a beauty as Heather for a wife. It's not just the film star looks and figure, either. She just seems able to draw men like a magnet.

'She could have had her pick of the social set, you know, and she is streets ahead of me when it comes to . . . well . . . you know, sex and that kind of thing. Why she chose me, I will never know. All I do know is just how hard it is trying to live up to her and keep her happy.'

The image of Dave, the spaniel, flitted across Vincent's mind again. He gripped his newfound friend and confidante on the shoulder.

'Well one thing's for sure,' he said. 'You can be certain it won't be *me* she chooses to run away and have it off with!'

With the ice well and truly broken, Dave stood up, giving Vincent a friendly slap on the shoulder and they went to rejoin the ladies.

Chapter 9

Mark's monthly Sunday visit was scheduled for the next weekend. Vincent had managed to keep the house purchase to himself until then but as soon as Mark arrived, they were off for a look. Vincent had casually said they had bought a small but very nice property for a hundred grand, and invited his close friend to have a look.

Even when Mark, as instructed, turned through the main gates at Foxglove Manor, he never realised what was on. As they drove up the 300-yard long drive, he looked this way and that. All he could see was a huge, old manor house in front of him.

He glanced at Vincent alongside him and saw the smug look on his face. Then he looked at the manor house and back to Vince, who was nodding his head and wearing a broad grin.

Mark was as envious as he was delighted for the couple. Ann showed their friend round the place whilst Vincent wheeled himself around the ground floor, once again making mental notes of what needed to be done. Then, for the first time since he had known them, Mark took Vince and Ann out for lunch, to the local village pub just up the road.

Mark spoke with the pub landlord, then brought him over and introduced 'the couple that had taken over The Manor.' This was the quickest way he knew of spreading the word locally about who the new owners were.

The time had come for the couple to enjoy a life of total luxury. Ann gave up her job and took driving lessons. They bought a small but nippy Ford Escort for her to drive around in. Vince had hand controls added to a sleek, new BMW for himself, and to finish off the set, they imported a customised recreational vehicle from America.

It wasn't a 40-feet long Winnebago, but a smaller version fitted with an electric side door and ramp, so Vincent could get himself aboard without help. Ann soon passed her test, and although initially nervous, did the driving of the motor home whilst Vincent could sit at a desk, either working or relaxing.

Ann suggested Vincent might like a motorised chair but he refused. He had become so adept at using his arms to propel himself along, it was quicker for him that way. Mainly though, Vincent realised that by using a motorised chair, he would become lazy and his muscle tone would suffer far too quickly.

They did, though, get him a motorised golf buggy, modified with hand controls, so he could get around the grounds.

On the way home from the Hansings' tiny unit the night they had celebrated the purchase of The Manor, Dave had told Heather all about Vince and Ann's bedroom.

'Who would have believed such a thing?' was all she could say.

Some weeks after that evening, Dave had to take Vincent to a business meeting. Heather went to the unit and stayed with Ann whilst the men were away. It wasn't too long before she managed to turn the conversation around to the mirrors. Ann was not at all embarrassed.

'Come and have a look,' she said.

Heather didn't need asking twice. Her already big blue eyes widened even more when she saw the toys on the bedside cabinet. Ann opened a few more drawers to reveal all sorts of equipment.

'Goodness,' said the bubbly, vibrant blonde. 'I knew Dave was the absolute missionary when it came to sex, but I never realised half these things existed!'

She saw the big screen and the videotapes.

'Can we play one?' she asked. 'I've never seen a blue movie before.' Ann drew the curtains and went to fetch a bottle of chilled white wine from the fridge while Heather selected a tape. None of the titles meant much to her, so in the end she just grabbed one that, from the pictures on the cover, looked interesting.

By this time, Ann was back with the drinks. She put the tape on to play and the pair of them propped themselves up on the bed to watch. Heather tried to be 'cool' and laughed at the excruciatingly bad acting but as things heated up on screen, she became very quiet.

Each of the girls was obviously becoming turned on. Ann noticed Heather's hand subconsciously slip down to her groin.

'Don't worry about me,' Ann said quietly, noticing the faraway look in her friend's eyes. 'I really don't mind if you want to play. Would you like me to leave you alone?' Heather turned and looked straight at her friend.

'Actually, I'd much prefer it if you stayed' she said, half smiling with embarrassment. Ann understood the message.

'Oh, what the hell!' she said, as she moved closer, slipping her hand under Heather's white mini skirt. The tanned, blonde beauty giggled guiltily as she moved her legs to make things easier for her friend. Heather's body jerked as Ann found the spot.

The embarrassed laughter quickly turned to a gentle moan of appreciation as Ann expertly aroused her even more.

Heather could not believe how another woman could make her feel this way. It was if Ann knew instinctively what to do and when to do it. It wasn't long before Heather suggested Ann slip her own jeans off so that they could enjoy each other. They lay there for a while continuing to watch the movie while both maintaining a highly charged state.

They were so relaxed about the situation, they chatted as they indulged each other. Heather admitted how she had often enjoyed her own fantasies but Dave always treated her body like a temple.

'Only to be visited on a Sunday, and then purely for communion!' she laughed.

From there, it was no distance at all for Heather to ask if she could test out a vibrator, and of course, Ann had to show her how to use it.

There was no question of either girl being lesbian. There was no undying love sworn nor even any mouth to mouth kissing. They had just been like a couple of teenage schoolkids trying things out.

It did bring them much closer together, though, and it didn't stop them from spending the odd hour or so here and there, having a bit of a rematch and stretching their activities.

Now that they had become so close, and Ann had developed Heather's education in the one direction, the blonde determined it was about time she returned the compliment and help Ann fit more neatly into her forthcoming new role as Lady of the Manor.

When they were not choosing decorator items for the house, Heather was giving Ann and her wardrobe an entire makeover. Ann was an enthusiastic student as Heather introduced her to the right hairdresser and beautician.

Into the Oxfam shop went all her old clothes from C&A and British Home Stores. Heather explained that not everything had to have a 'label' but it did have to be stylish.

Ann learned quickly. It took little time for her to abandon her glasses. On Heather's advice, she left them off entirely for a few days and was amazed at how her eyes readjusted themselves.

It had been Heather's intention to push Ann into using contact lenses, but a trip to the optician confirmed that her eyes, once having got used to doing without the glasses, were better than when she had been a youngster.

Both girls had their 'personal colours' checked and Heather had the beautician give Ann lessons on make-up. But for all of the designer clothes and the treatments, what made the most difference with Ann was her new inner-confidence.

She was happy to look men in the eye now – even flirt with them a little, knowing she was secure with Vincent. It was still Heather who would always turn heads because of the blonde hair and the beautiful eyes and captivating, vivacious manner, but Ann had also emerged as a beauty in her own right.

The transition hadn't escaped Vincent either and he was constantly telling his angel how proud he was of her. He even decreed the girls should do a makeover on his own wardrobe, although he decided not to bother with the make-up lessons!

It was all very well for Vincent to have said Dave should put his own business first, but this was not the way things panned out. The 'Lord and Lady of the Manor' were now keen to get into their new palace and everything needed to be done yesterday.

The first job was to get the modern extension designed. It would take a while to get it through planning and then built onto the back of the property.

The design would comprise a very private and plush study overlooking rolling countryside, a Hollywood-style bedroom with purpose built *en-suite* bathroom, a gym, and a small but perfectly equipped galley kitchen and dining area. This extension linked on to the Manor House via the back door to the kitchen and preparation areas, from where the large property opened up into the main reception rooms.

Whilst awaiting planning permission for the extension, an army of workers started at the top of the house, re-pointing chimneys, repairing eroded facias and gargoyles, and refurbishing the roof. At the same time, others were upgrading wiring, plumbing, ceilings and the like. Each of the huge bedrooms was given its own en-suite and the old bathrooms turned into what could best be described as

Roman baths, with plunge pool, jacuzzi, sauna, massage tables and reclining couches.

Downstairs was to be the jewel in The Manor's crown. It required very little adaptation to make the whole ground and first floors wheelchair-friendly. There were no steps except at the thresholds to the outside doors, and these were easily fixed with ramps.

The original idea of having a lift going up alongside the main staircase was changed. It would have spoiled the whole look of the entrance hall, and in any case, putting it alongside the back stairs off the kitchen and preparation areas was much more practical.

There was a huge entrance hall with a full cloakroom and toilet adjacent. The hall, along with most of the downstairs rooms, still had the original chandeliers, now wired for modern lighting.

The ornate ceiling mouldings, as with those in the rest of the house, had been restored to their former glories and the centrepiece of the hall, a beautiful carved oak fire surround matched the sweeping staircase and the heavy oak doors and surrounds perfectly. The minstrel's gallery, running the length of one wall from the top of the stairs, completed the picture.

The walls, adorned with fine art, had been painted a warm cream, with the plaster mouldings and lintels picked out in biscuit. A huge Chinese rug, with polished oak flooring showing around its perimeter, and heavy maroon velvet drapes, were the soft furnishing additions.

Rooms off the main entrance hall included a wood panelled library and study with magnificent fireplaces, a morning room where the light flooded in on perhaps the cosiest area of the house, a billiards room, and a massive dining room with The Manor's original oak table. All of these areas were lovingly restored with no expense spared and all mod cons sympathetically built in.

Best of all, though, was the formal sitting room, which was large enough to be a ballroom. Fully 50ft by 35ft, it was just breathtaking and needed the most careful of detailed attention to recapture its original magnificence. Running off the ballroom was a beautifully proportioned conservatory overlooking the formal gardens to the side of the house.

A little farther back on the same sunny side of the house was the walled kitchen garden, with orangery, greenhouses and large sitting areas. Vincent decided the orangery would go, and in its place, linked to the back of the house and enclosed by the privacy of the walled garden, would be a huge indoor swimming pool with glass concertina doors to the outside. The whole pool could be opened up onto a large suntrap patio area with pergolas and trailing vines.

Vincent and Ann were at The Manor every day. Maybe not all day, but enough to make sure things were progressing well. For the first time in their lives, they were not counting pennies on a project. There was no budget. 'Whatever it cost,' was Dave's brief.

He had never been a project manager before but he found it came easily to him. The surveying exams he had passed were helpful but he found the job was all about being organised and knowing the right tradespeople. He was proving himself a master of organisation and his attention to detail was absolute.

The mandate he had been given consisted of using the best materials and tradespeople available, and, where possible, drawing them from the local community. Of course, being able to give sweeteners and pay over the odds certainly helped to concentrate the minds of those people he contracted. The tradesmen even put up with Vincent and Ann's regular mind changing and general nuisance value.

The original head gardener to The Manor had been located and had jumped at the opportunity to come back to work at the Big House. Quite apart from his expertise in the garden, he proved to be a Godsend in knowing where to locate the various uncharted services and inspection pits.

Through Dave, Vincent instructed the experienced gardener to draw in all the short-term staff and contractors he needed to put right the years of neglect from which the grounds had suffered.

Ann and Heather had the job of decorating the whole place. They tried half-a-dozen interior design specialists before coming up with one they liked and could work with. The girls picked the themes and the designer created the finished article.

Most of the original furniture was kept, although it was virtually all re-upholstered. The soft furnishings, furniture, lighting and accessories were all matched together perfectly and whilst every modern convenience was built in, it was all intertwined sympathetically with the original character of the place.

Vincent wanted to see the cellars. Dave rigged up a pulley and lowered him down through the old coal chute. Once Vincent and then his chair had been lowered down, the two men wandered through the brick-vaulted areas together. What had seemed like a warren of rooms connected by brick archways ended up being a large central area with room-sized alcoves behind the arches all around.

The floor was made up of huge flagstones. Literally hundreds of years of debris was piled up in the main space and in the various nooks and crannies. Dave moved some of the tat here and there to find lots of trunks and cases from several eras ago. Vincent instructed Dave to open a few of the older looking trunks.

Aladdin's Cave rediscovered! Carefully packed and virtually as-new clothing, personal effects, manuscripts and documents were everywhere. None of the items themselves would have been considered as 'valuable' when they had been put into store, but time adds value to the most mundane of artefacts, and much of this stuff appeared to go back to the origins of the house.

'Secure this area immediately, find me a reliable historian and pay him to come down here and document everything as it is cleared out,' Vincent demanded. 'There's enough stuff in here to pay for the house!' Then he hesitated.

'No,' he said, 'let's check the legal side first. This stuff might have to go out of the back door and not the front!'

Chapter 10

Ann and Heather were despatched to the solicitors who had looked after the conveyancing on the property. They told the partner in charge of the sale they believed the dining room table could well be an antique worth several thousand pounds, and wanted to know where they stood on ownership.

The solicitor, a young partner in a well established firm, read through the papers carefully. He was no mug and guessed there was a bit more to this than the girls were letting on. When he had finished going through the details of the house sale he reached out his reference books and studied them for some time.

Eventually he looked up at the pair and smiled.

'You bought the house, and all of the chattels and personal effects within it,' he announced. 'There is nothing anywhere that puts a limit on the value of those effects.

'If you were to have bought the table at auction in a lot with other items for a few pence, and subsequently discovered it was worth thousands, this would simply be your good fortune. Exactly the same approach applies here. You bought The Manor and its contents.

'The only exception would be if we were talking about treasure trove.' Again, he looked knowingly at the girls before carrying on.

'Treasure Trove is defined as valuables that had been deliberately hidden and subsequently rediscovered. A completely new set of rules applies here.'

Ann took a chance:

'What about stuff stored in a cellar?' she asked as innocently as possible.

'First of all, we have to be talking about items containing gold or silver, any coins more than 300-years-old or gemstones. Artefacts, which we would not normally regard as treasure, do not count. If you wish, I will give you the official definition of 'treasure' but, as I say, generally we are looking at gold, silver, money, or gemstones. So I am confident that unless you have found a secret room full of

Spanish doubloons, then the purchaser of the property retains ownership of the contents.'

Vincent was quite right in assuming there would be plenty of stuff to be sorted. It took the historian and his two assistants a whole week to clear the cellars. They finished up with two full removal lorry loads of irreplaceable historical artefacts.

The historian had put an approximate valuation on the items as they were retrieved and catalogued. He pointed out most of the stuff belonged in museums rather than with private collectors. He gave what he thought was a reasonable mid-auction price for the material.

The grand total came to £375,000, less, of course, selling costs. Many of the items needed referencing at the British Museum, which had naturally shown an interest.

The Museum approached the Hansings asking if they would consider loaning or donating the find. Ann let Vincent make these decisions, and he was anything but philanthropic. In the end, however, he did strike a deal with the Museum, who paid him £225,000 for the whole find.

That was without the many beautiful dresses Ann and Heather had claimed before the consignment left the house. Vincent described it as 'a nice little windfall' – and wrote out a cheque for £50,000 to Dave as his share of the spoils.

Once the cellar had been cleared, Vincent had it refurbished to way above the standard it had been, even when new. The place ended up looking like all those artists' impressions of the cellars below the Houses of Parliament, just as Guy Fawkes was about to strike a match.

'This,' he explained to Dave, 'was going to be Ann's entertainment centre.'

Eight months to the day after the title deeds had been handed over, Vincent and Ann moved into The Manor. Vince never cared for the official name of Foxglove Manor. It sounded a bit feminine to him, given the magnificent stature of the place. He wasn't so put out as to formally change its official title, but the place was always known amongst the group as The Manor.

Apart from the £50,000 windfall from the sale of the contents of the cellar, Dave received a further £60,000 for his and Heather's parts in making the place what it had become. The bills for the work, inside and out, including paying Dave, were running at just over a million, less the windfall £225K.

If Dave was a little disappointed with his financial return, he didn't show it. After all, £60,000 for eight months' work wasn't bad in anyone's book. He realised he should also take into account the handout from the contents of the cellar. Somehow, though, he had come to expect Vincent to be more than just generous.

It felt strange when Vincent and Ann finally moved out of the tiny unit that had been their home for more than three years. The only things they removed from there, apart from their personal effects, were the mirrors. Everything else they left for the new tenant.

In fact, it was Dave and a labourer who stripped out the mirrors. Without the other paraphernalia on show, it was not difficult for the labourer to accept that the mirrors were simply part of Vincent's fitness regime.

With those mirrors safely stored away in an outbuilding of The Manor, the metamorphosis of Vincent and Ann from penniless paraplegic and helper to confident and well off property owners was complete. Dave joined Ann, Vincent and Heather in the library of the almost completed residence. Ann had a bottle of Dom Perignon and the glasses ready for his arrival.

'A toast,' declared Vincent, 'to our new house and to our new neighbours.'

Dave and Heather looked puzzled but Vincent merely handed them a document. It was a 99-year lease to the gatehouse at the end of the driveway. They were still looking nonplussed when Vincent explained.

He wanted Dave to retain all of the tradespeople they had used on the big house and for Dave and Heather to extend and renovate the gatehouse to their own requirements. The finishes should be equal to those of The Manor. Vincent would be footing the bill.

By this time, the entrance into the estate already had automatic gates and a voice link to The Manor. There would now simply be two security links and codes on the gates, one from the gatehouse itself and one from The Manor. And of course, Vincent would continue to pay Dave to be the site agent whilst the gatehouse was being developed. He was being paid to build his own property!

Ann and Heather went off to rustle up some food. When they had left the library, Vincent softly said: 'Just Ann's playroom to do now. I don't want to use any local tradesmen for that. I think we will go and get some ideas in Amsterdam, and maybe find some specialist outfitters there. They seem to have the lead in the kind of things I am looking for.'

Mark had found more and more doors opening for him in London, the money centre of the world. The snowball effect of his phenomenal success was now in full flow, and virtually any shares he bought would go up in value simply because people assumed he knew something they did not. Many a time he did.

One of his biggest attributes was his people-skills. He had quickly learned who the real inside men were. For some of these movers and shakers, money had become no real object and they simply enjoyed being fawned over and fussed with. He was happy to oblige them. Others were money driven, and the odd brown paper bag here and there kept them sweet.

His and Vincent's investments remained the priority, and their portfolios, whilst now far less risky, were still increasing considerably in value.

Money should never be a problem for either man again. But Mark suggested it was time to diversify their investments. It was all very well having all their money in the stock market where Mark could keep control of things, but as the amounts went up and up, so finding the right opportunities to invest such large sums became more and more difficult.

After several chats between the two friends, Vincent formed a new property company. Both he and Mark put two million into the new project. The company was, of course, registered in the Antilles, and profits were then diverted back to England via a holding company in Switzerland. This tax avoidance procedure was, by now, standard practice for the pair, who shared the same high profile London accountants.

The two investors needed a manager to run the new operation. They wanted someone in the business with estate agency experience who, when necessary, was prepared to cut a corner or two.

Because of all the work he had been doing for Vincent, David Scott's estate agency business had just about come to a dead stop. The work on the gatehouse had been completed for a while, and for Dave, going back to try and build up Scott Homes again was proving to be hard work. He jumped at the opportunity to become the manager of Vincent and Mark's new enterprise.

Vincent had the idea for the new property company to trade as

Scott Properties, which enabled Dave to carry on using the same shop-front until his lease expired. That way he could simply tidy things up with Scott Homes at his own pace and cease operations, without any raised eyebrows.

When Mark was on his way back to London after the arrangements had been agreed, Vincent spoke to Dave privately.

'Listen Dave, you know far more about the real estate business than I do. I know enough, however, to be aware of all the lurks and perks, and the fact that palms sometimes need greasing.

'I'll ask you two questions. The first is, are you strong enough to manage a property portfolio in order to maximise profits, and not to allow sentiment to cloud the issue? Second, are you comfortable working for Mark and me, rather than for yourself? I think you understand what I mean?'

Dave nodded, but Vincent repeated himself.

'Understand what I am saying, Dave. I need to know any and every move you make, above or below the table. I will then decide how to deal with these things. You nod your head now, but you must understand, if you ever let me down or try to double-cross me...'

The threat hung in the air for quite a few moments before Dave spoke clearly and calmly.

'Vincent,' he said, 'you are the best thing that ever happened in my life. You can trust me implicitly.'

'I'm glad you said that,' said Vincent, 'because I want you to do a very special, private and delicate thing for me. I need you to find me some 'special contractors...'

A little over a month later, Vincent and Ann were enjoying their evening meal.

'Did you hear the news on the local radio?' asked Ann.

'No. What did I miss?'

'Do you remember the brain surgeon, Mr Cohen, who was in charge of your case at Shelford General?' Vincent nodded.

'Well it seems he was set about by a group of young thugs last night. They broke both his legs.'

Vincent pulled a face.

'It comes to something when you can't walk down the street without being attacked, doesn't it?' he sympathised.

An eye for and eye, a leg for a leg, he thought to himself; very Old Testament. Vincent had fast come to understand that money is power.

What had amazed him was just how easy it had been. The hardest problem – finding the contractor – had been Dave's job. It had cost Dave £500 for the telephone number. He had covered the cost himself.

Armed with just the London number, Vincent had made the call. It had been brusque and businesslike. The person answering the call had simply wanted to know the details of who was to be the subject, and the damage to be inflicted. With that, he had given Vincent a non-negotiable, up-front cash price and they had made suitable arrangements for the money to be left in a rural location, just off the Newport Pagnell services on the M1.

That had been it. Vincent regarded his £10,000 as money well spent.

Mark had a far more laid-back attitude than Vincent to the running of the property business. As long as there were good profits at the end of it, he didn't want to be involved at all in the day-to-day stuff. His own life was far too full already.

He loved the fast cars and even faster women, the lavish parties, the boats moored in the Med and three-day breaks in the Bahamas. He had yet to find a girl from any background who could resist the offer of a few days on a yacht or at a tropical retreat. Money, he had decided, could buy you everything. Well, almost.

Although young, the whizzkid still kept close attention to business. He had now assembled a wonderful web of informants, helping him to come up with and then cross-reference information to confirm its accuracy. On the surface, he was a hotshot broker and the darling of the Chelsea Set, but he was still squirreling money away for himself and Vincent.

Mark adored Foxglove Manor and spent as much time there as he reasonably could. Vincent and Ann were great hosts. By now, there was a full-time housekeeper and staff to keep the place running perfectly. Mark's favourite couple had now reached sibling status with him. They spent a fair amount of time in their own quarters but nothing was too much trouble for them when he and his guests visited.

Mark turned up one Friday afternoon with yet another particularly young, vibrant and mighty attractive 'friend'. Her name was Amelia, and Ann, as with all visitors to The Manor, treated her kindly, even though she was aware this was just another of Mark's trophy girls.

After a wonderful meal, Vincent left Amelia with Ann for a short time, whilst he took Mark to sort out some business – except they didn't go to the study or the library.

Vincent led Mark to the rear stairs. He indicated to his broker friend that he should go down the stairs to the cellar, whilst he wheeled himself into the lift and descended quietly. They met at the bottom, where Vincent dialled a number into a keypad on the wall. Heavy oak double doors opened up onto the most amazing of sights.

The cellar was no longer a cellar - but a medieval dungeon! No cold stone walls or floor here, though, and no rats running around either. The original red brick arches could still be seen but the majority of the walls were covered with heavy red velvet drapes. Some alcoves around the outside of the huge central area were backlit to reveal all manner of erotic tableaux.

Some could be classified as magnificent pornographic art and sculpture, others were representations and reconstructions of various forms of lovemaking practices from around the world through the ages. Another section showed many of the various pieces of equipment one would find in a state of the art medieval torture chamber.

In the centre of this alcove was a black marble slab, 8ft long by 4ft wide and just 2ft off the ground. This too had a variety of belts, buckles and restraints hanging around and above it, creating a macabre spectre.

Another area was set up with all kinds of red velvet and black satin couches, benches, stools, bars, posts and seats with all manner of straps and stirrups, hoists and pulleys and other items of equipment dotted around.

In the main central area, there was a 10ft square roman bath with step down at one end and a ramp at the other, and a magnificent free standing, clear-glass shower big enough to accommodate four or five people, with at least 10 lots of water-jets, adjustable both for direction and intensity.

The biggest, strangest bed Mark had ever seen dominated the central area. It was circular, about 15ft in diameter, with a wheelchair-width channel about 3ft long cut into it. There were three spokes leading off the main circle of the bed, like handles on a ship's wheel. Each was about 5ft long but they varied in width from around 2ft for the smallest to 3ft for the widest.

The outer ring of the bed, about 18 inches wide, was deep-buttoned red velvet. The outer spokes were the smoothest of red suede; both the bed edge and the spokes were quite firm under their covers and padding. One side of the centre part of the bed looked like a huge white satin marshmallow whilst the other was topped with six-inch deep, pure black cashmere fleece. The bed was positioned up against a full-length mirrored wall.

Everywhere you looked in the place, there were brass handrails at wheelchair height and trapeze-style swings attached to a series of pulleys and tracks that disappeared in the murk of the ceiling.

The floor was black suede, soft, bouncy and warm to walk on, suggesting a sprung floor had been built underneath. The whole area had a glorious fresh fragrance to it. Wispy currents of air played around, but the room was wonderfully warm. It gave the impression of being inside a womb.

Mark whistled softly as Vincent wheeled himself over to a console near the bed.

'So what do you think?' Vincent said, as he pressed a couple of buttons and the handrails and trapezes slid out of sight.

'They are just to help me get about,' he added. A whole row of 30 sliders on the console adjusted lighting. Vincent played with the different settings. Piercing pencil beams, adjustable for width and direction on toggles, different colours of general mood lighting, adjustable speed strobes, or full psychedelia flashed on or off at Vincent's touch. He reset the controls to subdued mood lighting.

'With these, in conjunction with the sound system, you can pretty well put your mind where you want to,' Vincent said, 'but if you prefer the old-fashioned methods, there's most of the stuff you might need in this draw.' It was like a pharmacy, with a variety of drugs all neatly laid out and labelled with recommended doses.

'I tend to plan theme evenings with Ann,' Vincent went on. 'I pre-programme the whole lot including the movies.' Another button brought a huge screen down into position opposite the mirror wall. 'You'll find plenty of tapes and music selections over there in that alcove.'

'Let me know if you would like to use the room tonight,' Vince said nonchalantly. Mark needed no second invitation. He nodded vigorously.

'It might be a bit much to walk Amelia straight in here, though,' he suggested. 'Do you mind if I take some of this coke to make the introduction a bit easier?'

It was ten-thirty when the men rejoined the ladies. Vincent announced he was for an early night, and Ann dismissed herself shortly after.

'Hey, baby,' said Mark as he turned to Amelia and began to cut the coke into lines, 'have I got an evening planned for you!'

Vincent and Ann were already waiting when Mark and Amelia arrived. Ann was stretched out, naked, on the massage table in the secret viewing room while Vincent, still in his wheelchair, was gently stroking her. They turned to watch proceedings through the huge two-way mirror...

Chapter 11

Mark and Amelia had put on quite a good show considering they were a bit overawed by the sheer volume of the playthings. It took about two hours before they settled down to sleep and Ann and Vince went to bed.

When the four caught up with each other, mid-morning on the Saturday, Mark mentioned he and Amelia had decided to forego their planned walk in the woods that afternoon. Mark winked at Vincent.

Heather fielded the phone call from Ann.

'Do you want to come over this afternoon for a bit of fun?' Heather had intended doing some shopping but this sounded intriguing. She tried to ask for more information but was simply told to be at The Manor by 2.30pm.

Vincent delayed lunch a little and then engaged Mark in conversation until 2.15. Mark and Amelia then announced they were rather tired and were going for a lie down. Vincent assured Mark the doors to Ann's playroom were not locked, and said Heather was due to arrive at any minute. He and the two girls would be popping into town, so Mark and Amelia would have the place to themselves.

Heather arrived at The Manor within a few minutes. At Vincent's suggestion, they hurried down to the viewing room.

After Ann had moved into The Manor there had been far fewer opportunities for the girls to have their private moments. There always seemed to be workmen or staff around even when their men were away.

Heather had stopped over when Vince and Dave had gone to Amsterdam for a couple of days. The two girls had used one of the beautiful bedrooms with a four-poster. Yes, there had been a fair bit of horseplay, but it was more like a teenage sleepover, with its midnight feast and pillow fights. To be honest, both of them were so taken up with the work and planning on the house, even sex with their respective partners had taken something of a back seat.

Both girls had known about Vincent's intention to build Ann a playroom but Vincent had wanted the place itself to be a surprise. He had grilled Ann on all of her wildest fantasies and had tried to include them all in the layout.

Of course, there was one thing he could not give her, and Ann never included that on her list, although she did wonder what she was missing. The girls had laughed about it between them often. In Dave, all Heather got was a very straightforward portion of meat whilst Ann had every meal beautifully prepared, served up perfectly, and with any amount of fabulous sauces and side dishes.

But the fact remained, through none of her own making she was still strictly vegetarian when it came to physical sex!

Once the playroom had been completed, Ann had tried to describe it to Heather. During the construction, Heather had quizzed Dave about it but he wasn't letting on. The poor girl had been bursting to have a peep and this was now to be her chance.

Having quietly found their way to the rear entrance to the viewing room, Ann and Heather could see and hear the couple in the playroom chatting. 'Wow,' whispered Heather. It was all she could manage as her heart thumped and her mind filled with wild fantasies.

'No need to whisper,' Vincent said casually. 'The other room is wired for sound so you can hear clearly, but you could even bang on that glass and they wouldn't hear you.' Heather looked around the viewing room. It had its own couches, massage tables, and equipment, all set up so as all parties could continue looking through the one-way mirror whilst engaging in their own gymnastics. Vincent dimmed the lights in the viewing room to a very low glow.

Mark and Amelia were slowly walking around the room, stopping at each alcove to admire the tableaux inside. They played with sliders, switches and buttons to see what each did. There was little conversation except for when Amelia, wide-eyed, asked the occasional question about the equipment. Mark didn't know the answer to most and would simply reply:

'Don't know. We'll have to find out as we go along.'

As the unwitting performers helped each other out of their clothes, Vincent slid to the exit.

'I am sure you can manage quite well without me', he said, as he disappeared through the door.

It was almost five o'clock when the performers finally curled up on the soft cocoon of the satin sheets.

Sore, but happy, Heather and Ann dressed quickly. Heather had been incredibly surprised at how much of a turn-on being a Peeping Tom had been. Neither girl seemed to consider the morality of watching their close friend engaging in a sex romp.

As far as they could see, his and their gratification was just fun, as against anything to do with 'lovemaking'. In fact, the two girls had enjoyed giving Mark scores in a number of different categories. Both had agreed he was as much of a gentleman and a hunk in private as he was in public.

Dave came up to the house when he had finished his appointments and the three couples enjoyed a sumptuous meal that evening, washed down by plenty of the best drinks money could buy. It was a sparkling time. They all finished up in the oak-panelled study where they stretched out on leather Chesterfields in front of a roaring wood fire.

Dave and Heather stayed over. They used one of the guest rooms, Mark and Amelia another, whilst Vincent and Ann returned to their retreat. All of them fell asleep as soon as their heads hit the pillows and enjoyed a glorious night's sleep.

All of them, that is, except Vincent. As soon as Ann was off, he slid out of bed and expertly swung himself into his chair before gliding silently out of the bedroom and into his den. Tonight, more than most, his anger and frustration burned even brighter.

The next day he asked Mark if he could recommend a 'working girl' for a little job he had lined up. He would need her on call for about a month or so. It would involve a half-a-dozen or so sessions with the same man. But it would also require a good deal of role-playing. Mark immediately volunteered Amelia.

'I'll have one more session tonight in the cellar, if you don't mind,' he said. 'There are a couple of toys there I want to try out. After that, she is on her way anyway. She's becoming too much of a junkie for me. It would be perfect if I could buy her off with a little project.'

Before Dave left that day, Vincent asked him to rent a small, furnished bed-sit in a particular area of Shelford.

'How long for?'

'Say three months with an option.'

'Done!'

On the Monday morning, a decidedly worse for wear looking Amelia wandered around the house looking for Vincent. She finally found him reading quietly in the library.

'Mark says you might have a little job you wanted doing', she said sweetly.

The following Monday, Miss Amelia Harris walked into the small Coventry Road practice of Doctor McPherson, explained she had just moved into a bed-sit in the area and asked if she could register as a patient. This was no problem, and the very next day she was back in the doctor's surgery asking for birth-control pills.

Charles McPherson was in his mid-40s, married, with two teenaged daughters and a 10-year-old son. He had been at the practise for seven years and was well liked by his patients, although he had a constantly changing stream of receptionists. He and his wife enjoyed reasonable social lives and she had a wide circle of friends.

He checked Ms Harris' blood pressure and asked her when she last had a pap smear. At just 22, it was unlikely there would be anything to find, but he quietly suspected this young lady might have led a lively and very active social life. He supplied the prescription for the pills and that was it – another happy customer. He couldn't help but admire her tight little rear end as she disappeared out of the surgery, though. Doctors are people too.

A few days later Amelia contacted the surgery again. She needed a medical for a new job she had been offered. The receptionist explained such medical examinations were chargeable and Dr McPherson did them between normal surgeries. Not a problem.

'2.30 tomorrow?'

'Perfect.'

The medical was no great chore for the doctor. In fact, it was just the opposite. Amelia Harris was bright and lively. She had a wonderful smile and they got on splendidly. Hers was a sad story. She had worked hard to rise above a bad upbringing. Then, just when things had been going well, she had been forced to move to the Midlands in order to escape from a violent boyfriend. She was desperately lonely because she didn't know anyone at all locally.

What really attracted Charles McPherson, though, was how she was able to gently but clearly exaggerate each of their physical contacts as he went through the examination. He found himself taking much more time and trouble than he normally would have.

Did she ask, or did he offer? It didn't matter. Before they knew it, they were having a glass of Chardonnay in a small wine bar. Well, several glasses actually. He offered to run her home and, on the way, she told him she was having trouble with a dripping tap in her little bed-sit...

Vincent was mighty impressed. He thought it would have taken much longer. After the third visit to Amelia from the good doctor, it was time for the old-fashioned, but very reliable honey-trap to be sprung.

Amelia was nothing other than a perfectionist, though. In any case, she too had taken a personal dislike to this sad, slimy man who abused his position so easily. The cameras were set up and the videos taken, but she asked Vincent for one more take.

The poor doctor was well hooked by now and understood when this bright, young thing explained she had a habit. He was not prepared to leave anything with her, but would be happy to help her out when he called in. He thought he was locking her into allowing him to visit whenever he wanted.

The video showed the young girl apparently lying asleep in bed. The doctor came in, opened his bag, took out the syringe and phial, and injected her in the arm. He then put all the stuff back in his bag, undressed and got into bed with her. The tape carried on to show plenty more over the next half-hour, but the first few minutes would have been enough to satisfy Vince's requirements.

Amelia earned £10,000 for the deal, plus five thousand more as a bonus for the extra performance, with the promise of another five if she had to appear in court.

The *News of the World* loved it. They also covered fully the follow up story the next Sunday, about the respected family GP taking his own life after his drinking and womanising had been uncovered.

'That'll serve the bastard right for being too drunk to look after me,' was Vincent's only reaction to the shocking news. As with Cohen, he enjoyed what he considered nothing more than poetic justice.

For Amelia it was all in a day's work, Mark had known better than to enquire as to what Vincent's 'little job' involved, whilst Dave did what he was well paid for. He removed the cameras and promptly ended the tenancy.

Chapter 12

Dave and Heather had been living in the renovated and extended gatehouse for some months now. Spring was in the air, the property company was doing very well, and so was the stock market. Mark and Vincent decided to move another million each into the property side.

Vincent also moved a further half-a-million over into what he smilingly declared was his 'slush fund'. He had been making plans to use some money for a while.

At coming up to 25 years of age, he felt frustrated with just sitting about. It was about time to move ahead and take on new challenges. There were still some scores to be settled and then he could move on with his life.

Shelford Speedway was reported in the local rag as having run into financial difficulties. Although he had not been down to the stadium since his injury, Vincent had made a point of keeping up with the speedway scene. Jeff Harding was still the Racers' star man.

Vincent picked up the phone and spoke to Cyril Grant for the first time since the crash. The Shelford promoter was a short, squat man with a bouncy, irritating manner to him. The hideous comic comb-over indicated he was well into his 50s but thought himself still the man-about-town. Cyril Grant was not someone you could easily like.

Cyril was all over Vincent in a second.

'How are you?' he effused. 'I did come down to visit several times after your crash but they just wouldn't let me in to see you.' Vincent let it drift over him. He agreed that it would have been very difficult to get through the hospital security, knowing that Grant had tried just the once.

'I wasn't good company at the time!' he said lightly and they both laughed.

Shelford was one of the few speedway promotions left that owned its own stadium. When the place had been built in the 50s, it had been isolated some way out of the city, with nothing but green fields on all sides. By now, though, the urban sprawl had it surrounded by light commercial buildings on one side and medium density residential on the other. It's called the march of progress.

The stadium was dramatically underused. Apart from speedway each week during the summer, and stock cars once a month, the stadium lay idle. It had once staged greyhound racing as well, but that had since folded.

'They tell me you are struggling a bit financially,' ventured Vincent. Like all promoters in denial, Cyril rocked back in defence.

'Oh, that's just paper talk to try and reel in a big sponsor,' he countered.

'Tell you what,' said Vincent. 'I have a friend who might like to shove in a few bob. Would you like me to set up a meeting between you?'

'We start the season in a couple of weeks,' said Cyril. 'If he wants to become involved for this season, he'll need to be quick.' Got him! thought Vincent.

'Look, as you know, I can't get around much these days because of the old legs. Why don't you come over to his place now and I'll introduce you.'

'Can he make it in an evening?' Cyril shot straight back. 'I'm up to my neck during the days for the next few weeks.'

'Look,' Vincent suggested. 'I'm having dinner there tonight. How about you come round an hour or so beforehand and I'll introduce you? Say six o'clock?'

There was a pause. Obviously, this was anything but convenient, but the hook had been baited.

'How long do you think we'll be?'

'Oh, dinner is at seven-thirty, so that's the absolute deadline for finishing.'

Dave had been at The Manor since five-thirty. He didn't need too much putting in the picture. He had worked with Vincent long enough to be able to play the straight man.

Vincent explained The Manor was to belong to Dave as far as Grant knew. Other than that, they would play things by ear.

Cyril was a few minutes late.

'Sorry I'm a bit late, drove past it twice. Couldn't believe this was the place,' he said, obviously more than impressed, as Dave ushered him into the imposing library. Neither of the hosts excused his lateness. His words just hung there, limp in the air.

Vincent introduced Cyril to Dave, explaining that Dave used to be a big Shelford fan. Dave now wanted an opportunity to put something back into the club he had loved to support. What did Cyril suggest?

The promoter launched into his sponsorship pitch but Vincent soon stopped him. He pointed out that there was no real benefit in a sponsorship arrangement, because Dave's property company had little public exposure. In fact, he preferred it to remain relatively unknown.

Cyril was nonplussed. Short of asking for a straight gift, he had little to offer.

'Listen,' said Vincent. 'Dave is pretty good with accounts. Why don't you give him permission to have a chat with your accountants and make some suggestions as to how you can maximise returns from your business? That is really his specialist field and he could save you thousands – and he might possibly be prepared to inject some new money, if that is what is really needed. I'm sure all he would want in return is a couple of season tickets and a bit of a fuss making of him.'

Cyril had enjoyed three glasses of Dom Perignon in a short space of time and on an empty stomach. Foxglove Manor clearly indicated the fellow had more than a few bob and was no doubt a highly successful businessman. Cyril was comfortable and felt no threat. He admitted that cash flow was becoming an acute problem and that the speedway had lost a heap of money the previous year.

Dave and Vince carried on making all the right noises, allowing the promoter, relaxed by the alcohol, to ramble on about how the speedway had suffered a run of bad luck. Eventually, Cyril had talked himself out. Dave had been most sympathetic and Cyril was more than happy to let his new friend have a chat with his accountants, with a view to saving the speedway some money.

Vince glided out of the door and came back a few minutes later with a typewritten note.

'I forgot to ask the name of your accountants,' he said, 'so I just stuck on "To whom it may concern". It's just a clearance allowing your accountants to chat with Dave about your accounts. By the way, who are your accountants, and can you give them a buzz early tomorrow morning, to let them know to expect him? We fully understand time is of the essence.'

At 7.35, Cyril was on his way back to Shelford, convinced he had found a white knight. Vincent and Dave laughed out loud before joining the girls for a thoroughly enjoyable evening.

Just as they were settling into bed that night, Ann turned to Vincent:

'You do realise Dave has a crush on you?' Vincent was taken aback. Ann continued:

'Poor Dave just loves the strength and power you exude. I don't know what all the nonsense with that Grant character was about, but Dave has been doing everything barring wagging his tail and wetting the floor all evening!'

'Best I keep throwing bones in his direction, then!' smiled Vincent, remembering his first impression of Dave as a spaniel.

They both laughed.

'How would you feel if I was to move back into speedway, as a promoter this time?'

'Not with that nasty little man, surely?' was Ann's instant reaction.

'Heavens, no!' Vincent chuckled.

Next day, Dave Scott sent two of his staff, armed with the release note, to Cyril Grant's accountants. The secretary to the partner who dealt with the speedway account had already taken a call from Cyril telling them to expect a contact, and asking them to do all they could to assist. Dave's people left the office with several boxes of books and papers.

Vincent pored over the papers whilst Dave was sent on a mission to go and inspect the stadium. Cyril was too busy to give a guided tour but the experienced surveyor was happier to wander around on his own, anyway. That way he was less likely to lose count of his careful paces and could speak freely into his little dictaphone.

By the end of that day, Vincent knew far more about Grant's business than the promoter knew himself. He and Dave had also come up with an expert valuation of the company as a going concern, and a good idea of the actual asset value of the property.

As a going concern the place wasn't. If the figures in the accounts were actual and genuine, the company was running at a substantial loss. The freehold of the site, depending on planning being granted, and at what level, was worth between £750,000 and four million. With Dave's contacts in the local council, a minimum of two million was a realistic assessment.

Dave phoned Cyril the next day.

'Before we can talk, I need to know exactly how much you are taking out of the business in cash. It's all very well siphoning off a bit here and there from a profitable business, but it is lunacy to do so when the company is not making a profit and therefore not liable for tax anyway.'

'I wish,' said Cyril. 'Those days are long gone. I am afraid. I would be lucky if I had more than five hundred quid out last year. As you can see, I'm still drawing decent wages but I know it can't go on. I spoke to the bank manager about increasing the loan, but even with the stadium as security he is being cagey. He's reluctant to increase the current £250,000 loan, which I am sure you noticed is set against the stadium freehold.'

'Leave that to me,' said Dave. 'By the way, do you own your own house, what is it worth and is it mortgaged?'

'Yes I do, it's worth about a hundred grand. And no, it's not mortgaged. It's our only pension fund.' Music to my ears, was all Vincent, listening in intently, could think.

At seven-thirty that evening, Dave phoned Cyril at his home.

'OK,' he said, 'I think I've sorted things out for you. Be here at nine in the morning, and please don't be late this time.' Dave just loved all this stuff. He was even getting a hard on just thinking about the next day.

Cyril was 20 minutes early. He parked in the road outside the gatehouse, waiting until the time ticked around. Heather telephoned The Manor to tell Dave and Vincent he was there. They both enjoyed a good laugh at the older man's expense.

This time Dave showed Cyril into the study and then took his place behind the big antique oak desk. Vincent was there in his wheelchair at the side of the desk.

'I hope you don't mind Vincent being here,' he said, 'I thought he might be able to advise on the speedway side.' Cyril resented it like hell but kept quiet.

'OK,' said Dave. 'This is the plan. What you have at the moment are two businesses in one. What you must do is to separate the stadium ownership from the speedway business. I don't know what your relationship with your accountants is, but they have definitely not been working in your best interests. Tell me, have you been paying them simply to prepare and audit the accounts, or for business advice as well?'

Cyril hesitated.

'Just to do the accounts and audit, I think.'

'That's a shame. Had they been engaged as advisors, you could have had them for negligence. Even so, they should have seen so many simple things that would have assisted you. Before you leave this house, whatever happens, I want you to telephone them and discontinue their services.' Dave didn't wait for a reaction.

'What we will do is to form a new company to hold the freehold of the stadium. I have looked at the amount of interest and charges you have been paying on the £250K loan with the bank. Do you know that amounted to nearly 38 grand last year? I have spoken to the investment company I use, and they can improve considerably on that figure.

'The speedway and stock car operating company can stay as is. We will just transfer the property out of it into the new holding company. Now, Vince has been telling me you had a bad run with rider injuries and retirements last year, which caused you to finish near the bottom of the table. Obviously, looking at the figures, attendances collapsed towards the end of the season, losing you a lot of money.

'Also, I couldn't help noticing on my look around, the whole place looks shabby and run down. It looks what it is – a business on the edge of bankruptcy and closure. Vincent tells me there are lunatics around the sport who buy into such disasters but even if we were to believe these ridiculous valuations he says are bandied about, by the time you take into account your creditors, you really have little money left in the promoting business. It is close to being insolvent, and definitely is insolvent if you don't accept these absurd valuations you have placed on the riders.

'No auditor would accept these rider contracts as assets. I mean, as far as I can see, the contracts only run for one season at a time. You also have no insurance against rider injury and therefore loss of use. How in hell can riders be written into the books as assets when they are uninsured in such a dangerous sport? How much was Vincent worth after his crash?

'Clearly, what the place needs is a substantial injection of finance.'

Cyril had been loath to face up to it, but he knew that Dave was telling the truth. He had been trying to find a buyer, either of some or the whole of the business, but nobody would even think in the same financial terms as he was considering.

'OK, if you are agreed so far, here is the offer,' Dave continued. 'My people are prepared to become equity partners in the property.

What this means is, taking the bank valuation of half-a-million pounds, which my people consider a little high, they will pay off the bank loan for a 51% stake in the company. They won't charge a penny in rent whilst the speedway continues to operate, but they will benefit by 51% in any appreciation of the property and the return from its eventual sale. We could try for planning development on the stadium when you are ready to retire, and I have a few friends in the right places who can help with that...'

Dave touched his nose in a conspiratorial manner.

'So you will save £38,000 a year in bank payments and be putting yourself in line for a big pay-out at the end,' Dave continued. 'It isn't the house you should be considering as your pension fund, it's the stadium.'

'But if I give away half of the stadium...' Cyril stammered.

'Hardly give away, Cyril,' replied Dave, brusquely. 'Sell for £250,000 plus free rent, or carry on paying inflated interest on the loan. I'll tell you what the alternative is. The speedway will not be able to carry the loan repayments and will lose more and more money.

'The bank will call in the loan, you will not be able to pay, so they will bring in the receivers and sell the assets at distressed sale rates. You will be lucky to see a drink after all your bills are paid.

'Still, it's your decision . . .'

And with that, Dave stood up, apparently terminating the meeting. Cyril blustered.

'Come on, Dave, don't be like that.' he said, 'I only passed a comment. Please keep going.'

Dave sat down with a look of mock anger.

'Look Cyril, I'm trying to save your speedway here with nothing on the bottom line at this stage for me.

'Anyway, I'll carry on with the suggested plan. Stop me at any time if you don't like it or if you have any questions.

'As I said, the business has reached a stage where, not to put too fine a point on it, you have bled it dry. It needs a substantial cash injection to survive and become viable again. I reckon the minimum you need is £150,000. What you currently have, taking the property out, is a promotion that even a cashed-up, dreamy-eyed supporter would not pay £50,000 for. In real accounting terms its asset value is about five grand!'

This time Cyril wanted to say something but settled for squirming.

'What I am prepared to do is, if you put in £100,000, I'll put in £50,000 and take a third share of the operating company.

'I'll never be able to raise a hundred,' Cyril whined. 'My only asset is my house.'

'Well, how about we both put in £75K and go 50-50 on the business?' Dave suggested helpfully. 'I am sure I can use my contacts to get you a house mortgage for that much at a very good interest rate.' Cyril looked crestfallen.

'How will I be able to afford the repayments?' he moaned.

'Well, through the very reasonable salary you are currently paying yourself, which I am prepared to carry on with, and through profits.'

'That house is our pension plan,' wailed Cyril. Dave pointed out that, in fact, the half share in the stadium would be, but Cyril still looked unhappy.

Suddenly Vincent came to life.

'I've got it!' he said. 'Why don't I put in a share? I've still some of my compensation money left. What if I put in 50, Dave puts in 50, and you put in 50 and we'll all be equal partners?

'Done!' said Cyril triumphantly.

'So you have been,' thought Dave 'Like a kipper!'

Chapter 13

The paperwork was rushed through. Cyril Grant did not have a solicitor who was used to dealing in commercial law, so he was happy to let 'Dave's people' do all the work preparing the papers. He was also happy to let Dave's accountants and bankers replace his own. Suddenly, here was someone who had taken the pressure off.

True, Cyril did have difficulty talking his wife into mortgaging the house and resigning her directorship of the company but he was already planning which new riders he would sign and how else he would spend the new money.

The final paperwork was all signed in the solicitor's office a week before the start of the season.

'Whilst we are all here, could we call an extraordinary meeting, so we can get things moving,' Dave suggested. They agreed to waive the normal notification of meeting and the solicitor quickly drew up a note to that effect for them all to sign.

Then, in his proud position as Chairman, Cyril called the meeting open.

Vincent started proceedings.

'Item one on the agenda: "The Way Forward for Shelford Speedway Ltd."

'I propose Cyril Grant be removed as Chairman, director and manager of the company.'

Dave seconded the motion and both men looked at Cyril, who had turned white.

'You are supposed to ask for votes for the motion,' smiled Vincent. Cyril turned to the solicitor and demanded to know what was happening.

'Well, as far as I can see, you have been voted out of office,' was all he could say.

'There is a clear two-thirds majority of the directors and shareholders who have made the decision.'

'But it is *my* speedway, and *I* have just put another 50 thousand pounds into it!'

'Yes, and we will spend it wisely,' Dave volunteered.

'But with no guaranteed income from the speedway, how will I be able to pay the new mortgage on the house?'

'Hmmm. That is a bit of a problem, isn't it? And at 57 and with no qualifications, getting another job might not be too easy. Oh, and did I tell you the lending company you borrowed the money from are sticklers for their payments to be on time. I think you will find they will foreclose on you just as soon as you default.'

'Tell you what,' suggested Vincent helpfully, 'Dave's a very fair man. I bet if you ask him nicely he will be prepared to buy your 49% of the stadium holding company for £50,000.'

'As controlling shareholder, I intend making one or two changes there, anyway,' said Dave. 'I have to warn you, the changes just might have an adverse effect on the value of your shares.'

Vincent glanced at his watch.

'Ten o'clock already! Our people will have just moved in at the stadium. Dave and I had better get down there straight away. We've a lot of work to do. Oh, and just one more thing. Can we have the keys to the company car, please?'

Dave just loved the buzz he got from the events of the morning. He walked out there as stiff as a rod, having a job to hide it under his jacket, and beaming as if he had won the football pools.

True enough, Dave's people had informed the speedway staff of the takeover and suggested they wait until the new owners arrived to find out if they would be kept on or not. Meantime, nothing was to leave the stadium without permission.

The very first thing Vincent did, after assuring the staff that their jobs were safe, in the short term at least, was to organise a press conference. Given the general state of speedway by the spring of 1983, the editors of the national dailies did not rush their top men to Shelford. The only people at the conference were John Marchant, sports editor of the local radio station, and Mike Cox, the speedway correspondent of the local daily paper. Mike also covered Shelford Speedway for the weekly *Speedway Star*.

Vincent handed the pair of reporters a prepared text, the gist of which was that in order to save Shelford Speedway from closure, he and associates had put together a rescue plan.

They had tried hard to work with current promoter, Cyril Grant, but he was not prepared to make the sacrifices and changes it would need to keep Shelford afloat and restore the place to its former glory years.

Therefore, the takeover had ended up being acrimonious. Grant would remain as a minor shareholder until such times as the business side was restructured, but he would have no more connection with the running of the speedway.

To back up the prepared script, Vincent told the reporters – off the record – that Grant had totally cracked up and was raving. The pair of gullible lads agreed the middle-aged man had looked increasingly under pressure recently. They were not at all surprised he had gone over the top.

Next, Vincent telephoned the Chairman of the British Speedway Promoters' Association (BSPA). He knew the man, Alan Howard, was the promoter of Brighton Speedway, but not much more than that. He told the BSPA's main man more or less the same story he had given the journalists and asked if he could meet with the BSPA Management Committee as soon as possible to rubber stamp the change.

Howard was taken aback. He said he needed to speak with Grant, who held the promoter's licence.

'Oh,' said Vincent casually. 'According to my understanding, the licence is owned by the promoting company.

'True,' Howard admitted, 'Grant had previously been the holder of the promoter's licence, on behalf of the limited company, but the company had now materially changed. As such, the new office-holders would be subjected to full scrutiny and any application for a promoter's licence from anyone other than Grant would need to be approved by the Management Committee.'

'Surely this is just a formality?'

'I'll need to speak to Grant,' Howard repeated.

'Good luck, said Vincent. 'He's raving. Don't be too long, though, because I've an opening meeting to stage in less than a week and I would hate to imagine the mess speedway would be in should we not open. I promise you, if things are not dealt with inside 48 hours, I shall disband the team, sell off the assets and put the stadium up for sale. I'll also let the world and its mother know the BSPA will have been responsible.'

'I don't take kindly to threats,' was Howard's terse response. He had been the unchallenged Chairman of the Association for two years and, apart from his speedway interest, owned a large and successful building business. He was used to people deferring to him and getting his own way. Vincent had immediately got under his skin.

'Look, it is not a threat,' Vincent continued, appearing to be backing off.

'It would be incorrect for me not to put you completely in the picture. I would like to run the speedway but only if I can expect some support. At the end of the day, though, I am a businessman, and I'm just as happy to take a short-term profit out of the deal.'

It was a clear ultimatum, however carefully phrased, as Howard understood all too well. He spoke to Cyril Grant, who told him his version of what had happened. Howard could not believe the stupidity of the man.

'So all you own is a minority holding in the operating company and a minority holding in the stadium?' Grant was too embarrassed to admit he had sold out his share in the stadium holding company in order to get his £50,000 back.

'It seems to me that if Hansing and this other fellow were to go through with their bluff, your shares in the promoting company will become worthless, and with you having no controlling interest in the stadium company, hell knows what they can do to make sure you see little from any sale of the place.

'Whichever way you look at it, surely you are better off keeping your head down and hoping they make a success of the speedway. At least then you should get some kind of return from any profits?'

Howard was taking the easy option. If he could broker a smooth passage through from one promoter to the other, it would be the best thing for him and the best thing for speedway generally. On a personal level, he would also be able to save face with Hansing rather than having to back Grant in a lost cause.

'You could be right,' admitted Cyril. 'I still want to try and get my speedway back, and that will be difficult if it has closed.'

So, within an hour, Howard was back on to Vincent.

'I have spoken with Grant. He says he has no objection to the BSPA issuing you with a promoter's licence. Although we will need to interview you, I am sure that will be a formality.'

Vincent thanked him humbly for his assistance, pointed out his disability and enquired as to whether the 'interview' could be done over the phone.

'I'll get back,' Howard snapped. He spoke with the other Management Committee members, and the application was rubber-stamped.

Vincent's next call was to Bryce Penrith in Australia. Bryce had been a breath of fresh air as a rider when he had ridden for Oxford. He had the lot: looks, money, talent and so much charisma he had single-handedly pushed speedway into the mainstream sporting limelight in Britain.

Bryce had ridden in England for only five short years but had become so dominant by the time he had quit he had been just about unbeatable. During the two successive years that Bryce had been the World Champion, he had turned down attempts by the British media to pull him into a TV career. He had also rejected advances from the movie industry.

At the age of just 25, Bryce had retired from speedway to go back home to Australia, with his new English wife, in order to take over the running of the family business.

The centre of what was now a diverse group of companies was a cattle station the size of a small European country. His dad had developed muscular dystrophy and could no longer work on a day-to-day basis. He had needed to groom his son to take over before it was too late.

That was seven years ago and some promoters even pointed to Bryce's retirement as the time from when the sport had gone into steep decline.

'Hey Bryce, it's Vincent Hansing. Remember me? I was the mad-arsed kid from Shelford Racers who used to give you a bit of a run for your money!' Bryce had moved on from speedway. In fact he was now the local Mayor and well into politics in addition to running the family business. Dad had passed on, and Bryce now had his own five-year old lad, Ryan. It was quite a jolt to get a call from a British speedway promoter after such a long time.

Once the niceties were over, Vincent hit him with the deal.

'One season, just one more season, riding in the UK: One last glorious lap of honour. Eight months . . . no, make that seven (it was now well into March...), no, make that six and forget October . . . to come over with the family on an extended holiday.

'Just Shelford meetings and any invitation events you want to do,' Vincent pointed out. 'No internationals, no World Championships and no having to gallivant all around Europe.'

Vincent went on to explain that the Penrith family could stay as his guests, with car, equipment, his old mechanic (now the most respected engine tuner in the business) all provided, along with a no-limit credit card for him and his wife, and first class attention everywhere.

'Come on,' urged Vincent. 'Your boy has never seen you race. Why not treat him to six months' holiday before he has to settle down to schooling? I've already arranged for the first-class air tickets to be delivered to you tomorrow. All you need to do is book your flight.'

Many promoters had tried to tempt Bryce out of retirement in the first few years after he quit but for all of them the timing was wrong. And in any case, Bryce didn't want or need the commitment.

This time, though, it was different. The ambitious five times former Aussie champion was heading into Australian federal politics at the next election in 18 months' time. He had already groomed a management team to run the business without him and he was to be fast-tracked into a blue riband seat and parachuted straight onto the front benches.

It would harm him none to capture the public eye again, and this would be the last chance to enjoy such an extended trip for some time.

'If Molly says yes, I'll do it,' he said. 'What's your number? I'll phone back in half-an-hour.'

'Got him!' knew Vincent. Molly was English. She had met Bryce when he had been riding in England previously. Appealing to Molly was going to be Vincent's final ploy, but it hadn't been needed.

Twenty minutes later, Bryce Penrith had returned the call.

'You're on,' he said. 'I'll leave here in a week, have a few days' practice in California and will be with you by the end of the month.'

'Hell,' thought Vincent. 'Better do something about getting some tickets to him!'

Chapter 14

It was all over the media, both local and national, the next day. The first phone call was from Penrith's old promoter at Oxford, telling Vincent he couldn't do it and that he, George Magro would be getting Vincent thrown out of speedway before he had even started. Vincent didn't lose his cool. He simply explained that, in law, the promoter had no claims whatever to Penrith.

It was doubtful he even had any claims within the convoluted rules governing speedway. In any case, if he so wished, Vincent had no objection should Magro want to phone Bryce, sign him, and fit him into his own Oxford team.

At this stage Vincent knew this was unrealistic, and he was equally sure Bryce was a man of honour and would not consider other offers.

Vincent went on to say to Magro:

'Now, looking at it from your point of view, you have a good, young, successful team. Would it make sense to forego one of your top riders and gamble on a one-season contract on a has-been, with all of the problems associated with losing him again at the end of the season? And in any case, do you think you have the money to get him here?'

There was a pause.

'No, I didn't think so. I'll send you a cheque for 10 grand to ease the embarrassment of losing him. Have a nice day.'

Next on the phone was Alan Howard, the BSPA Chairman, again.

'You know it will be impossible to fit Penrith into your team without exceeding your team's overall points limit,' he said.

'Ah, I was meaning to talk to you about that, Alan. As you know, when Penrith retired he had the highest riding average ever in the British League, but that was five years ago.

'Don't you think we should consider revising that average down from nearly a perfect 12 to a more realistic seven-and-a-half? As you know, such revisions are not uncommon where a rider has been out of the sport for a substantial period of time.' Vincent ignored the exasperated noises coming down the phone and carried on speaking.

'Look, it really is wrong the way you lot run your business. Why do you need all these team restrictions? Why do you have to set up artificial and rigid barriers governing what riders a promoter can and can't sign? I'll tell you why.

'It's because not one of you trusts any of the others. Between you, you have an exclusive franchise to operate speedway. Nobody else can jump in. Well, not without running 'black' and setting up an unofficial league by themselves, and you know that is nigh on impossible.

'Instead of keeping on competing with yourselves over signings, why not work together? Surely it isn't that difficult, simply to say that all signings have to be in the best interests of the sport?

'Anyway, here's the deal. I am prepared to bring the hottest property speedway has ever seen to do a one-season reprise. It will cost me a small fortune. It will cost you nothing when he comes and rides at your track, but he will put several hundred extra people through your gate. You can also use him for invitation events provided he is prepared to do them and can work them around his commitments with me.

'On the other side of the coin, let me hazard a guess and say your worst crowd last year was when Shelford were the visitors. Just supposing Bryce Penrith scores 10 points a meeting? Just suppose, as a consequence, Shelford become serious challengers to win the league? Suddenly a dull, uninteresting visiting team will have become your top drawcard and I will have done it without affecting one other club's line-up.

'Believe me, Shelford won't be the League's whipping boys this year, regardless. Listen carefully. I will sign a top rider from somewhere. If you block this Penrith move, I will have to take a current rider from another track. Now, let me see, who have you got in your line-up this year....'

'You're not going out of your way to make too many friends, are you?' Howard spat out.

'No, but speedway will be the better for my being in it,' said Vincent', 'and the sooner you and the rest of your knitting circle understand that, the sooner we will all get on better. Can I presume that is a "yes" to readjusting Penrith's average, or do you want me to telephone every promoter personally with my thoughts?'

'I think you had better leave that to me,' the frustrated Chairman said wearily.

The next person on the list of people for Vincent to catch up with was Jeff Harding. He had read the news about Penrith and had been straight on the telephone, assuming he would be making way for the old superstar.

'Not at all, Jeff. You are a good rider and we need good riders. From what I read and hear, you are still as selfish as you always were and I shall, of course, be taking your captaincy and giving it to Bryce. In fact, I would have given it to the stadium cat rather than leave it with you anyway.

'Apart from that, you are in the line-up. I sincerely hope that as the season goes on, you will also become a part of the *team*. That, of course, is up to you, and I will not refer to this conversation again. Not until I get around to looking at the team for next season, anyway.'

'A pat on the head, followed by a kick in the teeth and then a slap in the face,' thought Jeff, as he put the phone down. 'I wonder if he still holds a grudge about Dianne? I'd better make an effort anyway. If he does kick me out at the end of the year, I will need to have put on a show in order to pick up a good contract elsewhere.'

Chapter 15

It was just like the good, old days when Shelford Speedway opened its doors for the 1983 season. The event was only a challenge match against local rivals, Thorden Heath, but the attendance was significantly better than anything the stadium had seen the previous year. Shelford won comfortably enough, with Harding unbeaten all evening, but the efforts of the lesser lights in the Shelford team really caught the eye.

In the home changing room after the meeting, the riders were clowning around, full of fun, when Vincent wheeled himself in.

'Well done, lads,' he said, 'especially Jeff and you two.' He nodded to the two youngsters, Alan Stewart and Reece Sullivan. I want to see both of you in my office when you are dressed. Each man in the team will find a 50 quid bonus in his paycheque for tonight's win, and the drinks are on me in the upstairs bar.'

The two lads stood nervously in front of Vincent's desk like a couple of schoolboys in front of the head after having been caught smoking in the bike sheds.

'You don't know me yet, and I don't know much about you, but you will find that if you do the right thing by me, you will end up in front. I want both of you on brand new bikes next week. Send the bills to me. Now, get upstairs, have a drink and find yourselves some birds to celebrate with.'

At ten-thirty, Vincent announced the office was closed. He dismissed the permanent and meeting staff for the evening by thanking them for their efforts over a long day. It had been years since the stadium had buzzed so much and they were all delighted with the new atmosphere.

Ann turned off the lights and locked the office door as Vincent started wheeling himself towards the back of the main stand. He was normally meticulous with his planning but with so many other things to organise, he had overlooked the question of getting up the back stairs of the stand to the main bar.

Two Shelford supporters, wearing anoraks, with their sew-on

badges, in the team's red and white colours, were coming down the stairs. They were both in their mid-20s and built like the proverbial brick outhouse. Without a word being said, they simply took a side of the chair each, picked it up, Vincent and all, and carried it up the stairs as if it was empty.

Once at the top, the lads turned to walk back down the stairs again.

'Stop right there,' demanded Vincent. 'I want to buy you a drink, and in any case, how the hell do I get back down if you two go home!'

By the end of the evening, Martin Kessler, better known as 'Lurch' to friend and foe alike, had become Vincent's new chauffeur, bodyguard, confidante and his eyes and ears at speedway's ground level.

Lurch was a classic speedway 'anorak'. Well, at least he was on the surface, and there was a lot of that. He would never be able to hide in a crowd. Six-feet four of solid muscle and a shock of disobedient jet-black hair made him a natural centrepiece.

Despite his size and the fact that he could obviously look after himself, he was one of those naturally clever, but non-conformist, characters you sometimes meet. He had wasted a grammar school education by spending his entire school life devoting himself to being as difficult as he could with the teachers. Not just the teachers, anyone remotely connected with authority in any of its many forms.

Leaving school at 16, he seemed to have done just about every job in the world there was to do, but none had lasted too long. Either the boss had resented his attitude, although he was always good at his work, or something would happen which forced him to consider compromising on his own particular set of priorities.

The first of these priorities was supporting Shelford Speedway; the second was supporting speedway in general.

They were the first and second priorities on the list, simply because that is where the list began and ended.

He scrounged and he scraped. At 22, he still lived at home with his parents, but somehow he always managed to follow his team, the Racers. He had no real mechanical training but had quickly grasped an understanding of speedway bikes – and many of the team men were happy to exploit the fact. He would do anything for them if it meant a free trip to a track, getting into the meeting for nothing, and a chance to be where the action was in the pits. Rarely a meeting went past where he hadn't been dragged in to help someone.

And now here he was, working for the boss.

Bryce Penrith and his family slipped into the country unnoticed. Lurch met them at Heathrow airport and drove them up to Foxglove Manor in the new Mercedes Vincent had leased for the Australian speedway superstar to use while in England.

Even Bryce and his family were impressed with The Manor. Vincent and Ann met them at the door and Ann showed the couple and their young son, Ryan, briefly around the main rooms.

She then took them upstairs where they selected adjoining bedrooms. One would be for themselves and the other for Ryan. The rooms they chose had a connecting door so they could have the outer door of Ryan's room locked. That way, he could only enter or leave via their room and, likewise, any visitors to Ryan had to get past them.

The new 'lodgers' were beginning to feel comfortable about the arrangements.

Ann explained that Vincent and her slept and spent a fair amount of their time in the extension.

'That's our bolthole,' she explained. 'It's purpose built for Vincent. Only he and I ever go in there. If we are in there and you want to speak to either of us, please use the intercom in the kitchen, and we will be straight out.

'Other than that, and the basement, where Vincent has his private rooms, the whole of the place is open to you. We have six staff available. They look after the inside of the house and keep it tidy.

If you want to cook for yourselves then feel free to use everything there is in the kitchen, both food and equipment. Otherwise, just give the housekeeper, Mrs Peasenhall, an idea of the times you would like meals prepared, and what you would like to eat, and she will do the rest. She has cleared out a fridge and a pantry for your own use, and will happily organise your food and any other shopping should you wish.

'We don't have formal maids, butlers and the like, but you can arrange with the girls who keep the place neat and tidy what you wish them to do about these two bedrooms and bathrooms.'

'Oh, I am sure I can manage them myself!' laughed Molly.

'Would you like a rest now, or shall I introduce you and this lovely boy to Mrs Peasenhall? I know Vincent is itching to catch up with Bryce.'

Ann had expected Molly to be a bit mumsy, dowdy even. The name 'Molly' had conjured up images of a slightly overweight middle-aged matron. The real thing was anything but that. She was trim, well read and had a terrific personality, with sparkling eyes and natural self-confidence. Her northern accent was still audible if you listened hard enough for it, but only just. Molly was clearly the product of a private education.

There were no signs that the 12-hour journey from California, albeit first-class, and then the trip up from Heathrow, had left any effect at all. The nicely tanned face needed little or no make-up and, like Ann, her hair was naturally black. Now in her 30th year, she was in her prime. Ann liked her instantly.

Bryce made his way to the library. Vincent beckoned to an armchair and wheeled himself around to be seated opposite at the other side of the coffee table.

'Drink of anything?' he enquired.

'Not yet,' said Bryce. The two were clearly weighing each other up.

Bryce Penrith was not a tall man but he was a wonderful specimen. He had broad shoulders and a narrow waist, and was obviously very fit. Even just from his movements it was clear he was a natural athlete.

He had been one of those kids who had been able to play all ball games, regardless of the size and shape of the ball. Whilst away at private boarding school he had represented Australia at schoolboy level in rugby union and could have done likewise at cricket, but had preferred to share his cricket playing with tennis, swimming and athletics during the long Australian summers.

Being brought up on a cattle station, Bryce had almost been born on a horse but, as a teenager, had moved from normal equestrian events to the more exciting and considerably more dangerous rodeo. At 15, though, he replaced horses with motorbikes. They were faster and more powerful. From the moment he sat astride a trail bike, he had felt comfortable and his love for two-wheeled motor sport had begun.

Outback living had already turned the Australian's face into a leathery walnut colour, giving the impression he was a little older than his 32 years, but for all of that, with piercing blue eyes and auburn hair bleached lighter by the sun, he was a real babe-magnet. Tall, he might not be, but he filled the room with his presence. It was clear why he had been offered a career in the media, and why he was being fast-tracked into politics.

Vincent took the lead.

'Here are my key thoughts on the role I am hoping you can perform for us. I know when you were here before, winning races was the most important thing in your life, but you also managed to understand the importance of public relations. I am gambling on two things.

'The first of them is that although winning races is still important to you, equally important now is being happy and settled in all you do. I am hoping speedway racing will be just a part of you wanting to enjoy yourself whilst you are here, and that you are also wanting to make more friends and contacts.

'I will not ask you to take unnecessary risks on the track, nor will I demand you win every race. What I want most of all is for you to help the younger team members, not just with their riding but also with all the other things that are involved with being a speedway rider. I want you to develop an ethic within the team of understanding that winning is not enough by itself. Winning in style and realising the importance of putting on a show is paramount.

'From my perspective, I have become involved in speedway again, when clearly I didn't need to,' he continued, glancing around at the library and grounds outside, 'but I do not intend to treat it as a hobby.'

Vincent continued: 'The older promoters, sadly dropping off the pace these days, always talked of a report from a Lord Shawcross. I have never seen the full report, let alone read it, but I have heard the first few lines quoted many times. *"Speedway racing is both a sport and a business. However, speedway promoters should always understand it is a business first and a sport afterwards."*

'If more promoters these days were to work on that basis, the sport would be a lot healthier than it is today.'

Bryce was nodding. In his own world of farming, he had similar balances to consider daily. Like where did the balance between putting food on the table for people at a reasonable cost, sit with the ethical questions of how animals are treated and the responsibility farmers had to the environment?

He was no tree-hugger by any means, but he clearly understood the difficulties of balancing responsibilities, especially as he wished to raise his public profile when he returned Down Under.

'Perhaps it is a bit conceited to see ourselves as trail-blazers in speedway's resurgence, but that is the way I would like us both to think,' Vincent went on.

'Because I have this kind of role in mind for you, and I want you to concentrate more on helping me set up a long term future at Shelford Speedway than simply riding your bike, I have no intention of paying you simply on your individual on-track results.

'Here are the credit cards I agreed to give yourself and Molly. They have a limit of 20 thousand pounds and the account will be cleared monthly. Please use them as freely as you wish. I do not expect you to have to pay for a thing whilst you are here. If ever there is a situation where the use of a credit card will not do the job, one phone call or word to me is all that will be needed.

'Beyond that, I will not embarrass you at this stage by talking money. I would simply want you to understand that if Shelford Speedway is profitable, then everyone associated with it will benefit.'

Again, Bryce nodded and went to speak, but Vincent continued,

'By putting this house at your disposal I have tried to demonstrate my commitment to having you here helping with my crusade. Please feel free to treat these arrangements as being as temporary or as long term as you wish. If you or Molly would feel more comfortable in a rented house or a hotel, then just say and it will be fixed.'

'I'll speak with Molly,' Bryce said. 'What I think will happen is that we will take up your kind offer but use this place simply as a local pad. As you know, I have many friends spread around Europe and I expect we will spend a good deal of time away. Also, we are bound to spend some of the time with Molly's folks and family. Therefore, I don't imagine we will be around here enough to become a nuisance.

'As far as the speedway goes, it's not my intention to be riding myself into the ground. I shall obviously honour all of Shelford's commitments but I shan't take on too many other bookings. Maybe a few meetings for old friends who have been good to me, both in the UK and on the Continent, but I shan't be a speedway slave this time around.'

Bryce stood up to leave.

'OK,' he said, 'when do we start?'

'If you are up to it, I have arranged for you to have a few private laps at the track tomorrow morning. Then, after lunch, I have asked all of the riders if they would like to come and have a run-out with you. I have also invited the press to attend.

'Most of the team are a good bunch of lads with a lot of improvement in them. Jeff Harding was last year's captain. He is a good points scorer. I'll let you make your own mind up after that. I've kept him on simply so that it will take some scoring pressure off you. Beyond that . . . well, as I say, you can make up your own mind.'

'I understand, thanks for the warning,' was all Bryce needed to say.

Vincent finished by telling Bryce that Lurch was hanging around The Manor, just in case he wanted a guided tour of the area.

Chapter 16

'I know it makes me sound like an old dinosaur,' said Bryce after a dozen or so very impressive laps, 'but these things are just so easy to ride compared to when I stopped! It's a wonder how anybody can get past another rider if they are all on these. I only hope my reflexes at the starts have not suffered with the lay-off.'

He modestly forgot to mention it had been three years since anyone back home had beaten him at squash.

Bryce then watched as the keener team members, who had arrived early, went through their paces. He had a ride around with them all, one by one. By this time, Jeff Harding had sauntered in. He got changed as his mechanic warmed up his bike.

'Just came along to try a few new things,' he said, before going out and putting in four blisteringly fast laps.

'Seems OK,' he said nonchalantly. 'Care for a few laps round, Bryce?'

'Oh, I don't think so,' said Bryce with a smile. 'You look far too good for me and, besides, this old-timer has done more than enough for today.'

Unlike the first press conference that Vincent had called a week earlier, this time some 30 media men had arrived. Local TV crews were there, most of the national newspapers and a posse of speedway photographers as well as the top men from the *Speedway Star*.

As expected, Bryce handled them all perfectly, telling them what they wanted to hear and posing for the many photographs the cameramen demanded. Vincent sent word, while the other team-men were getting changed, that he wanted the riders to hang about until Bryce finished with the press boys and they duly obliged.

After the press had been satisfied, Vincent and the team sat down with Bryce. The Australian's charisma fairly filled Vincent's private office. Even Jeff Harding was impressed.

There wasn't a great deal of detail in what the new skipper said. He carefully praised Jeff and thanked him for stepping down from the captaincy in order to let 'this old boy have one last fling' and then spoke generally about how enthusiastic the squad seemed, and how much talent he thought there was.

That was it really. The team members all drove away from the speedway feeling 10ft tall.

The first fixture after the new arrival was a league match at home to Sheffield. Vincent had rearranged the away meeting with Brighton planned for that week. For maximum impact and publicity, he needed Shelford to be racing at home when Bryce first wheeled out his bike for his second coming.

The place was heaving. Jeff Harding maintained his number one position in the team while Bryce had asked to be paired with the youngster, Alan Stewart.

'I'll be looking for you in the first turn,' was all the new skipper said, as they readied themselves for their first race in heat three.

In his excitement, Stewart messed up his start from the gate three starting position, leaving him at the back as the four riders approached the first turn. Bryce, off gate one, had got away marginally in front of the two Sheffield riders. Bryce glanced over and saw Stewart was behind the Sheffield pair, so he delayed his turn just a fraction, and then put his bike completely sideways in front of the two visitors in the middle of the turn.

The leading three riders all but stopped as the startled opposition pair had no option but to shut off their throttles and throw their own bikes sideways in order to scrub off speed and avoid running into the leader.

Stewart, with that split second more time, saw his chance and turned back inside the other three riders before roaring off ahead down the back straight.

When his partner had passed, Bryce just adjusted weight and throttle, put his wheels back in line, and happily followed the youngster around, with the Sheffield duo having no chance to mount a decent counter-attack.

On the last bend, Stewart looked behind him, saw Bryce was sitting comfortably second, and knocked his throttle right off, drifting wide as he did so. Bryce thought perhaps his partner had a problem, so also backed off his speed in order to cover any opposition attack down the inside. The Shelford duo crossed the line abreast, with Bryce marginally in front.

The crowd went mad as Bryce grabbed Alan Stewart's wrist and raised it as if he were a boxing referee declaring a winner at the end of a bout. He did this five times as the pair circled the track, much to the delight of the fans, who went mad, frantically waving their red and white scarves and flags.

As the two home riders dismounted, the youngster rushed over and gushed out his thanks to Bryce for the work he had done in the crucial first turn.

'*You* were the one who saw the gap and went for it,' said Bryce, 'but what the hell were you doing at the end of the race?'

'Letting *you* finish in front,' said the surprised youngster. 'Jeff says we should always give way to the senior rider in those circumstances.'

'Hmmm,' said Bryce. 'Well, Jeff isn't the skipper any more, and this captain says such a procedure is dangerous and unnecessary. You know very well, we both get paid for a win whichever way around we finish if we are lying in first and second place.

'I get three points for a win or two points and a bonus, making three points, if I follow you home. As far as I am concerned they are both the same, so in future you don't slow down like that unless it is to help a partner under pressure, OK?'

Shelford won at a canter, 48-30. Harding was unbeaten in the main match and was also victorious in the Rider of the Night second half final. Bryce was barely less impressive, dropping his only point in four rides to the visiting number one, Sven Helgusson, in his last race. He was understandably feeling the effects of not having ridden competitively for so long and, still lacking race-fitness, decided not to risk a crash by trying a risky pass. He also finished a diplomatic second to the visiting number one in his second half heat.

The packed crowd was jubilant at the end of the match as the winners paraded around the slightly banked, 375-yard circuit, with Bryce pushing the younger members of the team up to the front, where they could milk the applause.

Afterwards, in the changing rooms, as they were all in high spirits and skylarking around, Bryce raised his arms and asked for a few seconds of calm.

'You are a great team,' he said. 'Nothing is beyond us this year. That was wonderful riding, Jeff. We have a true number one and star rider in you!

'Can I just add one thing? Riders like Jeff and me are better than you lot! If you are in front of either of us, it is because we *want* you to be there. The next rider who insults either of us by moving over, so as to make it look like we can't do things for ourselves, will get stuck under a cold shower! Agreed, Jeff?'

Harding, revelling in the fact that he had gone through the card unbeaten on opening night, could do nothing but join in with the general merriment.

It had been clear to Bryce that, with such a young team, the question of each rider being able to maintain his own bike was of paramount importance. He had a chat with his own mechanic, ace tuner Eddie Campbell, and between the two of them, they teed up a plan to help.

Eddie invited all riders contracted to Shelford to a bike-cleaning clinic. All those who wished to take advantage were told to be at Campbell's workshop by ten o'clock the next morning, when he would hold a tutorial on how to properly strip down, clean and set up a speedway bike.

They had expected only two or three of the younger team-men to turn up. Instead, all of the team except Jeff Harding, and three junior riders had arrived by a quarter-to-ten. By the time Bryce got there, the acclaimed tuner had begun his lesson.

Eddie did the talking as he went through his regular cleaning and maintenance routine on Bryce's bike, demonstrating in detail exactly what he was doing, and why. Then each rider carried out the same procedures on his own bike, with Bryce and Eddie going around helping and advising as and when necessary.

Some of the lads learned just a few extra tips here and there whilst for others the whole session was an eye-opener.

Bryce pointed out that hopefully most of the team men would soon be earning enough to employ somebody to do the routine stuff for them, but they should be fully capable of doing it themselves anyway.

He spelled out the importance of having good equipment, and the responsibility each rider had to himself in assuring this was the case.

Most top riders through the years were incredibly secretive, even amongst team-mates about their bike set-ups, but Bryce no longer needed such secrecy. On that morning, and throughout the rest of that season, he passed on as much knowledge to his fellow riders as he possibly could.

As he mingled with the riders, Bryce had a chat with each one.

Just a few words here and there based on what he had seen of them the previous evening. Had this rider thought of adjusting his body position at the crucial start of the race? Had another thought of modifying his bike set up by altering the position of saddle and handlebars? Another rider learned the importance of varying the length of the bike overall by moving the back wheel forward or backwards.

By the end of the morning, each of the team members felt as if they were all friends rather than just team-mates, and all agreed Bryce Penrith was the best thing to ever happen to Shelford.

The Racers were to visit title favourites, Poole, as their first away meeting of the season the following Wednesday. This was a mighty challenge for such a young and inexperienced side but Bryce made a very good point to them at that maintenance clinic.

He pointed out that it was a distinct advantage going to a strong team early in the season. It gave the Racers a chance to catch the opposition cold before they had settled in properly. His sheer confidence was enough to put positive thoughts into all the riders' minds.

Vincent and Bryce travelled down to the south coast together in Vincent's fully fitted out motor home. Lurch did the driving, leaving the other two to chat about things in general, and to plan their strategy for the match. The chauffeur could not believe his luck. This was as near as he could get to his speedway heaven without actually being there, and he was being paid for it!

As was usual on the tight and slick Poole circuit, passing was at an absolute premium that night. Jeff Harding continued his excellent start to the season and again went through the evening unbeaten.

'Just goes to show what he has always been capable of,' thought Vincent. The threat of being dumped, along with the challenge to his number one spot from Bryce, had really livened him up. Now all Vince needed to do was to turn him into a good team-man – and he knew the fastest way to Jeff's heart in this respect was through his wallet.

By accident or design, Harding had moved the Poole riders over in one of his races. No doubt, the intention was to make room for himself but in doing so, he had also helped his partner, Tim Weston. Bryce showered praise on the selfish and conceited number one rider whilst Vincent pushed £200 into his hand. 'A bit like training a dog,' he thought to himself.

Shelford cashed in on some early season rustiness at the starts from the Poole Pirates' middle order to pinch an unlikely 41-37 victory. The Poole promotion was clearly unhappy but took the result with good enough grace, especially when Penrith got on the microphone, praised the local track, team and promotion, and said the visitors had been lucky to have stolen a victory against the run of play.

The Shelford team were ecstatic and the atmosphere in the local steak house, where Vincent took them all afterwards to celebrate, was one of complete elation and togetherness. Even Jeff Harding joined in the fun.

Once again, Lurch was left pinching himself at the excitement of it all, even though he was left to drive back to the Midlands as Vincent and Bryce strapped themselves into the vehicle's beds and slept most of the way home.

Another comfortable home win followed against Bradford on the Saturday. Not only did the Racers win, 45-33, but they also won with great style. Following on Bryce's lead, all of the team took to communicating with the crowd in a way they had never done before. The whole atmosphere of the place was upbeat and exciting.

What helped a good deal was for the supporters to see a programme of stadium improvements had already begun. Even the most sceptical of locals was now accepting the new promotion wasn't intending to asset-strip the place and flog it for development.

The Shelford Racers were the visitors at Birmingham the following Monday. The attendance there was the largest seen for three years or more. Many supporters in the area had turned out just to see Bryce Penrith again, but there must have also been a couple of thousand Shelford fans who had made the hour-long trip.

Again the sheer ebullience of the Shelford side got them another close victory, this time by 40-38, although Jeff Harding was beaten a couple of times on the night, and it needed an unbelievable piece of skill and daring from Penrith in the penultimate race to get them over the line.

Bryce had missed the start, and for three laps had followed, mid-track, behind the Birmingham pair who were team-riding, shoulder-to-shoulder, and presenting what seemed like an impenetrable wall.

At the beginning of the last lap the superstar had gone into the first turn very wide, turned close to the fence, and got his wheels in line extra early. As the riders were about to enter the third turn, because he had made a long straight, Penrith had just that tiny fraction of extra momentum.

Using nothing but sheer willpower, he ducked under the inside rider as they entered the turn, putting himself in at a ridiculously tight angle. He then flicked the rear of his bike out, turned incredibly tight and hung all his weight over the back wheel, reaching the finishing line whilst hanging off the bike.

Five yards past the line, the Birmingham pair, with more drive and momentum coming out of the turn, had passed him, but Bryce had timed his dash to perfection.

The local Brummies fans were disappointed to lose, but went home simply shaking their heads at the way Penrith had stolen the match from them in such a blinding fashion. The Shelford folk were just ecstatic. It had been a wonderful speedway meeting and a great night out.

Chapter 17

The following Wednesday, Vincent attended his first ever British Speedway Promoters' Association General Council meeting. Every Division One track was represented by one or two and, in some cases, three people.

Lurch saw Vincent to the meeting room and then went back for a kip in the motor home. Vincent was very much on his own and the atmosphere was cool.

Alan Howard, the BSPA Chairman, was a builder and property developer by day. He was a natural bully and used to getting his own way. Vincent had put him over a barrel both with the takeover of the Shelford promotion and the introduction of Penrith.

Howard was not one to forgive and forget. He was determined to even things up with this smart-arse somewhere along the line.

The Chairman wasn't the only promoter there who was unhappy either. Several had soon forgotten how Vincent had become a paraplegic whilst giving his best for the sport, and now regarded him purely as a Johnny-come-lately upstart who was getting above his station.

One of the first items on the agenda was to accept and ratify the minutes from the previous General Council meeting and to run through the decisions made by the Management Committee since then. Management Committee decisions needed to be ratified by the full council.

It was a nonsense thing really. Most times those decisions had been taken and already acted upon and certainly could not be reversed, but it gave the rank and file promoters a chance to sound off.

The two major decisions taken by the Committee since the pre-season meeting had been those of granting Vincent a promoter's licence and then adjusting Bryce Penrith's points average down to allow him into the Shelford line-up.

It took no time for the question of allowing someone with no previous promoting experience to be granted a promoter's licence to come up. This was allied to the fact that the previous Shelford boss, Cyril Grant, had been unceremoniously dumped.

It was suggested that Vincent had no right to be present in the meeting until the decision to grant him a licence had been ratified, and he was asked to leave the room whilst the question was discussed.

Vincent had been pre-warned that Grant had been stirring things up. When Howard asked him to leave the room, Vincent laughed. He pulled out of his pocket the promoter's licence he had been issued with, and laid it on the table in front of him.

'I believe,' he said softly, 'each track has a right to be represented at this meeting by a person holding one of these. I am here to represent Shelford, and I hold this. Now then, ladies and gentlemen, may I please ask every other person sitting at this table to produce his or her licence?'

There was silence and stunned looks. Nobody normally bothered with such technicalities and promotions sent all kinds of representatives to the meetings. Even the Brighton team manager was present. He had no promoter's licence.

The Chairman had a quick private discussion with the Association Manager, Rod Brown, who was sitting next to him.

After a minute or two, Howard said it was not necessary for the people at the meeting to show their licences. The Manager had a list of all licensed promoters with him, and could verify which of the representatives did or did not hold a current licence.

Silence descended once more. Several promoters had not yet got around to renewing their licences for this year.

'However, I have no alternative,' Howard continued. 'I have to ask that all those present who do not hold a current promoter's licence retire from the room.'

Bedlam broke out. Arms whirled like windmills and little groups of promoters convened private meetings in corners. After 10 minutes of this, during which time Vincent had sat calmly reading the *Financial Times*, the Chairman called the meeting to order.

'Gentlemen (and ladies) . . . Rod and I have been through the list of promoting licences issued so far this year. Looking at the people around this room, and comparing it against the licences issued, it seems that all but three tracks have at least one *bona fide* representative present, although they will have to ask their non-licensed advisers to leave.

'We have a clear choice. Those present who do not hold a current licence must leave the room. If enough other delegates also decide to leave and we then fail to have a quorum present, I will be obliged to abandon the meeting and reconvene it at another time.

'Given that I am required to give a minimum of 14 days' notice of a General Council meeting, it will be some three weeks before we can meet again.

'I now intend calling a short break. It is currently ten-thirty five. We will reconvene here at eleven o'clock.'

'You think you are so bloody clever don't you!' said Howard, who had stayed behind in the room with BSPA manager, Rod Brown, and a smug looking Vincent.

'If enough of the delegates walk out, then it will be at least three weeks before we can discuss the two issues, and if we carry on with the meeting short of representation from some tracks, we could end up getting a non-representative vote,' said an exasperated Howard.

'Oh, what you really mean is, you won't get the decision you want,' Vincent pointed out.

'Look, between you and me, it doesn't matter anyway,' Vincent continued, 'because if you vote to rescind my licence without good reason, I'll simply appeal to the Speedway Control Board, who will overrule you and hand it back to me.

'If you decide to rescind the decision for me to use Bryce, I'll hop straight over the heads of you and the Control Board, and slap in an injunction. This will put the whole of speedway into suspense in the first instance and then I will put the Association into receivership after that, when I sue you all. Your choice, Sunshine.'

Howard glanced at his manager who simply nodded back to him, indicating he thought Vincent once again had them over a barrel.

The Chairman left the room and came back 10 minutes later to tell Vincent and Brown that the meeting had been abandoned because a quorum could not be raised.

'Wouldn't care to give me a push, would you?' Vincent asked Brown, He could have managed easily by himself but wanted a chance to speak with the BSPA Manager.

Actually, Rod did the speaking to Vincent as he wheeled the chair down to the car park.

'Be careful,' he warned. 'The only side I am on is speedway's but all I can say is that you are running up any number of enemies.'

'I'm aware of that, Rod, but it seems to me there's a bit of deadwood that needs clearing out before speedway can move forward.

'If I win what looks as if it might become an interesting battle, speedway moves on. If I lose, only speedway loses, I make a killing by selling up, and end up with the freedom of Shelford instead of being an ogre. Howard would become the one everyone would blame, so I think I have all the bases covered. In any case, I really don't expect to lose.'

'Well, between you and me, good luck,' said Brown as they arrived at the motor home.

On the way home, Vincent composed the following letter to be circulated to all Division One promoters.

Gentlemen,

I would ask that each of you review what went on at the aborted meeting today. You will recall, the Chairman asked me to leave the room. I simply pointed out to him that I was constitutionally entitled to stay. All of the other actions and activities that took place were neither of my doing nor within my control. Therefore, I ask you not to blame me for your wasted day.

However, in order to try and answer as many questions as might have been raised during the meeting, I make the following points:

● *Those who challenge my right to hold a promoter's licence should ask themselves on what grounds? It is true that Cyril Grant was the subject of a boardroom coup but all procedures were legal and transparent. This will not be the first time, or the last, that speedway promotions have changed hands in acrimonious circumstances. I repeat, all procedures were correctly carried out.*

● *My promoting experience might well be limited but I have retained an experienced and professional staff around me. Many promoters in the past would have failed a good deal of the scrutiny to which I have been subjected. I have no criminal record, no history of any untoward business practices and can show financial means of substantially more than most.*

● *Gentlemen, what you should be saying is that Shelford Speedway, so close to being lost just two months ago, like so many speedways of late, is now a vibrant business again. This can only benefit speedway as a whole.*

● *As far as the signing of Bryce Penrith is concerned, his previous promoter was happy to enter into a financial arrangement with me for his use.*

● *It is true that in order to fit him into the team I needed a 'special dispensation'. Such dispensations are not uncommon where the net result is a benefit to speedway as a whole Ask the Poole and Birmingham promotions how many extra people they had through their turnstiles compared to the last few visits from Shelford. And it has cost the league nothing, either in poached assets or in any way financial, to have the best drawcard speedway has seen in 50 years or more, if not ever, appearing at their tracks.*

● *Shelford will not win the league this year but even if they were to, would that be so terrible? We have Penrith and Harding. After those two, we have a team of kids. For us to win the league, several of those kids will have had to improve significantly. They are all British, so surely this would have to be to the overall benefit of British speedway.*

● *Penrith will only be riding for this one season. Shelford will then be faced with having to replace him and will meet whatever team-equalisation restrictions are decided upon for next year.*

So gentlemen, I would ask you to at least accept the above logic, try to avoid personalities clouding judgements and simply allow us to continue adding value to speedway in general and each of your businesses in particular.

Best regards,
Vincent Hansing
Managing Director
Shelford Speedway Ltd

The aborted General Council meeting was not reconvened and the matter never referred to officially again.

Chapter 18

Shelford won again the following week, this time against the Byford Racers, in front of another bumper crowd, leaving them unbeaten at home in the league so far. Jeff Harding continued his unbeaten run but the team-riding skills of Bryce Penrith continued to steal the show.

Belle Vue was the next away trip. Molly's parents lived in Cheshire, so Bryce took his family up in the Mercedes. They would spend a few days with Molly's parents.

Vincent and Lurch went up to Manchester together in the motor home. Just before the meeting, Vincent and Bryce pulled the team together.

'This is not an easy track to come and win at,' said Vincent, 'but it is a wonderful track to ride. If we win, great, but the main thing is for everyone to enjoy their racing tonight. For those of you unfamiliar with the place, believe me, you will think you are going as fast as it is possible to go, and the home boys will still cruise past if you are not paying attention.'

Belle Vue was not Jeff Harding's favourite track. You had to stick your neck out to take on and beat the best of the locals, and that was not something he relished. Nevertheless, he got away well from the start in heat one and hung on to win the race.

The reserves predictably lost out in heat two but Bryce just loved the place and easily headed the local star, Peter Cullen, to win heat three.

Reece Sullivan was in heat four. He was trying desperately hard to take the lead when he clipped a back wheel, went over the bars, somersaulted in the air and landed part on his head, part on his back. Vincent sent Lurch out on the track to help. 'Damn these fucking useless legs,' he heard himself saying, before pulling himself back together.

Sullivan was taken to the hospital, unconscious. The rest of the team battled hard but succumbed by four points. It had been a mammoth match in front of yet another huge crowd.

Bryce had glided through the meeting unbeaten without getting a speck of shale on his leathers. Jeff Harding had battled uncharacteristically hard, as had the other riders. Vincent was mighty proud of them.

As soon as the match was over, he and Lurch were off to the Manchester Royal Infirmary. The staff at the hospital were unhelpful, but Vincent was having none of that. He and Lurch quickly located Sullivan, who was in a cubicle in casualty and still unconscious.

'Where is the Senior Registrar?' Vincent demanded, and despite efforts of the staff to fob him off, he was soon facing the man.

'Get this man to ICU,' he ordered. 'Now!'. The doctor was not used to being spoken to like this and his hackles started rising. He got as far as 'Now look here...' before Vincent held up his hand.

'A word,' he said pointing. 'In there.'

As soon as they were out of earshot of the others, Vincent said very quietly, but with clear menace:

'If you don't get him up there now, I promise you I shall break you as a doctor. And if the boy does not fully recover, I shall break you as a person. Don't mess with me, you are dealing with the wrong man here.'

The doctor was clearly spooked. He was not prepared for such mental intimidation and took the easy way out. He arranged for Reece to be admitted into ICU immediately.

Once the lad had been settled in and wired up, Vincent sent Lurch back down to the motor home to get some sleep. He would bleep if he needed anything. Vincent then settled in by the bedside for a night-long vigil.

The night duty nurse started chatting to Vincent as she checked all of Reece's vital signs.

'Younger brother?' she asked.

'I don't know him that well. I am just responsible for his welfare.'

'Oh, I see,' she said. She didn't see at all really but, clearly, the man in the wheelchair cared deeply.

'Can I do anything for you?' she offered.

'You can tell me where I can drain this bag off,' he said lightly, glancing down. She pointed out the disabled toilet and asked if he needed any help. He told her he thought not, but smiled and said:

'If I do, I'll press the panic button!'

When he got back to the bedside, there was a cup of tea and some sandwiches waiting for him.

Reece Sullivan regained consciousness just after four in the morning. Even before the medical staff had come to check on him, Vincent had got the lad to wriggle his appendages. All seemed to be functioning normally. He was soon out cold again but this time he was just sleeping rather than comatose.

Vincent allowed himself some catnaps from then on but stayed on. The consultant in charge of the unit finally came along to check all was in order in the morning. Reece had a king-sized headache, and there was always a danger of the swollen and bruised brain creating pressure in the skull, but the signs were promising. By nine o'clock. Reece's parents had arrived. Lurch had been hovering outside for some time. He took the parents up to the room and then he and Vincent left.

As the motor home swung out of the car park, Vincent took out his dictating machine.

'Memo: make an appointment with the local BUPA rep for tomorrow.' He couldn't believe he had been so remiss. He had organised extra injury insurance for his riders as soon as he had taken over but he hadn't thought about private health cover.

Given that most speedway injuries happened in the evening, he did not want his boys left to the whims of junior hospital registrars. He wanted consultants involved straight away. He put it a bit more basically to Lurch.

'Why the hell leave my lads in the hands of monkeys because the organ grinder can't be bothered to get out of bed?'

Vincent thought about lying down on his bunk on the way back to The Manor but with all the morning traffic it was stop, start, and in any case, right at that moment he felt fine, so he sat up chatting to Lurch.

'Excuse me, boss,' Lurch ventured during a lull in conversation. 'Can I ask you an impertinent question?' Vincent nodded, intrigued.

'Well, as you know, us Wallies out on the terracing all think we are better team managers than the experts, and I am sure that when we think a team manager has made a mistake it is really that we don't know all the facts, but . . .

'Here's the filled-in programme from last night. Was there a reason why you never switched Jason and Tony in heat 10? I'm not sure, even then, we would have won, but I reckon we would have stood a better chance.'

Vincent studied the programme carefully. Much as he hated to admit it, Lurch was right, and Vincent should have seen it himself at the time. He had allowed the situation with Reece Sullivan to cloud his judgement. Maybe he had also misjudged Lurch, this big mountain of a man. Perhaps there was more to him than just brawn and loyalty?

'So have I made any other errors so far this year? No, I'm not being sarcastic, I am being serious.'

Uncomfortable now, Lurch would only say that as they had won all their other matches, how could he not have done, but Vincent pressed for a fuller answer.

The conversation turned into a full critique of every team decision Vincent had made since the start of the year. Lurch was lucid, probing and very thorough. Most of his comments Vincent could counter with an explanation but one or two he could not.

'Lurch,' he said, 'you've just talked yourself into a job. I found out tonight, I am not mobile enough to do the job on my own anyway. As of now, you are the new Shelford team manager.' Lurch, taken aback, thought for a moment.

'If it's all the same to you, boss, I'd sooner be your assistant and simply help out where I can.'

'I'll be there with you, and my promoter's licence gives me the authority to stick my oar in when needed. But I have to concede that being a cripple (Vincent rarely ever used that word) is proving to be a handicap to my doing the team manager's job justice.

'If your name is not in the programme, you won't get full respect. I can fend for myself if I have to. And,' he added, pointing down to his chair, 'there are times when I can make *this* work for me.

'We'll do the job together but you will hold the official position of team manager. Do you think you can fit it in with the rest of your duties?' Lurch laughed. The biggest part of his duties so far had been sitting around waiting for his boss.

With no other damage except concussion and bad bruising, Reece Sullivan was released within a couple of days, and out of action for two weeks. As luck would have it, Shelford had no away matches during that time and managed to win their home match, against Glasgow, without him comfortably enough. They remained on top of the British League by a whisker.

All of the lads knew Lurch well, and his elevation to the position of team manager was universally applauded. All was going well in the Shelford Racers' ranks.

Chapter 19

Spring had turned into early summer. Molly Penrith was spending more time at The Manor than she had expected to. Ann was the perfect host and the two women got on very well.

Young Ryan loved Ann and the house, and had become good friends with the housekeeper's grandson, Andy, with whom he played quite often. He also went along to the nursery class of the local school whenever the family were staying at The Manor.

Molly also got on well with Heather. Ann, Heather and Molly had found themselves spending a lot of time together.

When Ryan had gone with Mrs Peasenhall to play with Andy, the three ladies were left lazing around the pool. It was a beautiful late-May day and they had opened up the glass concertina doors to the pool so they could sunbathe on the outside patio. Heather was applying sun cream to Ann's shoulders but in a slightly more than matter-of-fact manner.

'Something I should know about here, girls?' smiled Molly. She had seen the two of them exchange the odd intimate glance here and there before now. Both girls went bright red.

'Oh dear,' Molly added brightly, 'so that little secret didn't last too long, did it!'

'It's OK,' said Ann quickly, 'we are not actually gay and our husbands know all about it.' Molly wondered why that made it somehow OK, but she didn't say anything. Instead, she merely remarked:

'So I am the only one missing out around here, then?'

Ann looked at Heather and nodded downwards. Heather nodded back. They got to their feet and indicated for Molly to follow. The three of them made their way downstairs.

'Wow!' said Molly, 'I've not seen anything like this outside of Madame Tussauds!' When she saw the pool, she slipped off her swimming costume and marched in, hitting the power jet button as she descended into the water. Once again, she gasped 'Wow!' before adding: 'This water jet is really hitting the spot!'

Ann and Heather admired Molly's slender figure as she walked into the pool. 'Not bad at all for someone with a five-year-old,' Heather thought as they slipped off their stuff and piled into the glass shower, where they soaped each other down amid lots of schoolgirl giggling.

Molly climbed out of the pool, flopped face down onto a massage table and beckoned, before saying:

'OK, which one of you is going to oil me? Or better still, why not both of you?'

Nearly two hours later, as they went back upstairs, glowing and chattering like sparrows. Molly suddenly said:

'Oh, by the way girls, I don't think we will bother to let Bryce in on this. He's very… Australian!'

Ann told Vincent what had happened.

'That's fine,' he replied, 'but as Molly said, I'm not sure you need to let Bryce find out.'

The following weekend there was no home meeting because of the stock cars, so Vincent suggested a pool party and barbeque for the team and their wives and families or girlfriends.

It was another perfect day and everyone turned up. Lurch took it upon himself to entertain Ryan and the Hardings' son, Jack, who was just a little older.

Everyone seemed to be having a great time, especially the younger riders and their teenage girlfriends, screaming and clowning around in the pool. Jeff Harding was in the middle of them all, being Jack-the-Lad.

Dianne Harding was sitting on a sun lounge on her own reading a book. Vincent wheeled himself over to her to say hello. This was the first time they had spoken privately since she had walked out of the hospital, arm in arm with Jeff.

He quickly put her at her ease, asking if she was enjoying herself, and could he get her a drink? She answered yes, and no.

'No and yes look as if they would be nearer the mark,' he ventured. She laughed and said she would be driving home later, and she never drank when she was going to take Jack anywhere in the car.

'Oh, so it doesn't matter what happens to Jeff?' he laughed. Dianne blushed a little.

'I've lost the use of my legs, not my eyes,' he added. 'Things not as good as they could be at home, then?'

It was by way of a rhetorical question. Jeff Harding was famous for chasing young girls, and catching up with plenty. Indeed, the ever-vigilant Vincent suspected Jeff of making a quick, sneaky phone call to one of his bevy of 'groupies' while Dianne was chatting to the other girls. If Dianne had also noticed her husband suspiciously 'disappearing' inside the house for a good 10 minutes, she didn't express any concern.

'Oh,' she said, 'I'm happy enough in my own way. Jack is the one thing in my life. I live for him and, to be honest, I'm quite relieved Jeff finds his satisfaction elsewhere. It saves me having to...' She trailed off, leaving the words hanging in the air. Vincent couldn't resist it.

'So you swapped no sex with me for no sex with him!' he smiled, making his ex-girlfriend look very uncomfortable.

'Only teasing!' he added quickly. 'Let me know any time if I can help.' He wheeled himself away and she returned to her book.

Later, when everyone had gone, Vincent poured Ann a long drink.

'Do me a favour, darling,' he said. 'Can you see if you can add Dianne Harding to your frustrated ladies knitting club!' Ann knew better than to ask why.

The next time the 'knitting circle' met, Ann told the others what Vincent had said. All agreed it could be fun and admitted that Dianne looked well worth the invitation.

Sometime in late June, Dianne Harding got a call from Molly. 'Would she like to bring Jack over to play with Ryan tomorrow?' When Dianne and Jack arrived, Molly explained that Ryan wanted to take Jack to meet his friend, Andy, in the village. The housekeeper was given the afternoon off to take the two boys along.

Ann and Heather were also there at The Manor.

'It's a beautiful day. Let's all have a swim,' Ann said.

'Oh, I didn't bring a costume,' Dianne replied. 'I'll just watch.'

'Don't be silly,' said Ann, 'I'll find you one.'

'What the hell,' declared Molly. 'There's nobody about. We'll just skinny-dip!'

Before Dianne could argue, the others were all getting their gear off, laughing and chattering like excited schoolgirls.

Although she felt awkward, Dianne realised she would look silly if she were to refuse. All four ladies dived into the pool and splashed about. The water was lovely and warm and with all their frolicking and messing around with a beach ball, Dianne's embarrassment soon drifted away.

Ann was the first out of the pool. She opened up the glass concertina doors, stuck her head out, announced the coast was clear and stretched her arms over her head, whilst arching her body..

'Time for some serious sunbathing, girls,' she announced, and plonked herself, face down, on a sun lounge.

The other three women got out and shook themselves dry. There really was no need to towel off on such a nice day. There was no breeze and the sun's rays were warm and inviting. Dianne was the last one out. She slid, face down, onto a spare sun lounge between Molly and Ann. Heather was on the other side of Ann.

After just a few seconds, Ann said:

'Heath, be a dear and put some sun oil on me or my bum will burn like hell.'

Heather jumped up, grabbed a bottle of Ambre Solaire, and starting with Ann's shoulders, gently massaged the oil in. Dianne lay there bemused. This was not putting on sun tan lotion, this was more like an intimate massage. Ann looked straight into Dianne's eyes as Heather reached her buttocks and the insides of her thighs, gradually working towards the pleasure zone.

Molly had retrieved another bottle of sun oil and was kneeling next to Dianne with the lid off.

'I'll do you if you do me,' she winked as she poured some of the oil onto her hand and started on Dianne's back . . .

By the end of the afternoon, Dianne had become a fully paid up member of the knitting club. Molly thought she seemed the most enthusiastic of all the girls once she loosened up, although they had yet to show her the delights of Ann's play room.

Ann told Vincent of the encounter when she had the chance later that evening. He listened intently, and laughed along with her at the way Dianne had been embarrassed in the beginning but had soon got into the swing of things. He didn't admit it, but he was a little disappointed the group had not found their way downstairs.

He had left all the video cameras running down there in the hope of getting some nice explicit pictures of the girls. Of course, he would have carefully chosen those shots where only Dianne could have been identified to put into store for possible later use.

He had not yet made up his mind exactly what Dianne's punishment for her disloyalty to him would be but it was always handy to have ammunition tucked away. Never mind. From what Ann had indicated, there would be plenty of other opportunities.

Chapter 20

Shelford Racers continued to maintain their fine form. Reece Sullivan soon recovered his confidence and continued his improvement.

Bryce Penrith continued working hard with the youngsters in the team, giving constant tips and encouragement. Jeff Harding was determined to stay in front of Penrith in the averages. As a result, the team remained on top of the league and was progressing in the *Speedway Star* Knockout Cup.

Shelford was getting enormous press coverage – local, national and in the speedway media. Bryce had been an incredible ambassador as well as a yardstick for the youngsters to measure themselves against. Most of all, his infectious enthusiasm just seemed to rub off on everyone. Even Jeff admitted to himself the guy was special.

The other promoters had split into two camps. One camp thought Vincent Hansing was an over-opinionated smart-arse who had to go. The other half considered him an over-opinionated smart-arse who was doing a great job for speedway. BSPA Manager, Rod Brown, was still straddling the fence, but was quietly impressed with just about everything Shelford was doing. Most of all, the supporters were still turning out in droves to watch the Racers, both at home and on the away tracks.

Although he was having a great season, Harding missed out on becoming the British Champion with one bad ride. Lurch had been in his corner on the night and had advised him correctly. But Harding had no respect for the big fellow, thought he knew better, and disregarded Lurch's sensible advice in his, most important, third race.

The dash from the start line to the first turn was going to be critical in this heat because Harding was in the outside position, with the very fast-starter, Sam Butler, inside him.

Lurch had advised Harding not to get stuck outside Butler going into the turn, even if it meant dropping in behind the others.

Harding was much faster than the other three in the race, and could have picked them off, one by one, if needs be.

Instead of taking the advice, Harding had attempted to muscle his way around the outside of Butler, had run out of space in the middle of the turn, and had been forced to shut right off or hit the fence. By the time he had recovered, the other three riders had cleared off, and he had only been able to pass one of them before the end of the race.

Harding's 13 points saw him finish in third place, which moved him comfortably into the international knockout rounds of the World Championship.

Vincent called Jeff into his office the week after that meeting.

'I've had a full report on the British Final and how you managed to blow it. Having said that, I have been impressed with your riding in general so far this season.'

Before Jeff could start making excuses, Vincent carried on.

'Here's the deal,' he said. 'You are currently 26-years old. Let us say you have six years left as a top speedway rider. You have that amount of time to make all the money you can from speedway.

'I have to say, by and large, your attitude this year has been much better. Not perfect by any means, but at least a huge improvement.

'Do you feel I have done a good job as promoter here at the speedway? Do you feel, especially allowing for our history, I have been fair to you? Do you have confidence that I can make things happen – that I can make things work?"

'Yes to all those things.' said Jeff. He was not naturally humble and was finding it difficult to admit Vincent was doing a great job.

'Right,' said Vincent. 'I'm prepared to make you the World Champion. I can tell you right now, you will not manage it by yourself. You're just not good enough. But if I make you into the World Champion, what's in it for me? You'll forget who put you there and then stab me in the back, right?'

Predictably, Jeff blustered . . .

'Save it,' said Vincent. 'I have put together a package that will remove the embarrassment of either of us having to trust the other. I shall put it all down in writing, but, roughly speaking, this is the offer.

'You will sign a four-year contract, personal to me, not to Shelford Speedway. You will leave me to control your entire career both within and outside of speedway. You will leave all business decisions to me and do whatever I ask that's fair and reasonable in order to promote yourself, both on and off the track.

'In return for this, I will make you the World Champion within two years. I will increase your income from all sources by a minimum of 25 percent per year, year-on-year, taken from this year's base figure.

'I will guarantee you investment return of a minimum of 30 percent per year on your capital. If you have not become World Champion within three years, I will guarantee payment of all the above minimums, plus an additional 20 percent, and you will be free to leave the contract at that time.

'Be assured, presuming you do your part, and notwithstanding your spendthrift lifestyle, you will be a very wealthy man inside of four years. We can look at the situation again when the deal runs out.

'The only conditions to this agreement are that if in any one season you are injured for more than eight weeks, then your minimum returns for that year will not be guaranteed.

'Also, this contract will be based on you putting in your best efforts at all times. If this appears not to be the case, I will issue you with two written warnings before cancelling the contract. In that case, you will receive all of your guaranteed payments up until the cancellation.

'If you are happy with all I have said, I shall go ahead and get the contracts drawn up for you to refer to any advisor before signing. Jeff, you must understand that if you sign these contracts, we are both placing our future in each other's hands.'

Harding stood up and came forward to shake Vincent's hand. 'You are a big man, Vincent. We have a deal and I am truly sorry about this,' he said, nodding at the wheelchair.

'Not as much as you will be one day,' Vincent thought as he shook Jeff's hand warmly.

A week later, Vincent and Jeff signed a plethora of contracts and documents to tie up the arrangements.

Bryce Penrith was surprised when Vincent asked him to work with Jeff Harding towards winning the World Championships that year.

'You don't like the bloke, and I don't care much for him either come to that. Why in hell do you want *him* to become World Champion?'

'Business,' said Vincent, 'purely business. From your point of view, look at it this way. We shall announce that you are helping

Jeff and it will enhance your reputation all the more when you achieve the impossible and make a chicken-hearted dick-head World Champion.'

'You are very confident about this?' ventured Bryce.

'With you in his corner and me in the background, he can't fail,' laughed Vincent.

Jeff Harding sailed through the first two international knockout rounds, riding with plenty of confidence and carrying out all instructions from Bryce Penrith to the letter.

He was full of nerves in the final qualifying round, the Inter-Continental Final in Sweden. Fortunately, with 10 riders going through from a field of 16, and having gained a second place in his last ride, Harding scraped through to the World Final.

He either failed to notice, or preferred to overlook, that one rider in that final race who had already secured enough points to qualify pulled out with an engine failure and another ran very wide on the third lap.

It mattered not to this vain man. He would be riding in the 1985 World Final at Wembley in front of 90,000 fans and millions watching at home 'live' on television.

Chapter 21

Mark had brought one or two other young ladies down for long weekends at The Manor since Amelia. He had even asked Vincent if he could have a full-scale party in 'Ann's Room' one weekend. Vincent had made the place available and had kept right out of the way, but it was amazing just how many well-known business and political faces he had recognised mixing among all the young 'starlets' when he ran back the videos afterwards. He did think to himself that were he a bad boy, he could really have fun with the tapes! Had these people learned nothing since the Profumo and Christine Keeler affair?

Jack and Ryan, Dianne and Molly's kids, got on very well together and as a result, Dianne was becoming something of a regular at The Manor. On the weekend of the Inter-Continental Final in Gothenburg, Lurch had taken Bryce Penrith and Eddie Campbell in the motor home to look after Jeff Harding. This gave Molly the opportunity to take Ryan up and spend the weekend at her parents' place.

Vincent mentioned to Ann that Mark was coming that weekend on his own.

'Angel, how about asking Dianne if she would like to let Jack stay with his grandparents for the weekend and then Dianne could balance the numbers with Heather, Dave, and Mark?'

Ann gave Vincent one of her looks.

'Matchmaker, matchmaker, make me a match . . .' she sang at him. He responded with: 'Que sera, sera . . . Whatever will be, will be...' and they both laughed. Vincent was merely adding as much ammunition as he could to his arsenal, without being sure how he would eventually use it. He had to admit, though, he was beginning to soften his attitude towards his former girlfriend.

Dianne jumped at the opportunity for some decent adult company. She loved Jack madly, and spent just about every waking hour looking after him, but it would be nice to have a weekend off for a change.

Dianne had arrived first on the Friday afternoon, straight from dropping Jack at her parents. She was not certain what she should wear for the evening and wanted to seek Ann's advice. Ann put her into one of the four-poster bedrooms and recommended she go for a little black dress. They had a semi-formal dinner in mind, so the black cocktail dress was also what Ann and Heather decided on.

Ann presumed that as it was a nice, warm evening, the men would wish to be in shirtsleeves rather than jackets and ties.

As she was getting ready, Dianne began to feel nervous and insecure. She was out of her depth here. What had seemed like a good idea at the time was now becoming more like a nightmare.

Whichever way she looked at it, she had been set up on a blind date. Maybe, just maybe, that wasn't the case and it really was going to be an adult and genuine weekend. It was too late to run now but at the slightest hint of the odd man out making a pass at her, she would be out of there. It was one thing having a bit of fun with the girls, but she was not about to sink to the same levels as Jeff and start putting herself about.

Dianne had heard movements in the corridor and other rooms but was scared to venture out of her room. She had been up there for about an hour and ready for dinner for 15 minutes, not knowing what to do. At a quarter-to-seven, there was a quiet tap on the door. Dianne leapt off the bed and at the same instant said:

'Come in.'

It was Ann, elegantly dressed and carrying a bottle of Dom and a couple of flutes.

'I was ready early,' she said, 'so I thought we might get a sneaky start on the others.'

Dianne was so relieved. Her and Ann sat on a couple of Regency chairs in the window bay, gazing out on the beautiful evening landscape in its full summer splendour, as her hostess poured the bubbly.

'Thank you for being so thoughtful,' she said quietly.

'Don't be daft,' Ann said. 'I just fancied a drink – oh, and by the way, as far as I am concerned this is a purely innocent weekend. I will keep an eye on things but if at any time you want an escape route, just fiddle with your right earring and I'll know to come and get you out of any awkward situation. I just want you to enjoy yourself.' Dianne just smiled at Ann and nodded her appreciation.

'Isn't this a truly magnificent view?' she said, feeling far more relaxed and at ease.

At 7.15 they went downstairs. Heather, Dave and Vincent were sitting outside enjoying their own drinks. Ann emptied out what was left in her bottle into whatever glass she could find and flopped onto one of the cushioned swing chairs. Dianne sat down beside her and they let the swing rock them gently.

Vincent looked terrific in black trousers and a white silk blousy collarless shirt with puffy sleeves. 'A good deal more stylish than Jeff,' Dianne thought to herself. She swore to herself that Heather was getting even more stunning by the day. She looked breathtaking; a tanned goddess in a simple short, white dress.

Mark came down a few minutes later. All Dianne had been told was that he was a friend of Vincent's, was about the same age as everyone there and worked in the City. She really had not expected such a smooth, perfectly manicured hunk in the most expensive Armani gear imaginable. He even smelled rich!

Vincent did the introductions.

'Mark, meet Dianne,' he said. 'Dianne is a good friend of Ann and Heather, and she is MARRIED to Jeff Harding, my number one speedway rider.' Vincent clearly accentuated the 'married' bit and then carried on.

'Jeff is riding in Sweden this weekend and Dianne was at a loose end, so Ann asked her to join us.'

Mark walked over to the swing, giving Dianne a charming smile that rung bells in her boots as he correctly took her hand, saying:

'Hello, Dianne – how do you keep finding such fabulous friends, Ann?' He moved on and gave Ann a kiss on the cheek and a small hug.

'I know how really. It's because you are such a beautiful person yourself!' Finally, he walked over to where Heather was seated, put his arms around her shoulders from behind, and kissed her loudly on the cheek.

'When are you going to leave that husband of yours and run off with *me?*' he said. Dave laughed as heartily as the others.

Ann had been watching Dianne closely and recognised her immediate spark with Mark. She smiled quietly to herself, thinking how right Vincent had been with his idea of matchmaking

'Oh dear!' she suddenly thought to herself, 'I hope the poor girl has brought plenty of clean knickers with her!'

Soon they went into the dining room. Mrs Peasenhall had prepared a beautiful meal and two sweet, young things from the village acted as waitresses, with rustic good humour rather than in classic silver service style. Somehow, it made the evening all the more memorable.

Mark excused himself near the end of the meal, went to the kitchen and gave a £200 tip to Mrs Peasenhall and £50 each to the girls.

'Don't tell the others, they will want to reduce your wages!' he laughed.

The group moved to the library after the meal and lounged in the leather furniture, drinking, chatting and having a great time until well into the small hours.

Dave was the first to crack.

'Well it's OK for you lot, but I did a full day's work today,' he complained with a half-smile. 'Time for my bed I think. What do you reckon, Heath?' She had been yawning herself, and readily agreed.

'I think we are all a bit that way,' said Ann. 'Vincent, you can have just 10 minutes with Mark talking shop whilst I take Dianne up.'

Heather, Dave, Dianne and Ann trooped upstairs. The Scotts said goodnight and disappeared into their suite. Ann walked along with Dianne to hers, and plainly expected to be invited in.

'There,' she said, as they stepped inside. 'That wasn't so bad, was it? I thought I would leave Vincent and Mark together downstairs to save any embarrassment.'

'Thanks, that was very thoughtful again. I've had a fabulous evening. I cannot remember when I have enjoyed myself so much.'

'I wasn't saving any embarrassment,' thought Ann as she said goodnight. 'I was saving *you* from yourself, but tomorrow you are on your own my girl!'

Next morning Vincent was up with the lark as usual. He had worked out in his gym, had a swim, made himself some breakfast and done a couple of hours work in the study by the time Mark found him.

'So what's the story with the merry speedway widow?' Mark asked.

'Husband's a prick,' said Vincent. 'I felt she deserved a weekend enjoying herself with civilised people.'

'So is she out of bounds?' asked Mark.

'That's between you and your conscience!' laughed Vincent. 'I am certainly not her keeper, and from where I sit, she looks big enough and ugly enough to make her own decisions.'

By late morning, they were all lounging in or around the pool. Ann and Heather swapped the odd knowing look and enjoyed watching Dianne's coy performance every time Mark was around.

'Hey, let's go down to the antique fair at Swanborne Abbey this afternoon,' Ann suggested. Everyone agreed, so after a delightful cold lunch served around the pool, they all disappeared to get changed.

When they had reconvened, Vincent pointed out his motor home was being used to take the group to Sweden. 'Don't worry,' said Dave, 'you can come in the Merc with me.'

'We can't all get in there,' Mark pointed out. 'I'll take someone in the Porsche. Who's up for it?'

'Well, I'd love to,' said Ann, 'but I suppose Heath and I will have to go with our boring, old husbands.' She looked straight at Dianne and pulled her right ear lobe. Dianne ignored the signal and announced:

'If you can put up with me, Mark, I suppose I can put up with you.' Heather and Ann looked at each other and nodded.

After the group had returned to The Manor with their spoils and were enjoying drinks by the pool, Ann said, to no-one in particular: 'How about dress-ups tonight?' Dianne and Mark both looked puzzled. But Heather was excited and Dave and Vincent nodded their approval.

'Come with Heather and me,' Ann said to Dianne and the three women dived off.

'Don't worry,' Vincent said to Mark. '*We* don't have to dress up. Only the girls!'

The three men were changed, and on their second bottle of Dom when the girls reappeared. They looked stunning in their period dresses with tight bodices and breasts pushed up and out, trying to escape from the low-cut necklines.

Mark's jaw dropped. Even Dave and Vincent were impressed. The stage was set for an entirely different evening to the night before. It was fun, games and innuendo all the way. The wine flowed even more freely, and the cutlery was quickly dispensed with, all six deciding they would reconstruct a Henry VIII banquet. They ended up having an old-fashioned food fight.

Suddenly, fearing the worst, Ann whispered in Vincent's ear:

'Dianne doesn't know about the playroom. Tell Mark it is out of bounds and not to be mentioned. We'll just have a foursome downstairs tonight and leave those two to themselves.' Vincent nodded, mildly disappointed, and the message was passed on to Mark.

'So much for all my careful planning,' he thought, but shrugged it off.

By eleven-thirty, Heather, Dave, Vincent and Ann were all feigning tiredness. Eventually, they excused themselves, leaving Mark and Dianne together at the table.

'You look like you might need some help getting cleaned up and out of those dirty clothes,' Mark ventured. Dianne fiddled with her earring, but only because there was some food lodged in it.

On the Sunday, they all mixed together in and around the pool. Mark and Dianne flirted with each other all morning. After lunch, Vincent simply said out loud for all to hear:

'I would like to point out to you all, Jeff Harding is my number one rider. I trust his wife implicitly and could not possibly encourage or condone any impropriety that might cause problems between her and her husband.

'Fortunately, we can all say quite honestly, we have not seen anything at all to suggest such a thing might have taken place this weekend. Isn't that right, guys?' He winked broadly at Dianne as she blushed while the others all chorused their agreement. Mark and Dianne went upstairs to pack. It took them three hours.

Chapter 22

Shelford's success story was continuing unabated. It wasn't so much that they were winning their matches, but the way they were doing it. Despite being targeted by several of the opposition hard-men, the youngsters in the side had made huge strides.

Lurch had proved an inspired selection as team manager. The kids adored him. Bryce and he had struck up a real rapport, and even Jeff had finally come to appreciate his talent and effort.

Lurch had remained one of the lads as far as the supporters were concerned, though, and could always be found on the terracing and in the stands before and after matches, keeping up with the latest gossip supporters relish.

The whole place had become just one big, happy family and race nights were party nights for the patrons.

The nearest speedway to Shelford, some 35 miles away at Thorden Heath, was not having such a good run. Maybe some of their supporters had moved over to support the Racers? Or perhaps it was more to do with the weak Thorden Swords team and poor presentation on race nights? Whatever it was, although most speedways were just about holding their own, Thorden clearly wasn't.

Vincent sent Lurch to get amongst his contacts at the rival track on a fishing mission. Was Thorden Heath Speedway up for sale, or perhaps more importantly, could it be bought?

Jeff Harding was conceited enough to believe his own publicity. Bryce and Vincent, overtly and covertly had been playing up his chances at Wembley to such an extent that even the press now believed he was in with a good chance.

There were two riders in the World Final field, Denmark's Hans Simonsen and American Bobby Holder, who had won several titles between them over the years and who were very clear co-favourites. Other than those two, the field was pretty much wide open.

On the day of the event, the two favourites for the title were not seen all day. Their bikes, equipment and mechanics arrived at the stadium, but not the riders. Not until the last minute, anyway.

When they did finally arrive, both looked like death warmed up. They were as white as ghosts and looked as if they would keel over at any time. Had it not been a World Final, you could be assured they would have been either at home tucked up in bed, or even in hospital having tests.

They tried hard to produce their best but it was never going to happen for them. Both had to pull out of the meeting before their final rides. Food poisoning was the suspected cause. How they had both contracted it at the same time was a mystery.

With those two riders not in the picture, the meeting became something of a lottery. Jeff Harding had the dual advantages of having Bryce and Lurch in his corner, and being on specially prepared Eddie Campbell bikes. That put him a head in front of the other riders even before the start.

Listening carefully to Bryce and following his instructions to the letter, Harding won his first three races from the start.

Just like having to sink the eight-foot putt on the last green, though, winning the World Final is all about holding your nerve on the night when the pressure is really on.

Harding was last away from the starting tapes in his fourth ride. Somehow, he managed to pass two riders, but only finished second to Poland's Pawel Corbiceszky. That left him with 11 points with one race to go. His final race was heat 20, the last one of the night.

Before the start of that race, it was clear what was needed. The highest scorer of the night, Denmark's Jan Bergsen, had finished with 13 points from his five rides. If Jeff won his final race, he would have 14 points and become the champion.

He was up against a reserve rider who had been put in when one of the sick riders had withdrawn, and two riders who could not make the rostrum, even if they were to win the race. On any other day, he would have been a certainty to win.

With him again beset by nerves, Jeff's front wheel lifted as he left the start. He managed to get it down again and had cold fingers clutching at his guts, expecting the other three riders to have been long gone. But, to his amazement, he looked up to see all the other three had also made bad starts.

Somehow, he came out of the first turn in front and although he was all over the track, he managed to stay in the lead until the chequered flag was shown. The time for the race was a full second slower than any other that night, but it made no difference. He was the 1985 World Champion!

By the time Jeff got back into the pits after the on-track celebrations, he was disappointed to see that his promoter had already departed, having not even waited for the official presentation in front of the Royal Box.

Dianne wasn't there to see the full presentation for her husband's greatest achievement, either. Vincent and Ann had taken her, along with son Jack, home.

Jeff soon recovered from his disappointment. He was able to celebrate his success with one of the many speedway 'groupies' who hung around after the majority of fans had headed for home.

Next morning Bryce caught up with Vincent in the library at The Manor.

'I do hope you know what you are doing?' he said. Vincent nodded.

Chapter 23

It took Lurch a month to complete his investigations. He had discovered the situation was coming to a head at Thorden Heath and a change of ownership could well be on the cards.

Vincent decided his next job was to find a reliable front man. The idea of taking control of Thorden was interesting, but he would need to keep his involvement secret. Somebody needed to be found who could act, first in any purchase negotiations and then as ongoing promoter.

He went through the names of all those promoters who had left the sport in the last 10 years. There had to be someone in that lot.

The list was whittled down to three names and he decided to 'interview' them. The only thing was, they were not aware they were applying for a job! The pretext for contacting each was the same. He was asking advice about how to deal with the imminent departure of Bryce Penrith from the Shelford team. The actual dummy question was, what did the interviewee advise Shelford should do in order to alleviate the upcoming loss of Bryce Penrith?

The first ex-promoter he spoke to waffled on and was far too tied up in the past and his own self-importance. He had lost the plot.

The second character was much more sensible, but was getting on in years, very happy in his retirement and was considering a permanent move down to the South of France.

Vincent marked him down as someone he might well learn things from and made a note to spend time with the man in the future. The fact that the ex-promoter had left speedway suddenly, after a financial scandal, made him all the more interesting.

The third 'candidate' was the one. John Tindall was another of the old promoters who had left the sport under a cloud. It had been something to do with a VAT investigation. Tindall had been involved with several partners in his various speedway promotions, but had dumped each one along the way.

Vincent, perversely, saw this as a positive. It meant Tindall was a ruthless individual, a wheeler and dealer, ducker and diver.

Vincent doubted he would want to spend a great deal of time socialising with the man, who was both smarmy and unpleasant at the same time, but did consider he would be the one for the job.

Tindall had been out of speedway for some time and had been through a messy divorce. Currently, he was working part-time doing consulting work in his pre-speedway line of business but had clearly hit hard times.

The only difficulty Vincent could see was that the ex-promoter lived some distance from Thorden, and had always refused to move nearer any of the promotions he had owned, preferring to be an 'absentee' promoter.

There was no doubt he would adopt the same attitude this time. Again, Vincent thought things through, and decided that this would be no bad thing. Vincent could install his own people at the track to keep an eye on things on a day to day basis and keep an eye on Tindall at the same time.

He set up a meeting with John Tindall.

Following three long chats, Vincent arrived at the conclusion that Tindall was the perfect man for the job. His only concern was not knowing how much he could trust the wily old pro, especially 'when', rather than 'if', the relationship between them fell apart.

Tindall would be privy to Vincent's involvement and might decide to spill the beans. Even at this early stage, Vincent had little doubt a personality clash between the two would happen, sooner or later.

'Oh well,' he thought. 'I'll just have to get something over him fairly early on.' He was sure that wouldn't take too long. The word was, Tindall had a penchant for young boys; very young boys in fact, and Vincent would merely compile a damning dossier on him. He would keep it safe in case he ever needed to use it.

By the end of September, Tindall held one of his famous publicity stunts, dressing up as King Arthur, complete with 'Excalibur' and riding into Thorden Heath Stadium on a white horse, brandishing the huge sword over his head.

He announced to the assembled media people that he, along with the backing of a 'private' investor, was to take ownership of the Thorden 'Swords' at the end of the '83 season.

By this time, Shelford had reached the final of the *Speedway Star* Knockout Cup and were dicing with Belle Vue for the league title. The Racers were to meet Poole in the home and away final, whilst the league would be decided when Belle Vue Aces visited Shelford the week after that. The meeting against Belle Vue would be on October 20th and would round off the season's fixtures.

Vincent did not even have to ask Bryce to delay his return to Australia until after the deciding matches. This was too good for the Aussie to consider missing out on.

The euphoria of being the World Champion was beginning to die down for Jeff Harding. He had been in a constant whirl since the momentous event that had changed his life. One or two of his league performances had suffered a bit as he was still in his honeymoon period, but there was no doubt he loved all the attention.

The week before the two-legged cup final was due to take place, Vincent called Jeff into his stadium office. First, he showed Jeff how much his investment portfolio had increased in the few months Vincent had been looking after it. Jeff was more than impressed.

'Now the time has come to simply trust what I am about to tell you. I have your interests at heart, because your interests and mine are tied up together. So far, I think I have kept my part of the bargain. I promised I would make you the World Champion and I have…' Jeff chimed in to say *he* was the one who had done all the work.

'Don't be so bloody naïve,' Vincent interrupted, with a withering look.

'You will also have seen from those figures I have just shown you, I am more than keeping my deal regarding looking after your business affairs,' he continued. 'Now to tell you the reason I have asked you to come in. Shelford will *not* win the Cup Final . . .'

'Why not?' demanded the rider, totally bemused by Vincent's statement. 'We can easily beat Poole over the two legs!'

'Because it is not in yours or my best interests,' Vincent said quietly. 'You are going to have a shocker of a meeting at Poole, having bike troubles all evening, and then here at Shelford in the second leg you will ensure we lose on aggregate.'

A stunned Jeff Harding just sat there looking at Vincent.

'Then,' Vincent went on to add, 'you will ensure we lose at home against Belle Vue the following week. For these two losses, you will receive a £5,000 bonus.'

'But I'll get lynched!' stammered the gobsmacked rider. 'What the bloody hell are you up to? You must be fucking crazy!' Vincent simply sat there, unmoved.

'I'll make this easy for you to understand. I have specific plans in mind for you, which I will keep to myself for the moment. Just accept that you will benefit by far more than the five grand over time, and you don't want to dwell on what might happen if things do not go as I have planned . . .'

The threat was menacing and clear. After such a stellar season, Shelford was going to finish up with nothing . . . and Jeff Harding was to be the fall guy.

Harding duly had a shocker at Poole. The rest of the team, brilliantly led by Bryce, rode their hearts out. With clever tactical changes Lurch kept the losing margin down to 12 points but Poole were now at the top of their form and a dozen was a lot to make up in the home leg, against any reasonably useful team, let alone the very strong Pirates outfit.

For the first time in the history of Shelford Speedway, the 'full house' signs were posted long before the start of the home leg of the final. More than twenty-two thousand people packed into the stadium, with thousands left outside.

It was a fine and dry, but cold mid-October evening. Bryce walked his team around the track before the admission gates were opened. Normally very laid back, the rest of the team were shocked at Bryce's intensity. He pointed out to them he had stayed in the UK much longer than intended, simply to see the job through and collect some silverware for Shelford.

The Poole team were determined to sit on their lead whilst Shelford tore into them. Harding narrowly missed out on the track record in winning the first heat and within four races, Shelford had made up the 12 points deficit from the first leg. Then it became hard. Poole could bring in tactical substitutes in key races. They were not trying to win the meeting, just the tie, and that meant they could put their top men up against the weaker Shelford riders.

Shelford's lower order lads responded brilliantly to the pressure they were put under, and did very well to withstand the counter attack. The commitment from both sides was immense and neither team was able to take command.

Come the last race, Poole was 10 points down on the night but two points up on aggregate. However, Shelford had arranged their line-up to have Penrith and Harding paired together in the last race. Neither home rider had dropped a point so far in the meeting, and all the odds were in Shelford's favour. A first and second place finish in heat 13 would give them a 5-1 score and overall victory.

Jeff missed the start completely and even though Bryce, up front, slowed the opposition pair down to walking pace for the whole four laps, Harding made no impression. A 3-3 heat result meant Poole had won the Cup by just two points.

A stunned silence descended over the stadium. All the ashen-faced Harding could say to the press afterwards was that the same mystery problem he had been having with his bikes at Poole must have returned in that last race, because no matter how hard he had tried, the bike just would not respond.

Everyone was disappointed, Harding looking particularly crestfallen, and the youngsters in the team rallied around him, trying to make him feel better. Bryce Penrith was not so sure. He went to see Vincent with his thoughts.

'If I didn't know better, I would swear Harding had been bought off. Even on a pushbike, he could have made it through in that last race had he wanted. I never thought that mob at Poole would stoop so low as to nobble him. To be honest, for all his faults, I never thought that bastard, Harding, would do such a thing to us either.' The normally amiable and unflappable Aussie was incensed and unable to hide his disgust.

'I have the same suspicions,' said Vincent, glibly. 'I'll have it out with Harding during the week. You'd better stay clear of him or he'll sulk, and we will need him firing on all cylinders next week if we are to win the League.'

'Why don't you get him in here right now?' continued Bryce, his anger close to boiling point. 'If you won't deal with him, then *I* will. I've not come from the other side of the world, only to see that little shit ruin it for everyone.'

'Just leave it to me, Bryce. Please. I'll deal with him myself . . .' Vince insisted.

For the second time in a fortnight, the admission gates at Shelford Speedway were closed again the following week. Shelford got away to a good start but Belle Vue hung on in there in the League Championship decider.

It was a violent clash, with the Aces' riders determined to try and push the Shelford youngsters around.

The Racers were just two points up going into heat 11 and Harding was a mile in front, when his motor suddenly stopped. The Belle Vue pair managed to keep Alan Stewart at the back, giving the visitors a 5-1 heat win and putting them in front for the first time in the meeting. Two heats to go, and Shelford were down by a couple of points.

The Aces number one, Kevin Dixon, managed to win heat 12 but the Shelford boys packed the minor placings. The 3-3 again left Shelford, just as the previous week, needing a maximum 5-1 result in the last race to win the match and, this time, the League title.

Jeff Harding's mechanic warmed up his second bike for his last race in heat 13, while he sat in his corner of the pits, head in hands.

The bike was ready, and Jeff Harding slowly stood up and donned his helmet, facemask, goggles and gloves. The youngsters in the team all crowded around him, giving encouragement as he walked the few steps to the pit entrance and climbed astride his bike. Bryce was waiting for him.

'We have gate positions one and three. Which one do you want?' he asked Harding, tersely. 'I don't care how we do it, but we *are* going to get a result here, OK?' Jeff nodded back, holding up one finger to indicate he wanted the inside gate position.

Bryce held out his hand, Jeff shook it, and they were push-started out onto the track.

Here they were again, Bryce and Jeff, needing a 5-1 to win. Harding bolted out of the start like a frightened rabbit with Bryce tucked in behind. The crowd was going wild as the championship trophy came into view but their raucous cheers rapidly turned to groans of horror. On the third lap, Harding's second bike also mysteriously stopped.

A drawn heat, Belle Vue had done the seemingly impossible and snatched the league title from under the Shelford team's noses.

Jeff climbed off his bike on the third turn and left it there for his mechanic to retrieve. As he walked across the centre green back to the pits, he could hear the booing of the Shelford supporters ringing in his ears.

Disgusted fans were tearing up their programmes and throwing them to the ground. One irate lad tried to climb the perimeter fence to remonstrate with Harding before he was hauled back by a steward. They just could not believe what they had just witnessed.

The announcer, Dave Whitely, normally such an ebullient, wisecracking character, could barely steady his voice sufficiently to announce the result of the race that no-one wearing Shelford colours wanted to hear.

Many of the home supporters were already through the exit gates and heading for their vehicles in the car park before Whiteley congratulated the Aces on winning the title.

When Harding reached the pits, his team mates just turned their backs. All except Bryce Penrith. He walked up to Harding and floored him with a ferocious right hand, before stalking away.

Several hundred irate Shelford supporters gathered in the pits viewing area, booing and catcalling. Security staff kept a small group of hotheads from climbing the barrier and fronting Harding.

Unable to face the supporters or his own team, he had nowhere to hide. In the end, he decided to make himself as small as he could in the pits, nursing his sore and throbbing cheek, while his mechanics packed his gear away into his van.

Then he made the short dash from pits to van, and jumped into the back. His mechanics drove slowly through the angry throng, as they banged on the sides and rear doors.

'Sugar in my fuel,' was Harding's version of events next day. He claimed his bikes had been deliberately sabotaged. Far from backing him up, Vincent announced that Harding would never ever wear Shelford colours again.

'I told you before, and I'm telling you again,' Vincent said down the phone to a ranting Harding the morning after the final match. 'Trust me. Keep your head down and your mouth shut.'

Chapter 24

In succumbing to Mark's attentions, Dianne had done the unthinkable, but she really didn't care. She had all but forgotten what it was like to be loved at all, let alone so tenderly, expertly and long, in the way Mark had made love with her.

She had made her mind up the morning after the 'Henry VIII' night. Whatever the outcome with Mark, there was no future between her and Jeff. She would wait until the end of the season and then she would tell her husband, not certain if he would react angrily or with relief.

Dianne kept in touch with Mark but the distances involved, the complication of Jack, and Mark's jet-set lifestyle made it impractical for them to meet up. They did have phone-sex a few times, when Jeff was riding away from home. Dianne would phone Mark after going to bed, and they would talk dirty to each other late into the night, but that was it.

They were both sensible enough to realise the last thing either wanted was a scandal. In truth, also, although the pair enjoyed each other's company, they understood the attraction did not constitute deep-seated love.

Ann had waited patiently for Dianne to open up. Finally, whilst they were sitting on their own by the pool one afternoon in September, and Molly was playing outside with the boys, Dianne told Ann she planned to leave Jeff.

'About time too,' Ann said. She had wanted to suggest it to Dianne ages ago but Vincent had told her to let things run their course. He had also told Ann what to say to Dianne when the time came.

'Listen, time and time again you have been the injured party. Mark has merely opened your eyes to the fact that you really do have alternatives. Don't go throwing away the moral high ground by admitting things you needn't. I will speak to Vincent and he will deal with matters in a way that will see you come out of it on top. OK?'

Dianne thought she understood. Ann had been such a good friend and always came up with the right things to do. Dianne walked over to Ann. She gave her dear friend and figure of adoration an enormous hug.

'How much time do we have to ourselves?' she asked.

'Enough,' said Ann, taken aback, although she quickly regained her composure.

'Come with me,' she motioned. 'I've something I want to show you.' And with that, she took Dianne's hand and led her downstairs to the playroom . . .

Vincent had organised an end-of-season party at The Manor for the riders and their girlfriends. He told them it had originally been planned as a celebration for the team having won the double. As it turned out, it was just an end-of-season party. There was to be a barbeque in the afternoon, and then the ladies would be sent home so the riders could enjoy a stag night afterwards.

A deflated Bryce and Molly had left to go back to Australia. Bryce had kept well clear of Harding. He cheerfully admitted to Vincent that he was convinced the man had sold his team out, although he was suitably diplomatic when dealing with the press and public. As far as Bryce was concerned, the whole of his seven-month return to speedway had been wasted.

Jeff Harding wasn't invited to the party, although his wife Dianne was. Her parents looked after Jack that weekend. All the other Shelford riders who had represented the team during the season were invited, plus a couple of other riders Vincent had earmarked for fast-tracking into the team the following year. That made 10 young men in attendance, plus Lurch.

None were married, but each had brought a girlfriend with them, except the big team manager, so in all there were 11 men plus Vincent and Dave, and 10 girls plus Ann, Heather and Dianne.

It was a lovely late autumn afternoon and the pool doors were open so the young riders and their partners could splash around in the warm water and mess about on the large patio area. Alcohol flowed freely, and Mrs Peasenhall had laid on a fabulous barbeque that Vincent and Dave were happy to cook while enjoying the view.

The guys weren't the only ones admiring the assembled 'talent'. Like three old matrons, Ann, Heather and Dianne orchestrated proceedings. Quietly, and between themselves, they were having their own fun, marking each little chick with points out of 10. Both the peacocks and the peahens!

With the alcohol kicking in, several of the lads decided they would debag Lurch. Now, given his size and strength, this was a foolish thing to do and a potentially ugly situation could have developed, but he took it in good part, put up a token resistance and then gave in gracefully.

There was a collective and audible intake of breath as the swim shorts came off. Never mind the ladies, none of the guys had ever seen such an impressive set of tackle before!

Lurch managed to hang on to Alan Stewart. He tucked the wiry young man under one arm and ripped his trunks off with the other hand. Alan then grabbed his girlfriend and slipped the catch on her bikini top. It was only a matter of seconds after that before anyone in the pool was considered fair game. A couple of the shyer girls scrambled out of the water rather than submit, but seeing the others having such a good laugh, eventually gave themselves up.

Fun though it was for the three matrons to see the youngsters happily cavorting around, they just could not get over Lurch.

'Talk about hidden talents!' was Heather's first comment. Dianne was a little more forthcoming.

'That is a challenge I will take up one day,' she mused. The other two girls laughed.

As the watery sun slipped too low for comfort, the girls and boys got dressed and were herded along to the 'ballroom'. All manner of sweets and delicious treats, along with cheeses, fruit, and dessert wines were laid out and everyone mingled together well.

Dave and Heather had been flitting around sorting things out. Nobody had noticed the arrival of a coach whilst they had been finishing their meal. The 'passengers' had quietly gone upstairs to get prepared.

At seven, Lurch rounded the stragglers up until they were all back in the ballroom. The food had been cleared away. Vincent called the party to order and gave a short speech. He thanked all the team men for their efforts during the season and praised their dedication. He mentioned the absent Bryce, for being such an inspirational leader. He then talked about his disappointment with Harding, without actually directly accusing him of 'selling out'. Finally, he thanked all the girlfriends for having had to play second fiddle to a speedway bike all summer and suggested they catch up for lost time during the winter.

The ladies, who had made their own arrangements to go out on a hen night, were then packed off in taxis. Ann, Heather and Dianne were invited to join them, but politely declined.

As soon as the taxis disappeared down the drive, Dave led the party down the back stairs to the cellar whilst Vincent used the lift.

'Gentlemen,' he announced, as they stood at the bottom of the stairs, 'behave yourselves in here . . . but not too much!'

The big oak double doors slid open and what the young men saw was a harem scene straight from *Arabian Nights*. The 'dungeon' had been transformed. The sadomasochistic equipment was gone or hidden and the place was all pink chiffon, soft furnishings and Turkish delights. The scent was intoxicating and the hubble-bubble pipes inviting.

Not as enticing, though, as the dozen, young beauties covered in sheer chiffons and beads, posing in all manner of positions around the room.

Vincent and Dave withdrew, with the single word...'Enjoy!'

The two friends made their way up to the library, where they settled down to chat over a few drinks. They would check on their charges later, but had little interest in what was taking place. In fact, the whole evening had been Ann's brainchild, and she had planned it all.

Chapter 25

Vincent had crucified Harding in the press after the sickening losses to Poole and Belle Vue. Not too many of the press corps took Harding's claim of sabotage seriously – but where was the proof that he had deliberately thrown those key races?

Vincent's comments carefully avoided mention of 'fixing'. Instead, he referred to 'unprofessional preparation' and 'a lack of true commitment to the team'. His parting public shot was:

'Harding will never, *ever* ride for Shelford Racers again.'

The local and speedway press soon moved on to the next, big speedway story. This was about Thorden Heath Speedway having been sold to a company fronted by ex-promoter John Tindall. It was old news, but Tindall, always the showman, was nursing the media along with wonderful stories about what *he* was going to achieve and how *he* was going to push those upstarts from down the road, the Shelford Racers, back into their places.

Pretty soon it was time for him to announce his first piece of major news . . . The Thorden Swords had signed World Champion, Jeff Harding, to lead them into the new season, and had only given up their 17-year old find, Jamie Marlborough, in a straight swap exchange!

Harding had been forewarned of the transfer by Vincent and had been told why. He was made aware Vincent had 'an interest' in Thorden, which, because of the proximity of the two tracks, must not become common knowledge. Vincent explained that with Jeff moving to the rival track his presence in the opposition line-up would guarantee a big crowd every time the teams rode against each other. As part of the deal, Jeff's pay rate went up by 25%.

Jeff Harding's current young plaything, Jackie Bennett, lived in Shelford. Jeff had called in to the speedway in order to discuss his personal contract details with Vincent and how the change of team would affect them.

Whilst he was in Shelford though, he would obviously then use this appointment as an excuse to pop round and say 'hello' to his sweet, young and cuddly friend.

Vincent knew about Jackie. It was his job to know about any goings-on that could adversely affect his business. He warned Harding carefully about his illicit activities.

'Listen Jeff, you are playing far too close to home with your social life. Remember you are a high profile person now, a World Champion. You have already been subjected to a fair amount of negative publicity and if your penchant for young girls gets in the papers . . .'

'Don't worry,' said Jeff, 'I'm always very discreet. I think too much of my lad to wreck my marriage.'

Two hours later, Jeff Harding kissed the sixteen-year old Jackie passionately as he said cheerio on her doorstep.

"I love school holidays when both parents are at work!" he mused to himself as he got into his car and drove away, oblivious of the photographer.

The girl was certainly tasty but she wasn't the brightest lamp in the box, and was happy to sit down with the 'nice, young lady' who popped around shortly afterwards with a market research questionnaire. Soon Jackie was bragging about her affair with the World Champion.

The freelance journalist didn't just keep the story to one paper. There was enough to fill a whole page in all the sleazier Sunday tabloids. They splashed the story. Even reports of European champions Liverpool's new £1.5million signing from Manchester United was relegated to the inside back page in *The People*.

That was Dianne's cue. She had been given prior warning of what was coming by Ann. The same day the papers came out with the full explicit story, complete with photographs of Jeff and Jackie embracing passionately, Dianne and Jack were packed and gone, even before Jeff had risen from his Sunday morning lie-in.

She didn't leave a note. She just left the paper, back page up, on the kitchen top by the kettle. Over the next few months, Jeff would discover just how much money modern divorce settlements soak up.

Why, oh why, had he not taken Vincent's advice? He was so conceited, he never thought for one moment he had been set up. He had just assumed somebody had recognised him going into the house, and had telephoned the papers.

On the surface, it was absolute madness for Shelford to swap the current World Champion for a young, unproven kid, especially having lost another big star in Penrith as well. Of course, it was very doubtful Vincent would have done the deal if he hadn't owned both promotions. Even so, he had a special feeling about young Marlborough.

The boy had been a regular at Shelford's home meetings all of the previous season. Vincent had seen him hanging around the pits during meetings with a school exercise book and pencil in hand, scribbling notes. In fact, Vincent had him tossed out of the pits during the third home meeting of the season. The lad, then only 16, had come to the office after the meeting and asked to speak to Vince.

In the politest of terms he had explained how he was mad-keen on speedway and realised a chance to study Bryce Penrith close up and to learn from him would never come again. Therefore, he was simply trying to absorb as much as he could before it was too late.

Vincent had asked if he might have a look at the exercise book. The entries were in pencil and were anything but neat, but were entirely comprehensive.

There was a full report on every match. It started with a track and weather report and the names of the riders in both teams.

From then on, including diagrams where they helped, it broke each race down into what happened at the start, with notes on how the referee handled the riders, what the best riding lines seemed to be, and exactly how and where each pass – if any – was made during the races..

For the match that evening and for the week before, every move Penrith had made was logged. What he drank in-between races, did he sit quietly or involve himself with others, how much did he leave to his mechanics and how much did he check himself, was he first to be pushed away before a race or the last? . . . everything was in the book. Vincent had thought he was wholly dedicated when he first started, but this kind of detail was incredible.

Vincent studied this lad for quite a few seconds. He looked frighteningly young but he was very good looking for a 16-year-old and just had something about him that Vince took an instant liking to.

'Tell me a bit about yourself,' he said.

'My Dad died when I was three. That would have been a bit before your time but you might remember the name, Sid

Marlborough?'

As soon as the lad said it, Vince recalled Sid Marlborough being killed in a speedway accident around the time Vincent's own dad had started taking him to the speedway.

'Yes, of course I remember, but I hadn't made the connection,' Vince admitted.

'Well, Mum wouldn't let me do speedway, so when I had saved up enough to get an old bike, I kept it round my mate's house and told Mum it belonged to him.

I started going to the Thorden Heath training days . . . my mate's house was near enough to push the bike to the stadium from there.

On my 16th birthday, they stuck a contract under my nose and I signed it and forged mum's signature. Due to their early season injuries, I have been told I will get an extended run in the team, even though I feel maybe it might be a bit soon for me and a spell in the National League might have been to my advantage.'

'Listen, if you are good enough, you will make it OK,' Vincent reassured him. 'So if you are too young to drive, how do you get to away meetings?'

'I have an old wreck of a motorbike with a sidecar chassis on. The speedway bike and tools go on there and my mate goes on the back, behind me!'

'Alright, last question, does your mum know now?'

'Yep, saw my name in the paper. All hell let loose, but she let me carry on,' he grinned.

'Come and find me just before the meeting next week. I'll introduce you to Bryce and see if he can find the odd job for you to do for him during the meeting.'

With that, the interview was over. The young man, with his slightly unkempt look and faded denims, said his thanks and departed, leaving Vince to ponder on what it would be like to have a son of his own.

In the following weeks, the young Marlborough became something of a regular around the Shelford pits. He was quite a capable mechanic and had such an engaging personality, Eddie Campbell, Penrith's spanner-man, took him on full-time at his engine tuning business.

On his immaculately turned out, but aged racing equipment, young Jamie had made steady progress with the Thorden Swords but because the team and promotion were having such a bad run, his efforts seemed to go pretty much unnoticed.

Vincent had kept a close eye on the young man and had done something he knew he shouldn't. He had allowed personal feelings to affect his business judgement. He was determined, though, that as long as Jamie Marlborough retained both enthusiasm and effort, he would be fast-tracked to stardom.

That determination was intensified when Vincent went to see Jamie's mum. Even allowing for their combined dexterity and experience with the wheelchair, it hadn't been easy for Vince and Lurch to negotiate their way into the tiny council flat, but once inside, Vince was impressed with its neatness.

There was nothing to suggest speedway had ever played a part in this family's life. The only picture of Sid on show was a wedding shot of him and his wife, Joan. As most brides do, she looked stunning in the photo, and even in her careworn late thirties, she retained a natural attractiveness.

Vincent wondered why she had not remarried, although quickly realised it wasn't his business.

Joan had never seen Jamie ride. She had accepted that he wanted – no, *needed* – to do it, but the nightmare of her husband's death still haunted her.

Without saying it in so many words, she also made it plain that the presence of Vincent's wheelchair was living proof speedway was dangerous and that he could not guarantee her something bad would not happen to her son.

For his part, Vincent never tried to. He simply said he would look out for Jamie as much as he possibly could, and would ensure he was well treated. He also made the point that Joan would always be regarded as a special guest if she decided to come along to the speedway, but she steadfastly refused.

By the end of the discussion, though, Joan at least felt a lot happier. She was certain in her own mind that Vincent was genuine in saying he would keep a special eye on her only son. She resigned herself to the fact that, short of Jamie not riding speedway at all, signing for Shelford was the next best outcome.

Chapter 26

Dave had booked the tickets for the four of them, Vincent, Ann, Heather and himself: First Class to Los Angeles and then a private jet to Las Vegas. Finally, a stretched limo took them to Caesar's Palace where a suite had been reserved. They would only be there for a week, but intended to enjoy it to the full.

The two couples had only been in the suite for a few minutes, just long enough to phone down for a bottle of Dom, when there was a knock on the door. Ann answered it to find Bryce, Molly, Mark and Dianne standing there.

'We were just passing . . .' they laughed.

'What's going on?' asked Ann.

'Best ask Vincent,' suggested Dave. 'He's through there.'

Ann followed the direction of the pointing finger into their bedroom.

'If I tried to get onto my knees it'll need a crowd to pick me back up again, so will you settle for me just saying 'will you marry me, my angel?'

It was Ann who dropped to her knees, threw her arms around his neck, and unhesitatingly said: 'Yes, yes. YES!'

'Just as well, because it's all been booked for the day after tomorrow!' Vincent casually mentioned with a broad grin.

Mark and Dianne weren't 'an item' as such. Vincent had merely invited both of them along and they had accepted. They were, however, delighted to be able to spend a few days together. There was no suggestion they would be anything other than a couple, but only whilst in Vegas.

Bryce and Molly had joined the party from Australia. Mark had already booked for the group to see a show that night, and the eight of them had a whale of a time during the evening.

'It must be some kind of sixth sense,' said Mark. He had slipped a couple of 50 dollar notes into the hand of the man seeing the groups to their tables. The character had stuck the notes straight into his pocket and taken the party directly down to the best table in the house.

'I have to examine each note carefully to see if it is a one dollar or a hundred dollars. People in Vegas seem to be able to do it by touch!'

Next morning, the girls were off to get Ann fitted out for her special day. The men also organised some formal attire for themselves before spending a couple of hours at the tables.

'How in hell do you do it?' asked Dave, who was down several hundred. He was looking at the huge pile of chips accumulating in front of Mark.

'Dunno,' said Mark, 'just lucky I suppose.'

The men and the ladies met up briefly in the late afternoon before Molly announced the girls were off on their hen night. Then, she said, the ladies would all be spending the night in the suite, she declared. Vincent and Dave could make their own arrangements.

'Some kind of hen night that will turn out to be!' Dave said quietly to Vincent, with a grin.

The wedding next day in the bridal chapel of Caesar's was something else. It was a wonderful day and as she fell asleep that night Ann whispered in Vincent's ear:

'I love you more each day, my darling. You are my life.' Vincent hugged her tightly.

'You are now my wife as well as my guardian angel,' he murmured.

The Penriths returned to Australia next day. Dianne and Mark drifted in and out of the remaining group but spent some time on their own. They were only booked for another couple of days and had some catching up to do. Somehow, Dianne found Mark far more attentive when they were away from the others.

'Funny place, this Las Vegas,' Vincent commented as he pressed a large dollar bill into yet another outstretched hand.

'The whole system operates entirely on back-handers, from the bellboys to the top people, and yet the city is just so wheelchair-friendly and set up for people with disabilities. There's no doubting, I've had better treatment here this week than I could have dreamed of in England.'

Lurch brought Vincent up to date with the speedway gossip on the way from the airport back to The Manor. Rumour had it, another speedway promotion, this time at Marsdon, west of London, was up for sale. Vincent got Lurch to carry on sniffing around, whilst he organised John Tindall to make a formal enquiry.

'Dreamers,' uttered Vincent when he found out the asking price. 'They can keep it.' Not least in his thinking was that he had no automatic manager to put into the place and run it for him.

It was time, he mused, to do some serious homework and to sort out those sensible promoters who wanted to put the show on to a businesslike footing from the dangerous romantics and thick headed dreamers who just wanted to pose.

November was always a quiet month, so Vincent took the opportunity to despatch Lurch, with a speedway friend, to the States, where he managed to take in the last speedway events of the season in California. From there, they looked in on Las Vegas (hated it!) before moving on to Detroit. They weren't there for the Motown, but to order a replacement for Vincent's motor home.

The previous vehicle had been state-of-the-art but the replacement model, once it had been fully customised and fitted out, was simply magnificent. Nothing had been spared. There was a fully equipped office, complete with short-wave radio so Vincent could stay in touch with the world whilst on the road.

In addition, there was a small but fully functional kitchen and reclining sleeping couchettes that Vincent found far more comfortable in a moving vehicle than the old bunks. Lurch had his own bunk located above Vincent's desk. Lurch preferred to stretch out to sleep and figured that when he was resting, the motor home was going nowhere anyway!

The BSPA annual conference was to be held in Spain in early December. The promoters had discovered the age of the cheap package deal and had been inveigled into going abroad by an energetic and charismatic young travel agent, who had set up a deal to use a very ordinary three-star hotel in Benidorm as the venue.

Vincent telephoned the travel agent, Steven Bray, pointing out he had special needs and required facilities a three-star hotel probably didn't offer. He wanted a two-bedroomed suite in a five-star place with an assurance they could cope with a wheelchair guest.

You would have thought he was asking for the moon! Steve rolled his eyes and complained how difficult it would all be but he reckoned he had a special contact who could fix it.

'Listen, my son,' Vincent said, although they were much the same age, 'if it's too much trouble, forget it: Benidorm in early

December? The place will be almost empty. Now either cut the bullshit, and get on and do it, or I'll deal with someone who can.'

Crestfallen, Steve grumbled

'Consider it fixed.'

The travel agent got back the next day with first class airline seats and hotel accommodation and limo transfers booked.

'Here are my private and home numbers,' said Steve. 'Any problems or anything I can do, phone me, day or night.'

Next morning after he had woken up and sorted himself out, Vincent dialled the home number he had been given. Steve looked at the bedside clock as he reached over and answered the phone. It was a tick after six.

'Hello?' he mumbled, trying to get his thoughts into order.

'Morning Steve!' Vincent said brightly. 'You said 'any time' and I was just checking to see if you meant it'

'Bastard!' was the one-word reply, before both men put their phones back, laughing. Both had already decided each understood and liked the other.

Lurch held a promoter's licence now. He was no longer the team manager but the speedway manager at Shelford, and a trusted lieutenant. Vincent had wanted the big man alongside him at BSPA General Council meetings. Sadly for Lurch, he had to travel 'cattle class' on the charter flight and stay in the conference hotel with the other promoters. Vincent needed a presence in there with the other promoters all the time, especially in the evenings when the chatting was going on in the bar.

The big man was, despite his size, something of a chameleon and was able to wander in and out of groups without really being noticed. John Tindall was also there, meeting and greeting the few older promoters he knew from his previous stints, and making contacts among the new boys.

The first day of the conference dealt with clearing up outstanding business from the season just finished. The promoters were delighted that they each received a bonus payout of £25,000 each track, mainly from the profits made on the staging of the World Final at Wembley.

For some, the payment turned a poor year into an ordinary one; for others it turned an ordinary year into a good one. For Vincent and a few others, it was the icing on the cake.

Traditionally, the final business on day one was the election of officers who would see the Association through the next 12 months. Not so much an election this time as a re-election, as it turned out.

The Chairman, Alan Howard, was returned unopposed, and there was only one face-change on the rest of the five-man Management Committee. Neither the Shelford nor Thornden Heath tracks bothered to vote. The result was a foregone conclusion anyway.

Steven Bray, the organiser of the trip, was very much in evidence during the lunch break on that first day. Steve was a very ebullient character who would happily gate-crash any private conversation. He always tried to put himself about as much as he could during this kind of event. His company already handled many of the individual tracks' travel arrangements but this kind of personal networking allowed him to gain more business.

Vincent called him over.

'Just suppose,' he said, 'I wanted four first-class air tickets to Los Angeles. What is the best price you could get them for? And while you are about it, how much for the same deal to Sydney?'

'I'll have the answer by the end of the afternoon,' Steven replied.

'OK,' said Vincent. 'In the meantime, do me a little favour. Here are the names of four promoters. Would you like to discreetly ask each of these if they might care to join me for dinner in my hotel this evening?'

'Consider it done,' said the ever-helpful Steve.

By the time Vincent got back to his hotel suite that evening, there was a message waiting for him from his new-found friend.

The quoted prices for the tickets were very good - excellent, in fact. Not only that, but there was a complete list of flight schedules for each destination, with recommendations for stopovers on the Sydney flights.

In addition, the note confirmed all four promoters on the list had said they would take up the invitation for dinner.

Vincent telephoned Steve.

'Did I mention you are also on the guest list for tonight? Actually, it would be good if you could get here at seven. That will give us an hour before the others arrive.'

Steve had barely stepped through the door when Vincent started.

'I was impressed with both the prices you came up with and the speed. If you are stuck here in Spain, then presumably you must have some decent staff back home?'

'My girls are excellent, and I have a young fellow I have been grooming as manager for a little time now. It's all very well my going out and getting the business but I have to be able to back it up.'

'So at the end of the day, although everyone believes they are all getting personal service from you, it is the team you have put together that does all the work?'

Bray looked a bit put out.

'Listen,' he said, 'someone has to find and train the staff in the first place, and be able to keep them happy and loyal.'

'Oh, you get the wrong impression,' said Vincent. 'I wasn't having a go at you, just the opposite in fact. I think you are a good operator. I have been doing a bit of homework, and I get the impression you don't always do things...what shall we say... the conventional way?' Bray left that comment in the air.

'Well, this is the deal,' Vincent continued, 'I have several friends who lead jet-set lifestyles. If I put their business your way, first, can your company cope with the extra work? Second, would that still leave you, personally, enough time to increase your interest and involvement in speedway if and when an opportunity arose?'

'I would like to think the answer to both questions is yes', said the jovial agent, with a smile.

The dinner was served in Vincent's suite. Dave, Heather and Ann were there, along with John Tindall, Steven Bray, Lurch and the four other promoters, Richard Watts from Exeter, John Moore from Sheffield, Tony Jones from Eastbourne and Peter Morrison from Hackney.

The food was excellent and the wine flowed, with Vincent and Ann both on sparkling form. The conversation wandered this way and that but rarely settled on speedway. Eventually, Richard Watts brought the subject up.

'Now look here, Vincent,' he said. 'You've invited us five promoters here for a meal and on behalf of the others, I have to say we have enjoyed it very much, but there has to be a reason behind it . . .'

'Not really,' said Vincent. 'Of the 16 British League tracks represented at the conference table today, I glanced around and wondered whom I would like to get to know better and whom I felt I could enjoy working with. Sad, isn't it, that I could only come up with five names!'

They laughed self-consciously, but Richard Watts pressed the point.

'So are you saying the other 10 don't rate with you?'

'Well, I think it is no great secret that myself and Alan Howard don't see eye to eye on many things but he was elected unopposed, so that is that for another year.'

'We all had a reasonable year last year,' chimed in John Moore, 'and the twenty-five grand pay-out was good.'

'Two things on that,' said Vincent. 'Point one – Wembley only comes around once every three years; and point two – the money from the World Final was in spite of, rather than because of, Alan Howard.

'Now I don't know anything about your businesses, but when I took over Shelford Speedway less than a year ago, it was on its last legs. This year, even allowing for the huge bonus handshake I gave to Bryce Penrith, the speedway will have made just over two hundred grand, year on year.'

When he had regained his composure, Moore came back with:

'That was all down to Penrith.'

'Maybe,' said Vincent. 'I prefer to think it was down to me for signing him, but have it your own way. In any case, I reckon he single-handedly put between five and 10 thousand into each of your pockets during the course of the year, and yet you – or should I say, some of the promoters – tried hard to prevent me from signing him! Now does that make any sense to you?

'I'll just make this one more point about Howard and the way the sport is currently run and leave it there. I don't want to spoil a lovely evening.

'At just about every General Council meeting I have been to so far, the only things that have come up and have been discussed at length have been negatives. Why should so-and-so do this, and shouldn't we stop so-and-so doing that? Everything that is discussed hinges around trying to stop each promoter trying to steal a march on another. Nothing is ever discussed about how the promoters can help each other and work towards maximising returns from the product you control. I find it sad, very sad.

'You just listen carefully tomorrow and count how many things of a positive nature are discussed.'

With that, Ann asked politely if she could help people with drinks, and the conversation once again went back onto general subjects.

'What was all that about?' said Dave afterwards.

'It's called divide and conquer,' Vincent said, with a grin.

Discussion at the conference next morning was sedate, although the afternoon session was not so quiet. As the delegates settled into their seats after lunch, Chairman Alan Howard launched into an embittered diatribe about disloyalty and subversive elements within the Association.

He announced that he wasn't prepared to put up with promoters having clandestine meetings and plotting against him and the Management Committee. He theatrically resigned his position there and then.

There were enough sycophants to talk him out of it but there were also a good deal of raised eyebrows, especially from those who had dined with Vincent, over what was clearly paranoid behaviour on Howard's part.

Vincent merely smiled. Whilst on the one hand the promoters who had attended the dinner loudly protested at the attitude of the Chairman, those who had not enjoyed Vincent's hospitality the night before viewed the attendees as a dangerous breakaway faction.

Vincent spoke to Mark on his return to England. He suggested Steven Bray would make an ideal travel agent for Mark and his jet-set friends to use. Within weeks, Steve had to take on two more staff to deal purely with the new business generated. Just as important, the business was with the kind of high-profile clientele Steve had always craved. In return, Vincent was able to milk the gregarious agent of speedway information and gossip. There was little going on in the world of speedway the self-important travel agent let slip by him.

In fact, it was a tip-off from Steve that set up the purchase of Marsden Speedway. The asking price had tumbled since the original enquiry had been made. It was now almost at bargain basement price as the previous promoter battled with a very messy divorce. Vincent set up a new company to make the purchase, again with his name hidden behind a wall of nominees.

Steven Bray was named as the new promoter.

Chapter 27

The run up to the start of the 1984 season was quite interesting. The Shelford team looked desperately thin. Having lost the World Champion in Jeff Harding and last year's driving force and motivator in Bryce Penrith, the Racers looked like cannon fodder.

The signing of Jamie Marlborough from Thorden Heath went nowhere near to replacing either of the departed stars, and the supporters were even more amazed when the spare spot in the team was given to promising local youngster, Chris Andrews.

Marlborough already worked at Eddie Campbell's speedway engine tuning business. Vince arranged for Chris to spend a couple of weeks there in 'apprentice' mode. He was to do all the menial tasks around the place but listen and learn how things should be done properly.

Vincent organised brand-new Italian GM engines and top equipment for the two new lads on the understanding they would have to pay him back from their earnings. He doubted that he would see the full return of his outlay, but didn't want the young riders to feel things came too easily.

Both kids had struggled on out-of-date equipment up until then and Vincent was banking on the new machinery lifting them well above their previous form. He believed that, with constant attention from Lurch and himself, the lads would very quickly become key team men.

Chris, at 18, was a year older than Jamie. Jamie lived in Thorden Heath itself, while Chris was only 20 minutes from there, and the two became firm friends, travelling to most tracks together with their mates as 'mechanics'.

Time and again, Vincent took the opportunity in the media to blame Jeff Harding for the weak Shelford line-up. In his own mind, he and Lurch were confident they had put together a team of fast improvers but wanted to keep as much public pressure off them as possible.

However, the line taken was that this was a team in transition.

They might not be good enough to win the league this year, but every rider in the line-up was capable of making huge advances.

The team would be local, close-knit and exciting. Their supporters would be rewarded for their loyalty by seeing great speedway and by being in at the ground floor on what would turn out to be a very special outfit in a season or two.

Lurch was sure the other riders in the team, all still very young, but with the benefit of having spent a season being tutored by Bryce Penrith under their belts, would all revel in being given so much extra responsibility, and would drag the two new boys along with them.

This wasn't the universal opinion of many of the fair weather supporters the Racers had picked up during the final couple of months of the previous season. The usual flurry of letters suggesting Shelford had been one-year wonders appeared in the local paper. By and large though, the vast majority of the supporters were prepared to back the changes, sure in their own minds that the matches at their own home track would be close and exciting.

Thorden Heath supporters, on the other hand, were cock-a-hoop. They finally had a good promoter with a solid track record and, for the first time ever, a World Champion in their team. They felt, for the first time in a long while, there was a genuine chance for honours, especially with long-term injured rider Martin Mitchell back in the side after missing the entire previous season with a badly broken leg.

At Marsden, new promoter, Steven Bray, swapped a couple of riders with other tracks. The final line-up looked capable rather than exciting, but with his own special brand of bullshit and bluster, Steve was able to create a new and vibrant atmosphere around Marsden Speedway.

The 'Ravens' seemed to be once again a proud and enthusiastic outfit. The local supporters had never seen such enthusiasm and intensity. They took to the new man and his ways very quickly.

Vincent sat down before the start of the season with Jeff Harding. He explained to Jeff he expected him to do the same job at Thorden as Penrith had done at Shelford. He would be the captain and the 'go to' man, and he was to drag the other riders along with him.

Vincent spent a good deal of time explaining why Penrith had been so well loved by the supporters. It was because he always seemed to put the team first, he always said the right things in public and he never demonstrated any selfishness.

Vincent explained that a move from Shelford and a new start were essential if Jeff was going to reinvent himself and that he was sure he could. He also spelled out to Harding that he had set things up for Thorden to win the League, and that it was up to the new captain to make it happen. Following on the World Championship last season, it would be proof Jeff Harding could also be the perfect team man.

The split from his wife and son had hit Jeff very hard. Perhaps also, he was growing up a bit. Jeff Harding was a lot more thoughtful and a bit more humble this time around.

'Oh, one thing,' said Vincent. 'You hate me and you hate everything about Shelford Speedway. I want you to be very rude about me in public and to whip up plenty of bad feeling between the two tracks. As you know, I have set the ball rolling for you in that regard. Mainly though, I want you to back it up by winning every race you ride at or against Shelford.

'So you want me to play the bad guy when the two teams meet?'

'My word, I think he's got it,' thought Vincent, but he just nodded.

Reece Sullivan was given the job of captaining the Racers. Vincent and Lurch invited the team and the junior riders over to The Manor a few days before the season opener. No messing about this time, just a meal that Ann presided over, and then a few beers in the library.

Vincent gave a speech.

'I will speak to each rider individually later but I want you all to know, I am going to set each and every one of you your own individual goals this year. Those goals will incorporate the most important of all issues – the Shelford promotion comes first.

We pay your wages, and you will be paid far more and treated far better than your counterparts at other tracks. The reason for this is simple. We will expect more from you. We will expect absolute loyalty and discretion and within your own capabilities, you will always carry out the instructions of myself or Lurch.

'We will not win either the league or the cup this year, because we don't have a strong enough team, but if you all achieve your individual goals then we will finish high up and we will have a team to be feared next year.

'Achievements, individually and collectively, will be rewarded, and come the end of the season, if the business has done well, you will all benefit. I don't need to spell out to any of you, a failure to attain your targets without good reason could see you replaced. Before it comes to that, though, you will always be pre-warned and given the opportunity to pull yourselves around.

'Please bring any problem, to do with speedway, or in your private lives, straight to us. We will do whatever we can to help and, of course, always in the strictest confidence.

'Last year, you rode under the collective wings of Bryce Penrith and Jeff Harding. It is time to put their teachings and example into effect.'

One or two of the more cynical riders in the team sniggered under their breath at mention of 'bad boy' Harding, whom they still blamed totally for Racers finishing the previous season without any silverware. Vincent stopped the noise with just a long, cold stare.

'We open next week with a home and away challenge against Thorden Heath. More than anything else, I will be looking for the way you behave and play up to the crowd – at both tracks. I hope you all understand.

'Finally, this is a very young team. Young men are prone to doing rash and silly things. What I am asking is for you all to grow up fast. What you have to remember is that, whether you are wearing the Racers' colours or in civvies, you are always representing this team and this club. Please don't let it down.'

Vincent and Lurch then spoke to each rider in turn, giving him a file containing the full details of what was required of him as an individual. Some found they were expected to undertake extra fitness work, others needed to increase their technical knowledge, and they were collectively required to attend team clinics on personal presentation, public speaking and goal-setting.

Vincent had considered bringing in motivational experts but decided this might cut across Lurch's and his own roles.

John Tindall and Steven Bray were having similar conversations with their own teams at around the same time. Except that the Thorden team were informed that they were *expected* to win the league.

The Marsdon Ravens were to concentrate on the parts that had been missing most at their stadium over the previous few years and were expected to provide the supporters with a real evening's entertainment every week. They were also to make themselves available for every kind of public relations opportunity that came along in the semi-rural town of Marsdon.

Every help and encouragement would be given to any rider currently living out of the area if he was prepared to relocate to Marsdon.

The first of the home and away challenge matches between the Thorden Heath Swords and the Racers was to be the season-opener at Shelford.

The scores were level, 36-36, going into the last race. Harding had been unbeaten all evening but he missed the gate completely in that vital heat and the two Shelford boys got themselves out in front. Harding passed his own partner and tore after them.

On the last bend, he steamed under the team-riding Shelford pair and gave young Alan Stewart a huge nudge. Stewart all but lost control, and the following Thorden rider managed to nip through to take third place. A 4-2 heat win and a 40-38 victory to the visitors!

The crowd erupted with anger. Jeff Harding played up to the booing home fans, also to the thousands of visiting Thorden supporters.

Vincent, Lurch and John Tindall looked on, well satisfied that all four riders had performed their parts in that final, carefully choreographed, last heat. Reece Sullivan and Alan Stewart couldn't understand why Thorden had been allowed to win but knew better than to demand explanations.

Jeff Harding was also unbeaten in the return leg at Thorden Heath six days later. Somehow, though, Shelford managed to pack the minor placings, and in another breathtaking last heat, snatched victory by the same margin as in the first match. Honours therefore had finished even, but the two sets of supporters had seen two unbelievable meetings and the events were the talk of both areas all through the following week.

The Marsdon Ravens won their own opening fixture, also a challenge match against their long-time rivals, Birmingham, reasonably comfortably in front of an excellent crowd. The supporters reckoned it was the best presented meeting they had ever seen at the refurbished Marsdon stadium and went home happy. The Ravens lost a close encounter in the return match but won the two-legged challenge on aggregate.

Chapter 28

Mark and Dianne had spent a couple of weekends at The Manor during the winter but were still 'just good friends'. Mark had explained things to Vincent.

'Why the hell should I settle down?' he asked. 'I'm in the risk assessment and management business. The odds are far too high that something would go wrong and it would cost me an arm and a leg. In this instance, there's protection in numbers, and why would I want to limit my options in any case?'

Mark would not admit, even to Vincent, his real reason and determination not to settle down. He was already in love – and it wasn't with Dianne.

There was no disputing the logic, however, and in any case, Dianne was happy in her small house not too far from The Manor, living her life, in the main, for her son Jack. She really didn't see how the domesticity and lifestyle she shared with Jack and the wild, extravagant world of Mark's could ever mix.

She was happy to keep Mark and Jack in separate compartments, and there was always Ann and Heather to share her problems with in between.

She quite enjoyed her three-cornered existence and if she ever needed an escort, Martin Kessler, better known as Lurch, was always prepared to make himself available with no strings.

When the season had started, Jack insisted on his mum taking him to Thorden Heath Speedway to watch his dad race. The promoter there, John Tindall, was especially kind. He went out of his way to make them welcome. He seemed to take a real shine to young Jack. They hit it off straight away.

Dianne soon stopped attending the sport she had learned to loathe. It was left for Jeff to collect and return Jack, and to arrange for him to be looked after during the meetings.

Lurch knew the most important thing for his young, inexperienced Shelford team was to avoid injury early on. True, they needed to be competitive, so as not to become demoralised, but avoiding injury was crucial.

Telling a team of kids, the average age of which was below 20, to get stuck in and have a go was not difficult; telling them to take things carefully was not so simple.

Both Lurch and Vincent were aware there would be plenty of riders from the 'Old Brigade' in opposition teams who would be itching for a chance to put the young upstarts in their places. It was up to the management duo to steer their troops through the minefield.

The best way to do this was to make sure all of the team each maintained his bikes at the highest level. This way, once they were in front, it was doubtful the hard men would get near enough to do any damage.

In the early matches, it was the quality of their equipment and clever handling that chalked the team up a succession of close home victories. The young lads struggled a little away from home but this was to be expected given their lack of experience.

Vincent was able to 'organise' a victory for them at Marsdon, and the kids just loved the thrill of winning. OK, so they lost a couple of tight home matches but it was on their travels the team really started living up to its name of 'Racers'.

Of all places, their first 'genuine' victory was at Brighton. Admittedly, the home team suffered an injury to their top man in his second race but Shelford took full advantage.

Vincent simply loved it, especially the look on Alan Howard's face near the end of the meeting when the loss was looming. By the end of the last race, the home promoter, who doubled as BSPA Chairman, was nowhere in sight, thus avoiding his having to shake hands with either Vincent or Lurch.

Chapter 29

In May, Cyril Grant received a notice of the Annual General Meeting of Shelford Speedway Ltd. He presented himself at the stadium on the day, taking along a lawyer. Waiting for him were Vincent and Dave, with their own solicitor who had been appointed as the Company Secretary.

The accounts were produced and Cyril's eyes bulged when he saw how much the income had increased over the previous year. Then he looked over to the other column and was equally disbelieving of the expenses. The two figures on the bottom line were almost identical. According to these accounts, the business had only just broken even.

Cyril demanded to see a full breakdown of the accounts.

'I'm sorry, detailed accounts are for the directors only,' the Company Secretary said, 'but I will be happy to answer any questions where possible.' After being assured by his advisor that this was correct procedure, Grant pointed to the figure of £185,000 for 'consultancy fees'.

'What in hell's name are these?' he blurted out.

'Exactly what they say,' said the solicitor. 'Fees paid to an agency for consultancy. If you look in the notes, you will see both directors have declared a financial interest in the management of the agency.

'From that, I do not think it unreasonable to infer that the fees were paid for consultancy services performed by either or both of the directors and/or others.'

'In other words, instead of declaring the money as profit and paying it out as dividends to the shareholders, the directors have paid it to themselves,' wailed the hapless Grant.

'It is true, the directors do not recommend the payment of a dividend this year, but the auditors have examined the fees, along with the rest of the accounts, and have no difficulty with them.'

'Well, if there are no more questions, perhaps we can vote on the continuation of the directors and auditors for the coming year?' Dave suggested.

Grant looked at his advisor, who merely shrugged his shoulders. With that, the angry ex-promoter jumped up, knocking his chair backwards, and stormed out of the office.

'I'll take that as an abstention, then?' Dave shouted after him, laughing.

Meanwhile the property market was in full swing. Vincent and Mark had moved more money into the property portfolio out of the increasingly overheating share market. Dave was doing a brilliant job in managing what had now become a property empire. Such was the intensity of the housing market that a new word had entered the industry. 'Gazumping' was now becoming commonplace.

Vincent and Mark had decided to give the market another six months before clearing out a lot of their property portfolio and only keeping the best, high earning assets. Dave was given even more licence to turn properties over, and given his knowledge and position in the local property market, was making big money for the company.

Here and there, he was doing a few deals for himself, but only with Vincent's blessing. Not that he needed the money really. Dave's continued alliance with Vincent had already made him a rich man. He was now able to live the same lifestyle as the others without having to rely on handouts, but he was also very happy to remain subordinate to Vincent's powerful personality.

Vincent was at the Scott Properties plush new offices. He suddenly asked Dave how much he was worth in cash and property assets, not counting the leasehold on the gatehouse. Dave guessed at about half-a-million pounds. Vince then asked what the property company was worth. The answer was, at fire sale values, something over £12million but, realistically, £14-15million.

Previously Mark had made a suggestion to Vincent, which he had totally agreed with.

'Mark and I have been mighty pleased at the way things have been going. We reckon a double figure percentage rental return on investment, even without the capital gains, is exceptional for a property company.' All three of them, Mark, Vincent and Dave were well aware the annualised capital gains for the last eighteen months had been more than 100%, but they also knew such a figure was not sustainable in the long term.

'How about you toss your assets into the fund and take a directorship and 20% of the company in return? That way you won't need to be side-tracked doing deals for yourself.'

Twenty percent of £15million was three million. In one casual sentence, Vincent had made Dave a multi-millionaire! Not bad for a lad his father-in-law had said wasn't good enough for his daughter.

Dave suspected Heather enjoyed the money and the more lavish lifestyle even more than he did. She could act up to her father, and she could certainly maintain parity - and more - with the County Set. Not that she bothered too much with them these days. Her and Ann were still as close as ever.

Dianne was fine and fun but as far as Heather was concerned, Ann was her favourite. Neither Dave, putting more and more into his work, nor Heather, enjoying her carefree lifestyle to the full, understood the pair of them were slowly slipping apart.

Chapter 30

Vincent took centre-stage for a while at the first BSPA General Council meeting of the season in June. Up until that time, he had maintained a low profile at these talk-fests.

'At the AGM I tabled a motion to have the riders' personal injury insurance pay-outs lifted considerably,' he reminded his colleagues, 'but in your wisdom you decided to reject the idea. For the record, I have sourced a broker who will come up with better rates than the company you are presently using.

'I am aware the arrangement with the current BSPA brokers has been long-standing, and I would not wish to get involved there, but if any promoter wants to increase his riders' personal insurance, they can contact me privately.

'What I want to mention today is the new legislation concerning wheelchair access in public places. I doubt too many of you have given this a thought but I suspect each and every one of you is currently open to prosecution.

'Apart from the matter of wheelchair access and toilet amenities, there is a phrase you will hear more and more in the future. This is "duty of care".

'It is all very well you pointing to your million pound public liability insurance cover – but I promise you, in the event of a multiple injury claim, that amount will not be nearly enough. And in any case, the question of negligence, maybe even criminal negligence, will arise.

'It will be of no surprise to you all that this is an area I have considerable interest in. In fact, I reckon I am just about up to speed with what is required by law.

'Would it make sense if I were to travel around to each track, check it out and prepare a private and confidential report for each promoter? It will then be up to each individual promotion as to how much he wishes to do in order to comply with the new laws, and in the case of those who rent their stadia, how much they wish to lean on their landlords to do.

'To show how strongly I feel about this, I am prepared to make these inspections without charge to the Association. To me, it is a personal thing.'

There was high suspicion in one or two quarters but it was an emotive subject, and such a gift horse could not be looked in the mouth. Only Vincent's old foe, Alan Howard, the BSPA Chairman and Brighton Speedway chief, turned the offer down.

'What are you up to, Boss?' Lurch asked as they were driving home.

'Lurch, we have achieved three things today. We have made ourselves the good guys for those who have yet to decide; we have given ourselves licence to go and examine every nook and cranny of every speedway stadium in the land; and we have given ourselves the opportunity to chat with all the promoters on a quiet one-to-one basis. I'd say that was a good day's work!'

The Bystone track was of great interest to Vincent. Located on the western side of East Anglia, it had recently changed hands and the speedway business was now owned and being run by a consortium of businessman supporters after a couple of very rocky years when it had looked certain to fold.

As is usual in these cases, this consortium was rapidly beginning to shake out. Running a speedway promotion by committee is fraught with problems and like most supporter consortiums, those at Bystone just didn't have the sense to put the job in the hands of a capable manager and then watch from the stands.

It soon became clear one of the three remaining members of the original group was far keener on running the business on a professional footing than the others. Vincent had several chats with him and decided Harry Grahame, who owned a local tyre retail franchise, was the one to back and someone with whom he could work . . . or, more to the point, he could control.

It didn't take long for Grahame to buy the other partners out, once Vincent made the money available. They were more than happy just to have received most of their money back. Vincent was prepared to take a secret 49% stake through one of his many offshore companies, leaving Harry Grahame in charge of things.

Vincent now, with this new arrangement, either directly controlled, or had sympathetic liaisons with, eight of the 16 tracks in the British League.

He then switched his attention to the Second Division, or National

League as it liked to be known, and soon located two ambitious promotions that both fancied a go in the top flight.

The only thing stopping them was the necessary extra capital, so Vincent was happy, for an interest in the operations, to finance, underwrite and support their plans to move forward.

The beauty of what he had created was that nobody other than him (and Ann) at this stage was aware he now had financial involvement in no fewer than six tracks, and had acolytes in four others.

Presuming the senior league would have 18 teams next season, Vincent would have effective control of 10 of them, and therefore a clear majority within the BSPA General Council.

The 1984 season flew by. The Shelford supporters stood by their team whilst the kids all fully established themselves. The atmosphere at every Shelford meeting was electric and both the racing and the matches always close and exciting. The Racers won most of their home matches and a few away from home.

The main thing was, they avoided serious injury, and from mid-September onwards, made a real charge up the table, seeing them finish in a very creditable sixth place.

Both Jamie Marlborough and Chris Andrews had done everything expected of them and more. Most importantly, they had both evaded injury other than minor bumps and bruises.

Although a little younger, Jamie had emerged in front of Chris. Many put this down to the experience he had gained with Thorden but Vincent and Lurch had both decided young Marlborough had what it took to reach the top.

Quite apart from his ability and determination, there was just something special about him. He seemed to soak up information like a sponge and, best of all, had a brilliant attitude and a disarming manner with everyone. Had anyone mentioned it, Vincent would have been indignant to a suggestion young Marlborough was receiving special treatment. But clearly this was the case.

Vincent had popped round to see Jamie's mum, Joan, several times during the season, just to keep her updated on her lad's progress and to reinforce his invitation to come along to meetings. She still refused but Vincent thought she was beginning to weaken in her resolve.

He nipped around again in September, during the day, when he knew Jamie would be at work. He asked how Joan felt about Jamie having a month or so in Australia during the coming winter, doing a bit of racing and expanding his horizons. She was not one to put her own feelings first and agreed it would be a good opportunity for her lad to gain more experience, so Vincent telephoned Bryce who set up a short riding tour for Vincent's protégé.

That evening, over dinner, Vincent told Ann what he had arranged.

'Of course you do realise what this is all about, don't you?' she said in her quiet, sweet voice.

'You know I am pretty thick, Angel, you will have to explain . . .'

'You must realise you are treating him far better than any of the rest of the team? You loaned him the deposit on that car of his and stood guarantor for the payments. You got him his job, you bought him his bike and new leathers and now you have arranged a trip to Australia for him, which no doubt *you* will pay for.

'And all because the lad reminds you of yourself when you were the same age. Your parental instincts have come out and you've virtually decided to adopt him!'

Vincent dismissed the notion and said it was simply because the boy had a lot of talent and all he was doing was protecting his investment. But in his heart, he knew she was right. He *did* feel something special about young Jamie Marlborough.

Marsdon had been a revelation under Steven Bray. Every week he had pulled another headline-grabbing stunt, and with the local football team having dropped down the divisions, the Ravens had become the darlings of the local media. They only finished halfway up the league, thanks to several mid-season injuries, but were always fun to watch, and totally unpredictable.

At Thorden Heath, Jeff Harding was a changed man. He grew in stature and became an exceptional captain and number one. He carried several younger, less experienced team mates with his unselfish riding and the Swords finished the season with a flurry. They won the league title in their last match of the campaign. Harding had once again held his team together with a masterly display in that final meeting, ironically, against Belle Vue.

Harding had reached the World Final in Poland but relinquished his title to a local favourite, Marek Szcekowski, the Brit having to settle for fourth on the day.

Shelford's Reece Sullivan also made it into the final in Katowice, although he only scored five points. Still, everyone was pleased with the lad, who had not yet reached 20 years of age.

Both of the second division clubs that had applied for first division status for the following season were quietly informed they would be welcomed into the senior ranks. They would have to pay an entrance fee, the amount yet to be determined, but an 18-team league gave a far better balance to the fixture list.

When it came to the Annual Conference in early December, back in the same Benidorm hotel, Alan Howard again nominated for the position of Chairman. This time though, John Tindall put forward Vincent Hansing for the position and Steven Bray seconded the nomination. In the usual secret ballot, Vincent was voted into the job.

Howard and his few remaining followers were horrified. Only two of the previous year's Management Committee nominated to retain their places, and they both lost out.

The new committee consisted of Vincent, John Tindall, Steven Bray, Richard Watts and Tony Jones. Watts and Jones were two of the promoters who had been invited to the dinner in Vincent's hotel suite just 12 months previously. In fact, all five of the new Management Committee had been there that night. This time, Vincent decided against a private meal in his own hotel suite.

An entirely new era in British speedway was about to begin.

Chapter 31

Vincent had now reached a second crossroads in his life. His original idea in getting involved in speedway again had been purely vindictive. It had been his intention to take control and then destroy speedway in the same way it had destroyed his life.

Now he was not sure what he wanted. Now he held speedway in his hands, should he destroy it or not? Apart from Jeff Harding, the burning desire for revenge was dying down.

Vincent had begun to feel much the same about speedway as he did about Dianne. Since she had become part of 'the gang', Vincent's bitterness towards her had softened.

But there would be no second chance for Harding. His future was mapped out, and Vincent was merely getting maximum use out of him for the time being.

When he had still been vengeful towards Dianne, Vincent had some time ago outlined in his mind what was to be her fate. Her weakness was her boy, Jack, and the powerful speedway entrepreneur had intended to use him as a way of evening things up.

However, the close relationship that had developed between Dianne and Ann, and the fact that he himself was losing his anger towards her, had complicated things. He would wait and see for a while on that one. After all, she had all but admitted to him that summer day at The Manor, she had made a bad error in getting involved with Harding and had paid for it.

Vincent finally made similar decisions about both Dianne and the speedway. He controlled the Management Committee and the General Council. Effectively, he was speedway's dictator. The potential profit on the sale of the freehold at Shelford more than covered the monies he had outlaid to date, so he couldn't really lose.

What he would do is to run speedway how he thought it should be run. If it proved to be successful, then so be it. If not, then he had enjoyed the fun and was none the worse off for it.

Likewise, he would consider Dianne 'off the hook' unless, and until, something happened to change his mind.

Mark's stature as the darling of the markets grew and grew and he continued to make serious money. Vincent decided it was now patently unfair to expect Mark to devote a couple of hours a day giving him personal service, so they had pulled out of the options markets completely.

They had several million in blue chip portfolios by now, though, and the property business, although quite well cashed up, was worth about £18million in cash and property.

He and Mark knew there were both a property and a stock market slump coming. Both markets were overheating badly, so the pair were now cashing in and storing money in bonds, waiting for the inevitable crash, when they would jump back in and pick up the bargains.

Vincent had discussed the speedway situation with Ann earlier that evening after his elevation to the Chairman's job.

'I look at it this way, my love,' she said. 'The speedway is something to keep you occupied and you patently enjoy the cut and thrust. Really it gives you a nice little interest, so why not carry on with it, at least until you get bored? Besides, knowing you, you won't be content until you have seen Alan Howard in tears!'

She was right, of course. Howard had been mighty upset that afternoon when he had been outvoted in the conference, but not nearly enough to satisfy Vincent. Quietly, he mused to himself just how much he depended on his Angel for her common sense and sound advice.

The new Chairman cancelled the next day's morning session of the conference. He reasoned that the completely new Management Committee needed a good, long session together and some time with the BSPA Manager, so he could bring them up to speed.

By the time the General Council reconvened, Vincent had rewritten the rest of the agenda and felt comfortably in control. Not only did he have his two secret 'employees' on the committee with him, but he had also captured the hearts of the other two members of the new committee completely.

This was to be no normal afternoon in the history of British speedway racing, though. In the next two hours, Vincent tackled the biggest problems that had blighted the British League for several years. He put into place revolutionary plans to solve speedway's biggest ongoing problems.

Effectively Vincent abandoned the old methods of team equalisation by numbers. He had been given a mandate to create the equivalent of the 'draft' system employed by American professional sports.

He also abandoned the paying of transfer fees by contracting riders to the BSPA administration rather than with individual promotions.

Further, he decreed that, except for the final stages of World Championship events, any riders from any nationality who raced in the British League were required to commit to putting their British fixtures first.

These moves, along with the banning of fixture changes except to accommodate rained off fixtures, went a good deal of the way to solving the question of riders being absent from matches. Vincent also came up with a system, vesting power in the BSPA manager, Rod Brown, to alleviate the difficulties individual promotions had in coping with teams being hit by injury to key riders. Effectively, the use of 'guest riders' in speedway would cease.

Speedway had not seen such a dramatic shake up since the establishment of the British League in 1965. Some promoters called it visionary, whilst others dwelt upon all the possible problems that could arise. Rod Brown was elated! Quite apart from his title having been upgraded to that of Chief Executive Officer and his having been given executive as well as administrative duties (with a commensurate rise in salary), he really believed the changes were for the better. At last, he thought, speedway can begin to move forward.

There was significant reaction from the overseas federations during the months before the beginning of the 1985 season. It would be fair to say they were less than happy at the hard-nosed stance taken by the new British regime, but the BSPA stuck to its guns and ended up losing only the two Poles who had ridden in Britain the previous year.

Sweden, Denmark and the USA had issued ultimatums to their riders, but by the start of the speedway season their bluffs had been called.

All of the riders had decided, if it came to the crunch, they would take out British racing licences and cut speedway ties with their own countries. Faced with universal solidarity, the federations had backed down and agreed to arrange their own fixtures around the British domestic calendar.

There was also plenty of drama between the two British domestic leagues. The Division One promoters refused to pay any transfer fees to second division bosses for riders who wished to step up . . . despite their best efforts, the second division promoters were still unable to prevent the migration of their best and most ambitious riders to the senior league, although their promoters received no 'compensation'.

Once the season got underway and the new procedures Vincent had put into place on how the meetings should be presented were adopted, speedway flourished. The fixture list, so carefully put together this time around, was locked in, and the only changes allowed were those needed to accommodate rained-off matches. This one thing went a long way towards stabilising the sport and making it more supporter-friendly.

The new BSPA Commercial Department was also a huge success. The Commercial Manager, John Watson, carefully selected by Vincent and Rod, covered his costs purely with the profits from the newly introduced BSPA merchandise.

In addition, the staging of the special events on the speedway calendar, the international series and the various finals and competitions, were a huge success. Once the BSPA Special Events team began to work with the staging promotions, these fixtures were transformed into real blockbusters, adding significant revenue to the BSPA coffers.

Most important of all, promoters started being honest and open with each other. Publicly, they carried on the little local feuds and spats, but these were mainly for show.

Vincent even pulled all the referees together before the season, treated them all to a leisurely day at The Manor, and over fine food and wine, got through to them that they were as much a part of the entertainment as they were there to see fair play.

Some of the older referees resented the intrusion into their own little power base, and were quietly sidelined when the allocation of meetings was made, but in general the bulk of the refs joined in the with this 'new image' of speedway.

Starts of races were cleaned up and, where possible, rider exclusions were limited to the minimum, which meant meetings were run at a much smoother rate.

The few original Vincent detractors had to admit it was a brilliant year, with every speedway showing much higher attendances and increased profits. Even the riders were happy. Vincent had pushed through a substantial rise in their basic payments and a significant increase to their injury benefits.

As Shelford's young local team developed, they won more matches, and this year finished third in the league. The best part about it was that every one of the riders improved on the previous year.

The shooting star had, of course, been the long-haired Jamie Marlborough. He was popular with everyone and always in demand for individual events and extra bookings.

Vincent arranged meetings for him on the Continent and his mum finally began to come and watch him race. The youngster failed to make the World Final by just one point but, in anyone's terms, he had enjoyed a brilliant year. For a lad barely 19, it was incredible.

Ann was again put in charge of the end-of-season riders' party at The Manor. In fact, it became two parties. The first was a mixed fancy dress evening, not just for the riders and their partners but also for all of the helpers who had made Shelford Speedway the envy of the league.

One hundred and eighty people, between the ages of 16 and 60 were invited and the whole Manor (except the cellar!) became the venue. Caterers set the food and free bar up in the entrance hall, a live group played in the ballroom that had been emptied of furniture, whilst those who simply wanted to chat gravitated to the morning room and the library.

Later on, the younger, more outgoing party-people found the pool, this time with the concertina doors to the outside all closed up, and they had a great time in there, frolicking and posing.

The odd few illicit couples were also seen creeping up the back stairs to the bedrooms. Everyone had a great time and all agreed it had been the best party they had been to.

The riders' 'traditional' stag night was on the following weekend. Once again, the wives and girlfriends had organised their own night out, leaving the riders to their own devices.

The ever-inventive Ann had organised a 'Roman orgy' for this year. The riders were required to get into the swing of things by donning either Roman soldiers' tunics, or decidedly short togas before being allowed into the 'Roman villa', where three slave masters were in charge of plenty of slave maidens, scantily clad and bound together in a line. The crack of a whip kept the girls in order.

Most of the riders headed straight for the exquisite and exotic foods and fortified wines, figuring the slaves could wait. Jamie Marlborough and Chris Andrews decided to inspect the goods. They figured they would like first choice, besides which, they just loved to show off their capabilities. Ann, Heather, and Dianne settled in to enjoy the show.

Lurch looked decidedly ill at ease. As manager, he felt obliged to accompany his charges, but he was uncomfortable with the idea of simply having sex because it was there and available. This was a minor disappointment for the three onlookers, who were still in awe of the size of his wedding tackle.

At the height of the activities, Lurch slipped away. He had intended simply having an early night and headed straight for one of the guest rooms upstairs. On seeing him depart the party, Dianne was off like a jackrabbit. She saw him disappear into a four-poster room, and followed him in . . .

Next morning, after all the stragglers had been rounded up and despatched, Dianne emerged. Ann was keen to hear all about her evening coping with the big guy, but Dianne went all coy and would merely say it had been a night to remember.

Shortly after the Christmas and New Year break, Mark telephoned the Manor to give Vincent some hot news. Greyhound Racing Incorporated PLC owned five dog racing stadia. It was a public company and Mark had heard the whisper it was in a good deal of trouble financially. Those in the know thought if the company didn't offload at least one stadium it could go under.

Vincent picked up the phone and got through to the Managing Director of GRI, using his relationship with Mark to ensure the call was answered.

'I am interested in buying Brighton Stadium,' he said. 'Can you give me a price and access to the books so that I can carry out due diligence, please?'

The Managing Director, Peter Lowe, did not insult Vincent's intelligence. If he was a friend of Mark Breeze, he was clearly in the know. If GRI could unload a stadium quickly and quietly before the rest of the market got wind of their plight, he could avoid a run on their shares.

He named a price.

'I'll send my man down for a look at the stadium and books, tomorrow if you like. Who should he liaise with?'

By the next evening, Dave had done all his homework. GRI wanted £2million. The break-up value of the place was about £1.5m. The business was running in the black but represented a poor return on capital if you didn't take appreciation of the freehold into account.

Vincent contacted Peter Lowe the next day.

'You and I both know the value of the place is a million-and-a-half. However, this is a distressed sale. I can get the money to you by tomorrow if necessary. It will be one point four million.'

'I'll need to speak with my Board.'

'Be my guest,' said Vincent. 'The offer is on the table for 24 hours.'

First thing the next morning the deal was done. Vincent was going to enjoy telling Alan Howard the name of his new landlord . . .

Over the previous couple of years, Brighton Speedway had appeared to have experienced a series of setbacks. Nothing Howard could put his finger on, but enough to make him believe Vincent was behind them. He was certainly fast losing his enthusiasm for the sport.

Vincent phoned Howard the moment the deal was signed and sealed.

'Alan,' he said. 'Guess what? I'm your new landlord!' There was a shocked silence.

'It says here you are due for a rent review within the next couple of months. Just thought I'd let you know there will be an appreciable increase, and I've been glancing through your lease agreement. I see there are several things down here you don't seem to be fully complying with. Perhaps we can catch up and have a chat about it sometime?'

A couple of weeks later the beleaguered Howard received a phone call from John Tindall.

'Alan, I hear on the grapevine that bastard Hansing has bought Brighton Stadium and is giving you a hard time. I hate him, but because we are so close geographically, I have to make it look as if I am getting on OK with him.

'Listen, my company is looking to make a couple of raids on some speedways with the idea of unseating Hansing. Your promotion wouldn't be for sale at all, would it? We ought to do what we can to stop Hansing getting his hands on Brighton

Speedway, even if he owns the stadium.'

When the deal went through, once again using a proxy company, Vincent asked Tindall to run Brighton Speedway, in addition to Thorden Heath, until they could find a suitable man to put in at the Sussex track.

He resisted the temptation to phone Howard and tell him who was behind the purchase. That could lead to Tindall having problems with Howard's cronies down there. Vincent would save that final dig at Howard for another day.

Vincent had held the Management Committee and General Council meetings at the Manor all season. He was also fed up with going abroad for the annual conference and determined that it, too, would be held at his grand home. It was his way of making a point. *He* was in charge of the Association. In any case, he wanted to limit the traditional talk-fest. Now things were running smoothly, two days was plenty of time for the AGM.

The attic rooms at The Manor had all been made into nice, single bedrooms a while back. Occasional staff used them if they struggled to get home after late shifts. Then there were the main bedrooms in The Manor, and a couple of guest rooms at the gatehouse Dave and Heather were happy to offer up as one-off accommodation for the conference.

Vincent suspected the Midlands-based promoters would want to go home and spend the night in their own beds anyway, which meant he could just about accommodate all of the other promoters on site.

As a back up, there was an excellent guest house in the village and in early December it would be virtually empty.

For the first time since anyone could remember, this conference did not break into factions. Vincent was re-elected unopposed and received a standing ovation for his efforts over the previous year that had seen British speedway return to its position of strength.

Most of the meeting, after rubber-stamping the way things were running, was devoted to discussing how individual tracks could assist each other in their promotions and how they could all improve the running of the sport.

It was great to find all promoters were pulling in the same direction, sharing ideas and happy to work for the common good.

Vincent picked up on one thing. One promoter mentioned he had been approached by his stadium owners, who were dog racing and betting people, and asked why there was no gambling on speedway.

'Could this be pursued as an extra line of revenue?' he had wondered. Vincent set his mind to exploring all the possibilities and put it to the BSPA's commercial department to make further enquiries.

The Head of the BSPA Commercial Department, Chris Wright, soon reported back to Vincent. The betting industry would like nothing more than a chance to develop ties with speedway.

The gaming industry had struggled and they were looking to every avenue for additional opportunities. It wasn't just the traditional horse and dog racing people they wanted, it was punters from a whole range of sports, both mainstream and niche.

Vincent could not believe it. 'Sheer stupidity,' he thought. Then he stopped to consider the other sports on which betting was now permitted. In particular, the one-on-one sports like boxing, tennis, snooker . . .

Not surprisingly, he determined that if the bookies were daft enough to offer betting opportunities on speedway, then he was daft enough to take them. Vincent took the decision himself to dispense with speedway's 'no betting' regulation.

With the regulations determining team make-up remaining unchanged, Shelford were able to track the same seven riders in their team again for the following season. All of the kids wanted to stay together and all were still moving forward, so there was no point in making changes for the sake of it.

Vincent and Lurch spent the winter working on ways to improve presentation. With the collapse of the Speedway Riders' Association, Vincent invited all of the team captains to a meeting at The Manor. Many of the skippers were abroad for the winter but most tracks managed to send a representative.

The riders were all unhappy about the constant technology changes to racing equipment and the fact that this brought with it rapid obsolescence and a constant need for them to have to upgrade perfectly good machinery. Sadly, yet typically, they disagreed amongst themselves on how the problem could be tackled.

Vincent had to accept that, unless there was common ground amongst the riders, it was asking for trouble trying to foist his own solutions upon them. He would wait until either he was more established or the riders a little more in harmony.

The 1987 season exploded into life with even more razzmatazz than usual. Shelford and Thorden Heath continued their perpetual feud, with neither seeming to wrest the upper hand completely.

Dianne's son, Jack, had his ninth birthday during the season. Although Dianne had little interest in the speedway herself, she was happy for Jack to go and see his dad ride each week. John Tindall was always prepared to put himself out for the lad, keep an eye on him and make sure he got home safely.

Vincent watched Tindall's care of Jack with interest. Was he the only one to realise what was happening? Should he step in and sort things out? He could easily warn Tindall off on the one hand or, on the other, warn Ann of the dangers and get her to tell Dianne of Tindall's predilection for young boys...

But Vincent still had yet to decide where he stood about Dianne and whether or not he had forgiven her entirely for leaving him and running off with Harding.

The boy Jack was living proof of the way she had treated him. He rationalised it to himself this way. What was going on with Tindall – if it was – had not been instigated by Vincent. Dianne had a duty to look out for her son. It was not Vincent's place to stick his nose in. He decided to let things take their natural, or perhaps unnatural course. Que sera, sera . . .

Martin Kessler – Lurch – was becoming more and more of a key person in the running of Shelford Speedway. He spent many hours each day at the stadium, organising track preparation, press and public relations, and team matters. He also spent much time driving Vincent around and acting as his sounding board in dealing with the day to day dealings of the BSPA.

Most evenings, when he wasn't needed for Shelford matches or to ferry Vincent around, he was to be found on the terracing at other speedways.

Again, Vincent spoke to the man who had begun as his chauffeur but was now his speedway right hand. He was concerned about Lurch's workload.

The big fellow laughed it off.

'Boss, you and speedway give me all I want from life. Provided I can get a few hours sleep each night – or day – then I have all I need.'

'How about we get an assistant driver then, so you at least don't have to do so much driving?'

'Boss, how on earth can we have our private conversations having someone else within earshot? Are you saying you don't think I am up to the job any more?'

Vincent realised, instead of showing Lurch how much he was appreciated, he had, in fact, hurt his feelings. He backed off fast but made a mental note to increase his pay by 25% and upgrade his company car to something more executive.

The two men rarely said so in as many words, but they were mighty proud of what they had achieved. Reece Sullivan and Alan Stewart, whilst still youngsters themselves, had become genuine team leaders. The other kids in the team were wild, loud and precocious. They took risks on the track and, more often than not, got away with them. They were always full of fun and nobody was safe from their pranks.

More important to Vincent, the team was totally irreverent. They backed away from nothing, be it difficult tracks or rider reputations. Here and there, youthful enthusiasm saw over-robust riding, but at any sign of potential trouble, the whole team would stand shoulder to shoulder. Having Lurch standing in front of them helped in that respect!

With this kind of approach, staying injury-free was unlikely, and injuries to key men at vital times caused losses they could not afford if they were to win the league, but Vincent wasn't at all disappointed about that.

He knew that winning the championship would signal the end of the fun development stage for him. Sooner or later, individual personalities would take over from togetherness within the team. Vincent was aware that winning the title would accelerate that change, so he was happy to leave it a while.

Already, his own particular favourite, Jamie Marlborough, had been showing signs of discontent here and there, whenever someone else in the team stole the limelight.

Vincent and Lurch never attempted to interfere with the results of meetings that year. They didn't need to. The injuries and odd aberration did the job of keeping the Racers just below the top, quite nicely.

He and Lurch enjoyed themselves taking money from bookmakers, simply because they were clever enough and well informed enough to know how results would go. They used their winnings as a 'slush fund' for rider treats and bonuses.

Shelford did finally put a trophy on the board though, taking the knockout cup in a classic home and away encounter with Marsdon.

Jeff Harding had led the Thorden Swords to retaining the league title. He had continued to grow into his role of undisputed top man and team leader. He had also come to love the kudos that went with it. Vincent had seen to it that Jeff's investments had performed well, and Jeff, having recovered from the divorce, was living a Hollywood lifestyle.

'Enjoy it while you can, my friend,' thought Vincent as he presented the British League trophy to the man he detested above all others.

All promotions had reported a continued increase in attendances and greater profits. Even the overseas promoters had been casting an envious eye in the direction of British speedway, which was once again sitting firmly at the top of the international tree.

Away from the speedway, both the stock market and the property market had turned upwards again. Mark and Dave had both been given the green light to fully invest, and both portfolios were showing substantial gains.

All things considered, Vincent had reason to consider it had been a really good 12 months.

Chapter 32

Ann's 25th birthday fell on December 6th. Vincent had made up his mind what her present was to be. First, the four close friends, Ann and Vincent, and Heather and Dave, enjoyed yet another sumptuous meal. Heather had fussed and fretted over Ann all day. They played dress-ups again for the evening, but Heather spent twice as much time on getting Ann ready than she did on herself.

The four were on great form when they stumbled downstairs to the playroom. On cue, Dave and Heather disappeared, leaving Vincent to lavish every intimate affection he could muster on his beloved Ann. She was soon steaming. Vincent moved up to stroke her breasts, and to kiss her face and lips for a few moments.

Then he lifted his head from Ann's face for a few seconds to reveal a masked Adonis standing over them, with his huge member erect and ready for action. 'This is for you,' Vincent whispered, as he lay across her chest and continued to kiss and caress her.

She remained relaxed and surprisingly unshocked by the powerful, young man's sudden presence. If this was Vincent's idea of a perfect birthday treat, who was she to argue? She had wondered for long enough just what the experience would be like.

Vincent continued kissing and caressing Ann's face whilst the man entered her. Ann felt it slide in, bit by bit, inch by inch. It started to move in and out, stronger, further, faster. Ann tried to work with the strokes, arching her body to aid penetration. She tried to time her movements to coincide.

Somehow, though, it wasn't happening. She wasn't in charge. She had always been in charge before. She had always controlled what happened, where and when. This was not the same. Yes, the cock was big and bold and probing every fraction of her tight, tender space, exploring places no man had ever been before. And yes, the warmth and feel, like hot velvet, was nice. But where were the fireworks?

The pulsations quickened more. She and Vincent were being jogged up and down. Ann was now anything but in control and didn't care much for having her body taken over like this.

'Now,' she whispered, and then, much louder 'NOW!' Spurred on by the invitation, and mistaking the command for climax, the invited guest launched into a frenzy of action, his groaning increasing with every thrusting movement. But she was unmoved when he reached orgasm. In fact, she was pleased it was over.

The mystery man in the mask disappeared as fast as he had arrived. Ann grabbed Vincent in a ferocious hug, sank her teeth into his shoulder, and hung on. When she finally let go with her teeth, but not her arms, she could hear herself saying: 'I love you, I love you...' over and over again.

A few moments later, once she had caught her breath, Ann said quietly and sincerely: 'Vincent, my darling. I love you so much. I know what it cost for you to do that, and I needed to find out what it was like, but I do not need to do it again. I enjoy our games far more.' And she hugged her man again.

Towards the end of April, Heather sidled up to Ann.

'Guess what?' she said. 'I've just come back from the doctors, and . . . guess what!'

For the next few weeks, Ann and Heather were inseparable. Ann applied daily non-intimate massage, often with Dave around. The two girls began getting the nursery ready as the four friends all joined in what was to be the next great adventure in their lives. Vincent and Ann were as excited as Dave and Heather. When Ann had telephoned Mark to tell him the news, she had been surprised at his initial negative reaction.

'Come on, Mark, don't be jealous,' she chided. 'You know you would hate to be a family man, with its responsibilities and restrictions on your lifestyle!'

None of that initial negativity was present, though, when Mark saw the expectant couple. He flirted with Heather even more than usual, and insisted she have a boy, so he could be a Godparent, along with Ann and Vincent.

The fun and planning wasn't to last.

At just about three months gone, Heather and Ann had been enjoying a swim. As they climbed out of the pool, Heather doubled up with stomach cramps.

That was it really. Ann nursed her dear friend until the ambulance arrived and then went to the hospital with her, but the signs were obvious. Even at that stage, they both knew the baby was gone.

Both couples took it badly but Dave's reaction was extreme. He seemed to turn right away from Heather, being curt and formal with her. Gradually, he began working longer and longer hours.

Ann could see there was a problem and even tried to talk to the grief-stricken man about the situation. It did no good at all. Even Vincent couldn't get through to him that Heather was in no way to blame and was even more of a victim than Dave.

Instead of turning towards each other for comfort, the distraught pair became like strangers.

Heather began spending more and more time at The Manor, often staying overnight when Dave was working late. Dave also spent a good deal of time there but mainly in the library or study with Vincent, where business dominated conversations.

It wasn't too long before word got back to Vincent that Dave had started dabbling with one of the young girls in the property company offices. He had also become much more ruthless in his business dealings.

Fearing his friend could crack up at any time, Vincent felt he should let Mark know what was happening. He was reluctant to talk about it over the phone, so merely asked if Mark could pop up to The Manor for a 'business chat'.

Such a call from Vincent was uncommon to say the least. As soon as the markets closed that day, the high-flying broker jumped into his car and drove up the motorway, arriving by late afternoon.

Vincent opened the door himself and took Mark straight into the library.

'Are you staying over tonight?'

'I'll make this a strong one then,' he said as he received an affirmative nod on his way to the drinks cupboard.

Over the next hour, Vincent explained all that had happened. Mark was aware of the loss of the baby but other than that, this was all news.

'OK, what do you suggest?' the broker said, when Vincent had finished filling him in.

Vincent had the advantage of having been able to brood on things.

'Look,' he began, 'apart from yourself, Dave and Heather are the only people I care about. Us five people are a family.

'One thing I will not do under any circumstances is to make judgements or to take sides. I love both friends dearly (Vincent had never ever used that word before, except with Ann) and I simply want what is best for them both.

'In the meantime, with so much tied up in the property business, you are entitled to be aware of the situation and to have a say in anything we do. In fact, given my emotional involvement, I intend to give *you* the last say on what we decide, businesswise.'

Mark studied his gin and tonic carefully, turning the glass round and round in his hands.

'Let's look at possible worst options,' were his first words.

'If Dave were to crack up completely and suddenly vanish from the business at any stage, what would be at risk?'

'Little of consequence,' replied Vincent. 'Maybe it could compromise any work in progress but the bulk of the assets are safe. Dave has a cheque-signing facility. I can easily have a chat with the bank and get them to ring me should there be a significant and unusual movement of funds.

'I mean, I would hope neither of us would worry too much about the odd 100 grand, and in any case, Dave has his own money involved these days. I really can't see him trying to rip us off under any circumstances.'

'Next question,' Mark continued. 'Is the business suffering as a result of Dave's state of mind?'

'Just the opposite really,' assured Vincent. 'He is throwing all his energies into work. I don't regard his dalliances as anything more serious than a release valve. I can keep a close eye on that side of things and quickly nip anything in the bud I feel might be a problem.'

'In which case, we needn't worry about the business side of things, except to consider looking around for an emergency replacement should that become necessary?'

'That's not a problem. Dave has some good staff there who could cope quite well.'

'In that case, we can concentrate our minds purely on the domestic side of things,' Mark summed up. 'Does Heather know he is putting himself about?'

'That's a good question. She has not confided in as many words to Ann, so I presume she is not aware of chapter and verse, but she is no fool and I'm certain she will have reached her own conclusions.'

Ann appeared in the room.

'Hello Mark, sorry to interrupt but Heather just phoned. Dave is working late again so she will be joining us for dinner.'

Ann disappeared as fast as she had arrived. With that, Mark

reached over and gripped Vincent's wrist.

'Vincent, you need to know this. Ever since the first day I set eyes on Heather, I have been in love with her. I have never said a word to anyone before and I have never allowed it to show. I shall continue to keep my thoughts entirely to myself but I feel you and Ann – I know you will tell her – should be aware."

It wasn't often Vincent was caught napping but he had never picked this one, and neither had Ann. He managed to hide his surprise.

'Too much information,' said Vincent, pulling his hand away and holding it up like a traffic cop. 'For a bastard though, you aren't a bad sort of bloke!'

Despite the combined efforts of Vincent, Ann and Mark to keep things light and easy, dinner was a subdued affair. As soon as it was over, Mark stood up, took Heather lightly by the elbow, moved her chair for her as she stood up, and simply walked her out of the dining room, guiding her with his hand.

Vincent and Ann remained at the table for another hour.

'We dare not leave it any longer in case Dave turns up,' Vincent pointed out. The two of them made their way to the study, talking loudly, and knocked gently before going in.

Mark and Heather were sitting on a Chesterfield. Mark was holding both of Heather's hands, except for when she used the one holding a wad of tissues to dab away more tears as they formed. It was clearly a 'Dutch Uncle' scene rather than a romantically charged one.

Dianne stood up and sobbingly embraced Ann, who took her out of the room.

'I hope you don't mind,' Mark began. 'I figured you and Ann were too close to both of them as a couple for Heather to open up to either of you, so I took on the duty.

I didn't need to tell her about the girl in the office. I don't think she knows directly but she understands enough to make the who, where, or when unimportant. I think now the dam has burst, she will find it easier to talk to Ann.

'As for Dave, I like the bloke, but I am not the one to become involved there. That is strictly *your* duty, Vincent.

'I promise you I will not allow my own feelings for Heather to interfere with the situation at all, but I would appreciate it if I could be kept in the loop.'

Not long afterwards, the telephone rang. Ann answered. It was

Dave, phoning from the gatehouse. He had just arrived home.

Both Vincent and Mark glanced at the mantle clock: just coming up to eleven. Ann poked her head around the door to say she was going to take the dogs for a walk and see Heather back to her place at the same time. She felt lousy leaving the still unsettled girl at the door to the gatehouse but she knew equally well that anything she tried to do or say would only inflame things more.

Chapter 33

Vincent was not looking forward to having to stick his nose in where Dave was concerned. There was one thing being asked for an opinion, but it was a different thing entirely to wade in without an invitation.

He decided two things were needed. The first was a private, and more or less neutral location, and the second was alcohol. With this in mind, he manufactured a reason to go to Dave's office at the end of the working day. Lurch took along Vincent's briefcase and then withdrew to the motor home.

As soon as Dave had said goodnight to his secretary and they were settled in his private office, Vincent took a bottle of champagne from his case and opened it. 'I thought we would celebrate that deal you tied up last week,' he began. 'It was quite a nice little earner. I hope the tenants weren't too upset!'

'Fuck 'em,' Dave responded, as he collected a couple of glasses from the drinks cabinet. 'My concern is to make money for *us*, not to worry about stepping on corns.'

They drank to that and the conversation drifted around business for a while. Vincent was waiting for the drink to kick in. He waited until the conversation began to dry up and the first bottle was empty.

'So how are things at home?' he ventured. It was a clear invitation for Dave to get things off his chest but Vince was not sure how it would go.

'So-so. They could be better. Still, knowing how close the girls are and that Ann and you discuss everything, I expect it would be more sensible for me to ask *you* that question.'

'Ouch!' Vincent replied. 'I'll tell you what. I'll tell you everything I know and you tell me everything you know. Deal?'

He then went on to outline how Heather was upset at the amount of time Dave had been spending at work, how she felt there was a significant problem between them, and how it was upsetting her. Not only upsetting Heather, but also Ann and himself, because they hated seeing both their best friends so unhappy.

'I suppose she also said we're not having sex?'

Vincent wasn't prepared to lie. 'Yes, but how much of that is a by-product and how much is a central issue I don't even think Heather knows.'

Ann had briefed Vincent before this meeting. She didn't consider herself to be a psychiatrist but she had always been of the opinion Dave had a repressed homosexual side. At first, she had put it down to his devotion to Vincent, but it also explained a great deal more, not least of which had been his paranoia about losing Heather.

Ann had reasoned that Dave needed Heather, with her ultimate looks and sexuality, as a constant assurance of his own masculinity.

Ann reckoned the miscarriage had seen Heather fall from the pedestal of perfection Dave had always placed her on. The 'affair' he was having was obviously Dave simply trying to prove to himself that there was 'nothing wrong' with him but that Heather was somehow now 'damaged goods'.

Ann had made it clear to Vincent that it wasn't their job to simply do all in their power to keep the couple together, but to try and do whatever was best for the both of them.

'I've been having a bit of a dabble with Maggie, the receptionist,' Dave blurted out. Vincent decided to say nothing at this stage.

'She's only 18,' Dave continued, taking another good slurp of bubbly before he added:

'Anyway, it's over. I suggested we spice up the sex a bit and she was off like a frightened rabbit. No problem really, though. I mean, she is a tidy sort, but there's not that much between the ears.'

Vincent finally spoke up.

'Dave, how you spend your lunch times is of no real concern to me. What is a concern is the welfare of you and Heath. Let me spell that out. Both Ann and I are worried about you, Dave Scott. We are equally – not more so or less so – concerned about Heather Scott.

'What we are not at all concerned about is pointing fingers or laying blame. We simply want what is best for *you two*, both as individuals and as a couple.'

Dave sat up straight in his chair with a look of absolute horror on his face.

'Are you trying to tell me something? Is she thinking of leaving me?'

Tears welled up in his eyes.

'Dave, I have no idea. All I know for certain, is that you are a mess, she is a mess and as a direct result of this, Ann and myself are very sad. We'll do anything we can to help you two resolve things. What we will never do, though, is dictate to either of you or take sides.'

Dave was in full floods now, crumbling before Vince's eyes.

'Dave, you need to figure out who or what the tears are for. Are they for you, are they for your lost baby, are they for Heather, or are they for a lost relationship?'

'Dunno,' was all Dave could get out from between sobs.

'Well, it's clear you and Heath are not on the same wavelength at the moment. How about the four of us all sit round a table and try to make some sense of it?

'Whatever the situation, one thing is clear. We all love each other in our own ways and there has to be enough goodwill between us all for a chat between us not to degenerate into a slanging match. You never know. Maybe something positive just might come out of it.

'Now how about I phone Ann and tell her to have tea with Heather? Ann can talk her into a meeting of minds for tomorrow, whilst you, me and Lurch can take ourselves out for a meal somewhere tonight.'

The next evening Vincent and Ann went down to the gatehouse. They could feel the tension as soon as they arrived, even though everyone was being ultra nice. Vincent had already told Ann he would let her make the running and would only support her as and when needed.

Ann switched into 'nursing' mode as soon as the niceties were out of the way. She handled the situation delicately and with sympathy, carefully avoiding any suggestion of 'blame'. Vincent was hugely impressed and despite the situation, he was sure his friends appreciated her efforts to be fair to both parties and not at all judgemental.

The bottom line was the couple really loved each other – in their own way. What the miscarriage had done with Dave was to identify the fact that love had always been there, but not passion. Heather also admitted Dave was not really the same man she had fallen for as a starry-eyed kid.

Vincent came forward at this stage and made the point that virtually all marriages started as a strong physical relationship but ended up with the couple remaining happily in love with or without sexual attraction.

The four people then entered into a long discussion about marriage, about the fact that most couples stayed together because they were trapped into it by parental responsibility or the lack of financial independence, or both.

Was it a blessing or a curse that these people did not have those artificial reasons for staying together; that they were 'free' to make their own choices?

By the time Ann and Vincent had left the gatehouse that evening, Heather and Dave were close again. Their problems had been laid out in front of them and they each understood how the other felt. This understanding was enough for them to be loving friends again but was it enough for them to be married lovers?

That question had not been resolved.

Ann and Heather were holding a post-mortem the next day. Gradually it became clear, what both Heather and Dave needed was a trial separation. Hardly original, but maybe something both parties might benefit from.

It seemed to Ann as if they both liked each other but needed to discover if that was enough. The question they both wanted answering was, surely, did they *need* or even *want* each other? Heather pointed to the relationship between Ann and Vince. Now that *was* true love.

Ann came up with a good way to give the trial separation a go, without making it obvious. She suggested that to avoid any kind of embarrassment or loss of face, Vincent and Dave simply go for a holiday.

Vincent had been promising himself a trip to Australia for quite some time and could tie it up with speedway business. Nobody doubted Dave both needed and deserved some time off from work.

Heather and Dave were responsible enough adults to be able to avoid any flings by either party having any long-term effect on their relationship. Both promised faithfully they would be 100% 'responsible' whilst apart, and would neither enquire of, nor admit to, any step from the straight and narrow. Most of all, they would respect each other and not cause any embarrassment at all.

Jamie Marlborough had already planned to go out to Australia again in the winter and this time Vincent also organised for his team-mate, Chris Andrews, to spend a couple of months there as well. Vincent again funded their trips and intended going over himself to have a look. It was a perfect opportunity to get Dave away for a while.

Vincent, Dave, Steven Bray and Lurch headed for Australia as soon as the season was over and tidied up. By this time, Bryce was the Australian Minister for Sport and rarely at home on his huge spread in Northern New South Wales, but he had promised to catch up with the group somewhere along the line. To that end, Steven had sent Bryce a detailed itinerary of the trip.

Although the first-class cabin on the 747 was spacious and the service excellent, Vince didn't fancy doing the trip to Sydney in one leap, so they stopped off in Singapore.

Before arriving in the island country, Vincent's knowledge of the place was limited, but he was mightily impressed with what he saw.

It didn't take him long to pick up a potted history of the place, rapidly coming to the conclusion that Sir Stamford Raffles, who 'discovered' Singapore and turned it into an important part of the British Empire, and latterly, the current President, Lee Kuan Yew, were the two island nation's greatest achievers.

He vowed to learn more about modern-day Singapore. He realised that, with its geographical location, relative political stability and historical connections with both East and West, the tiny island country was ideally positioned for the future. It was a place to invest in.

On arrival at Sydney Airport, the group of four were taken aback when they were met off the aircraft by top airport officials and whisked through VIP channels. In a matter of minutes, they were in a government car and heading for their superb hotel overlooking the harbour. Bryce had certainly not forgotten them!

For the next few days, the group did the sights, but Vincent was a reluctant tourist and wanted to get up to Queensland, where there was some decent solo speedway taking place and where the two Shelford lads were racing. Vince had also heard about a Kiwi rider based up there.

Country Queensland was some distance, and not just geographically, from metropolitan Sydney. Vincent found it difficult coping with the Backwoods nature of the place that provided little by way of assistance for wheelchair people.

Fortunately for Vince, the ever-present Lurch was always on hand, even if it meant the odd loss of dignity to be carried like a child here and there. This was true pioneer country and Vincent often found himself needing assistance with what would be routine for non-handicapped people.

The heat and humidity were oppressive and the insects a bitch but despite all the discomfort he was happier here than in Sydney. The same could not be said of Dave, who was a town-mouse through and through.

Jack Miller, the New Zealander, was, in speedway terms, a giant of a man. He stood 5ft 11ins but was almost as wide as he was tall, and all solid muscle. He was a rough and ready type of character with an almost permanent smile and an equally permanent obscenity on his lips.

Even before he had seen Miller on a bike, Vincent had decided to give him a job. In-between speedway meetings, the big Kiwi was responsible for looking after track preparation and routine stadium maintenance, and Vince had never seen anyone so hard working or adept at modifying mechanical equipment to make it work better.

On the Saturday night, when it came to the racing, Miller was a real eye-opener. The two Shelford lads were mounted on far better bikes and had more ability and technique than him, but through sheer guts and determination, Jack just terrorised them into making mistakes.

It seemed he never, ever, shut off his throttle on the big, fast track, using whatever he collided with, be it fence or opposition, to turn off. Vincent had seen raw aggression before, but never on a scale quite like this.

Jack was delighted to have set up a deal for riding in England so easily and even happier when he realised he would also have a steady income from working on the Shelford track. At 25, he was not your average bright-eyed, bushy-tailed raw recruit. He had bummed around seemingly all his life and only found speedway a couple of years previously when his first love of drag racing had become just too expensive.

The four English travellers stayed on in the 'bush' for another week so that Vincent and Lurch, in particular, could take in another speedway meeting. There was to be no racing the week after, so Miller declared he would take Dave and Steve down to Surfer's Paradise where, according to Jack, the 'babes queued up to be serviced'.

Vincent had agreed to take up an offer of a few days on the Penrith's sheep station and insisted Lurch go and enjoy himself on the coast with the others whilst he was taken directly to the isolated homestead in a small, private plane.

Molly was out at the private airstrip waiting for the plane to touch down. She was in a farm 'ute' (utility or pick-up truck) with Joe, the station manager. Between them, the pilot and the manager lifted Vincent, together with wheelchair, onto the back of the ute.

The manager sat alongside Vincent on the back of the vehicle to hold the wheelchair steady, while Molly drove. Vincent loved feeling the wind rushing past his face again as they made their way to the main house. There was a loading and unloading ramp in the yard and Vincent was able to wheel himself straight off the truck.

Somebody had organised for temporary ramps at all entrances to the house in order to make things easier for him to come and go. The only problem he had was with the outwards opening flyscreen doors, but he quickly realised that if he kept a stick on the side of the wheelchair, he could use it to hold the flyscreen open whilst he wheeled his chair through. The self-closers on the screens did the rest as soon as he took the stick away.

That evening Vincent enjoyed a nice, home-cooked meal, just himself and Molly. Lucy, the latest addition to the Penrith family, was tucked up in bed by then and Ryan was away at boarding school. He would be coming home at the weekend to meet Bryce again, and to spend a few days with dad. Bryce was due in on Wednesday having decided to take a week off from official duties.

Suitably dowsed with insect repellent, Vincent had adored sitting on the veranda watching the sun go down and enjoying a drink with Molly whilst they took it in turns to relay three years of gossip in one hour.

When they went inside it was as if they had entered another world. The air-conditioned comfort of modern living was so different to the crackling hot, dusty and stark environment outside the immediate confines of the homestead yard.

Vincent slept like a log that night. It was the first time he had slept well since leaving his 'cocoon' at The Manor.

He was finally woken by the sounds of the outback. The oasis of the homestead surrounds, with its many leafy trees and buildings and manicured gardens, contrasted with the dry wilderness of the surrounding areas. Every bird for what seemed a million miles around seemed to have been attracted.

The constant and angry squawking of the parrots and cockatoos was enough to waken the dead, so Vincent was soon ready to get out of bed. He looked at the bedroom clock. Five o'clock. Could he manage to get up and make it outside without waking anyone?

As he wheeled himself past the kitchen, a polished timber floorboard creaked. Molly sang out from inside:

'Good morning! Breakfast won't be a minute.'

'Out here, nature dictates what times we keep,' she said. 'We usually work to the sun. This is the best part of the day so we tend to be early to rise and early to bed.'

'Exactly my kind of life,' said Vincent.

After breakfast, Joe, the station manager, pulled up on a quad bike.

'I thought you might care for a look around,' he said. 'I'm sure we can get you up on the pillion behind me.'

'Bugger that,' Vincent replied. 'If the controls on that thing are standard motor-bike controls, there's no reason why I can't ride it.'

Joe was taken aback but agreed to give it a go, and soon Vincent was on board.

'What about the foot controls?' the concerned manager said.

'I expect it will pull away in third if I slip the clutch a bit, and that will give me enough speed for now. I have a front brake and we can worry about the back one when I want to go a bit quicker.'

With that, Vincent started the bike up, reached down and put the quad into third gear with his hand, and was away.

He was soon back.

'Have you got a workshop around here?' he asked. 'We can soon rig up a hand-change facility and a method of using the rear brake by hand. I also need a back support.'

'I'll take it around to Johnno,' Joe suggested. 'He is a whiz when it comes to bodging.'

An hour later, he was back with a lever on the left-hand side to operate the back brake and a hand-change facility cobbled up on the other. There were also bars that could be locked into position, to save Vincent tipping out when he hit bumps, and a rudimentary backrest. Slung on the back of the quad was a trials bike.

'I'll take the bike, you use the quad, and I'll show you around.'

It was lunchtime when they got back. Vince was sore in his back and shoulders, and badly bruised lower down. Between them, Molly and Joe had to make running repairs to superficial damage on his legs and rear end, but he couldn't remember having had so much fun since the accident. Having one of these machines customised with an auto clutch and hand-controlled braking was going to be his first job when he got back home.

He had found 'Johnno', a weather-beaten Aboriginal, during the morning. Between them, they had changed a few things here and there, especially fitting straps to stop him from bouncing about too much. After that, Joe had found it difficult to keep up with the natural motorcyclist who relished this rare chance to turn back time.

Vincent spent the afternoon resting and recovering from the exercise of the morning. He hated to admit it, but he was missing Lurch. Not just for the routine assistance but also for the company. This quiet time gave him a chance to realise how he took the bloke for granted and expected him to be on call all day and every day. He determined to make sure his faithful right-hand man had more opportunity to have a life of his own in the future.

Bryce arrived the next day in his own light plane. He looked for all the world like a cabinet minister when he arrived, but within minutes he was into shorts, short-sleeved check shirt and bush hat – just one of the boys.

They were soon racing around on quads like a couple of teenagers. Again, Vincent had a rest in the afternoon whilst Bryce caught up with the happenings around the station before the pair of them spent the late afternoon and evening on the veranda, putting the world to rights.

Bryce collected Ryan from his boarding school on the Friday and early on Saturday morning the family and Vincent squeezed into the plane and nipped down to their 'shack' by the sea. Vincent had expected something quite primitive but when they arrived, he found an impressive beach house with local staff to look after the place whilst it was not being used, and to look after the family when it was.

Vincent struggled on the sandy beach but Bryce made up a sledge from a body-board to get him to the water, where he was far more comfortable.

Strapping him onto a jet ski wasn't as easy as the quad but they managed it, and again Vince was in his element. The jet ski was as near to a speedway bike as he was ever likely to get. Bryce was never far away and had to get there quickly to right him after wipe-outs, but once again Vincent found he was having the kind of fun he had not experienced in years.

Back at Surfer's Paradise, Lurch was feeling very much the odd man out. Jack Miller was the best – or worst – thing for Dave. He was into everything involving having a wild time and was happy to use Dave's plastic to achieve it. For his part, Dave was more than happy to be towed along in Jack's wake.

Late nights and tanned beauties were followed by crazy antics by day for the odd couple. Lurch contented himself with the hotel pool. Not that he lived like a monk. A group of up-for-it girls 'adopted' him, and he picked himself one of the half-dozen to spend some private time with.

On their last day, the other five girls gatecrashed his farewell session with his selected lady. They had heard about his 'special gift' and wanted to see for themselves. The session ended in a no-holds barred romp with Lurch as the major prize!

For all of that, Lurch was happy to fix up for a light plane to take him to the Penrith's place on the Monday, leaving the other two at Surfer's. He was pleased to meet Bryce again, albeit not for long, as the Aussie Larrikin switched back to high-powered politician and returned to Canberra on the Tuesday.

A few more days was all both Vincent and Lurch wanted away. Dave, though, had other ideas for himself. The Crazy Kiwi had brought out all the alter-ego within the normally reserved and uptight character Dave had become.

With a contract to ride in the UK in his pocket, Jack was happier spending Dave's money having a good time than going back to North Queensland, so the pair of them packed their bags and headed for Thailand.

Not before Vince had a word with 'Crazy Jack' on the phone, though. He pointed out that Jack's contract with him was subject to Dave returning to England with no exotic diseases, and without any problems with Thai police or authorities.

'Dave is naïve in the ways of the world, Jack. I am making you responsible for his wellbeing. Do you understand?'

Jack got the message.

Chapter 34

The day Dave had left for Australia, Heather felt as if a weight had been lifted from her shoulders. For all of their tiptoeing around each other, things had remained tense in the Scott household. Before the group of men was out of sight on their way to Heathrow, Heather was loading her car with stuff to move up to The Manor, where she would base herself while Dave was away.

'First on the list is some retail therapy,' she declared to Ann. 'What do you reckon – local, London, or abroad?'

'Let's start with London,' came the answer. 'I'll phone Mark. We'll do some shopping, dump the stuff at his place and then let him take us to a show!'

A few hours and several thousand pounds later, Heather was stretched out in the bath and Ann was lounging on the sofa in Mark's apartment. Both were armed with glasses of bubbly when Mark arrived home. He had arranged for the porter to let them in.

The place was everything a bachelor pad should be. Overlooking Tower Bridge in the modern Elizabeth Quay development, the place just reeked of quality and luxury. Heather wandered through into the lounge, head in turbaned towel and wearing a bathrobe.

'Did you design and furnish the place yourself?' she enquired.

Mark shook his head.

'Fraid not,' he said. 'Just not enough hours in the day really, although I did set the people who did it strict guidelines.

'Now, I've managed to get us some great seats at Covent Garden for this evening, so it will give you a chance to posh up. Do you want a snack now and a meal after, or a meal now and light supper later?'

The girls looked at each other and both said the same thing at once.

'Hair!'

'I guess we'll have dinner after then,' Mark said with a smile. 'By the way, girls, do you want me to arrange to balance the numbers or are you happy with a *ménage a trois?*'

'I think just the three of us tonight, if you can cope!' joked Ann. 'Oh, and don't expect any menaging from us! Quite apart from anything else, we'll be knackered!'

Mark went into his study and made a couple of calls. Fifteen minutes later, a character with a lisp and extremely weak handshake, followed by two young girls lugging various bits of equipment with them, took over Mark's large and impressive main bathroom.

They were soon followed by a stream of smartly dressed young men, who laid out the most wonderful array of cold cuts and sweetmeats you could imagine. Mark asked them to spread the platters around the spacious lounge.

By the time the Rolls Royce arrived to take them to the opera, the girls were looking breathtaking in the new designer dresses they had bought. Both would have outshone any parade of film stars at The Oscars.

Mark, in modern formal attire, played his part, and heads turned everywhere as they stepped from the car and up to the private box he had arranged, where yet another bottle of bubby appeared from nowhere. They really did feel like royalty.

Mark had been to the opera before but the girls had not and didn't really know what to expect. They needed the bubbly to sustain them for a while, but as the performance built up, they were swept away by the sheer power of the music and the performances.

A trip to the bathroom was needed to freshen up their make-up, affected by the odd tear, before they were turning heads once more as they made their way to the waiting car and then to the Park Lane Hilton. Here, in the Starlight Room, they were once again the centre of attention. The girls had become accustomed to enjoying the good things in life, and Heather in particular was used to turning heads but this was much more.

Mark had greased some palms as they had entered but really hadn't needed to. The waiters fell over themselves to help, the restaurant manager served them himself and they were clearly the talking point of the entire room.

When the three of them had finished a fabulous supper, Mark offered the girls a chance to go to a nightclub or casino but by then they were exhausted, and suggested they save that for another night.

'I'd better tell the driver to get the pumpkin ready, then.' Mark commented, looking at his watch. It was 12.15.

Although the girls were very tired from all the excitement of the evening, they were also still on a high when the three friends arrived back at the apartment.

Mark put on some gentle music and made hot chocolate in large mugs. They sprawled around the room talking about the evening and enjoying the sheer magic of the moment for another hour-and-a-half.

By that time they had wilted to nothing, Mark kissed them both goodnight and disappeared off to bed.

The two girls didn't make it out of their undies. Despite having chosen their bedrooms earlier in the afternoon, they just both collapsed into the same bed, happy to be aware of another body sleeping next to them.

Both knew, in their own minds, as their friendship had deepened and they had grown up a bit more, the sexual activity between them was pretty much consigned to the past.

Mark had left for the office by a good couple of hours when the pair finally surfaced next morning. He had left a note.

'Do you need to go back home today? Why not stay 'till the weekend? Anything you need, just phone Albert, the *concierge*, on 900.'

He finished the note with his private number at work.

'That would give us all day today for more shopping and then Saturday and Sunday here, before going home Sunday evening,' was Ann's first reaction. 'What do you think?'

Heather didn't have to think. Yesterday had been such a release for her. She had forgotten how to have so much fun. Ann telephoned Mark and then the girls made up a shopping list of routine requirements for Albert. By 11.00am they were on their way to Knightsbridge.

Mark arrived back at the apartment before the girls. He had not been in long when there was a knock on the door. Three assistant porters were standing there with armfuls of bags.

'The ladies sent these on by taxi, sir,' the first one said.

The shoppers arrived at 4.30pm with more armfuls of bags from Harvey Nicks, Harrods and other chic places in Sloane Street.

'You've three-and-a-half hours to unwind and then get yourselves tidied up,' Mark announced. It seems we were spotted last night and you two were the talk of the office when I got in this morning.

'They didn't seem to believe you were my 'nieces', so I've

carefully selected a handful of the young bucks to meet you this evening. We are going for a meal and then on from there, I expect.' He just laughed when they both protested that they were happily married women who had to consider their reputations.

'Girls,' he said, 'these kids are straight out of kindergarten. Just enjoy the attention, and if any of them is a nuisance, tell him you are both sleeping with me!

'Oh, and can we dress down a bit tonight? My dress shirt is in the wash!'

Heather and Ann's idea of dressing down meant short dresses instead of long, and short they were, but no less head turning than the night before. They did the black and white thing. Heather was all in white with gold trimmings, Ann in black with platinum trimmings.

The restaurant, San Lorenzo in Knightsbridge, was where all the 'beautiful people' ate, and the *Maitre-de-Cuisine* escorted the three of them around to a semi-secluded alcove where five men, all in their mid-20s, and all superbly groomed and turned out, were sitting at a table laid out for them all. They all leapt to attention as the girls approached, and the loud exhaling of air was audible.

'Tongues in, gentlemen,' said Mark. 'My blonde is called Heather. She looks after me on Mondays, Wednesdays and Fridays. My raven-haired beauty is Ann. She fills in on Tuesdays, Thursdays and Saturdays. On Sundays, we all muck in together!

'You may all introduce yourselves individually once we have sat down. No more than 20 words in the 'CV' though!'

Mark had chosen well. Both at the restaurant and afterwards at the nightclub, the consorts acted perfectly.

They never allowed conversation to involve business or anything the girls could not hold their own about. They were polite and attentive, without being forward or fawning, and they were happy to share their time with the ladies, even down to the late-night dancing.

Several of the pretty, young things at the club knew the lads and engaged them in conversation or a dance, but none of the five roamed far. Heather pulled all five men together.

'Look,' she said, 'You fabulous young men are all angels and Ann and I love each of you dearly, but we are married women. You have been wonderful company but we will be happy to see you getting yourselves paired up and away.'

Come 1.30, though, the five bucks were still in close attendance as Mark decided it was time to call it a night. All eight revellers found their way back to Mark's place. This time Mark left them to it, and the two ladies held court until four o'clock, when they finally showed their admirers the door.

By the time the girls had surfaced at eleven o'clock, the next morning there was a complete nap hand of five gorgeous bouquets waiting for them in the porter's lodge. Two were to 'Heather and Ann', two to 'Ann and Heather' and one to 'Both fantastic ladies'. The attention hadn't harmed Ann's self esteem any but it had done a massive amount of good to Heather. Her old, bubbly self was beginning to show through again.

Saturday afternoon, Mark took them to see the England/France rugby union Test match at Twickenham. The ladies didn't understand everything they saw but they loved the atmosphere of the event and the excitement of the match.

In the evening, Mark took them along to a very high profile party, warning them beforehand that 'rich and powerful did not always mean well behaved'.

Once the girls had got over their celebrity-spotting, and that took a while, they found things a little less fun than the last couple of days had been. They spent most of the evening warding off unwanted advances from the men and clear resentment from several of the women. But, again, it did their egos no harm at all.

Come midnight, Mark realised things had not gone as well as he had hoped, so he took them to his favourite burger stand on the Embankment and they sat, all rugged up, enjoying the passing parade, along with the food.

When they got back to the apartment, Ann feigned a headache and beat a hasty retreat. She didn't know what would or would not happen, but felt it only fair she should not get in the way.

Mark and Heather stayed up until very late. Heather had draped herself along the sofa, while Mark arranged a small mountain of loose cushions on the lambswool rug and then immersed himself in them.

It was one of those situations where both were enjoying themselves so much that neither dare break the mood by making a move.

There was no contact whatever. But clearly the couple was being intimate. If ever you could have intercourse without sex, they had it that night.

Heather had found herself drawn more and more towards Mark over the last few days. For his part, Mark had slowly allowed himself the luxury of moving from dear friend to prospective suitor.

Heather, too, was allowing her emotions to escape from the strait-jacket of marriage. Whichever way you looked at it, they had always been soul mates, kept apart only by their respective regard for Dave.

Eventually, though, Mark said it was bed time, walked Heather to her bedroom door, kissed her sweetly and held her gently, before turning and going into his own room. Heather debated about following him, but decided against it.

She slept alone that night, still not comfortable in her mind about 'deceiving' Dave, although she was equally certain she would be deceiving herself if she thought they would ever get back to being man and wife again.

Once back at The Manor, Heather Scott did an awful lot of serious thinking over the next couple of days, some aloud with Ann and some to herself.

Unlike Dave, she didn't consider a 'trial separation' to be defined as 'sleeping around'. When she had given her marriage vows, she had meant them, and a mental block was still there.

She knew just how close she had been to breaking those vows, and was grateful to Mark for not having taken advantage, which he clearly could have done.

Was it time to concede defeat as far as Dave was concerned, or should she leave it to him to make the decision? She would have happily gone through life with the Dave she had married but was *that* Dave ever likely to resurface?

That was the first conundrum.

Once that was decided, and presuming the decision was to move forward in her life, how should she do it? She had enjoyed herself over the weekend, and it was good to know she was still considered attractive by men, but she really did not want to put herself back onto the 'singles' scene?

If she and Dave did divorce, then she would become independently wealthy. That being the case, she would be able to make decisions without having to worry about financial consequences.

How did she really feel about Mark? They had been 'good mates' now for over four years. In that time she had never, until a few days ago, considered him as a lover. Was that because she had been under the impression her and Dave were happily married, or was it because she had felt no magic towards him?

Ann helped her answer that one.

Heather's best friend's gently prodding questions forced the rare beauty to realise she had simply built up a wall of resistance in her mind to all other men because of her loyalty to Dave. She had allowed the sexy fun shared with Ann to fill in that particular gap without leaving any guilt.

Heather had simply never before allowed herself to look at Mark as anything but the loveliest of good friends.

She had seen him making love to other women, including Dianne. Heather certainly didn't want to upset her other friend for the sake of it, or be just another notch on his bedpost.

On the other hand, there had clearly been chemistry between her and Mark over the weekend. Surely, she wasn't imagining that? If he had wanted simply to chalk up another score, the chance had been there, but he had not taken it.

Ann was in a very difficult position. One thing she did not want to do was to be disloyal to Dave. The part involving Heather and her husband was for Heather and her alone to decide on. In her own mind, Ann could not see the couple getting back to where they were. She had always questioned Dave's sexuality in her mind and wondered if this was now beginning to show through.

For all that, though, she didn't feel it was *her* place to influence her dearest friend in *her* decision-making.

Her next problem was even more difficult. Heather had asked Ann what she thought Mark's feelings towards her were.

An honest and forthright answer might well have been disloyal to Dave, and might even betray a confidence with Mark. Equally, obfuscation and evasiveness might not be fair to Heather.

Even worse, she could not plead the fifth. She could not refuse to answer the question, because to do so would start all kinds of alarm bells ringing in Heather's head.

Ann decided to try and be fair to everyone. She correctly pointed out that whilst Mark had tried to make a fuss of both girls equally over the weekend, Ann had felt he had been far more of a friend towards her and a suitor towards Heather. She also reinforced Heather's opinion that if he was simply after a one-night stand, it had been there for the taking.

'Would it make sense for Ann to invite Mark up for the

weekend?' she suggested. Heather was concerned Mark would see that as a direct invitation from her.

'Look,' Ann pointed out, 'you two know each other well enough. Bugger what he might or might not think. Why don't you simply tell him all the things that are going through your mind? After all, he was brave enough to help you when you needed it before. It would then be up to him to put his cards on the table or not.'

'The only problem there is that if he does, then I have then to make a decision myself,' Heather responded.

'Or ask for more time?' Ann pointed out.

Heather accepted the point and Ann invited Mark up for the weekend if he was at a loose end. Mark was never 'at a loose end', but told Ann he had nothing planned and then cancelled his previous arrangements.

Ann, again trying to maintain a balancing act in her loyalties between Dave and Mark, explained he should not read anything into the invitation either way. She made Mark aware that Heather had not yet given up on her marriage, and that he should respect this. Mark thanked her for her advice and promised to tread carefully.

The three friends enjoyed walks in the country, pub food and ferreting around in antique shops. In the evenings, they lounged around an open fire chatting about nothing and everything, but Mark always made sure he disappeared off to bed whilst Ann was still around.

Heather saw Mark to his car as he was leaving on the Sunday evening.

'Thank you,' she said. She kissed him on the cheek and gave him a hug. Despite his having made no attempt at a pass over the weekend, it was crystal-clear how much he cared, and Heather was now smitten herself.

'Please give me a bit more time?' she whispered, 'I still need to make adjustments in my mind.'

Chapter 35

Vincent was lucky. On his arrival back, he discovered Dave had telephoned Heather to say he was staying on in Thailand for a while with Jack Miller, so Heather knew all about the extension to Dave's trip, without him having to explain her husband's absence.

Just how many of Dave's activities Vince should tell Heather about, he didn't know, but decided if he kept quiet on the subject, Heather could draw her own conclusions and they would almost certainly be correct.

The two ladies had another long chat and the result was, Heather contacted Dave in Thailand.

'I just want you to answer me one question,' she said in as calm and sweet a voice as she could manage. 'Do you see a future for us together?'

'I will never, ever stop loving you, Heather. But as a brother and sister would. I've found out more about myself in the last few weeks than I ever knew before and things can never be the same as they were with us previously.'

Dave had rehearsed these lines many times, and cringed waiting for the reaction.

'Dave, I feel exactly the same way,' she said. 'I care for you so much, and I just want you to be happy. I shall begin to get on with the rest of my life but we will always be close. Whatever happens, you must understand we have a special bond nobody can replace.'

It was Dave, not Heather, who had made the decision, and it was he who broke down in tears.

'I'll come back for a while to sort things out before Christmas – and I *do* love you,' he added before the conversation ended.

With that, Heather packed an overnight bag whilst Ann phoned Mark and said rather cryptically: 'Cancel any arrangements you have for this evening and go straight home after work . . .'

Mark left his office a little earlier than usual that afternoon and when he arrived back at his pad, Heather was already in his bed. He had waited the best part of four years for this moment with his dream lover. The couple had finally abandoned their inhibitions and enjoyed two hours of frenzied passion, followed by a whole night of tender love.

Mark took a few days off work and came back with Heather to spend time at The Manor. The question of how to deal with the situation regarding Dave, Heather and himself needed to be handled very carefully.

Having got this far without any spilled milk, they wanted to avoid alienating Dave, who might well feel he had been isolated and conspired against. All four friends agreed it would be best to wait until the wanderer returned before making any announcements.

They didn't have to wait long. Mark was still at the Hansings' when Dave telephoned from the airport to say he would be there in a couple of hours. Heather said she would wait for him in the gatehouse. Mark wanted to be with her when she told Dave about them but Heather quickly pointed out this was not about bravado and needed handling with kid gloves. He should trust her to deal with Dave herself.

Before Heather had a chance to tell her husband about her and Mark, Dave had his say. The words 'gay' or 'homosexual', or even 'bisexual', were not used, but Dave explained he had found a different way of life in the Far East and had decided he wanted to make his home there.

This caught Heather by surprise. She decided to play for time.

'You look all-in,' she said. 'Why don't you have a couple of hours sleep? I'll go on up to The Manor and you can come up when you are ready. Mark is there, and I daresay you will need to discuss what you are going to do about business with him and Vince.'

Dave was happy with the idea. Both were aware it meant he didn't have to be there in front of the others when his news was passed on. Even now, with her marriage all but collapsed, Heather was still being considerate.

This was not a time to be thinking in terms of 'truth' and 'honour'. This was a time to be expedient and to get out of a tricky situation with as much as possible of Dave's pride in himself still intact. Only the four of them were aware of their small deception regarding Mark and Heather and all agreed it would serve no purpose to let Dave in on the secret.

Vincent had discussed more than once with Mark, his thoughts about investment opportunities in Singapore. He wondered out loud if there was a chance of involving Dave in any plans they might have in that direction?

Dave was welcomed like the Prodigal Son. The fatted calf was preceded by a celebratory glass of Dom and soon it was just like the good, old days. After dinner, Dave had them all laughing at some of the scrapes Jack Miller had got the pair of them into and then out of.

'Boy, you'll have your work cut out with that one,' he said to Vincent, laughing. 'He's staying out there with me for another month or so. He's as rough as guts but he is just so good at opening doors.'

'...Or knocking them down!' Vincent laughed.

Come bedtime, Mark set the ball rolling by going up first. Dave then announced he would wander back to the gatehouse, suggesting it would be sensible for Heather to stay at The Manor, where the majority of her clothes had gravitated to over the past month. Mark was a relieved and happy man when Heather slid in beside him and cuddled up.

Next morning, Vincent telephoned down to Dave at the gatehouse, and then he and Mark went down there to have a business meeting with their co-director.

Dave had obviously given the business situation some thought.

'Look,' he said, 'the lad I left in charge, John Pringle, is very good. He's still got that college-boy attitude to him but he has a very good brain and is well educated. As he learns the real world is not cast in black and white, he will do very well.

'As for me, if you are agreeable, I'll be happy simply to sell back my shareholding for the same amount I put in when I became a director, and I'll resign the directorship, of course.'

Vincent asked Dave what the particular attraction in Thailand was. Dave blushed, looking to the floor, so Vincent quickly rephrased the question. He asked if there was any significant difference between living in Thailand and living in Singapore.

Dave didn't know the answer but asked why it was important.

'Because Mark and I like the idea of investing in Singapore. Quite apart from the potential for making money, we believe the currency there will only get stronger. We need someone we can trust to spend some time there sussing the place out and looking for opportunities. From your point of view, it could give you the best of both worlds, western-style living with eastern style, erm . . . attitudes.

'We would reckon you could use Jack Miller to get you settled initially, and then you would need at least one, and maybe a couple of people from the region, to act as assistants.' The implication was clear.

Mark added: 'Vincent and I have always been impressed by the way you have managed to use your initiative and people-skills to smooth paths over here. We suspect those skills will be even more important over there.'

The more Dave thought about it, the more he liked what he was hearing.

'If I was self-sufficient out there, at least I could leave Heather with the gatehouse and the money from the property company here.'

'Dave,' Vincent said quietly, 'you know me well enough not to worry about money. We owe you for the way you set up and ran the property company anyway. You can either cash in your 20% shares in the company for their current value or let the money run, but the shares are yours to do with what you will.

'You have enough money for you to lead a life of leisure in Thailand if you wish and still be able to leave Heather rich. If you take up the Singapore offer, we want it to be because you fancy it, rather than need it.

'Why not brood on it? An idea might be for you to spend a few months in Singapore, just checking it out from our viewpoint and yours, before making any kind of medium-term commitment?'

'You're on!' Dave confirmed. 'If you agree, I would like to retain my shareholdings and directorship, as much for Heather as for myself. If you agree with me about retaining and promoting John, I will spend a couple of days going through the loose ends with him and then I will go to Singapore via Thailand.'

Everyone agreed on the deal. Mark was due to return to London later that day, so he asked Vincent if he could find his own way back to The Manor. Then he sat down with Dave.

'As I understand it, and tell me if I am wrong, although you care deeply for Heather, the marriage, as such, is over?'

Dave didn't budge.

'Look Dave, I am going to confide in you. I have strong feelings for Heather. I have always kept them to myself until now but given what has happened over the last couple of days, I am taking you into my confidence.

Would you mind if I . . . you know . . . made a play for her? I

213

promise I would never hurt her, and I promise that, regardless of her reaction, I will look out for her and ensure she is OK. I need your blessing, though, Dave. Without that, I will keep away from her.'

It was a gamble. But Mark made his living by gambling and rarely misread the odds.

'Mark, don't worry, you have my blessing and my support. Please look after her for me, and I wish you the best of luck.'

'A win/win situation,' Vincent exclaimed when Mark returned to The Manor with his news. 'You have to stay over tonight now, Mark, but should go back to London first thing in the morning.'

'Oh, and just one other minor thing, who is going to let Dianne know what is going on?'

Dave had disappeared back to the Far East again within the week. The gatehouse was effectively mothballed as Heather split her time between Mark's place in London and the Manor.

At that stage, she was reluctant to commit herself entirely, and anyway she soon tired of shopping all day but didn't want to cause Mark to take his mind off his work.

Heather was convinced Mark was the man she wanted to spend the rest of her life with but she was not sure London was where she wanted to spend it.

Ann took on the task of telling Dianne. Whatever her inner thoughts, the girl accepted the news with remarkable good grace. Her son, Jack, was becoming more and more the centre of her world anyway. What Dianne did not know was that Vincent had now decided she was off the hook as far as revenge was concerned. He had decided life had punished her enough.

Meanwhile, Dave was finding Singapore a real conundrum. In theory, the law and politics were based on the British system. In practice, the British way of doing things was being sidelined by the Asian ways.

On the one hand, the indigenous Malays felt they were owed special consideration but didn't actually want to do anything to earn it. The ethnic Chinese, the descendants of the original imported labour, were the political and commercial power base driving the new order. In theory, the President, Lee Kuan Yew, headed a democracy. In reality, those who stood up against him did not stay around for too long.

'Mr Fixits' were everywhere but sorting out the genuine door openers from the charlatans was not going to be easy. Backing the right horses, though, could prove to be very profitable indeed.

Dave suggested, in the first instance, the three men needed to form an investment company, stick enough money into the local market to be accepted as genuine investors, and then just let him leave his calling card around here and there to wait for a bite.

He did point out, though, there was 'serious' money being invested in the place, and their own budget would see them very much as small players. They would need to find nice, little niche boutique investments where the main aim would be minimising risk rather than maximising return.

Whatever else, Dave had clearly not lost his business acumen. Mark and Vince organised for one of their offshore companies to incorporate a division in Singapore and they put five million pounds into it for Dave to use as their initial investment.

Chapter 36

The two young Shelford speedway stars, Jamie Marlborough and Chris Andrews, returned to England shortly after Christmas. Vincent had been round to see Jamie's mum as soon as he had got back from Australia to let her know things had been going well for her son, and to make sure the widow would not be alone at Christmas. He had been relieved to discover she was spending the festive season with friends.

Two weeks after Jamie arrived back, the office manager at Shelford Speedway, Peter Green, telephoned Vincent to tell him he had received a copy of written transfer request to the BSPA from Marlborough. He wanted to take his chances in the 'draft'.

The young rider would have had no idea just how badly Vincent would take the news. The Shelford promoter didn't even bother to telephone Marlborough and ask him why. He was just heartbroken. This was the worst thing to have happened to him since the crash.

Lurch, not an aggressive person by nature, went and sought the boy out to ask why he wanted away from Shelford. The flippant answer was that he needed 'a new challenge and a bigger track'. He felt his progress was being restricted at Shelford and wanted to have more 'space' to establish his own identity.

Lurch wanted to smack the cocky smile from the kid's face, but just held himself back. Both Lurch and Marlborough knew a dirty deal had been done somewhere along the line. The lad he and Vincent had nursed so carefully was throwing it all back into their faces.

The normally placid manager tried hard to get to the bottom of things, but eventually reached the conclusion that Marlborough no longer wanted to be a 'team player'.

'I don't know what Vincent will do about it,' he said, 'But I, personally, promise you I will make this the worst decision you ever made in your life.'

Marlborough arrogantly dismissed the threat as bravado and sour grapes on Lurch's part.

Two weeks after the transfer request was made public, the front page of the local *Shelford Sentinel* paper carried a report about the young rider. Marlborough had been pulled over by the police in an unmarked car for speeding.

A 'routine stop-and-search' had brought to light a large amount of marijuana resin and a substantial amount of cash concealed in the glove compartment of his BMW.

Lurch smiled at the now 20-year-old rider's eventual sentence. He imagined the lags in jail rubbing their hands and smacking their lips at the thought of such a pretty, young man joining them for three months. After that, Lurch would make certain the cocky upstart would find it more than a little difficult to restart his speedway career.

After the initial disappointment of Marlborough's defection from the Shelford team, Vincent became even more ruthless. 'I must have been going soft in the head,' he decided. 'No more Mr Nice Guy from now on . . .'

To the speedway supporters Vincent was still a great man of the people and the saviour of Shelford. The loss of Marlborough had no effect on crowd numbers or enthusiasm on the terracing. Just the opposite really, and when the drugs story broke in the paper, it was a case of 'good riddance'. Marlborough's attitude had a lasting impression on Vincent, though. Never again would he let a speedway rider get under his skin.

The new hero, or villain, depending if you were a Shelford supporter or not, was Marlborough's replacement, Jack Miller.

'Miller the Killer', as Jack had soon become affectionately known as by the home crowd, did not immediately cover Marlborough's point-scoring abilities but he was perhaps even more popular. The bull of a man knew no fear and seemed to enjoy mowing other riders down just for fun.

Initially this was because Jack was simply trying to come to grips with the smaller British tracks, whilst not being prepared to change his aggressive approach, but he quickly cottoned-on to the notoriety it was causing and enjoyed being the centre of attention.

The two opposition riders he had put into hospital in separate incidents after only the first three weeks of the season were less happy, but Jack had broad shoulders.

Vincent noted the Kiwi's success with disdain. However, this was the man Vincent had been looking for, and right on cue. He had already decided this was going to be the year the Shelford Racers were to win the league. He might as well have a folk-hero in the team when they did it. There was also another little job he had in mind for 'Miller the Killer'.

Chapter 37

Jeff Harding was in the last year of his contract with Vincent. Everything he had been promised had happened, and then some. Harding missed his lad, who was now coming up to 10-years-old, but he saw young Jack each week at the speedway, and he and John Tindall had spent a couple of weeks in California with him in the winter.

Other than that, life was good. Jeff was a well-respected star rider who had been able to transform himself from the selfish, greedy character of his youth.

At least, he had done so on the track. Away from the stadium, and now in his late 20s, he still enjoyed surrounding himself with teenage girls too young and naïve to know any better.

Thorden were on their first visit of the season to Shelford. Just before heat nine Vincent called Jack Miller over.

'Here's the deal, Jack. You will start from gate one and Harding will be off two. Ten thousand pounds in cash to you if you take him out. I'm not talking about just knocking him off, I'm talking about really hurting him – and the more the better. The 10 grand is yours if he goes to hospital. From then on there are extra bonuses according to the amount of damage done.'

'Shit, man, you really don't like him, do you?'

Vincent looked down at the wheelchair and back up at the giant Kiwi.

'It's personal,' Vincent said.

'I get the message,' Jack nodded. 'You're the boss.'

All four riders went down in the first turn. Three got back up, but Jeff Harding stayed on the deck having suffered a badly broken right leg. Jack Miller was the first one over to Jeff, apologising desperately and explaining his throttle had jammed.

Two days later Vincent visited Harding in the hospital. 'I'd just set up a really big deal for you,' he said, shaking his head. 'Bang goes this season now, though. They tell me it really is a nasty break involving the knee joint?'

Three months later, Jeff had been discharged from hospital and was at his large, detached house, being waited on by a barely 17-year-old girl when Vincent arrived. Vincent noted, with satisfaction, the rider could still not get around without crutches.

'Thanks for coming,' Jeff started. 'To be entirely honest, I'm running short of funds. The mortgage and outgoings on this place are high and, as you know, I lead quite an expensive lifestyle. Can you give me an advance on this year's payments, please?'

'Well, not really,' Vincent replied. 'You see, you have been off now for three months, so the 'more than eight weeks out through injury' clause has cut in on this year's deal. All you will receive from speedway this year will be your insurance payments and I can't see them maintaining this lifestyle.

'Tell you what, though, you can draw on some of your investment earnings. They are looking very healthy.

'Oh, and by the way, you know our contract runs out this month, don't you? I think it would be a bit rash of me to sign you up again on a riding basis, given that we don't know how the leg will finish up. But if you like, I'll carry on looking after your investments on an ad hoc basis.'

'Would you, please,' Jeff came back. 'Thanks a lot.'

'I'll tell you what,' Vincent added, 'given that you might have to rely on the investment income for some time, do you think it would make sense to take the money out of the boring stocks it is in now and get it working a bit harder?'

'Would you do that for me? You're a real friend.'

'No problem, I'll send someone round tomorrow with some new documents for you to sign.'

Armed with all the waivers and carefully worded powers of attorney, it took Vincent just four months of carefully recorded bad share option gambling to turn Harding's £800,000 into just under £50,000, which was close to the amount he owed his creditors.

Vincent sent a minion around to break the news, and refused thereafter to take any calls from a shattered Jeff Harding. The injury to his leg never healed well enough for the former World Champion to ride again.

Six months later, his house was repossessed and he was declared bankrupt.

With 'Miller the Killer' in the side, the Shelford Racers had added backbone and aggression to a very talented and determined outfit. Alan Stewart and Reece Sullivan were regular internationals by now, and the team began to have that air of would-be champions about it.

Personally, Vince was not mad about the loud, foul-mouthed, Kiwi, with his lack of manners and disregard for protocol, but he realised the bloke had become his best ever signing since the brilliant Bryce Penrith.

Shortly after his arrival, Miller had set about remodelling the track equipment at the stadium to make best use of it. He had also worked with the Shelford track maintenance staff and come up with several really good ideas and work arounds, to improve the way the track was prepared.

There were hardly any more rain-offs at Shelford and every week the track surface drew more praise.

Initially there had been resentment from the stadium staff but Jack just ignored the early sour faces. As the wisdom of his ideas emerged, allied to his on-track worth, he soon became accepted.

With his solid scoring and having 'earned' £15,000 for sorting out Harding, Miller became reluctant to do a full-time job. Actually, this quite suited Vincent, who sent the track preparation expert around, one by one, to each of the tracks in which he had an interest.

Miller's reputation for track expertise was soon established, and he loved the lifestyle. Two weeks here, two weeks there, staying in nice hotels and with a fresh source of female opportunity at each place, it suited Jack fine. Best of all, he loved the notoriety he was generating with his riding exploits, and also having money in his pocket.

Vincent could not believe how quickly the Shelford team 'adopted' the wild man. Not only adopted him, but also began to put far more 'devil' into their own riding.

These were no longer kids who were going to be pushed around by anyone - and it had to be said, having Lurch and 'Miller the Killer' on their side of the pits gave the lads a good deal of confidence they would be protected against too many physical repercussions to their sometimes over-exuberant racing.

Shelford supporters continued turning up in droves, loving the new steel the team was demonstrating. Other promotions were mixed in their reactions to the new, aggressive Racers. The sensible ones appreciated the extra business Shelford now generated, on a par with the year Bryce Penrith rode for them, but some felt the competitive edge had become too sharp.

Most bookmakers now included speedway in their odds lists. Vincent had been bemused when the arrangement was first mooted but, not one to look a gift horse in the mouth, had supported it all the way. He was, by now, a very rich man, but saw no reason not to cash in on this foolishness.

He had placed a heap of money on Shelford to win the league with a variety of different agencies. After the departure of Marlborough, he had been quoted odds of between 10-1 and 8-1 on his bets. He reasoned that it would take very little by way of outlay to ensure which way the occasional close meeting would finish, especially when he controlled so many tracks himself, so this wasn't so much a gamble as a bonus payout.

In between, he indulged himself on spread-betting here and there, predicting the winning points margins of league matches, just for kicks and also to raise some fun money.

He had heard how some insiders had profited in a similar way from international cricket matches, where it was impossible for the sport's authorities to prove any wrong doing by a team losing (or gaining) runs or wickets at a suspiciously rapid rate.

Match fixing in cricket had been rife for a few years – and Vincent seemed to be the only person in speedway to identify how similar scams could be exploited in his sport.

In speedway terms, it was very easy for Vincent to simply instruct one of his riders – or even one from each of his teams if they happened to be in opposition – to 'throw' the occasional race to ensure the right result on the night.

The bookies were helpless to prevent big losses in that first season after betting restrictions on speedway were lifted, because Vincent never actually placed the money himself.

He didn't bet on speedway meetings so much to win money – his winnings were obviously peanuts by his standards – but he did so for the sheer pleasure it gave him to put one over on the likes of Coral, William Hill and Ladbrokes, plus the small, independent bookies who almost went out of business thanks to Vincent's carefully orchestrated coups.

Much of the money was channelled in various ways to Lurch. The man had proved to be a revelation and the more work and responsibility Vincent piled onto him, the greater appeared to be his capacity to adjust and cope with it.

Several times Vincent had told him he was now far too important to the organisation to be driving the motor home around, but Lurch was reluctant to give up that part of his duties.

Over the last few years, he had stayed over at The Manor more and more, and not just when they had arrived back late from speedway meetings or social functions. He had taken to sleeping in one of the attic rooms.

In fact, the room had pretty-well become 'his'. Lurch spent more nights at the Hansings' than he did at home, especially during the summer. It was something Vincent encouraged. Having Lurch on call around the clock was ideal.

Martin Kessler had long since been the Mr Fixit for Vincent. With the discharging of his many different roles, there wasn't much Lurch didn't know about 'The Boss'. The only thing he did not know about was Vincent's involvement in Jeff Harding's 'accident' but the chances are that he would even have approved of that.

Several times the big man had acted as Dianne's consort at social functions, and she had done the same for him, but since that one special night, she had kept him at arm's length.

Dianne had decided it would not be fair to her son, Jack, for her to keep having lovers. Maybe she still carried a torch for Mark?

Jack had become moody and difficult. Everyone told Dianne this was a stage all lads Jack's age went through and that she should not worry, but it was unsettling. The injury to his father had upset the boy badly but he had insisted on continuing to support the Swords.

A mixture of the Shelford Racers being a strong team, Jack Miller de-tuning many an opposition rider and Vincent manipulating races as and when necessary all combined to ensure Shelford would win the league, provided they won their final home match.

The fixture list had been kind, with Marsden the visitors for that league decider and season closer. The Racers won the meeting in fine style to take the league title in front of a 22,000 full house.

Fireworks erupted and the whole stadium went wild as the riders crossed the line at the end of the last heat. This was Vincent's finest hour as a promoter. As soon as the fireworks had finished exploding, tractors drew an assortment of equipment onto the centre green and the riders were sent into the crowd in order to invite the supporters to join them on the infield for a celebration party.

Free beer was handed out and a massive sausage-sizzle set up.

There were sweets and gifts for the kids, who were further delighted when three bouncy castles appeared from nowhere, along with a mobile disco for the adults.

The extravagant party, initially for 20,000 people, went on until one o'clock in the morning. Even at that time there were at least 10,000 revellers still celebrating. That night was one of those never-to-be-forgotten, spur of the moment, spontaneous evenings Vincent had planned and choreographed for weeks beforehand.

It was during the celebration after that final meeting Vincent asked Lurch to check with the riders for the traditional end of season stag night.

Lurch was somewhat sheepish the next day, when he explained to Vincent that, with several of the team now married, and others in long-term relationships, it was the majority view of the lads that the end of season 'do' should be limited to just a social evening for riders and their partners.

'The sands of time are moving fast,' thought Vincent. He passed the riders' decision on to Ann, who wasn't overly disappointed, and they arranged for the team and their families to spend two weeks in one of the top hotels in Disneyworld, Florida.

British bookmakers had generously but unwittingly paid all of the costs for this trip and even more.

Jack Miller was the only rider to turn down the invitation. He was back off Down Under to enjoy his new-found fame and finances in Australasia, incorporating, of course, a stop-over with his old mate, Dave, in Singapore, straight after the last meeting of the season.

Vincent and Ann decided to spend one of the two weeks in Florida with the riders. They then planned to spend Christmas in Australia as guests of the Penriths. Mark and Heather were invited on the Florida trip but decided they would 'house-sit' The Manor, so Ann asked Dianne if she would like to take Jack along.

It had not been the most perfect of ideas. Jeff Harding had convinced young Jack that all his problems had been brought about by Vincent. Even at the tender age of 11, Jack couldn't quite believe that, but loyalty to his dad was enough for him to give Vincent the cold-shoulder, which caused difficulties. Fortunately, the ever-reliable Lurch had spent a good deal of time taking Dianne and Jack around, keeping Jack happy and limiting his opportunities to upset Vincent.

Vincent and Ann were sitting enjoying the last of the late Autumn

Florida sunshine over a couple of strawberry daiquiris on the terrace of the luxury resort hotel.

Vincent slipped his arm into Ann's.

'Are we getting old?' he said. 'We are not even 30 yet, but things are changing so fast around us. We seem to be living our lives around others. We scarcely use your playroom any more, and I felt like a dirty, old man when the riders decided not to have a stag party at ours this year.'

'Take things in order, dear,' she said sweetly, trying to reassure him. 'The most important people in our lives are Heather, Mark and Dave. They have had a sea change in their lives, and it is natural we will have become caught up in it.

'We don't use the playroom much these days because we don't need to. You have finally come to accept that I love you for you, and you don't have to spend your entire life simply trying to please me in that way. I still enjoy being pampered but it's not an essential part of my life. I need more tenderness and less action these days!

'So far as the riders are concerned, since when did you get much out of the parties anyway? Be honest, sitting here in this idyllic setting sipping cocktails isn't a bad way to spend some time now, is it?

'In fact, I wonder if we should consider putting the cellar to more productive use when we get back home?'

Vincent squeezed her arm and kissed her cheek.

'Do you regret not having kids?' he asked. With that, Lurch and Dianne turned up looking decidedly harassed.

'Where's Jack?' Ann demanded with some alarm.

'I don't know and I don't care,' Dianne replied dismissively. 'He's been a pain in the arse all day and as soon as we got back here to the hotel, he scuttled off.'

Ann smiled at Vincent again. 'The answer to your question is no!' she said.

Chapter 38

Vincent and Lurch were having one of their long chats about speedway. They had been back from Florida a few weeks and were on a journey to London.

'We seem to have speedway running quite smoothly now, don't you agree?' Vincent knew tossing out such a leading question would set Lurch off.

'Well,' Lurch began, 'what are the most important things in speedway from a supporter's point of view?'

Vincent thought for a while. He was well aware how Lurch would soften him up with such comments.

'Let's see . . . good, close racing, crashes, personalities, close meetings . . .'

'OK, Lurch went on, 'let me stop you there. What were the first two things you said? Close racing and crashes, I believe?

'Now, second question, what is the biggest expense in speedway promotion?'

'Riders' costs, naturally.' Vincent was confident on that one.

'And, what drives rider costs?'

Again, Vincent considered his answer.

'We'll leave out greed!' he joked. 'I suppose two things really. The first is – or was – the concern that they were not being paid as much as the next rider, but by and large we have that in check these days. I suppose the driving force now is their own costs.'

'Good. Now what is the biggest driver of costs?'

'The purchase and maintenance of equipment?' Vincent ventured.

'Wrong! It is the competition between the riders to have the *best* equipment. Every time one rider steals a march on another by finding a better but more expensive piece of equipment, within weeks everyone has rushed out and caught up by buying the same thing. The biggest cost to riders is self-imposed obsolescence of perfectly good equipment.

'Also, this results in riders going faster and faster. This means they get spread out more on the track and it means the safety tolerances are reduced, so they are not game to take as many risks. This means the racing is not as close or exciting. Also, each time the power and speed of bikes is increased, so the need for greater and more expensive maintenance is increased.'

'So you are suggesting we should bring in stricter regulation on what can be done on engines?' asked Vincent.

'Pointless,' Lurch said. 'That way, you are always trying to put fires out after they have already started. The only way it would work is to put the riders on standard equipment.'

Lurch waited for a reaction. All Vincent said was: 'And...'

'Simple really. You supply the equipment . . . Or at least, the engines.'

'Let's see,' Vincent said, warming to the prospect. 'Say two engines per rider and allow nine riders per team, times 18 teams . . .'

'No, you are not going to give the engines to the riders. Instead, you are going to make them available to use. You have a team of mechanics who take the engines from track to track. The engines are numbered and the riders draw lots for them each night.

'The mechanics fit them before the meeting and take them back afterwards. Each engine has its own history sheet and either gets serviced after a set number of races, or sooner if it appears there might be a problem. But every engine receives exactly the same parts and treatment.

'What's the busiest night of all? Saturdays, when up to five meetings might be taking place on the one evening. That's 10 teams of seven riders or, in theory anyway, a maximum requirement of 70 engines. In fact, you would need a 'float' of surplus engines and spare engines available at meetings, but a hundred would do the job.

'As for things like clutches, electrics and the like, they are far easier to police, and in any case could easily be bought in bulk by the BSPA and supplied to the riders.'

Vincent suggested there would be an adverse reaction from the riders but Lurch felt the package could be 'sold' to the riders simply because of the enormous savings they would make.

He conceded that the few star riders sponsored by equipment manufacturers would object, but he pointed out it was these riders, acting as test pilots and shop windows for the suppliers, who were the ones actually driving the costs up.

'There would be some squealing but the majority would be in

favour. And if you were to lose one or two of the prima donnas, then maybe that wouldn't hurt the business, long-term.'

Vincent decided to give the matter some serious thought.

What Ann had failed to mention to Vincent during their conversation in Florida was that speedway was now taking up far too much of Vincent's time and grey matter.

Within limits, he had done what he had set out to do. He had speedway within his complete control. He could dictate every result, every move and every situation. There was no challenge left. Speedway was now just routine.

Building puppets and making them come to life had been one thing, but being a full-time puppet master was another. She had mentioned this on the flight home, causing him to give the whole concept of speedway, and his role within it, serious examination.

Jamie Marlborough's defection had been a serious blow. Although he tried not to admit it to himself, let alone others, Vincent knew he had developed a strong affection for the lad – and had been kicked in the teeth for his troubles.

Life now was bearable. In fact, with Ann so solidly behind him, life was good. He had settled his scores with the track doctor, the hospital and the consultant who had consigned him to the body-part hunters, plus Jeff Harding and speedway generally.

He remained consistent in his earlier thoughts that he would let Dianne off. After all, if she had not run off with Harding, then he might not have finished up with Ann. Besides, it would upset Ann if he were to do anything against Dianne. In any case, truth be told, he quite liked the girl. In fact, he decided, it was time to clear that side of things up.

He picked up the telephone and dialled John Tindall's number.

'John,' Vincent here. 'How do you like the south coast?' There was a short, puzzled silence.

'Because as of now you are the stadium manager and speedway promoter at Brighton, with a substantial increase in salary and expenses and a considerable resettlement allowance.'

'Sounds good to me. I'm not that far away from retirement myself. I could fit in well down there.'

'One condition,' said Vincent. 'You never lay an eye, never mind a hand, on Jack Harding again.' There was another long silence before Tindall's voice trembled as he simply said:

'I understand.'

'Just to spell it out, John,' Vincent went on in a matter of fact tone, 'go near him again and you are a dead man.' Tindall was shocked and started shaking as he sat at his office desk. He had never heard Vincent speak like that before but, equally, he knew this was not an idle threat.

'Like I said, I get the message,' was all he could manage to say.

'Good,' Vincent said, lightly now. 'You are off on holiday next week, aren't you? Give me a ring when you get back and we'll finalise the arrangements.'

Next, he phoned Steven Bray. After the niceties, he asked how the travel agency was going. 'Great,' said Steven. 'I've now got a dozen staff, the young lad who I put in charge is still here and has turned out to be a great manager. I also have a full-time tours manager who has his own department and staff.'

'So, essentially, you enjoy yourself swanning around the speedway scene, then?'

'Well, yes, if you put it that way, although I have to say I think I do a terrific job at Marsdon, and the bottom line certainly bears that out.'

'I agree. In fact, I want you to become the next BSPA Chairman. I have been in the seat long enough and it is time for someone else to have a go.'

This came as a bolt out of the blue to Bray. He quickly regained his composure, though.

'The job doesn't carry any money with it, does it?' he asked tentatively.

'I might have guessed!' Vincent laughed. 'I'll see you're not out of pocket, and think of the posing you will be able to do around the world!'

Steven Bray was already warming to the idea.

That afternoon Lurch was sitting in Vincent's study. Unusually, he had been summoned. He and Vincent normally did their chatting in the motor home or around The Manor, as their paths crossed.

'Lurch,' Vincent started. 'I'm going to give up the chairmanship of the BSPA in favour of Steven Bray. I've also asked John Tindall to go down and take over the running of Brighton for me.

'What I want you to do is to tell me where you see speedway going over the next 10 years or so and what you would do to change it for the better. Do you need time to think about the question?'

'Not really, boss.'

Vincent effectively just sat and listened for the next two hours whilst Lurch presented what amounted to a tutorial on the direction speedway should take.

In the four years or so since Vincent had declared, on behalf of the BSPA, a unilateral declaration of independence from the international body of the sport, feelings had thawed significantly between the British promoters and the FIM, and its member federations.

The iron curtain countries had begun to integrate more in speedway terms and several of their senior riders had been given spells of absence from their domestic commitments in Poland to earn much needed hard currency for the cash-strapped Soviet bloc.

Lurch reasoned that the political situation in Eastern Europe was fast coming to a head, and British speedway should recognise this and act now to ensure it retained its position of strength.

'I think British speedway should become far more involved in international speedway affairs,' he added.

'I'll give you two scenarios. You can decide which you like . . .

'Look at the current set up of the international controlling body of the sport, the FIM. There are 30-odd nations represented on the small oval racing section (the CCP) alone. Each has an equal voice and an equal vote. By my count, there is one genuine professional league. That is ours here and, don't laugh, we have no direct representation at all, let alone a vote, at the FIM!

'You could make a case for Sweden and maybe Denmark, along with Poland, having genuine speedway leagues, although very much club-run. Other than that, you have a few meetings in Australia, a few in America, even fewer in New Zealand, and the odd meeting in places like Italy, Germany, Hungary and the other Nordic countries.

'Just who are the power brokers at the FIM? They are people from Italy, Germany, Norway and . . . Holland! Believe me, these people are only there to empire-build, either as individuals or on behalf of their minnow countries.

'The genuine speedway nations of Britain, Sweden, Poland and Denmark should form their own association. Otherwise, they will lose control of their own sport. It would perhaps mean including Denmark in the World Final rota but, in fairness to them, Danish riders are beginning to dominate the scene anyway.

'The new federation of four nations should then lay down their own rules for competing in the World Championships and should either wrest the title from the FIM or simply stage their own version of it.

'Scenario number two:

'I look at other sports and I see an increasing number of travelling circuses featuring the elite players. Golf, tennis, motor racing, on two wheels and four . . . cricket is now entirely Packerised, and all other professional sports are moving in the same direction.

'I also foresee more and more sport being shown on the television and I think the public are becoming armchair fans except for when the big events come along, in which case they seem to want to be a part of the action regardless of the cost.

'I look at the pop stars filling huge outdoor stadia and I see all the people at Wimbledon tennis and the motor grands prix (on two wheels and four) and the golf Open Championships . . .

'I also see the amount of money being pumped into advertising and sponsorship in televised sport, and I think that speedway is, by its very nature, not getting its share. You have dragged it a long way, but as long as the sport is organised and decisions made solely by a disparate group of individuals, all with vested interests, it will never take the hard, long-term, commercial decisions.

'So, scenario two means you unloading your current speedway interests now, at the top of the market. Then signing up the top 20 or so riders in the world, Kerry Packer-style, and forming a world-wide circus.

'You would run the troupe around the globe, following the sun, as the motor grand prix people do now. There are a million little tin-pot nations itching for a bit of space on the world stage. It wouldn't be difficult setting up, say, 30 or 35 events a year.

'You could run a couple of rounds in each of the main speedway countries and then punt the rest around the less obvious speedway nations. All you would need to do is to sell the idea to a TV network and once you have guaranteed TV exposure, the rest just follows.

'There's you and me to set the thing up and run it. Then there's Steven Bray to look after the travelling, Rod Brown to do the admin, and we could easily head hunt the commercial and special events departments from the BSPA along with Rod. Effectively they are our people anyway. We put them there.

'We currently have the Formula One Grand Prix and the 500cc Motorcycling Grand Prix. Why not the Speedway Grand Prix? Even if, like Packer did in cricket in the early years, we have to run outside of the establishment and lay our own one-off circuits in non-speedway venues, we have enough track maintenance specialists to do the job – and do it properly.'

It was breathtakingly simple.

Vincent loved it. 'We'll start unloading our speedway assets during this season and engage a specialist to sort out a TV contract. For the time being, though, Lurch, this is between you and me, and Ann when I tell her. Meantime, you are in overall charge of the running of all my current speedway interests whilst we dispose of them.'

The next day Vincent arranged for Dave's replacement at the property company to informally sound out the planning officers at Shelford and Brighton with a view to putting in development planning applications. It was time to move on . . .

Chapter 39

Ann quite liked the idea of a renegade Grand Prix series. It would give Vincent a new challenge, and she didn't care much for the current speedway set-up. To her it was too airy-fairy, and not easy enough to manage and control. The new idea would involve a much smaller group and be far easier to keep on top of. It would also be more fun and not become routine, as the domestic speedway had.

She was pleased to see Vincent bubbling again. He seemed to have finally put the unhappy Jamie Marlborough episode behind him.

They might all be a bit older now, but that summer things seemed to drop back into place.

Vincent missed Dave far more than he expected. Dave would certainly have been handy to have around in helping find buyers for the various stadia. Vince took Ann to Singapore a couple of times. Molly Penrith had met them there once and the pair of ladies had done some serious shopping while Dave took Vincent around on a meet and greet exercise.

Their 'Far Eastern Office' was doing well and Vince was impressed with the manner in which Dave had established good contacts. He and Ann noted the ever-present fresh-faced young men who seemed to be Dave's 'assistants', but they decided not to pry into Dave's personal arrangements.

The upside to not having Dave around was, they saw a great deal more of Mark.

With Vincent and Ann's blessing, Mark and Heather held three parties at The Manor during the summer. The guest list was becoming very exclusive, and the parties more 'interesting'. Mark was now moving in very high circles and having a stunner like Heather on his arm had turned out to be a huge asset.

Vincent told Mark of his speedway plans and asked if any high-ranking TV executives happened to figure among Mark's social circle.

It really took very little to sort out a TV contract from there. The deal with a national TV network, with broadcasting rights likely to be sold off to a significant number of countries around the world, was struck over two weekends at the Manor.

Vincent had been the perfect host, supplying all amenities and playthings for the executive to enjoy, in between contract negotiations.

Halfway through the season, Vincent and Lurch called in on Steven Bray at Marsdon. Steven had noticed Vincent's significant loss of interest in the running of the sport. He had expected to have had the man looking over his shoulder all the time and attempting to influence all decision-making. This had not happened and it had left Steven feeling puzzled.

The conversation that afternoon explained why. Steven was quite enjoying the kudos of being the head of the BSPA, maintaining what had turned into a long period of success and stability in the sport. Every one of the 18 Division One tracks was doing healthy business.

However, he certainly saw the advantage of setting up an independent international 'travelling circus' both for Vincent and for his own travel business. Vincent reminded Steven that Marsdon Speedway had cost £50,000 to purchase nearly four years previously.

Since then, its profits had rocketed along with the increase in attendances. Vincent reasoned the business should now be worth about £120K. In his own mind, Steven thought that figure a bit low, provided word did not get out about the 'circus'.

'You are in the best position to find a buyer,' Vince pointed out. 'There must be business people among all of those locals you have carefully nurtured, who would want a nice, little very profitable cash business.

'You have from now until the end of the season to find a buyer. I want £100K. You keep anything you can get in excess of that. I would suggest you tell people the holding company that owns the speedway simply wants out, and you should hint you are happy to stay on and run the place if required. Then again, I'm happy to leave that side of things up to you.'

Steven Bray had found a buyer within two weeks. The price finally settled on was £140K.

It wasn't difficult for Vincent to tidy up the outstanding debts from the two clubs he had loaned money in order for them to join the first division. Indeed, they had already paid some back, and Vincent's offer of a small discount for immediate repayment, claiming he was 'temporarily cash-strapped', had them both keen to assist.

To each promotion, unaware of Vincent's assistance to the other, both the loans themselves and then the vibrancy, stability, and success he had brought to the league, had provided them with substantial profits.

Likewise, when Vincent proposed to Harry Grahame, at Byford, that he was prepared to sell his 49% holding for a 'sensible' price, Grahame leapt at the chance. The shares were probably worth three times more than Grahame eventually paid, but Vincent was happy to take a 50% profit on the deal for a quick sale.

With very little effort, Vincent had managed to clear all of his investments in speedway at a substantial profit. All the investments except the two places where he actually owned the stadia that is – and, of course, he knew he could make very substantial profits there also. He figured a minimum land valuation of three million for each place, and that was without the value of the speedway licences and the tangible assets.

There was no doubting, speedway had been good to Vincent, but he held no remorse about the ambitious, new venture he was about to undertake. He had put the sport back onto a much firmer footing than it had been before he had become involved as a promoter.

The decisions the remaining promoters took from the time he launched his travelling circus would see them either continue to rise or fall. He might be intending to 'rob' the league of its top riders, but provided they were sensible, the promoters could reduce their outgoings substantially and also benefit from the higher profile the sport would gain once his troupe was up and running.

The only fly in the ointment was Dianne. Well, not so much Dianne as Jack. Never a strong boy and always on the frail side, over the last month or two he had become even paler and thinner. Dianne had taken him to the doctor, who had been dismissive of her concerns, indicating Jack was around the age when hormonal changes were likely to begin kicking in.

Jack had not been entirely truthful to either his mother or the doctor though. As Vincent had suspected, Tindall had indeed 'taken advantage' of Jack, but far more than Vincent had imagined. It had been in the worst possible way, and not just the once either. The adolescent was now having real difficulty with his urinogenital system, but was scared to admit it to anyone.

Ann kept an eye on the lad over a few days from the time Dianne had first mentioned her concern, and it was clear to the ex-nurse that all was not well. By this time, Jack's complexion was changing from pale to a golden yellow.

She decided to take matters into her own hands, and as soon as the opportunity arose, she sat Jack down in private, put on her most authoritative nursing air, told the lad any secret he had was safe with her, and asked him what was wrong.

By now, the pain of just urinating had become so bad that Jack had stopped drinking liquids. He had constant and agonising back pain, night and day. Even he knew his secret could remain that way no longer. He began by admitting he had a serious problem 'down there' and then, reacting to Ann's sympathetic and kindly manner, eventually, in a great torrent, told her about the physical abuse he had endured from John Tindall during the last speedway season.

It was clear to Ann that Jack had merely started with prostatitis, but, untreated, the infection had migrated to the kidneys. She could only imagine how much pain the poor lad must have been in for months.

Once Ann had explained there wasn't necessarily a direct connection between what Tindall had done and the infection, and that the infection could have come from elsewhere (although, in her own mind, she was pretty sure the two things could be linked), Jack was much happier about getting medical treatment.

Ann promised she wouldn't tell his mother about their conversation, provided Jack told his mum he was having problems 'with his waterworks'.

Dianne was happy to be swept along by the tide of Ann's activity. That same afternoon, renal specialist, John Cohen, examined Jack. He was admitted into the consultant's private clinic, and put on a drip containing a cocktail of the most powerful antibiotics available.

Dianne stayed with Jack at the clinic, while Ann did the running around. Finally, late in the evening, Ann left mother and son together, returning home to The Manor.

Ann had it in mind to keep her knowledge about Tindall completely to herself, but as soon as she told Vincent about Jack's condition, he had pointed the finger straight at the Thorden promoter.

Taken aback, Ann repeated to Vincent what Jack had told her, begging him to respect her promise. Managing to hide the worst of his anger, Vincent obviously agreed. In his own mind, he was aware that he could have prevented this from happening. He was the one to blame for the poorly young man's condition.

Ann, Vincent and Lurch were all at the clinic by eight o'clock the next morning. There had been no repeat of Dianne and Lurch's dalliance since that one-off night a long time ago now, although he remained close friends of both mother and son.

By nine, the specialist had finished examining Jack, and had placed him on a dialysis machine. He asked Dianne if he could have a word in his office. Dianne asked both Ann and Vincent to go with her, while Lurch stayed with Jack.

'I am terribly sorry,' Cohen said, 'the treatment has come too late and the kidneys have ceased to function.' Dianne had turned pure white. Ann took over for her.

'Does this mean, when he recovers from his current state, he will be able to live a more or less normal life having regular dialysis until a suitable kidney turns up for transplant?'

'Well, in theory that is the position, but I am not going to sugar-coat this. There is a serious likelihood of further infection spreading if those kidneys stay in place. We really need to find a kidney, and very soon.'

Dianne emerged from her shock.

'He can have one of mine.' She said without hesitation. 'That is possible, isn't it?'

'I cannot say without tests, but the closer the relationship, the more likely the match'

'OK, can we do it now?' she replied.

While they were waiting for the results of the tests, Ann suggested to Dianne she should think about letting Jeff know about his son's condition. The response took Ann by surprise. It was an absolute and categorical 'No'.

Gently, Ann pressed the upset woman, saying the boy's father had a right to know. Dianne remained adamant, but Ann kept on going, finally provoking a violent outburst.

'Jeff Harding does not need to know, because *he* is not Jack's father!' Vincent and Ann stared at Dianne, as the potential significance of what she had said began to sink in. Eventually, as if reading their minds, Dianne broke the shocked silence.

'And no, in case you are thinking it, I was not so much of a hard-faced tart as to cheat on both Jeff and you, which means that – yes, Vincent, *you* are his father.'

Ann immediately stood up and, without speaking, walked away, leaving Dianne and Vincent alone. She did not trust herself to be diplomatic and needed to sort out her own feelings.

Vincent was caught in the middle. Still reeling from Dianne's words, he was caught between his love for Ann, the irony that he had allowed Tindall to do this to his own child, and the state Dianne was in.

He had decided to go after Ann, but just as he was about to excuse himself from Dianne, a grim-faced Mr Cohen approached them.

'Mrs Harding, are you aware you are a diabetic?' Dianne shook her head.

'Well, I am sorry to say it, but you are. Not enough to be insulin-dependant. Careful diet control is all you need, but I am afraid this rules you out as a kidney donor.'

'It looks like me then, doesn't it, Doc? I've just discovered I am the boy's father!'

The consultant looked down at Vincent and the wheelchair.

'Mr... er...'

'Hansing,' interjected Vincent.

'Well, Mr Hansing, as I am sure you realise . . .' Vincent cut right across him.

'Do you mind if we have this conversation in private, please, Doc?' Cohen looked at Dianne, nodded, and turned away. Vincent followed him down the corridor and into his office.

'I know what you are going to say Doc. Wheelchair cases have a history of renal problems. All I can say is that I keep myself fit, have regular check-ups, and I understand I am currently in pretty good shape, so I reckon it should be alright.'

'Mr Hansing, you know very well, even if your kidneys are in good shape at the moment, losing one of them in your condition will, at the very least, reduce your life expectancy significantly: At worst, it will put such pressure on the remaining kidney, you could easily become an invalid overnight.'

'And I am not now?' Vincent asked, with a quizzical expression. 'Why don't we do the tests now, and worry about the consequences later?'

Mr Cohen shrugged his shoulders, and buzzed for a nurse.

Ann had returned to Jack's bedside after walking away from

Vincent and Dianne. Lurch had been telling the lad dirty jokes, whilst the youngster had been trying to put on a brave face.

Ann's anger disappeared when she looked at the sick lad, not yet quite a teenager. How could *she* be angry with *him*? The same feeling did not extend to Dianne, though. Both herself and Vincent had been entitled to have been told about the paternity earlier – at the very least when Dianne and Jeff had split up.

When Dianne composed herself and returned to the bedside, Ann said there were things she needed to do at The Manor. Waving away the offer from Lurch of a lift back, she grabbed a taxi instead.

Heather was in London at Mark's place. Ann telephoned with the news about Jack's illness. She was not prepared to mention the rest of the news over the phone, but burst into tears halfway through the conversation.

This was so unusual for the normally implacable Ann that Heather cut the conversation short, rang Mark at work to let him know what was happening, and jumped into her car. She was at The Manor in just over two hours and before Vincent had arrived home.

Not surprisingly, Vincent's kidneys proved to be a good match for Jack. Vincent and the consultant had another long conversation, or perhaps, debate would be nearer the truth. On the one hand, Vincent was adamant the transplant should take place. On the other hand, Cohen was equally determined he would not risk Vincent's own life.

In the end, they reached a compromise. It would be several days before Jack would be stabilised enough to undergo the transplant. From that time on, Cohen reckoned there was a two-week window within which it would be safe to perform the operation.

The two men decided to spend the next three weeks trying to locate an alternative donor source. In the event of no match being available at the end of this time, both parties would review the situation.

Vincent finally returned to Jack's bedside. He assured the boy everything was going to be alright. Then he pulled Dianne to one side. He told her that the ideal time for Jack to have a transplant would be in three weeks' time, and that unless a 'healthier' kidney became available beforehand, the lad would have one of his. Although it pained him to be deceitful to Ann, he asked Dianne not to disclose this backstop position.

Vincent was relieved to see Heather's car outside the house when he and Lurch made their way up the driveway. He had hated putting Ann second in all of this, but had made the decision that he needed to prioritise his time during the day in order of urgency. Having Heather there would have given his angel a shoulder to lean on.

Ann wasn't at all angry with Vincent. She saw him as the main victim in all of this. She had talked things through with Heather. Dianne's original subterfuge might have been understandable, given the circumstances of the time. Indeed, Ann wondered how she had failed to spot the date correlation herself.

The first thing she had done on returning to The Manor was to sit down with a calendar. The dates were at the outside edge of possibility, but as a nurse, she should have been smart enough to have worked it out for herself, even if the most likely father looked to have been Jeff.

Even if the original lie was understandable, Dianne should have told Vincent and Ann when she had begun to socialise with them. Illness to Jack or not, Ann would have to have it out with the woman she had come to regard as a very good friend.

As it turned out, such a confrontation turned out not to be necessary. While Vincent had been waiting for the result of his tests, Dianne had sat down with him and explained her reasoning for keeping quiet.

She had explained that she hadn't been remotely aware of the pregnancy when she made her fateful decision to abandon Vincent for Jeff. She did admit, it was a decision made while her mind had been in turmoil, and that Harding had taken advantage of her distraught mind the first time they had sex.

Dianne had been in a bad way, with Vincent still in a coma and not expected to live. She had been leaving the hospital after a visit when she had bumped into Jeff in the hospital entrance. She had reasonably assumed at the time he had been trying to get in and see Vincent. In fact, the 'chance' meeting had been no coincidence at all.

Jeff had offered to drive her home and they had stopped off at a pub on the way, where she had too much to drink. Jeff had then taken full advantage of the effect of the alcohol and Dianne's mental vulnerability.

This is where she had originally thought the conception had occurred. After all, the dates all seemed to pan out that way.

Dianne made no excuse to Vincent for her continued relationship and then marriage to Jeff, other than that he had been attentive in the first year and she couldn't get her head around what had happened to Vincent.

By the time she had realised her error, the young girl had already been married, and Vincent had settled down with Ann.

It had been a chance conversation with a nurse when Jack had been admitted to hospital with pneumonia in his second year that had set Dianne thinking, and she had quietly carried out her own investigations after that. This is when she discovered who Jack's real father was.

Given the circumstances at the time, she had decided it would not have been fair to Ann, Jack, Jeff or Vincent to say anything at that stage.

The next time she had met Vincent was when Jeff had bullied her into attending the barbeque at The Manor. She had realised then just how wrong she had been, but trying to rectify matters would only have meant upsetting a whole group of people, especially Ann, whom she had liked immensely from the outset.

She had felt then though, Jack and Vincent were entitled to at least get to know each other, so she had not discouraged closer contact. It was something she herself had wanted anyway.

Finally, when she had managed to get rid of Jeff, she had felt it would have looked as if she was a gold-digger, had she then admitted the situation.

She was very aware of how much disruption such an announcement would cause and felt it could jeopardise her relationships with Jack, with Ann, and with Vincent, whilst also causing upset between Vincent and Ann.

She had determined that she would wait until Jack reached the age of 18 and then she would tell him. It would then be his decision what he did about it and at least she could not then have been accused of trying to cash in on Vincent's money.

She was deeply sorry to have blurted it out like that. Her only excuse was that she was not thinking straight at that time and she would understand fully if Ann wanted nothing more to do with her.

Ann, Heather, and Lurch had listened carefully to Vincent. Heather and Lurch both quietly thought the explanation sounded both reasonable and sensible, but it wasn't those two's opinion that mattered. Ann sat there for a full thirty seconds. Nobody dared speak. Then she stood up.

'Where are you going?' Heather asked, looking concerned.

'Somebody should be at the hospital helping Dianne with Jack,' Ann said quietly. I'm going to change my clothes and then I shall go down there.' Heather went with her. Apart from Mark needing to be told, they all decided it was then entirely up to Dianne who else was informed of Jack's father's real identity.

Lurch stayed with Vincent. They had a few drinks during the evening. Vincent was aware Lurch had volunteered as a kidney donor, but was not a match.

'Don't have too much drink tonight, Lurch. I'll need you to drive me down for a chat with Mr Tindall tomorrow. I need to take him his Christmas box.'

They arrived at Tindall's flat just before noon. Vincent had two brown paper bags on his lap as Lurch pushed him into the lift.

'This is as far as you need to come, Lurch. Go and have some lunch. Don't be longer or shorter than an hour, and then park in that car park opposite and wait.'

Once welcomed in to Tindall's beautifully decorated flat, Vincent was offered tea.

'Fuck the tea, John, we're here to celebrate!' and Vincent pulled a bottle of Dom Perignon from one of the bags. Tindall's eyes lit up as he reached for a couple of glasses from the cabinet.

'Well, how are you enjoying your retirement here on the south coast?' ventured Vincent, as they clinked glasses.

'I've brought along a little Christmas box for you.' He pushed the other brown paper bag across the table. It contained £20,000 in cash.

'You have done a fantastic job for me, John, and I thought I would show my appreciation.' They raised their glasses again, and Vincent then topped them up.

The bottle soon emptied as they sat there reminiscing. Vincent had two more bottles in the other bag.

'Oh, Hell,' he said. 'I meant to put these in the fridge. I'll stick the spare in the fridge. If we don't get around to it, you can have it later. And I'd better open this other one over the sink.' Tindall offered to do it for him, but Vincent waved him away.

'Don't treat me like a cripple, John! Besides which, I pride myself as having become something of an expert where opening champagne is concerned.'

Tindall heard the cork pop. A minute or two later, Vincent emerged, apologising for having spilt some, but saying he had cleaned it up. He filled Tindall's glass, but not his own.

'I've still some in my glass,' he said, I'll stick this bottle in the fridge to cool until we need it.'

Champagne at lunchtime on an empty stomach has an almost immediate effect, and Tindall was already slurring his words. Vincent raised his glass again, and they downed them together.

'I don't think the second bottle is as good as the first,' offered the slightly drunk host.

Vincent avoided the comment. After another 10 minutes, Tindall appeared to be totally drunk. He tried to stand, saying he didn't feel too good, but slumped back down.

'Oh, there was something else I wanted to discuss with you, John.' Vincent had lost his expression of bonhomie.

'It's about Jeff Harding's young son, Jack.' Tindall looked at Vincent, suddenly alarmed.

'What about him?' he said, with obvious concern.

'Well, it seems that after you had finished doing obscene and diabolical things to him, he contracted an infection that has cost him his kidneys. Oh, and by the way, *I* am the boy's father, not Harding.' Tindall was struggling to take this all in.

'I did wonder if you would like to donate him one of your kidneys, but knowing what a nasty prick you are, I will have to use one of mine instead. Besides which, yours are shot away now anyway.'

'There's nothing wrong with my kidneys!'

'Wanna bet?' Vincent replied. 'They are fucked, like the rest of you. According to my research, you have about 10 more minutes to say your prayers.'

Tindall once again tried to get to his feet. Vincent leaned over and, with one hand, easily pushed him back down.

'Come on now, John, don't spoil it. We've had such a nice drink.'

Tindall looked in horror at the empty glass. Once again, he tried to stand up, but couldn't. Vincent took the empty glasses into the kitchen, picked up the remainder of the powder in its small envelope, opened the third bottle of champagne and emptied half out, before washing both glasses and replacing one back from where Tindall had taken it. His victim had almost passed out.

'Listen John, please don't be sick until I have left?' he asked brightly, whilst pouring fresh champagne and some powder into the clean glass, holding it with a cloth, before pressing it into Tindall's useless hand. He then let the glass drop, before carefully putting

Tindall's prints, along with his own, over the two bottles. He then put the envelope with the remaining powder on the coffee table next to the bottles and finished cleaning up in the kitchen. Finally, he collected the brown paper bag with the cash, and carefully put the poisoned bottle of wine and all its packaging inside.

By this time Tindall was vomiting, and had knocked over the bottles with his convulsions.

'Great stuff John! Very realistic! Now, die, you bastard!'

He wheeled his way out of the apartment, down in the lift and across to the car park, where Lurch was waiting.

'Lurch, there is no reason to think they will, but in case anyone should ever ask, we came here today to drop off a Christmas box of two bottles of the finest champagne. During my chat with John, I told him about his good friend, young Jack Harding, being very unwell. He seemed to take it badly.'

In February, the coroner came up with an open verdict. John Tindall had consumed a bottle-and-a-half of Dom Perignon, but the remains of the powder that actually killed him were still on the coffee table when his cleaner found him on December 11th. The police doctor thought he had been dead around two days. It was clear the man had been poisoned, but the coroner could not determine if it had been by his own hand or by person or persons unknown. There was no note or other evidence to help him decide.

Chapter 40

It had been five days since Jack had been taken into hospital. The tight group of friends had formed a roster for visiting, so there was always at least one person at the hospital, day or night. Ann had insisted Dianne move into The Manor for the time being. At least that way she would get regular meals.

The dialysis and the antibiotics had done their job, and Jack looked much better. In fact, he admitted he hadn't felt so good for many weeks, and was becoming frustrated at having to stay at the clinic. Several of his school friends had visited, and he was looking forward to Christmas. No kidney had shown up though, and the clock was ticking.

Vincent and John Cohen tended to avoid each other, but when Vincent saw an opportunity during his visit, he confronted the consultant. His first question was the one all of the group had been asking each other. If Jack was looking so well, why wasn't it possible for him to continue on the same regime he was on now?

The doctor carefully explained that the antibiotics Jack was being administered were so strong that they could only be used for a short period before they started doing more harm than good. He re-iterated the timescale he had already outlined.

Vincent again raised the question of his being the donor, if and when push came to shove. Cohen was again evasive but Vincent was not prepared to be fobbed off this time.

'Doctor,' he said, 'either you agree to perform the operation, if required, or I have to search around for someone who will. I reckon that will take at least a week, so I need to know your answer within the next day or so.

'In the meantime, I would like to take Jack home for a Christmas party. As you know, my wife is a fully qualified nurse and she will keep a careful eye on him. What do you say?'

'Ask Mrs Hansing to come and see me. I will give her a treatment regime. I see no reason why he cannot be away from dialysis for two days. We are both on the same side Mr Hansing. We both have the lad's best interests at heart.'

Both Ann and Dianne were delighted with the idea of a party for Jack. Vincent left it for the boy's mother to tell him he could have a couple of days away from the hospital, and he was not at all disappointed to be staying at The Manor instead of home.

Mrs Peasenhall arranged for her grandson, Andy, who was a regular playmate of Jack's, to join the party that had been arranged for the next day, also bringing a couple of his school friends. Jack selected some of his own friends, and Lurch telephoned around their parents, arranging to pick them up after school.

Neither Jack nor Dianne were used to the 'money no object' world of Vincent and Ann. The sick lad came up with some interesting and imaginative ideas for Christmas gifts, both for himself and his friends, but he was totally indulged.

Lurch was able to meet every request, barring one. Jack asked if his dad could come to the party, but Dianne was adamant she wouldn't even be telling Jeff, who had not been near either her or Jack for months, so it was decided to tell Jack his dad was out of the country.

It was a wonderful party. Mrs Peasenhall and her helpers came up with the whole Christmas package from nowhere and still had time for the traditional jelly and ice-cream type stuff for the kids. Not that Jack had much appetite. Several of the Shelford and Thorden riders looked in, a magician appeared from nowhere and even a premature Santa arrived to give out the gifts.

When the party was finally over, Jack fell asleep and his mother settled in to keep an eye on him, Ann all but dragged Vincent into their private quarters. Just as soon as she had closed the connecting door, she set upon him.

'What is all this nonsense about you giving a kidney to Jack?' she demanded.

'So what happened to the doctors' oath of secrecy?' retorted Vincent.

'Don't try to deflect things. Mr Cohen naturally assumed I knew about your plan and was trying to persuade me to talk you out of it! I've never heard such a ridiculous idea in my life. Don't you think for one moment I saved you from becoming a posthumous donor so you could go and deliberately kill yourself a second time!'

Vincent began to laugh at the absurdity of the situation, which he hadn't fully taken into account before. His laughter only inflamed Ann further. In the 13 years they had been together, this was the very first time she had raised her voice to him and he loved her the more for it, but had badly misjudged the situation.

'Angel . . .' he began, but got no further. Ann stalked out of the living room and into their bedroom, slamming the door behind her. What Vincent did not know was that Ann, Heather and Mark had all been tested as possible donors, and all had been rejected as not suitable.

By the time Vincent ventured into the bedroom, Ann was asleep, or at least, acting that way. He went to the bathroom and then slid in alongside her, but she made no movement.

Next morning he was, as usual, in his study before anyone was about. He had made several telephone calls to the US, trying to locate a suitable donor kidney, but with no success. He then switched his attentions to England.

Right at the outset, he had made enquiries as to which the best surgeons for a kidney transplant were. Nobody had come up with a stronger recommendation than John Cohen, which is why Jack was still under the man's care.

This time, though, Vincent began checking to see if he could find someone who would be prepared to use him as a donor, should Cohen refuse.

He was not surprised to run straight up against the British Medical Association self-protection mechanism whereby nobody would take on a patient without the blessing of the current practitioner.

Finally, and without speaking to Ann, Vincent rang John Cohen at the clinic. He made the point that the surgeon had broken his confidence, albeit by accident. Then he demanded Cohen make a decision, warning him that unless he was prepared to perform the transplant, Vincent would fly the boy over to America.

Faced with such an ultimatum, and knowing Jack would suffer from such an arduous flight, Cohen put his patient's care first and conceded that, in the event of all else failing, he would perform the operation.

Vincent then searched for, and found, Ann. This time he was as contrite as he possibly could be. He explained that it really was not his wish to play the martyr and was banking on a donor kidney becoming available. However, he did go so far as to ask Ann to suggest an alternative if the worst came to the worst. It was not a question she had an answer for.

Jack spent half of the next two weeks in the clinic and half at The Manor. Unknown to him, the adults were all waiting for the telephone to ring. This was the other side of the donor equation.

They were, effectively, waiting for someone to die.

Dianne's parents were in bad health and therefore in no position to help. As Christmas approached, John Cohen extended his deadline until after the New Year. Jack had managed to avoid re-infection so far, and the holiday period was a 'good' time for road accidents.

Heather had been keeping Dave up to date with proceedings. He had been planning a trip home over the Christmas anyway and decided to bring it forward.

Vincent didn't care to admit it, but he had missed his friend a lot, especially during this difficult time. Dave's regard and admiration – love even – was complete, unqualified and unquestioning. Not even Lurch could give Vincent such blind loyalty as Dave could provide.

Mark too, took time off. He and Heather moved into the gatehouse, leaving Dave to stay close to Vincent in the Manor.

Christmas celebrations were subdued. As each day ticked past, Ann understood more the dilemma Vincent was in. She was bitterly unhappy about the situation, but she understood he could not sit and watch his only son die.

The operation finally took place on January 6th, Ann's birthday. All went according to plan, although, much to Vincent's annoyance, he was kept in hospital far longer than a normal fit donor would have been.

Three full weeks after the operation, both father and son were released on the same day, with the strict understanding that they would abide by the regime Ann was given by the surgeon.

Vincent and John Cohen had developed quite a rapport. Vincent was sure he would be able to maintain a healthy lifestyle, but promised he would attend for regular six monthly check-ups. He also understood that he would be an absolute fool if he did not give up alcohol.

Cohen made a point of being around when Vincent was preparing to leave. They shook hands firmly, and Vincent thanked the man sincerely, going so far as to tell him this was the first time he had felt proud to know a medical man.

'You might not be so happy when you receive my bill,' joked the dedicated surgeon.

'John,' Vincent replied, 'I have discovered money cannot buy everything. Even so, my people will contact you with a view to some kind of trust being set up for the benefit of the clinic.' They shook hands again and John Cohen pushed Vincent's chair to the exit.

'Remember,' he said. 'No wheeling yourself around for another three weeks.'

Lurch took over from the doctor, muttering that it was going to be a long and grumpy period.

Chapter 41

It was mid-February. The Manor no longer resembled a sanatorium. Dave was leaving to go back to Singapore at the end of the week, Mark had gone back to London and Jack was up and around. He was looking forward to going back to school. He and Dianne would be returning to their own house when he finally received the all clear.

Vincent had arranged for he and Ann, and Lurch if he wished, to travel out to Australia as soon as he was fully fit, although he appreciated there would be no high jinks on quads or jet skis again for a long while – if ever again.

Speedway had taken a back seat. Even Lurch was reluctant to broach the subject until Vincent had fully recovered, although he was beginning to do some quiet planning.

The weather had turned lousy. Clear, frosty nights and bright, sunny days had given way to gale force winds, with driving rain and sleet.

Just after eight o'clock on the Thursday evening, following a particularly bad squall, there was a power cut. Lurch soon started up the standby generator and telephoned the electricity authority.

The blackout was not widespread, so it pointed to either a problem in the local substation or, more likely, tree damage to the overhead power lines. Either way, emergency crews were busy trying to repair bigger outages, and it would be some while before The Manor could expect to be back online.

Lurch nipped down to the gatehouse in his car to collect Heather and open the drive gates manually. She had intended waiting until the weekend to move back up to the big house, but the power cut had brought a change of plans. She had started to clear out fridges and freezers, and put the place into mothballs again when Lurch arrived. Lurch took the foodstuff back to The Manor with him, Heather said she would only be an hour or so, and would then bring her own car up.

The generator at The Manor was big enough to run the oil-fired central heating boiler, the fridges and freezers, a few electrical gadgets like TVs or stereos, and a minimum of subdued lighting. The occupants were perfectly happy – cosy, in fact, with the howling wind and lashing rain outside adding to the calmness of the dim lights and warm comforts.

Dianne had taken Jack up for a bath and bed and the others were sharing a drink in the library overlooking the front drive when they saw the headlights of a vehicle approaching the house. It was obviously travelling too fast and erratically for the conditions.

As it slid to a halt outside the entrance, in the semi-dark, they could see someone jump from the driver's seat of what had turned out to be a Transit van and run towards the front door.

Dave went to let the late-night visitor in. As the group in the library heard the outer door open, there was a commotion, and a few seconds later, Jeff Harding burst into the room, followed by a flustered Dave, who had been unable to restrain him.

Lurch and Ann immediately jumped to their feet and formed a protective barrier in front of Vincent. Harding was obviously the worse for wear. He was either drunk, or on drugs, or, more likely, both. His eyes were as wild as the weather and it looked as if he hadn't washed or combed his hair in a month.

As soon as he was through the door, he started yelling that he wanted to see his son, and demanding to know what they had they done to him.

He was raving and totally out of control but knew he would never get past Lurch, should he try to attack Vincent. By this time, Dave had also joined the protective wall around the wheelchair.

Vincent shooed them away, although Lurch remained close enough to intercept Harding, should he try anything silly. Ann decided she would be better off out of the way. She whispered to Vincent that she would go and warn Dianne, and slipped out of the room, almost unnoticed by the out-of-control intruder.

'Don't be such a prat,' Vincent said quietly, 'sit down and Dave will get you a drink.' Dave looked at Vincent, who nodded towards the drinks cabinet.

'Whisky?' Vincent asked. His calm and controlled manner threw Harding completely. All the sad character could do was drop into the nearest chair, clearly just about at the end of his tether.

There could have been a case for having some sympathy for the man, but this was nowhere in Vincent's mind. The unwanted guest would feel the effect of the fury that had been building up since

Dianne's revelation about Jack.

Nobody spoke, while Dave more than half filled a whisky glass and passed it over. The drink was gone in three gulps. The glass was refilled and handed back again.

Finally, Harding began to speak, half shouting, half shaking, and close to tears.

'What have you done with my son? Is he still alive? Why is he here?' Vincent was not going to make this easy. In a perverse way, he was enjoying himself.

'First, Mr Harding, he is not *your* son but *my* son. He was conceived just before you tried to kill me, but, as is typical of you, failed to do a decent job.

'Do not, for one moment longer, labour under the misapprehension that you are capable of fathering a child. You are a mule, Mr Harding, and mules are sterile.'

Ann stuck her head around the door. Seeing things relatively calm, she told the assembled group that the telephone now appeared to be out. She had tried to contact Heather without success, so she was going to rug up and walk the dogs down to the gatehouse whilst there was a break in the rain.

This interruption had given Jeff the time to think. His brain processes were not moving too quickly by now. He had been given two huge pieces of information. The first was that Jack was not his child and the second was that Vincent knew the crash had been no accident.

'I don't believe you,' was the best he could come up with. 'I love my wife and my son, and they love me. You have poisoned them towards me.'

'Not so my friend,' replied Vincent, after yet another long silence. He was enjoying spinning the moment out as long as possible.

'I will tell you about Jack now. *You* introduced Jack to John Tindall, didn't you? *You* left him in John Tindall's care. *You* encouraged Tindall and the boy you thought was your son to spend a significant amount of time together.

'John Tindall assaulted Jack, over a long period, and he finally ended up buggering him – not just once, but several times.

'He buggered him so badly that the boy's kidneys failed as a result, and he was within a few days of death. That is what *you* did to the boy you claim you love.'

Tears were now beginning to roll down Harding's cheeks. He held out the empty glass, which Dave refilled.

'It gets better,' Vincent continued. 'Whilst *you* were off shagging little girls yourself, because you are not man enough to cope with proper women, I was looking after *'your'* Dianne and Jack.

'I saved the one you had allowed to be buggered's life by giving him one of my own kidneys. *That* is love, you wretched specimen, not your pathetic mouthings.'

The front door banged shut, and they watched Ann, wrapped in her long duffle coat with the hood up, fighting her way down the drive, with the two Alsatians bounding around her. With Ann outside, and Dianne upstairs, Vincent no longer felt the need to moderate his voice.

Beginning slowly and quietly, he started talking again.

'So you say Dianne loves you? Do you think she is still saving herself for you? Don't make me laugh. She told me five years ago, she couldn't stand you and that your idea of lovemaking was pathetic compared to what she and I had shared.

'Who do you think orchestrated that exposé in the Sunday papers about you and that young girl?'

Vincent was now beginning to lose his own self-control. Like rolling thunder, his voice began gaining momentum. Each new peal built in the last. Only the final jibe was delivered with lesser force, as if the thunder was rolling away . . .

'Now then, let me see, Dianne saving herself for *you*? You know I fucked her before you, but did you know my partner Mark has fucked her? Did you know that Lurch, here, has fucked her? DID YOU KNOW MY WIFE HAS FUCKED HER?

'That only leaves my two dogs, and I'm not certain about them!'

Even Dave and Lurch were stunned. They had never, ever, seen Vincent like this.

'Your *wife* has fucked her?' was all Harding could say, as they all looked down the driveway to where Ann could just about be seen, battling against the driving rain that had started up again.

Harding suddenly jumped up and dashed to the door, catching Lurch unawares. He slammed the library door behind him, gaining valuable seconds, before running across the hall and out of the entrance. He jumped into his van and spun it around, the wing mirror knocking Lurch off his feet as it went.

By then, the other two men were in the doorway. They watched, unable to do a thing, as the van, without lights on, thundered towards the dimly lit isolated figure of Ann, wrapped up tight and hearing only the wind roaring in her ears...

The impact was loud enough for the three men to hear over the top of the wind and rain. Her body was thrown hard and high.

Vincent instinctively hit the panic button on the side of the doorway to close the main gates. Nothing happened. The power was out.

He needn't have worried about Harding. After ploughing into Ann, the van veered off the drive, slewed across the meadowland and smashed head-on into the trunk of a huge oak tree.

The three men just froze there, transfixed, for a full five seconds. Vincent was the first to react. He began to try and wheel himself down the drive. Dave grabbed the chair to stop him.

Lurch began to rush for the telephone in the house, but suddenly realised it was not working. He told Dave to try it anyway, while he pulled Vincent out of the stinging, sheeting, rain. Dave came back out, shaking his head.

'OK,' Lurch shouted, 'Dave, you take my car keys and go find a phone. The keys are hanging up on the key board inside the door.

'No, hang on. I'll get them; Boss, I'll go get the buggy and we'll go down the drive in that.' As he was speaking, he was running back into the house to grab both sets of keys.

He was just about to reach the keys from their hooks when a movement on the staircase caught his eye. He blinked, wiped his eyes with his sleeve, and looked again.

There, halfway down the stairs, was . . . Ann!

Lurch grabbed at the doorpost. On seeing him, and the wide-open entrance door, Ann called out, causing both Dave and Vincent to spin around.

'What's going on?' she asked, continuing her descent. 'What is all the noise about? Where's Dianne?'

'Dianne?' Lurch said, incredulously.

'Yes, she wasn't prepared to stay under the same roof as Harding, so she took my coat and went down to the gatehouse for me . . .'

When the emergency services finally arrived, Lurch, Dave and Heather were gathered around Dianne's body. Ann was in the golf buggy with Vincent.

It had taken them no time at all to establish the brave girl, whose life had been such a succession of heartaches, was dead.

The whole group were just numb with cold and disbelief.

The police had found Harding some distance from the van. He

had gone through the windscreen and hit the trunk of the tree.

He was taken to Shelford General with severe head and spinal injuries. It didn't take too long before he was consigned to room L4 in the intensive care unit. The one at the end of the corridor . . .

Vincent sat in the library, looking down the drive. The storms of two days ago had gone. It was a beautiful sunny day.

Although none of the others had spoken about his final, goading words to Harding, Vincent himself had decided he was responsible for Dianne's death.

His mind drifted to the day he had suggested Ann invite Dianne for the weekend.

'Que sera, sera', he thought to himself.

As he sat there, he allowed himself to rerun the video of his life.

Just like the weather, nature seemed to have a way of balancing things out. Call it 'Kismet'... 'Ying and Yang'... 'The will of God'... No matter how you tried to control things, they always seemed to balance out in the end.

As he held his head in his hands, Vincent thought of himself and Ann, and their marriage.

'The Angel and the Devil,' he said out loud. Even on the sunniest day, storm clouds always seemed to lurk on the horizon.

About the Author

John Berry earned a reputation throughout the 1970s as one of the most respected, forthright and successful speedway promoters of his generation when he moulded the Ipswich Witches into one of the greatest teams in British League history, winning back-to-back championships in 1975 and 1976.

Berry also had three spells as England speedway team manager, leading his country to the World Team Cup in 1977. He also managed the British Lions touring team to Australia.

JB retired from speedway in 1987, when he emigrated to Perth, Western Australia, where he now lives with his wife, Linda, and son, Alex. Berry remains an outspoken critic of speedway and is a regular contributor to the *Backtrack* retro magazine.

Also from John Berry...

CONFESSIONS OF A SPEEDWAY PROMOTER
John Berry reveals the truth about speedway in the 70s & 80s

Published November 2004
256 pages, softback, £14.99

"Explosive, emotive, pulls no punches"
– Speedway Star magazine

"Most compelling and controversial speedway book ever written – Backtrack magazine

MORE CONFESSIONS
Speedway Revelations and Memories from the 70s & 80s

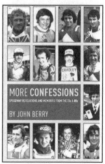

Published November 2005
256 pages, softback, £14.99

These books, and *Backtrack* magazine, can be ordered from the publishers Retro Speedway by post at: **Retro Speedway, 103 Douglas Road, Hornchurch, Essex, RM11 1AW, England.** Credit Card Hotline: **01708 734 502.** Or via their website: **www.retro-speedway.com**